D1429589

LEARNING FOR ONE'S SELF

Neo-Confucian Studies
Sponsored by the Regional Seminar in Neo-Confucian Studies
Columbia University

Learning

for One's Self

Essays on the Individual in Neo-Confucian Thought

Wm. Theodore de Bary

COLUMBIA UNIVERSITY PRESS   NEW YORK

COLUMBIA UNIVERSITY PRESS
NEW YORK   OXFORD

Copyright © 1991 Columbia University Press

Library of Congress Cataloging-in-Publication Data

de Bary, William Theodore
Learning for one's self :
essays on the individual in Neo-Confucian thought /
Wm. Theodore de Bary.
p.   cm. — (Neo-Confucian studies)
Includes bibliographical references and index.
ISBN 0-231-07426-3
1. Neo-Confucianism.   2. Self (Philosophy)
I. Title.   II. Series.
B127.N4D397   1991   126'.0951—dc20   90-44575
                                                    CIP

Casebound editions of Columbia University Press books are Smyth-sewn and printed
on permanent and durable acid-free paper

Printed in the United States of America

c 10 9 8 7 6 5 4 3 2 1

Book design by Audrey Smith

To the Columbia College Class of 1941
On the Occasion of their Fiftieth Anniversary

Neo-Confucian Studies

Contents

Preface   ix

1. Learning for One's Self   1
2. The Self in Neo-Confucian Discourse   25
3. Getting It Oneself   43
4. Individualism and Holism   71
5. Learning for One's Self in the Yüan and Early Ming   99
6. Wang Yang-ming: Sagehood and the Self   119
7. Wang Chi and the Freedom of Innate Knowing   139
8. Wang Ken and His School: The Common Man as Sage   155
9. Li Chih: Arch-Individualist   203
10. Lü Liu-liang's Radical Orthodoxy   271

Notes   365
Glossary   413
Bibliography   433
Index   441

Preface

A common misconception about Confucianism, held even by persons thought to know something about it, sees the Confucian ethic as little more than role-playing, with the roles, for the most part, socially defined. Akin to this is another notion: that Confucianism is a shame ethic rather than a guilt ethic, and social relations operate pretty much on the basis of "face," behind which stands no morally responsible self or rationally understandable person but only an inscrutable Oriental, masked by an ingratiating smile or impassive countenance.

Such misconceptions do not arise from ignorance or cultural barriers alone. Behind the first notion lies the truth that in Confucianism much importance attaches to the fulfillment of specific roles or duties, often defined in terms of personal relations and social obligations. No one, in this view, can be thought truly human whose regard for others is expressed simply in a vague humanitarianism, undefined and undisciplined by the fulfillment of specific duties and obligations. In the second case, the truth about "face" as it concerns the Confucians, is their great sensitivity to personal feelings, not just to matters of right and wrong rationally defined. They consider it of great importance in human relations that one not needlessly damage another's self-respect by causing him obvious public embarrassment—"loss of face."

Awareness of such sensitivities, however, is no ground for supposing that another people lacks a sense of right and wrong or of personal responsibility. And as regards Confucianism, its central and utlimate concern, even as a social ethic, is with understanding the self, with shaping a self into a responsible person, and with helping one to make a life for oneself (not always, it must be admitted, a living) in the company of others.

Confucius, as a teacher in the *Analects*, starts not with indoctrination but with "learning." In the opening lines he speaks first of learning as something to be done, to be delighted in, and to be shared with others. It is not simply to be imparted by a teacher and absorbed by a student. Later in the *Analects* he says that "learning among the ancients was for one's self *(wei-chi)*, but now it is for the sake of others" (meaning to impress others or gain their approval). Here "learning" *(hsüeh)* is an active pursuit, and *wei chi* tells us for what purpose it is to be pursued, namely to do something *(wei)* for the self, to help make it or shape it into a person, rather than simply to have it take something in or put something on to satisfy others. This has nothing directly to do with either selfishness, self-sacrifice, or altruism, but implies that none of these is conceivable except on the basis of some proper understanding of the self and what it can be. Without that one can neither relate to others, give of oneself to others, or even act out of real self-interest.

Understood in this way, "learning for one's self" links up with what Confucius has said about learning in the third line of the opening passage: "To be unsoured even if one is not recognized—is this not to be a noble man?" The nobleman *(chün tzu)*, in Confucius' day, was supposed to be a leader, a person of some cultivation, of some learning. But, for Confucius, unless such learning enabled him to stand on his own feet even when disappointed in his personal ambitions, it would not be true learning, nor would he be a truly noble man. I hasten to add that "standing on one's own feet," for Confucius did not mean standing apart from other men. For neither the self nor the noble man was it possible to be completely free-standing; a radically independent individual in the modern Western manner (as for instance in "doing it *my* way") would have been an absurdity for Confucius. His idea was to achieve self-fulfillment in the company of others.

There have been many interpretations of Confucius and Confucianism but none I know of that would deny the central importance of self-cultivation and self-fulfillment in his teaching. I do not deal here with all aspects of the matter, or with all times and places in which it was of some importance. The period I do attempt to cover, from the twelfth to seventeenth centuries in China, including roughly the Sung, Yüan, Ming, and early Ch'ing dynasties, is also the period in which "Neo-Confucianism" held sway. The name attaches to new developments in Confucian thought, occasioned by important changes taking place in Chinese society and culture. The challenge of Buddhism, which raised fundamental questions about the self, was one of these. Political changes in the status of the leadership elite, reopening old questions about the concept and role of the *chün-tzu*, was another. Economic and social, as well as cultural and technological change (the spread of printing especially), posed questions with respect to literacy, book-learning, and education.

Contrary to a widespread impression that China somehow got stuck in a rut or fell into a trap during these years, in my view significant change did continue to take place. It is true, however, that the main lines within which development would take place down into modern times were already well-established, and the terms of Neo-Confucian discourse were fairly well set, during the period treated herein. Where one breaks off one's account of such continuing developments is arbitrary in any case, but the seventeenth century is often taken as a major transition to a new stage of scholarly thought and my final chapter suggests how that new stage could have been set by developments from within Neo-Confucianism. In the *Message of the Mind in Neo-Confucianism* I have extended the discussion of related developments down to the nineteenth century. Here my time-span and choice of representative figures are guided by a desire to focus, in a more concentrated period, on a diversity of views within Sung-Ming discourse, thereby to show how certain key assumptions about the self were shared even by those whose philosophical positions differed widely in other respects.

The question of the individual in Neo-Confucian thought is one I stumbled into some years ago while pursuing other lines of inquiry, historical and political, which, it turned out, could only be dealt with adequately by addressing first the problem of the Neo-Confucian self. In doing so, I found myself using terms like "individualism" or "liberalism," not because of any predispositon to read Western values into Chinese thought but because, against my original assumptions and preconceptions, certain resemblances could not be ignored. Used with significant qualifications to fit the Chinese case, such terms serve better to approximate the Chinese case than any others in common parlance—that is, short of coining a wholly new, quite technical, and probably no less problematic, vocabulary.

My first attempt to deal with these matters appeared in *Self and Society in Ming Thought*, now out of print. Other aspects were first broached in my Ch'ien Mu Lectures at the Chinese University of Hong Kong, later published under the title *The Liberal Tradition in China*. Since then I have developed the main themes in greater detail, added further to the discussion of leading figures in the school of Wang Yang-ming, and balanced this by a lengthy study of Lü Liu-liang, who led the intellectual resurgence of the orthodox Chu Hsi school in the early Ch'ing period. Some of the essays presented here have appeared elsewhere in books or conference volumes now either out of print or difficult to obtain. I apologize if their reappearance here gives to some of my most attentive readers a feeling of *déjà vu*, but it seems important to bring as much as possible of the relevant material together in one compass, and to update earlier writings in the light of perspectives gained form further research. Moreover, chapter 4, though originally written as part of the present study, and to my mind indispensible to an understanding of issues subsequently raised concerning Chu Hsi's view of learning and the self, has already appeared in a conference volume on *Individualism and Holism* edited by Donald Munro (Ann Arbor: University of Michigan Press, 1985). Not to have it available here as well could, it seems to me, seriously inconvenience not a few of my readers.

This project, long delayed in completion, has now extended over thirty years. Originally my thought was to include the Korean and Japanese in the discussion, since they too became important contributors to the Neo-Confusian discourse on Learning for One's Self, but it is clear to me now that I could not do justice to these aspects of the problem without delaying the project much, much further.

It is also beyond my power here to acknowledge all the many debts incurred over the lifetime of this work. I can only ask those who have shared most in these endeavors—my wife Fanny above all—to understand that my sense of indebtedness to them, acknowledged on many previous occasions, remains undiminished. Meanwhile I have incurred new debts in the process of preparing this book for publication, especially to Irene Bloom, Marianna Stiles, Martin Amster, Tsay Heng-ting, and to my old and dear friend Okada Takehiko, for the calligraphy that graces the book jacket.

LEARNING FOR ONE'S SELF

1. *Learning for One's Self*

Individualism—the lack of it or the excess of it—has often been considered a major problem in the modernization of China. In the early decades of this century reformers championed individualism in opposition to traditional authority in both thought and social life, and especially in opposition to the "Confucian" family system.[1] Others contended that what thwarted China's modernization was not the absence of individualism but rather a surplus of it. Sun Yat-sen's experience trying to organize the Chinese people, first in a revolutionary movement and then in a modern state, convinced him that the excessive individualism of the Chinese made them just a "heap of loose sand" unable to achieve the cohesion necessary for true nationalism.[2] Still others, ardent exponents of greater individual freedom in the early reform movements, later found such freedom almost meaningless in a chaotic society, and succumbed to an authoritarian control more intense than any China had known before.[3]

The common term for "individualism" in modern East Asia (in Chinese *ko-jen chu-i*) represents a Western idea, and implies that no such "ism" existed in traditional thought. Thus it symbolizes the challenge of a new idea to traditional values and suggests the conscious advocacy of change. Nevertheless, in the earlier Chinese tradition the problem of the "individual"—his relation to the group, his role in society, his "rights" in the sense of the respect that is due him as a human being, or in such and such a status—has been the subject of as much thought and discussion as in the West. In this sense the problem of "individualism" has existed in China's past as well as in its present.

Confucianism from the outset had been deeply involved with the problem of the self or person, and Confucius himself had set guidelines for the discussion. An incident in the *Analects* reveals his basic stand. Once the Master was traveling with his followers (in the context of the book, if not of actual chronology, he had just left the court of an unworthy ruler), and one of his disciples went off to ask directions from a farmer. The latter, however, gave him advice of a different sort. "The whole world is swept along in a great flood, and who can change it? As for you, instead of following one who flees from this man [i.e., the ruler] and that, you would do better to follow one who flees from this whole generation of men." When the disciple reported this to Confucius, the latter replied sadly, "One cannot flock with birds or herd with beasts. If I am not to associate myself with humankind, then what am I to do? If the Way prevailed in the world, what need would there be to change things?"(18:6).

"To associate oneself with others" is a fundamental premise of Confucius' thought. There can be no fulfillment for the individual in isolation from his fellows. To think of oneself as an island apart, or as an individual abstracted from humankind as a whole, is impossible. Nor is it just a matter of human beings as social animals; what distinguishes them from birds and beasts is their moral sense, the inborn, Heaven-endowed sense of a mission to make the Way prevail in the world, which compels Confucius to associate his own fulfillment with the fulfillment of others.

Another passage elaborates this theme when Confucius is asked what it takes to be truly human: "The humane man, if he seeks to establish himself, will help others to succeed. To be able to judge others by what one knows of oneself is the method of achieving humanity" (6:28).

Reciprocity, then, becomes the basis of self-cultivation. One defines one's "self" in relation to others and to the Way which unites them. Thus is constructed the web of reciprocal obligations or moral relations in which one finds oneself, defines oneself. Apart from these one can have no real identity. And yet these relations alone, it is equally important to recognize, do not define one totally. One's interior self exists at the center of this web and there exercises its own autonomy. In the opening lines of the *Analects* Confucius speaks of his delight in learning and in the company of friends, both social activities, but then asserts that the true gentleman or noble man must be prepared to stand on his own even if others fail to recognize or appreciate him.

Confucius was not constantly burdened by his responsibilities to others or his mission to the world. He not only "delighted in truth" with a joyful spontaneity (*Analects* 6:18); he was enraptured by the music of Shao so that he lost his taste for anything else (6:13), and forgot all his worries in the enjoyment of learning (8:18). He said, "Personal cultivation begins with poetry, is made firm by the observance of rites, and is perfected in music" (8:8). And his disciple Yen Hui said of Confucius that "he has broadened me with learning and restrained me with rites" (9:10). Here learning stands for culture generally, and rites for moral discipline. They are equally essential to self-cultivation, complementary aspects in the process of intellectual enlargement and moral self-control.

These few examples may suffice to illustrate how for Confucius the individual exists in a delicate balance with his social environment, reconciling his own self-respect with respect for others, his inner freedom with the limiting circumstances of his own situation in life. It is this delicate balance which becomes most central and most crucial, both in the self-development of the Confucian individual and in the development of Confucianism as a whole.

In Confucianism this development focuses on the self-cultivation and self-fulfillment of the person in a cosmic or social setting. In this respect it might better be referred to as Confucian "personalism," which does not set the individual over against state or society. The question I try to address here, however, is the extent to which, in the Neo-Confucian phase, this personalism came close to Western forms of individualism. It was particularly in the Sung and Ming periods that the question of the individual became a lively, indeed crucial, issue, and came closer than at any other time, past or present, to the kinds of questions asked more recently about the nature and role of the individual in the modern West. Indeed, some Chinese and Japanese scholars are convinced that the Sung-Ming experience in this regard was crucial in determining the direction China would take in the modern world.[4]

My procedure here, instead of starting from a definition of individualism based on Western concepts or experience, will be to explore the developing awareness of the individual in Sung and Ming China in order to see how, in what context, and under what aspect the individual emerged as a central concern of Neo-Confucian thinkers. Rather than a preconceived definition, what we require here are only a few distinctions as to our use of the term "individualism." For one thing I would distinguish between individualism and "individuality." The existence of the latter does not always imply the presence of the former. Many flourishing cultures have recognized individuality in arts and letters, for instance, without affirming an equal right to individuality of expression in other fields of endeavor or among all classes of society. Aristocratic societies have often encouraged more individuality among the elite than democracies have tolerated among the masses. Nor is it difficult to recognize the extraordinary degree of individual creativity or mastery exhibited by artists, craftsmen, and performers in traditional cultures. Japan, with its strong aristocratic tradition and hierarchical society, fostered this kind of individuality in the arts without conceiving of individualism as a value to be more widely extended. In China the great cultural flowering of the Sung is a similar case in point.[5]

Further, in regard to the assertion of individualism itself, we may distinguish two main types in traditional China. There is, first of all, the individualism of the hermit or recluse, who has largely withdrawn from society. This we might call a detached or "private" individualism. Though it has a positive aspect in affirming the individual's freedom from society and his own transcendent value, from the standpoint of society this has no effect on the status of other individuals.[6] It makes no positive claim within society. It establishes not so much the right to engage in political dissent or to advocate social reform as the right to secede from human society. Some forms of Taoism and Ch'an (Zen) Buddhism tend in this direction and historically their type of individualism has had little positive effect in terms of basic political or social institutions.

By contrast, there is a more affirmative and socially defined individualism which seeks to establish the place of the individual or self in relation to others, to secure his status in some institutional framework or on the basis of widely declared and accepted principles.[7] Here we face the paradox that, in order to establish and secure its own claims, such an individualism must be "social." Confucianism attempts this in relation to the family and state. In the process, some modern critics have complained, Confucianism made a bad bargain for the individual. He was made to sacrifice more to the group than he got in return, and there is a real question whether this kind of "individualism" could ever be equated with the types of individualism known in the West. However this may be, it remains true that the Confucian almost alone in traditional China concerned himself with defining and establishing some positive role for the individual in society, and, while this was not to be equated with the advocacy of individual rights in the modern sense, it was by virtue of this active social and political endeavor that Confucianism became a vehicle for the growth of a new humanism and individualism in Neo-Confucianism.

At the same time, the question of the relation between this new trend and tendencies deriving from Buddhism and Taoism remains a real one throughout this period. This is because none of these systems falls wholly within one or the other of our categories. The Confucian conception of the self is not without a metaphysical aspect, nor the Buddhist and Taoist wholly without some social orientation. All three have a common ground insofar as they deal with one or another aspect of the human condition.

Another distinction which may be useful is between the advocacy and the effectuality of individualism. Confucius is reported in the *Analects* to have said: "In education there should be no class distinctions" (15:38). In principle this would seem to carry the implication that the individual's right to an education overrides social and economic differences. Yet Confucius and his followers, while asserting this as a seemingly universal principle, appear to have accepted the fact that social and economic circumstances would prevent many from receiving any formal education, and that politically effective learning would remain the business of an elite. In the Ming this assumption was openly challenged. And yet the question remains: how effectively was it challenged, how much actual change was brought about through the advocacy of the new individualism?

The type of individuality recognized by Confucianism, especially in terms of moral character and intellectual attainments, had been manifested to a remarkable degree by certain individuals in traditional Chinese society. In the Sung (960–1279) we observe a striking increase in the number of independent and creative minds and an unprecedented expression of individual interests and tastes in art and culture. Nevertheless, this development too appears to have been confined largely to the social elite: the scholar-officials, the bureaucratic gentry, and such members of the merchant class as might approach the latter status. It becomes an appropriate question then what signs there are of this type of individuality finding wider expression in the Ming through the advocacy of a humanitarianism extending to all classes of society.

While this minimum in the sorting out of terms has been necessary as a preamble to further discussion, it would be a mistake if we let Western concerns establish the whole agenda. For Neo-Confucians that agenda was largely set by Chu Hsi (1130–1200), the dominant thinker of the age, and his was set to a large extent by the priorities already established in Sung society and culture during the Confucian revival of the eleventh century. Indeed, if we can identify the Confucianism of this and succeeding periods as "Neo-Confucian," it is because we have a reformulation of traditional values to meet new problems and challenges, and the Neo-Confucian discourse, as it emerges from this process, introduces new concepts, philosophical formulae, literary genres, and pedagogic strategies in the revitalization of tradition.

The title of the present work illustrates this. "Learning for One's Self" is an expression from Confucius' *Analects* that came to have a special meaning and importance, as we shall see, for Chu Hsi. But the two main themes here, "learning" and "self," were already central concerns of Confucius. As we have seen, the opening lines of the *Analects* bespeak Confucius' belief that the truly noble person—one capable of leadership—is someone whose learning and self cultivation enable him, with a strong sense of his own inner worth, to withstand rejection by others. In the conversational form of the *Analects*, this is put in the form of a question rather than the enunciation of some profound doctrine; but as one reads on in the *Analects* one realizes that it does indeed sound a keynote of Confucius' teaching. As to why "learning for one's self" should have become so significant for Chu Hsi, about 1500 years later, we must look for at least a good part of the answer in the context of Sung life and thought.

THE SUNG CONTEXT

Seen in the perspective of Sung thought, the phrase "for one's self" should be taken as expressive, not of a radical individualism which asserts the complete autonomy of the self or sees the individual as in opposition to society, but of the Confucian personalism referred to above which affirms the importance of the self or person *(shen or tzu)* as the dynamic center of a larger social whole, biological continuum, and moral/spiritual community. In the Sung this Confucian view of the person or self becomes noticeably enlarged, in ways that reflect the expansive economic, social, and cultural trends of the times. If one thinks of Confucian tradition as the larger continuum of which Neo-Confucianism is its later, mature phase, one may say that Neo-Confucian individualism represents a subspecies of Confucian personalism (understood as the effort to cultivate, make, or shape a self). On the one hand, it partook of individualistic tendencies broadly manifested in Sung thought—in Ch'an Buddhism, for instance, and in Confucians outside the Ch'eng-Chu school like Su Tung-p'o and Lu Hsiang-shan. On the other hand, Confucian tradition imposed upon these tendencies certain restraints which, along with limiting factors in the physical and social environment, shaped and contained this individualism so that, as compared to modern Western varieties that have stressed freedom from any form of constraint, i.e., in terms of "liberty," "liberation," etc., it might be viewed as remaining for the most part within the more modest limits of Confucian personalism, which saw the individual as fulfilling himself through the social process and in a moral and spiritual communion with others.

Often this process was described as "getting or finding [the Way] oneself" *(tzu-te)*, a concept discussed in chapter 3. Here it may suffice to explain that "getting" or "finding" the Way in oneself suggests the Way as embracing the self and others and implies the essential harmony of the self, the Way, and others as something to be realized through one's efforts at self-cultivation. There is no fundamental opposition here between the one and the many; nor is there, in the end, a loss of personhood or individuality through the total absorption of the self into the one. Instead, what Chu Hsi seeks is a self-realization in which man fulfills all that is distinctively human while participating in the creative work of heaven and earth. The individualism under discussion here is in keeping with that larger conception of Confucian personalism.

In his writings Chu Hsi addressed an educated elite which thought of itself as occupying positions of leadership in the family, the school, the community, and the state. Traditionally, Confucians had viewed these as primary roles of the individual, corresponding to the moral duties which Confucius said must have first claim on one's attention, after which, if one had time and energy to spare, one could devote oneself to "letters" *(wen)*. The Neo-Confucians reconfirmed this priority in the Sung, but as a class in more comfortable circumstances they also enjoyed more leisure for cultural activities than most of their forebears; along with it there came increased material and technical means put at their disposal. Generally speaking, the centers of Neo-Confucian scholarship were also areas which led in agricultural production, trade, and population growth in the late T'ang and Sung period, i.e., modern Kiangsu, Chekiang, Kiangsi, Fukien, Szechuan, and—for political and cultural reasons rather than economic—the capital region in north central China.[8] Whatever it may have lacked in military prowess, the Sung certainly did not want for brilliant cultural achievements, and it is no surprise that the outburst of individual creativity in arts and letters, especially the greater freedom of individual expression in painting, calligraphy, and other arts taken up by scholar-officials, should have expressed itself also in Neo-Confucian thought.[9]

The term *wen* represented something more than letters and polite culture, however. A follower of Hu Yüan (993–1059) spoke of *wen* as the literary expression or cultural transmission of the Confucian Way.[10] In this sense *wen* stood for the highest values of the culture, human civilization as carrying out the Way and the will of heaven. Confucius had talked of his own mission in the world as bound up with "this culture" *(ssu-wen)*, and many Neo-

Confucians likewise took it as their personal responsibility in life to make the Way manifest in the world through "this culture."[11]

In so doing, the Neo-Confucians, as an educated elite in relatively prosperous times, dedicated their new affluence and leisure to serious purposes, attempting to convert them into a higher form of culture. They did this with a sense of vocation as leaders in the society who felt keenly their responsibility to meet the social and cultural crises of their time. It was this humane concern which led them to reinterpret and revitalize tradition so that, instead of merely perpetuating antiquarian studies, it would express the highest aspirations of the Confucian elite as bearers of that culture in the Sung.[12]

In this broader and deeper conception of *wen*, the cultural activities of the Neo-Confucian scholar ranged from the substantive business of moral self-cultivation to the study of classical texts, literary activities, and historical or practical learning of some social benefit. In the Ch'eng-Chu school these were viewed as complementary activities, sometimes summed up in terms of "dwelling in reverence and fathoming principle" *(chü-ching ch'iung-li,* i.e., spiritual/moral and intellectual pursuits); or "quiet-sitting and book learning" *(ching-tso, tu-shu,* i.e., contemplative practice and scholarly study); or "preserving one's moral nature and pursuing scholarly inquiry" *(tsun te-hsing, tao wen-hsüeh).* These activities went hand-in-hand. Book learning was meant to enhance and enrich one's moral cultivation, while the latter served to deepen one's scholarly understanding. Thus, even "learning for one's self" was intimately bound up with how one read the classics; and classical studies, always a major occupation of the Confucian, involved not only textual research but also the application of textual learning to practical activities through which the Neo-Confucian pursued his self-cultivation. In this sense, "learning for one's self" was to be understood, not as opposed to activities on behalf of others, but rather as a constant attention to one's self-development and self-integration in the midst of such activities.

Accordingly, it is through these activities that we find the Neo-

Confucian celebrating certain individualistic qualities associated with the autonomous mind—self-consciousness, critical awareness, creative thought, independent initiative, and judgment—which find their way into the basic texts and commentaries of the Ch'eng-Chu school. In other words, Sung individualism asserted itself as a natural outgrowth of the high degree of cultural activity sustained in the Sung by the members of the scholar-official class and by the classes supporting them. Likewise, in Sung politics, Neo-Confucians advocated a more independent role for scholars at court. Meanwhile, in the social sphere, there was no doubt less allowance made for the individual; rather, a greater accommodation to others was stressed.

To sum up, then, the types of individualism asserted here reflect the following features of Sung society and culture: (1) the special status and functions of the scholar-official class; (2) the rising affluence and rich culture of the period; (3) a religious atmosphere pervaded by a Ch'an Buddhist spirituality which had already put the problem of the self high on the human agenda; and (4) the interaction of these factors with a Confucian humanistic tradition already disposed to value highly the cultural and political contributions of the individual scholar.

In Chu Hsi's terms, the essential nature of the self was the same in all these contexts. It is not he, but we who, from the hindsight of history, find most fully expressed this individualism more in certain areas significant for his class than for society as a whole. In principle Chu Hsi would probably still insist that, whatever the limiting factors in particular situations, the highest priority should always attach to the fulfillment of the person, i.e., to the fullest development and exercise of individual human capabilities within the given circumstances.

"LEARNING FOR ONE'S SELF" IN CHU HSI

The thought of Chu Hsi begins and ends with the aim of "learning for one's self" *(wei-chi chih hsüeh)*, understood to mean that learning should be for one's self and not for the sake of others (i.e., to gain acceptance by others and improve one's standing in the world). This aim, which set a high priority on self-understanding and self-fulfillment, was put before Chu early in life by his father. It was what motivated his studies under his teacher Li T'ung (1093–1163), what guided him in official life, and what stayed with him to the end of his scholarly career. For many of his later followers it was what distinguished true Confucian teaching from any other.

Mencius, much admired by Neo-Confucians, had not used the same terms but had made a similar distinction when he spoke of cultivating the nobility of Heaven in contrast to the nobility of man. He says, "In ancient times men cultivated the nobility of Heaven and nobility among other men followed in train" (6A:16). By the "nobility of Heaven" he means distinction in the personal virtues of humaneness, rightness, being true to oneself, and trust-worthiness—all in contrast to the distinctions of rank in the political and social hierarchy. Those who pursue the latter without recognizing the primacy of personal virtue, says Mencius, are certain to fail.[13]

Hsün Tzu, often misunderstood as completely subordinating the individual to the group and viewing education as simply a process of socialization (i.e., conforming to external, socially imposed norms), makes it clear in his important first chapter on the "Encouragement of Learning," that this learning should be for the sake of one's self. Quoting from the *Analects* he says: "In ancient times one studied for one's self; nowadays one studies for the sake of others. The gentleman's learning [today] is meant to serve as a bribe to win attention from others."[14]

Thus the two main wings of classical Confucian teaching shared this basic premise of the learning process as rooted in a true conception of self or personhood. As will be seen presently, Chu Shi, who thought of the Ch'eng brothers as the direct heirs of Mencius in the repossession of the Confucian Way, would have frequent occasion to quote their views on "learning for one's self," inasmuch as his own early education had come from a succession of scholars in the line of Ch'eng I, including his own father.

In 1148, at the age of eighteen, Chu passed the civil service examinations at the capital and won the advanced *(chin-shih)* degree. He was already a success by the standards of the age, having achieved the goal coveted by most educated men in Sung China but not often attained by them so early in life. Soon thereafter he received his first appointment to office as a subprefectural registrar in the T'ung-an district of Fukien, where his varied duties included responsibility for the local school and presented him with the occasion to address the students there. "Learning should be for one's self," he said, "but in today's world what fathers encourage in their sons, what older brothers exhort in their younger brothers, what teachers impart to their students, and what students all study for is nothing more than to prepare for the civil service examinations." Then he urged that they should aspire to emulate the ancients' "learning for one's self" instead of "studying for the sake of others," meaning that they should aim at understanding and fulfilling their own true selves, rather than let their studies be directed toward winning the approval of the official examiners.[15]

In 1165, when Chu and Lü Tsu-ch'ien compiled *Reflections on Things at Hand (Chin-ssu-lu)*, in the important section on the Pursuit of Learning which sets forth the overall aims of the work, they cited Ch'eng I's (1033–1107) amplification of Confucius' remark: " 'In ancient times one studied for one's self,' that is, Ch'eng said, to 'get it oneself *(tzu-te)*; nowadays one studies for the sake of others,' that is, in order to gain recognition from others."[16] Here Ch'eng I's reference to "getting it oneself" echoes Mencius' doctrine that the "noble man steeps himself in the Way because he wishes to get it himself. When he finds it in himself, he will be at ease with it; when he is at ease with it, he can draw deeply upon it; when he can draw deeply upon it, he finds its source wherever he turns. That is why the noble man wishes to get it himself."[17] Here "learning for one's self" is explained in terms of finding the Way in oneself and deriving deep inner satisfaction from it.

Later, in commenting on the original passage in the *Analects*, Chu Hsi again referred to Ch'eng I's comment that "when the ancients studied for their own sake, it led in the end to the fulfillment of others; nowadays studying for the sake of others leads in the end to the destruction of one's self,"[18] an observation which Chu Hsi praises highly for its aptness and succinctness.[19] Further, in the *Essential Meaning of the Analects (Lun-yü ching-i)*, Chu includes commentaries from other Sung masters which explain the meaning of "for one's self" *(wei-chi)* as "being true to one's self," "rectifying the mind and making the will sincere," and as not ending in self-love but taking self-cultivation as the starting point for reaching out to others.[20] In these ways Chu distinguishes true self-fulfillment from mere selfish satisfaction, identifying the latter with self-destruction and the former with the fulfillment of others.

Chu Hsi returns to the same theme in chapter 6 of *Things at Hand* which deals with the Regulation of the Family. At the very outset of this discussion of the family, he points to the primacy of moral relations in learning for the sake of one's self, again quoting Ch'eng I: "Master I-ch'uan said, 'If young people have energy to spare after the performance of their moral responsibilities, they may study arts and literature (making reference to *Analects* 1:6). If they do not perform their moral duties, and study literature and art first, this is not "Learning for one's self *(wei-chi chih hsüeh)*."[21] Here a certain tension is set up between moral learning and the pursuit of arts and letters, at least to the extent that the latter might lead to neglect of the former.

Chu Hsi reiterated this aim on another occasion significant for the expression of his views on education: the restoration of the Stone Drum Academy *(Shih-ku shu-yüan)*. In a commemorative inscription of 1185 he recalls the noble ideals which inspired Northern Sung scholars during the great days of the Hsi-ning period (1068–77), and contrasts their aims with the attitude in his own time, which is completely absorbed with study for the examinations, as personified by the education officials appointed to each prefecture and county. This, he says, causes men to have an eye only for personal gain and not to appreciate the scholar dedicated to right principles and to "learning for one's self."[22]

Toward the end of his fitful and frustrating official career, on the very eve of his official condemnation for heterodoxy, Chu revisited the Academy of the White Deer Grotto which he had been instrumental in reviving when he was prefect in Nan-k'ang, Kiangsi, in 1179–1181. The lecture which he gave on that occasion later became celebrated as one of the most authoritative statements of his mature position in philosophical and educational matters. He began it on the same theme with which he had launched his educational efforts as a fledgling official in T'ung-an many years before:

> I have heard that "in ancient times one studied for one's self; nowadays one studies for the sake of others." Therefore the sages and worthies, in teaching men to pursue learning, did not have them patch together speeches or compose literary pieces simply with a view to obtaining civil service degrees and official emoluments. Only "investigating things, extending knowledge, making the will sincere, rectifying the mind, and further extending these to regulating the family, ordering the state, and pacifying the world," [in the *Great Learning*] can be considered correct learning.[23]

In this brief passage Chu summed up many of the ideals of his age and of the educational philosophy which he had developed over a lifetime: the "correct learning" *(cheng-hsüeh)* which had been the dominant ideal of Northern Sung reformers; the "learning of the sages and worthies" which in the Ch'eng-Chu school was to be increasingly encapsulated in the "Great Learning"; and "learning for one's self," which Chu saw as both beginning and end of all the rest. Early and late, Chu had put this moral and spiritual "learning" forward as a genuine alternative to the spurious literary learning for civil service examinations, and also, in citing Ch'eng I, had espoused it in opposition to any pursuit of art and literature at the expense of moral learning.

Later in the Yüan dynasty, when the issue of resuming the

examinations arose in the court of Khubilai, those who supported the idea were known as the "literary party," while the followers of Chu Hsi who spoke in opposition to it were said to have advocated "learning for one' self."[24] It was Chu Hsi schoolmen such as these who first established his works as basic texts in the school curriculum under the Yüan dynasty, again under the banner of "learning for one's self."[25] Similarly, at the founding of the Yi dynasty in Korea when the same issue arose with regard to the examination system, advocates of Neo-Confucianism attacked bureaucratic scholarship as "learning for the sake of others," in contrast to Confucius' "learning for one's self."[26]

CONQUERING ONESELF AND RESTORING RITENESS

Another view of the self in Neo-Confucianism, and one which at first sight seems radically opposed to that just presented, is found in Chu Hsi's treatment of the theme of "Conquering oneself and restoring riteness" *(k'o-chi fu-li)*.

Here Neo-Confucians understood *chi* in the negative sense of "selfish" or "self-centered" (rather than in the positive sense it has in "learning for one's self"), while rites represent, as Chu says in his Commentary, "the measured expression or defined form of Heaven's principle," i.e., norms governing one's conduct of relationships within the world at large. As a member of society the person must subordinate his selfish desires *(ssu-yü)* to the good of the community or public good *(kung)*. His true personhood is thus achieved by disciplining his desires so that they mesh rather than conflict with the public good. Whether desires are seen as good or bad depends entirely on how they meet this test, just as self-fulfillment depends on how one overcomes any contradiction between the self and others.

Neo-Confucians often invoked the dictum of Confucius in *Ana-*

lects (12:1) in response to Yen Yüan's question about perfect virtue or humaneness *(jen)*.

Confucius said:

> It is to conquer oneself and restore riteness. "If a man can for one day conquer himself and restore riteness, all under Heaven will ascribe perfect virtue to him." Yen Yüan then said, "May I ask what it consists in?" The Master replied, "Look not at what is contrary to rites, listen not to what is contrary to rites, speak not what is contrary to rites, act not contrary to rites."

Here what I have translated as "restore riteness" *(fu-li)* might also be translated as "restore the rites" or "return to the rites," and in some contexts these might serve well. Confucius did indeed wish to restore the rites of the early Chou dynasty, insofar as they had lapsed; and insofar as they were still known, he wished individuals to return to their observance. But in Confucius' terms, while "rites" are definite forms to be observed or practices to be studied, and thus represent an objective measure or standard for individual and society, *li* is also spoken of by him in association with other virtues, as here with humaneness. In this sense *li* expresses an inner disposition toward the *rites*, a moral habit of according with the rites, an achieving of spiritual attunement or communion with the ritual order as a sacrificial order. Since Confucius recognized that coded ritual had changed from dynasty to dynasty, each among these having the holy aura of antiquity, the rites were not fixed forever in one mold, but were subject to some adaptation as circumstances of the dynasty or individual changed. Hence it was important to enter into the essential spirit of the rites, to cultivate "riteness" as a virtue, and not simply to conform to established practices.

Confucius' classic definition of the concept of *jen* was given heightened significance by its central role in Neo-Confucianism, and especially by the attention Chu Hsi gave to it in a key chapter of *Things at Hand* and in his commentary on the *Analects*. The chapter in *Things at Hand* has to do with self-examination and self-correction, the basic moral discipline which Chu Hsi focused on when he featured the *Great Learning* as a main text of instruction. The title of this chapter in *Things at Hand* is variously rendered in different versions, but as translated by Wing-tsit Chan it draws upon the edition of Yeh Ts'ai (fl. 1248), an early compiler of commentaries on this important manual of Neo-Confucian teaching. Yeh's title and description read:

> On Self-discipline, 41 sections. In this chapter the effort to practice what one has learned is discussed. Having clearly investigated principles and having deeply preserved one's mind and nourished one's nature, one is about to extend one's understanding and cultivation into personal practice. At this point one should devote the utmost effort to self-discipline.[27]

Here Yeh Ts'ai's explanation of the sequence of learning follows along the lines already given in Chu Hsi's discussion of "learning for one's self," i.e., self-understanding should be linked to one's conduct toward others and does not stop with the self. Professor Chan's translation of *k'o-chi* as "self-discipline" is in keeping with the general nature of the contents, with the emphasis in Neo-Confucianism on rational, moral control, and is also in keeping with the tone of Yeh Ts'ai's own description. Indeed, in the text itself *k'o-chi* is often equated with *tzu-chih,* "self-control."

If I translate it, however, as "conquering oneself," there are, I think, good reasons for this. For one thing, "conquer" is closer to the original sense of *k'o* as "to conquer or overcome," and this is the sense in which Chu Hsi understands it in his commentary on this passage in the *Analects:*

> Humanity is the complete virtue (full power) of the mind-and-heart. *K'o* (subdue) means to conquer or overcome. *Chi* (self) means one's selfish desires. *Fu* (restore) means to return. *Li* (rites) are the measured expression of Heaven's principle. To become humane is to perfect the virtue (powers) of the mind. The complete virtue of the mind is all heaven's principle, and yet

it cannot help being spoiled by human desires. Therefore to become humane one must have the means to overcome selfish desires and restore riteness, so that one's conduct of affairs will be in accord with Heaven's principles and the virtue of the original mind will be perfected in oneself. . . . If day by day one overcomes selfish desires to the point where it ceases to be difficult, then the desires will become completely purified, Heaven's principles will flow forth unobstructed and one's humaneness will become unconquerable.[28]

In this passage *fu-li* may fairly be rendered in the Neo-Confucian context as "return to decorum or propriety," yet *li* has strong residual overtones of its original religious significance in ritual sacrifice, as the ritual order by which the members of the class, community, or state were joined together in the service of the common cult, each in a manner befitting his own rank and status. Hence *fu-li* can also be understood as "to restore the practice of ritual order," meaning "to restore one's conduct of life to a state of vital communion with the sacral order." We must not dispense too quickly with the religious overtones of this key concept, or yield to the modern taste for a moral and rational humanism at the expense of the traditional religious aspect, for the latter is strongly retained in Neo-Confucianism along with the rational and moral. It is in the original connotations of the terms that *k'o-chi fu-li* allows for two distinct possibilities. One is a deeper awareness of the weakness and fallibility of man which Chu Hsi referred to as the "human mind" or "mind of man" *(jen-hsin)* and spoke of as being prone to err, precarious, insecure, etc. The other refers to the "mind of the Way" *(tao-hsin)*, which is always correct but not always easy to perceive or follow. Here the emphasis could be on a strict and severe testing of oneself, for a rigorous religiosity aspiring to self-transcendence through self-conquest, i.e., through overcoming of the ego-self and its wayward (rather than Way-ward) tendencies.

The pertinence of this interpretation is brought out by the number of Neo-Confucians for whom this religiosity had a strong appeal, as well as those others for whom it was to become an abomination. Some early Neo-Confucians (or proto-Neo-Confucians, if we are to include Li Ao [774–836?] in this), perhaps reflecting the prevalence of a "medieval" Buddhist view of the desires as selfish or egoistic, tended to see human desires as selfish and to emphasize repression of the desires. Chou Tun-i speaks of the sage, or aspirant to sagehood, as being "without desires" *(wu-yü)*.[29] Chu Hsi, for his part, stressed the distinction between desires that are selfish *(ssu)* and partial, and natural human emotions that are held within the bounds of what is "shared in common," unselfish or "impartial" *(kung)*. Yet Chu Hsi also accords Chou Tun-i a high place among the patriarchs of the Sung school, and the latter's guide to the attainment of sagehood, *Comprehending the Changes (I-t'ung shu)*, remained a classic text of the Neo-Confucian canon. Thus such an influential and seemingly authoritative proponent of Chu Hsi's philosophy as Chen Te-hsiu (1178–1235) quotes in his *Heart Classic* Chou Tun-i's doctrine of desirelessness as if it were a cardinal teaching of Neo-Confucianism, to the point indeed where it would seem to incorporate within the latter an extremely rigoristic, if not puritanical, view of the desires.

Subsequently other "orthodox" Neo-Confucians like Yi T'oegye (1501–70) in Korea, who was much influenced by Chen Te-hsiu's *Heart Classic*, reiterated Chou Tun-i's injunction against the desires, and further intensified this rigoristic strain of Neo-Confucianism among its adherents in Korea and Japan.[30] Indeed the essential ambivalence of Neo-Confucian teaching on this score is indicated by the cases of those who exhibited both of these manifestations in one life-experience, first embracing the ritual with zealous intensity and then later repudiating it. Negative indications of this also came from protests in popular literature against a harsh ritual discipline prescribed in the name of Chu Hsi, which is far more repressive than simple self-discipline.

Yet another, less pessimistic, view of the matter is revealed in Chu Hsi's quoting of Ch'eng I in chapter 5 of *Things at Hand:*

One's first act is to see. If one looks at what is contrary to rites, then, as the saying goes, whenever he opens his eyes, he makes a mistake. Hearing comes next, then speaking, then action, in proper sequence. If one can "conquer oneself," his mind will be broad and his heart generous, and his body will become big and be at ease. Looking up he will have no occasion for shame before Heaven, and below he will have no occasion to blush before men. We can understand how happy he will be. But if he lets up in his conquest of self for even a moment he will starve.[31]

At this point we encounter again not only an enlarged conception of the self *(chi)* but also a larger view of *li*, or rites. As we have seen, in the context of Confucius' response to Yen Yüan above, where he speaks of virtue directly in relation to daily conduct: "Look not at what is contrary to rites, listen not . . . speak not . . . act not contrary to rites," *fu li* can be understood as "to restore," "renew," "revitalize" one's relation to a ritual order that unites one to the whole human community and, in its most expansive form, to the cosmic order and process. In his recent studies of key classical concepts of the self, body, virtue, etc. Roger Ames has discussed the significance of *k'o-chi fu-li* in the following terms:

the corpus of religious actions, beginning as a set of practices initiated to give human beings access to otherworldly realms, became an apparatus for personal spiritual integration within the broad cultural community of this world. The religious element was sustained in this process of evolution in that ritual actions were consistently interpreted as a formal construct directed at relating part to whole. The quality of the religious component in the ritual-structured experience is a function of the extent to which one is able to overcome a preoccupation with ego-self (i.e., to *k'o-chi*) and to achieve the level of person-in-context. In that ego-self is delimiting, it is seen as an unfortunate inhibition to the fundamentally religious experience of integrating part with whole. Similarly, to the extent that the personal body can be construed as a dimension of the ego-self, it too must be overcome. Yet when extended out into the world, body has an analogous religious function in relating part to whole. To appreciate this paradigm it is crucial to resist equating ego-self with particularity. That is, the process of integration, far from being a surrender of part to whole, is the extension and celebration of the particular in its integral, organismic relationship to the whole.[32]

And again, putting it more specifically in Confucian terms, Ames explains:

> The *jen* [truly human or humane] person is someone whose personhood extends out and is definable in terms of his human community. As his personhood is extended, his range of possibilities and the influence or power of his person are proportionately extended. He becomes a "large" person in that he encompasses a sphere of psycho-physical energy that goes far beyond the range of any ego-self. (Insertion mine.)[33]

If one compares this language with that of Ch'eng I, as quoted above by Chu Hsi in *Things at Hand*, one can see that the Ch'eng-Chu understanding of this crucial concept is remarkably close to the classical one as interpreted by Ames in its own context. What is new in the Neo-Confucian case is the fuller articulation of the part-to-whole relationship in the doctrine of the "unity of principle and diversity of its particularizations" *(li-i fen-shu)*, in which the reality of the particular (individuality in self-realization) is affirmed along with the universality of principle (the moral nature). In this view the legitimate expression of individual feelins is not impaired in the "conquering" of selfish desires, and the sage or worthy is no less of an individual for having fulfilled the common human nature.

Recently in the People's Republic there has been some discussion between Fung Yu-lan and Ren Jiyu as to whether Neo-Confucianism is a religion or not.[34] Part of the debate has centered on the view of human desires and ritual discipline, with Professor Ren citing the repressive view as typically religious and Professor Fung calling the "expressive" or expansive view of the human self and desires in Neo-Confucianism, cited above, as non-religious. Whether "religious" or not, it is clear that these two views are each grounded in different views of the self and self-conquest, reflecting the actual ambivalence of Neo-Confucian tradition on this matter.

On either reading some transcendence of the ego-self is involved. As Ch'eng I and Chu Hsi see it, "self-conquest" through according with rites is a process whereby one's acceptance of certain limits, and the transcending of them, overcome the distinction between self and others, and join one to a moral and spiritual community. Here a radical modern individualism would be ruled out, but what I have called Confucian personalism—a concept of the person as most truly itself when most fully in communion with other selves—would nevertheless allow for the distinct personality differences Chu Hsi celebrates in the final chapter of his manual for the achievement of sagehood, *Reflections on Things at Hand*.

2. The Self in Neo-Confucian Discourse

When in the nineteenth century superior Western power brought to the "Far" East such far-out ideas as political freedom, free trade, liberty, liberalism, and individualism—ideas typical of the expansive, enterprising, and even aggressive spirit of the West in those days—nothing quite like its brash, rugged "individualism" was to be found in East Asia. There the most recent "modern" culture, the Neo-Confucian, had been inspired by what, to its adherents, were the central and no less vital values of self-understanding, self-reliance, personal responsibility, and highly disciplined individual performance. New words had to be coined to represent Western notions like "liberation" and "individualism," since they had no precise equivalents in Chinese or Japanese parlance.

The new Chinese term for this [Western] individualism, *ko-jen chu-i* (actually borrowed from the Japanese neologism *kojin shūgi*), emphasized the discreteness, uniqueness, and separateness of the individual, rather than his relation to the group or society. This stood in some contrast to earlier Confucian views of the self or person, and to what I have called in chapter 1 a Confucian personalism. Invented to represent "liberalism" was the modern term *tzu-yu chu-i* (Japanese *jiyu shūgi*), which emphasized the autonomy of the self and the idea that one should be allowed to follow one's own inclination, but suggested little of the liberality and generosity of spirit associated with "liberalism" in the minds of its Western proponents. Nonetheless *tzu-yu* appeared in many modern compounds rendering different aspects of "liberty" and "freedom" in Western legal and political thought. The term currently used for "liberalization" in the Peoples Republic is an instance of this, and it too has easily been misconstrued as a form of selfish, irresponsible individualism, so rampant and undisciplined, say its critics, that its pursuit leads to nothing less than anarchy.

Awareness of these incongruities in terms and values has led some East Asian writers and thinkers to delve further into Western culture for a deeper understanding of the new concepts. Other East Asians early became persuaded that this radical individualism of the West was fundamentally alien to Eastern cultures—an idea still current in the frequently expressed fear of Western liberalism as a form of "spiritual pollution." Such reactions, in turn, evoked their own response from Westerners, some of whom, noting the apparent artificiality of these new expressions, or seeing that such concepts were easily misconstrued, became convinced that the ideas and values themselves were essentially foreign to East Asian cultures; as delicate hybrids, they could not be expected to survive transplantation. Just one more step along this line of thinking, and one was led to the conclusion that the whole historical and cultural experience of East Asia rendered it resistant to democratic values.

Recent history, with the success of democracy in Japan, its gradual spread elsewhere in East Asia, and the ready identification of other peoples with basic human rights, belies any such sweeping judgment, and warrants a reexamination of at least two of its basic premises. One of these, of course, is the assumed fundamental incompatibility of values, and the other the validity of an approach which restricts the terms of the discussion to Western concepts and how they are expressed in East Asian terms, instead of asking whether there may not be, in the indigenous East Asian discourse on key human issues, native concepts and terms which share some common ground with rough Western counterparts—concepts which may suggest some convergence of thinking between the two, rather than radically divergent orientations of mind.

Anyone who examines the East Asian record, and especially the Neo-Confucian discourse in China, Japan, and Korea, becomes aware of these resemblances—kindred problems, and similarities in the proposed solutions to them. One need not in fact search them out; they thrust themselves upon the attention of anyone who takes the trouble to look at that record. Unfortunately too few have gone to this trouble, given certain prejudicial earlier assumptions, namely, that the thought traditions of East Asia have for long been dead or dying; that they are of no more relevance today than mummies in a museum; and that at best, even in the past, they only represented ideas, not the real stuff of history.

What follows, here, is an attempt to get at the terms of the Neo-Confucian discourse about the self and individual, observe how Chinese thinkers defined the issues, and see how these were debated among them. Not only are these ideas of intrinsic interest, but they have a bearing also on East Asia's reception of related ideas from the West.

The *tzu* of the *tzu-yu* in the modern word for "liberalism" is a term for "self," frequently used in combination with *chi, shen* or *ssu*. Like *chi* and *shen, tzu* is often translatable simply as "self." In classical Chinese usage *tzu* also has the connotation "from, in, or of itself," much like our prefix "auto." This sense of self-originated or self-motivated gains added emphasis when used in combination with *yu*, "from" or "out of." Thus *tzu* readily forms compounds corresponding to ours with the prefix "self-." For instance, in the *Great Learning* it says: "To make one's intention sincere means allowing of no self-deception *(tzu-ch'i)*, as when we hate a bad smell or love what is good-looking, which is called self-satisfaction *(tzu-ch'ien)."* In both cases, self-deception and self-satisfaction, the implication is that the source of value lies within the self and the immediate, affective, visceral response to things is the authentic one. The Neo-Confucians proceeded on this assumption to develop a vocabulary of terms with the prefix *tzu-* which recur frequently in their discussions. A few of the more common examples follow:

Tzu-jan means "natural" in the sense of what is so of itself, and not made to be so or appear so to be *(wei)*. In China the Neo-Taoists of the fourth and fifth century A.D. had made almost a supreme value of naturalness *(tzu-jan)* in the sense of uninhibited spontaneity or an amoral, pragmatic adaptability. For their part Neo-Confucians were unwilling to concede that moral effort and rational calculation were unnatural to man. They followed Mencius in trying to steer a middle course between a laissez-faire, value-free pragmatism on the one hand, and a tendency toward moral compulsion, forced effort, or conscious manipulation on the other. They often cited Mencius' eschewal of the opposing extremes of either "forgetting" or "abetting" the moral nature—i.e., either neglecting moral cultivation altogether, or consciously straining to "do good." Both were equally prejudicial to a natural process of growth in accordance with the inner-directedness of things. How to sustain a moral life that is spontaneous, non-manipulative, and unfeigned was a central concern of both Sung and Ming thought. Thus Wu Ch'eng (1249–1333), in explaining the opening lines of Chu Hsi's commentary of the *Great Learning*, points out how naturally the cultivation of the moral nature leads to the "renewing of the people" because it evokes a ready response in accordance with the inherent propensity of their own natures.[1]

Tzu-chia: In contrast to the terms discussed above, *tzu-chia* (lit.: one's own family or household but meaning "oneself" or "one's own") is a colloquial usage which became common in the Sung period, but is now preserved mainly in coastal dialects and in Korean and Japanese dictionaries of Chinese.[2] It appears frequently in Chu Hsi's *Classified Conversations (Yü-lei)*, reflecting the vernacular speech of his time, as for instance in the following: "In reading one cannot seek for moral principles simply by looking at the written page; one should turn, look for it within, and find its application and corroboration in oneself *(tzu-chia).*"[3] Or again: "The Way is a general term whereas the nature *(hsing)* is used with reference to one's own self *(tzu-chia shen).* . . . The Way is the principle inherent in all things, whereas the nature is the principle inherent in the self *(chi).*"[4]

Since for the most part our discussion of terms in this section has emphasized the autonomy of the self, we may note here that even when reference is made to the individual's innermost self, it retains some sense of continuity with a collectivity such as the family, household, or school. No doubt this colloquial usage reflects a basic view that the life of the individual is rooted in the family and that one does not draw attention to himself as a freestanding individual. Though much used, the term does not, however, derive from any classical philosophical depiction of the self or individual, nor is it the focus of attention in Neo-Confucian philosophical discussions.

TAKING RESPONSIBILITY ONESELF

Tzu-jen or *chi-jen* means "taking it upon oneself" or "bearing the responsibility oneself." This is in accord with voluntarism in the moral life and of action that is in keeping with "learning for one's self"—that is, with the idea that one must take full responsibility for one's own actions, since actions undertaken simply with a view to pleasing others lead, as Chu Hsi said, to "self-destruction."

The locus classicus for the term *"tzu-jen"* is *Mencius* (5B:1), where it refers to "taking on the weight of the world." In Neo-Confucianism this is closely associated with the conception of the moral hero and becomes a key concept in Neo-Confucian moral individualism. In turn the idea of taking upon oneself responsibility for the Way, or accepting the duty to uphold it, is predicated on Chu Hsi's view of the individual as a self-determining moral agent.

The moral agency here is the mind, or more particularly the "master" *(chu-tsai)* in the mind which controls human impulses and desires, and sees that they do not conflict with reason, or what is proper to a given relationship or situation.[5] Most importantly, however, the mind is the agency of self-determination in that it decides the direction of one's self-development or one's self-dereliction. This is done either through making, or failing to make, a moral commitment that establishes one's aim in life and fixes the course that will guide one's learning and self-discipline. At fifteen, Confucius had said, he set his mind-and-heart on learning, a life-long, life-directing process. Chu Hsi too greatly stressed the need for making such an early and crucial commitment:

> All men should take responsibility themselves for becoming a sage or worthy. Many men think becoming a sage or a worthy is too lofty a goal and regard themselves as unworthy of it. Therefore they make no effort to advance toward it. . . . Yet the natural endowment is the same in all human beings, and since it is the same for ordinary persons, how can one not take responsibility oneself for becoming a sage or worthy?[6]

Moreover, in language reminiscent of the *Analects* and of "learning for one's self," Chu says: "In ancient times those who pursued learning started with the thought of becoming leaders *(shih)* and ended with the thought of becoming sages."[7] Chu goes on to explain that the pursuit of this ambition requires application to study; it is not something that comes without effort. It is rather the outcome of a primary life-orientation following from a deliberate decision and commitment on the part of the individual.

In Chu Hsi's view one has a natural disposition toward the good but it must be nurtured by reverence and cultivated by the practice of propriety or rightness *(i)*. Through that nurturing and practice one achieves an ease and effortlessness in the conduct of the moral life which is spoken of as "natural" *(tzu-jan)*. In contrast to this is any kind of straining at results, forcing or manipulating things *(an-*

p'ai) out of an impatience to obtain some preconceived selfish end. Far from precluding noble ambitions, however, the former view encouraged a belief in the compatibility of high ideals, and even engagement in great struggles to attain them, with a spontaneous, and in the end serene, way of life. Such a natural ease of moral conduct in all life situations was also characteristic of one who had "gotten it oneself" *(tzu-te)*. Yet by the same token, according to Chu, one who wished to "get it himself" could only do so by undertaking such a responsibility and making such an effort.[8]

The educated man, Sung Confucians understood, should be prepared to serve in government and develop specialized skills where appropriate to serve humanitarian purposes. For its part the Ch'eng-Chu school held that the essence of government lay in universal self-discipline, beginning with the ruler's self-rectification. This obliged the minister, in his relation to the ruler as defined in the Five Constant Relations (i.e., "Between prince and minister there is [a bond of] rightness"), to assist the emperor in his self-cultivation and in the conduct of a moral life. In other words, he is to be a minister in the sense of counselor, mentor, preceptor, and not just a subordinate or subject of the ruler.

This was all the more the case with the Ch'eng brothers and Chu Hsi, who as court officials often served in preceptorial roles such as "lecturer from the classics mat," discussing current affairs in the light of the values and principles set forth in the classics. They directed the counsel given in their memorials and lectures toward the primary motivation of the ruler: his need to take full personal responsibility for the conduct of the Way. Often this is expressed in terms of *tzu-jen*, "taking responsibility oneself," closely accompanied by the ideas of learning for oneself, making up one's own mind, and making a definite decision or commitment in behalf of the Way.

Ch'eng Hao told the Emperor: "To rule with a sincere mind-and-heart is to be a true king. . . . Your majesty has the natural endowment of Yao and Shun, but only if he takes it as his personal responsibility *(tzu-jen)* to have the mind-and-heart of Yao and Shun can he fulfill their Way."[9] Neo-Confucians at court often echoed this sentiment in later ages.

Here the close connection in Ch'eng Hao's mind between sincerity, making up one's own mind, and taking personal responsibility is evident. Ch'eng I, for his part, speaks in much the same terms and to the same point: "The way of government may be discussed in terms of its fundamentals and of its practice. In terms of its fundamentals it is nothing but 'rectifying what is wrong in the ruler's mind'[10] and 'rectifying one's mind in order to rectify the minds of the officials at court.' . . ."[11] In terms of its practice nothing can be done if the ruler does not want to save the country."[12]

In a lengthy memorial to the throne Ch'eng I reiterated the need for the Emperor to make a definite decision and commit himself to the Way. Three things were most needful in rulership: for the emperor to commit himself, to share the responsibility he personally accepted for the Way, and to find worthy men able to accept the same responsibility.

> Committing oneself means to be perfectly sincere and single-minded, to take up the Way as one's own responsibility *(i-tao tzu-jen)*, to take the teachings of the sages as trustworthy, to believe that the governance of the Kings can be carried out, to avoid either following rigidly the advice of those nearby or being swayed by public clamor, but to be determined to bring about a world like that of the Three Dynasties.[13]

In Chu Hsi's sealed memorial of 1162, an early expression of his approach to government, he urges the emperor not to rely even on what he is told by Chu, but by objective study, subjective confirmation, and discussion with others, to find out and get for himself *(tzu-te)* the truth of the Way.[14] In this and many other passages Chu Hsi stresses mind-rectification as the essential method by which the ruler fulfills his personal responsibility for the conduct of the Way. In one sense it can be said that this approach is derived from the view of education discussed earlier, extending it into the domain of politics. On the other hand, it is significant that key elements in this doctrine of the examination of conscience or rectification of mind were voiced first by Chu Hsi in this memorial, i.e., in a political context, before being developed in his preface to the *Mean* as a more generalized doctrine for human cultivation. It was via the public man and the political function that the more fundamental human problem was first addressed.

It has often been asserted that the distinctive feature of Sung political life was the increased centralization of authority and bureaucratization of dynastic rule. Sometimes this has been spoken of as "Sung autocracy," a new stage in the long-term development of an increasingly autocratic dynastic system. Yet it can also be argued that the Sung represented a new stage in the rise of the scholar-official class as well, and in the extension of their influence in government.[15] Modern scholars have confirmed the impression given by the Sung statesman and historian Fan Tsu-yü, when he credited the Sung with encouraging freer discussion and debate at court than any previous dynasty.[16]

These trends were concurrent, and coexisted in a relation of complementarity as well as in a state of tension. There was an increasing centralization of bureaucratic rule, but in certain areas and on different levels of government this thrust greater responsibilities on the managerial class as well as concentrating greater power in the hands of the ruler. By the new class of educated, civil-oriented, Confucian officials this power of the ruler was perceived as both an ominous threat and a promising possibility. When lecturing the Emperor, they stressed how crucial it was that he use his power for good rather than ill, trying to bolster his confidence in the power to do good and impress on him the consequences of failure.

In the Northern Sung especially there had been an air of optimism concerning man's ability to accomplish great and good things by the creative use of human reason. Economic growth and cultural affluence encouraged this optimism, and to some extent sustained it even through repeated frustrations and failures to achieve the idealistic goals of Sung reformers. Thus, with the Ch'eng brothers, and even with Chu Hsi in more trying circumstances later, there is a sense of political and cultural crisis but also a stubborn, idealistic faith that man has it within his power to meet the challenge.

No doubt the readiness, indeed resoluteness, of scholars like the Ch'engs and Chu Hsi to express themselves so vigorously in writing and to speak out with great frankness at court, reflected some of the trends of the times and the characteristic attitudes of their class. The economic development of the country, especially in central and south China, supported a significantly larger number of educated persons in the performance of their political and cultural functions, and gave them a new sense of their own importance, a lively esprit de corps, greatly reinforcing their own self-image and self-confidence.[17] This is seen not only in the Ch'eng brothers but in their opponents, like Wang An-shih and Su Tung-p'o, as well.

This self-confidence cannot be compared with the more aggressive and expansive attitude of the Western bourgeoisie in later centuries. If the scholar-officials of the Sung can be thought of in any sense as performing the political functions of a middle class, it is only because as local gentry they had one foot in the land and one in the bureaucracy.[18] The "sprouts of capitalism" that have been detected in the China of this period did not grow and flower into anything like the economic and political pluralism of the West.[19] Available evidence suggests that Chu Hsi was not propertied or well off[20] and their later followers saw the Ch'engs and Chu as having led lives of great hardship.[21] This was no doubt possible, even within a generally rising trend for the gentry as a whole, because of differential rates of growth in some regions and the varying fortunes of individuals and families. Nevertheless Sung scholars did have the leisure to pursue cultural interests, enjoyed the immunities and protections which their class had managed to win in return for its performance of essential bureaucratic functions, and were supported when in difficulty by other members of that class.

The essence of the Ch'eng brothers' own situation is captured in an episode involving Ch'eng I's stipend as lecturer from the classics mat. The convention at court was that the lecturer should submit an application for his salary to the Board of Revenue—in itself an example of the increasing bureaucratization of life. Ch'eng refused to do this, even though he had to borrow money to live on. When asked about this, he replied that to apply for his salary as if for a favor from the throne was demeaning, especially for the lecturer from the classics mat who was supposed to serve as mentor to the Emperor and should be treated with appropriate respect. "The trouble is that today scholars and officials are accustomed to begging," he said. "They beg at every turn."[22]

The matter was eventually handled by proxy, in typical Chinese face-saving fashion, so that Ch'eng I did get his stipend, but for us the story registers several significant points: first, there is Ch'eng I's attempt to assert an independent role for the scholar-official at court vis-à-vis the increasing power of the ruler; second, there is his own acknowledgment that the principle or standard he wishes to uphold was not in practice widely respected; and third is the fact that he was only able to make this rather striking gesture with the help he received from his colleagues. Class solidarity supported him in this rather strained affirmation of self-respect, but the net effect, if any, was more to register a moral point than to score a political gain. Thus, when Ch'eng I and Chu Hsi urged the emperor to emulate the sages, and to take full personal responsibility for the conduct of the Way, it was a projection of the same sense of individual integrity and self-respect that they wished to assert for themselves.

Much the same purpose was served by Chu Hsi's strong emphasis on the relationship between prince and minister as essentially one of agreement on basic principles. It tried to establish the moral parity of the two as well as their collegial solidarity, in contrast to the prevailing view of the minister as the servitor or virtual slave of the emperor. In this respect it sought to gain moral leverage on the ruler, for want perhaps of a politically stronger position for the minister at court. Ch'eng I, reaffirming the stance of Mencius, insisted that the relation between prince and minister was based on a shared commitment to right principles and obliged the latter to depart from the service of a ruler with whom he had fundamental differences on what is right. "Unless the ruler honors virtue and delights in moral principles . . . it is not worth having anything to do with him."[23] In Chu Hsi's *Things at Hand*, Ch'eng I is quoted as saying, "When a scholar is in high position, his duty is to save his ruler and not to follow him in wrongdoing."[24] And further, "When one has resolved that 'if he can hear the Way in the morning, he will die content in the evening,' he will not be content for even a single day with what should not be acquiesced in."[25]

Julia Ching has characterized the stance of the Neo-Confucians in these terms:

> The authority to which they gave adherence was higher than the state, which saw itself as guardian of classical exegesis, higher even than the classics. They relied primarily on their own authority, as self-appointed interpreters of the sacred message. Their claim was to solid classical learning, but particularly to their own insights into the spiritual meaning of the texts. For this reason, in the political realm, they acted as moral judges of their sovereigns rather than as dutiful ministers.[26]

To this one amendment may be made, concerning the word "rather." In the view of the Ch'engs and Chu Hsi, it was precisely by judging the sovereign, by holding him to the highest standards of political morality, that they served as "dutiful ministers." This is what they meant by saying that the relation of ruler and minister was fundamentally a moral one or one of rightness *(i)*, i.e., a relation between two individuals who had freely joined in taking responsibility for the way of governing.

To assert this high standard of political rectitude may have accomplished little politically, but as embodied in the lives of the Ch'engs and Chu Hsi it set an inspiring example for many of their later followers, some of them scholar-statesmen who themselves manifested a great personal initiative, strength of purpose, and stalwart independence against overwhelming political odds. Fang Hsiao-ju (1357–1402) and Hai Jui (1513–87)[27] in the Ming are two examples among many that could be cited. Against the formidable pressures operating to compel conformity, this side of the Neo-Confucian tradition upheld a lofty conception of the dignity, integrity, and independence· of the individual scholar-official. It had a high estimate of the moral and spiritual resources of man, and while its celebration of the heroic virtues may seem hopelessly idealistic to modern minds, it aimed, like *Mencius* (6A:16), at the "nobility of Heaven," i.e., the moral nobility of man, judged on the basis of individual worth rather than special rank or social status.[28]

THE SAGE AS IDEAL SELF

Sagehood and how to attain it is the central theme of Ch'eng-Chu thought, which is to say, of "learning for one's self." It was already the unifying conception of Chou Tun-i's (1017–73) major work *Comprehending the Changes (T'ung-shu)*,[29] and from it Chu Hsi drew the initial selection for "The Essentials of Learning," which set the pattern for his *Things at Hand (Chin-ssu-lu)*.[30] Ch'eng I contributed to the development of this theme by his youthful essay, "What Yen Tzu loved to learn" (i.e., how to become a sage),[31] which Chu likewise quoted early in the same chapter of *Things at Hand*. Consistently with this, Chu's own work concludes with a discussion of those qualities in the sages and worthies which make them fitting models for the individual.

Sagehood had long been a dominant ideal of Chinese thought, for classical Confucians and also for Taoists and Neo-Taoists. What gave special significance to its discussion in the Sung by the Ch'eng brothers and Chu Hsi was their view of the sage as not just a lofty and remote ideal but a model for their own times. They shared a conviction that sagehood could be "learned" by anyone, and Chou Tun-i's positive assurance to this effect became one of the most quoted, and later one of the most disputed, passages in later Neo-Confucian literature:

"Can one become a sage through learning?"
"Yes."
"Is there any essential way?"
"Yes"[32]

What follows in Chou's own work and in other major texts of Neo-Confucianism sets forth this "essential way." Thus sagehood not only was a generalized human ideal of symbolic value but became specifically a model for self-cultivation. The meaning of this is especially clear in Ch'eng I's discussion:

The way to learn is none other than rectifying one's mind and nourishing one's nature. When one abides by the mean and correctness and becomes sincere, he is a sage. In the learning of the noble man, the first thing is to be clear in one's mind and to know where to go, and then act vigorously in order that one may arrive at sagehood. . . . Therefore the student must exert his own mind to the utmost. If he does so, he will know his own nature. And if he knows his own nature, examines his own self and makes it sincere, he becomes a sage.[33]

This message, directed to any and all students, could not be more straightforward or matter-of-fact. No one lacks the essential capability for sagehood if he will just make up his mind to achieve it. Ch'eng adds:

In later years people thought that sagehood was basically due to innate genius and could not be achieved through learning. Consequently the way to learn has been lost to us. Men do not seek within themselves but outside themselves and engage in extensive learning, effortful memorization, clever style, and elegant diction, making their words elaborate and beautiful. Thus few have arrived at the Way. This being the case, the learning of today and the learning that Yen Tzu loved [i.e., learning to be a sage] are quite different.[34]

Again the relevance of this "learning to be a sage" to "learning for oneself" rather than "for the sake of others" is evident. The requisites for the one are the same as for the other; both are contrasted to the prevalent forms of literary learning and indiscriminate erudition. The path to sagehood, practically speaking, represents the method of "finding the Way in oneself," and the sage becomes the ideal self for purposes of Neo-Confucian self-cultivation.

The meaning of this is twofold. When Chu Hsi explains the point of "Reverencing the self or the person" *(ching-shen)* in the *Elementary Learning,* he says, "This section presents a basic model for emulating the sages and worthies."[35] Elsewhere, however, Chu stressed that sagehood came from within the self. In answer to a question about relying on the teachings of the sages as a guide to one's own learning and conduct, he said, "In talking to students we can only teach them to act according to the teachings of the sages. When after making some effort they realize something within themselves, they will know naturally (of themselves, *tzu-chih*) what it really is to be a sage."[36] In other words, one draws on one's own experience as well as on the model put before one, and the result partakes of both individuality and commonality. The sage is the self writ large, but in both of these senses: an internalization of others' representations of sagehood (in the classics, histories, etc.) and a projection, an objectification, of one's own experience.

In this process the experience of one's own age and the preconceptions of one's own generation enter in. Chu Hsi himself understood this when, at the end of the *Things at Hand,* he drew more heavily on the personal experience and example of the Sung masters than on the ancients as a guide to sagely learning. Indeed, the point of compiling *Things at Hand* was to demonstrate the contemporary relevance of sagehood by drawing on the teachings and achievements in self-cultivation of his near contemporaries. In turn, much of the effectiveness of this work and its appeal to Chu's followers lay in its modernity or contemporaneity. Its readers could identify with the Sung masters whose experience of life was closer to their own. Thus sagehood, instead of remaining a lofty abstraction from the past, became defined, and the ideal self to some extent delimited, in ways characteristic of that age.

Some of these delimitations are more apparent to us, with the hindsight of history, than they were to Chu Hsi. He believed deeply in the perfectibility of the moral nature in all men. Philosophically this was based on his doctrine that each man possessed the moral nature or principle inherent in all, sharing a common nature that could form a unity with Heaven and earth and the myriad things, while at the same time each had his own individuality. Chu Hsi sometimes used the metaphor of the moon and its reflection in different bodies of water to illustrate the universality and particularity of principle (or man's nature) expressed in the formulation "principle is one but its particularizations are diverse" *(li-i fen-shu)*. But this metaphor, drawn from Hua-yen Buddhism, had the defect that, since the one moon was real while its many reflections were only passing phenomena, the particular nature manifest in the individual might be taken as only an insubstantial and imperfect reflection of some transcendental reality. In that sense self-realization could only be understood as abandoning all individuality and becoming an exact mirror-image of the transcendent ideal. Wishing instead to affirm the substantiality of the individual in his concrete humanity, morally as well as physically, Chu later chose to express it in terms of the metaphor of growing grain:

> One substance is expressed in the myriad things, but the one substance and the myriad things are each integral by themselves, while the largeness and smallness of each has its own definiteness. . . . The myriad objects embody in themselves, each and every one of them, their own principle. This is what is meant [in the Ch'ien hexagram of *the Changes (I-ching)*] by "changes in the Heavenly Way resulting in each possessing its correct nature and destiny. . . ." It is like a grain of millet, which gives birth to a seedling, which gives birth to a flower. When the flower bears seeds, which become millet again, the original fig-

ure is restored . . . they will go on producing like this eternally.[37]

Here the reality of principle as particularized in each individual, which is the basis of his self-perfection and his aspiration to sagehood, is made clear in a most concrete way. There is no human being not similarly endowed and individually defined.

This universal principle and potentiality in all men is much in the mind of Chu Hsi as he addresses them in his written works. His preface to the *Great Learning* and the opening lines of his Commentary stress universal education as the basis for renewing the people and leading each person to the perfecting of his individual nature. In a preface to *Reflections on Things at Hand (Chinssu-lu)* he expresses the hope that it could serve as a guide to the cultivation of self and sagehood even for "young lads in isolated villages."[38] Likewise, when he recommended the *Elementary Learning* and its "Reverence of the Self" as a guide to sagehood, he spoke of it as "serving for the edification of unlearned *shih*."[39] Just exactly what *shih* meant to him in contemporary terms is not clear; probably Chu thought of this class as not essentially different from the scholar-knights or scholar-officials of ancient times in regard to their leadership functions and commitments, even though he knew that conditions of life had changed since then (for instance, in regard to the performance of rites, the conduct of education, and the institutionalization of the examination system). We today would probably be more conscious of the elite status and leadership functions of the *shih* as differentiating them from the common man in the country village, but Chu seems to emphasize the common human potential rather than the class difference. Each and every individual had it within himself to fulfill this aspiration, even though, as a matter of fact, not many would.

3. Getting It Oneself

In the Neo-Confucian understanding of "Learning for One's Self" no concept was more important than "getting it oneself" as a way of expressing how one achieved self-realization of the Way, and how the Way, especially as revealed in the Classics, was actively repossessed by oneself.

Tzu-te means literally "getting it by or for oneself." This was understood in two important senses. One, relatively low-keyed, is that of learning or experiencing some truth for oneself and deriving inner satisfaction therefrom. Here *tzu-te* has the meaning of "learned to one's satisfaction," "self-contented," "self-possessed." The other sense of the term is freighted with deeper meaning; "getting or finding the Way in oneself," as referred to by Mencius: "The noble man steeps himself in the Way because he wishes to 'get it' himself. When he gets it himself, he will be at ease with it. When he is at ease with it he can trust it deeply, and when he can trust it deeply, he can find its source wherever he turns. That is why the noble man wishes to get it himself" (4B:14).[1] Chuang Tzu also uses the term in the sense of a deep inner fulfillment in accord with the Way.[2]

Another Taoist work, the *Huai-nan tzu* also uses the expression *te* "getting" (the Way), with or without the prefix *tzu*, in contexts where the main subject of discussion is one's self-discovery of the Way.[3] The term *tzu-te* itself is used for finding the Way within oneself, in such a manner as to "complete the self," achieve the "mutual realization (lit: "getting") of the self and all things under Heaven" and "unite one to the Way."[4]

This view of "getting" as "finding the Way in oneself" or as a process of self-realization which overcomes the opposition between self and other, or self and the world, is confirmed by the recent studies of Roger Ames which deal with *te*, "getting," in relation to rightness and virtue in the context of Chinese classical thought. Discussing "getting it right" *(te-i)* in *Mencius, Hsün Tzu,* and the early Han philosopher Tung Chung-shu, Ames, after citing the latter's views on *yi*, states:

> Tung Chung-shu goes on to state that *yi* is the condition of personal identity and uniqueness inasmuch as conduct which expresses a person's *yi* is self-realizing *(tzu-te)*, while conduct which does not disclose *yi* is self-negating *(tzu-shih)*.
>
> *Yi* means appropriateness to one's own person. Only once one is appropriate to his own person can this be called *yi*. Thus, the expression *yi* combines the notions of "appropriateness' *(yi)* and "personal self" *(wo)* in one term. If we hold on to this insight, *yi* as an expression refers to personal self. Thus it is said that to realize *yi (te-yi)* in one's actions is called self-realizing *(tzu-te)*; to neglect *yi* in one's actions is called self-negation *(tzu-shih)*. A person who is fond of *yi* is called a person fond of himself; a person who does not like *yi* is called a person who does not like himself. Considering it in these terms, it is clear that *yi* is personal self *(wo)*. The difference between *yi* and human-heart-

edness is that while human-heartedness means proceeding outward, *yi* means coming inward; while human-heartedness is
distant, *yi* is very close at hand; while love invested in others is
human-heartedness, love in and of one's own person is *yi;* while
human-heartedness focuses on others, *yi* focuses on oneself. The
expression "self-realizing" *(tzu-te)* which occurs in this passage
and is equated with "realizing yi" *(te-yi)* appears frequently in
the corpus of early Chinese literature in discussions that center
on the achievement of personal identity and the uniqueness of
that achievement.[5]

Chu Hsi's commentary on *tzu-te* in *Mencius* 4B:14 says that the
noble man should cultivate himself deeply in accordance with the
Way, so as to have a firm direction or method to hold to, and by
silent recognition and penetration of the mind, naturally (of oneself) find it in oneself *(te chih yü chi)*. He cites Ch'eng Hao's view
of it as "learning that is unspoken and is acquired naturally is truly
'getting it oneself.' Learning that is contrived and forced is not
'getting it oneself.' "[6]

What I have translated above from the text of Mencius as "steeps
himself in the Way" (following D. C. Lau)[7] is explained by Chu
Hsi as "reaching" or "meeting" the Way, i.e., advancing unceasingly in accordance with the direction and method of the Way.[8]
Unless one can reach or meet it within, says Chu in his *Questions
on the Mencius (Meng-tzu huo-wen)*, learning remains mere sense
knowledge, external to one. Neither can it, on the other hand, be
found in a vacuous state, apart from everyday life. This "reaching"
is found only in the subtle, inner workings of the mind as the
principles in things and in the self come into dynamic accord.[9] It is
a process not unlike Chu's explanation of the "investigation of
things" as an arriving or meeting, in his commentary on the *Great
Learning*, which emphasizes the correspondence or resonance between principles in the self and principles in things, rather than the
pursuit of one to the exclusion of the other.[10] But here Chu particularly emphasizes that the "getting" must come naturally (the

expression *tzu jan* occurs frequently in the context) without any straining or calculation to obtain a predetermined result or to acquire something not already one's own. Chu also stresses the contentment that comes from finding the Way within, as if one were thoroughly at home with it, like the rich man who has everything he needs at home and does not have to look elsewhere.[11] These are key points, as we shall appreciate later on when we encounter the concept of "getting it oneself" as applied to book-learning.

Also deeply revealing are the comments of the great nineteenth century scholar James Legge in his translation of the *Mencius*. Legge translates the first part of the passage quoted above as: "The superior man makes his advances in what he is learning with deep earnestness and by the proper course, wishing to get hold of it as in himself."[12] The standard pre-Sung commentary, by Chao Ch'i, had explained this last expression in terms of wishing to reach one's original root or essence, as if one's nature originally possessed it; and Chao reiterated this idea further in commenting on the final portion of the passage about resting content, "as if it were something inherently possessed by him . . . as the root of his being."[13] Legge, who captions his own comment "The Value of Learning Thoroughly Inwrought into the Mind," thereby opts for a somewhat different interpretation emphasizing the appropriation of something external to one, as if to make it what we might call "second nature," and there are indeed passages in the writings of Ch'eng I and Chu Hsi which, by themselves, could be so understood. Nevertheless Legge is scholar enough to acknowledge that the traditional commentators incline to another view. What he has translated as "advancing in learning" *(tsao)* literally means "reach" or "arrive at," and the *tao*, which he renders here as "course of study," has a much broader and deeper meaning for most earlier commentators. Hence Legge concludes:

One may read scores of pages in the Chinese commentators, and yet not get a clear idea in his own mind of the teaching of

Mencius in this chapter. Chao Ch'i gives *tao* a more substantive meaning than in the translation [i.e., Legge's]: thus: "The reason why the superior man pursues with earnestness to arrive at the depth and mystery of Tao, is from a wish to get hold for himself of its source and root, as something belonging to his own nature." Most critics understand the subject studied to be man's own self, not things external to him. We must leave the subject in its own mist.[14]

Legge's more matter-of-fact interpretation attempts to demystify the matter and render it more comprehensible to Western readers, but his scholarly conscience compelled him to acknowledge that the almost unanimous judgment of Chinese commentators saw in this a much deeper, more mystical significance, one which, well before the Neo-Confucians appeared on the scene, would lend itself both to Chu Hsi's view of it as a method of learning which involves an interpenetration or convergence of the Way within and without, and to the more radical or mystical view of those who would reject the trivialization of the Tao as a mere "course of study."

The centrality of *tzu-te* in the Ch'eng-Chu system is indicated by the fact that Master Ch'eng's discussion of it is the first-cited passage at the head of the "General Introduction of Learning" in the *Great Compendium on Human Nature and Principles (Hsing-li ta-ch'üan)*, the Ming dynasty compilation long accepted as the official "bible" of Neo-Confucian philosophy. Here Ch'eng speaks of learning as seeking within oneself and says "the most refined of principles should be sought and found in oneself *(tzu ch'iu te chih)*.[15] Hence among the possible translations of *te* as "acquire," "obtain," "possess," any of which may be appropriate in a given context, I have in general used "get" as the most basic meaning, despite its colloquial tone, but sometimes "find" as in "finding the Way in oneself" or "finding [satisfaction, contentment, joy] in oneself." Just as *te* had the advantage of generality and was open to different interpretations, "get" avoids over-determination. It can be used for different kinds and levels of experience, ranging from the intellectual, methodical, and gradual (which Chu Hsi tends to emphasize) to the more intuitive, spontaneous, and total.

Both *tzu-jen* and *tzu-te* recur frequently in descriptions of the crucial learning experience or decisive conversion experiences of leading Neo-Confucians.

Much of chapter 4 in Chu Hsi's *Things at Hand*, on "Preserving One's Mind," is concerned with the problem of naturalness and getting the truth or the Way for oneself as a matter of practical self-cultivation. This was a particular concern of Ch'eng I. Of the many passages quoted from him, the two following will help to clarify the point.

> Master I-ch'uan [Ch'eng I] said: "The student should revere and respect the Mind. He should not anxiously try to force it. Instead he should cultivate it deeply, nourish it richly and steep himself in it. Only thus can he get it for himself *(tzu-te)*. If one anxiously presses in pursuit of it, that is mere selfishness *(ssu-chi)*. In the end it will not suffice for attaining the Way."[16]
>
> Nowadays students are reverent but do not get it for themselves *[tzu-te]*. All this is because in their minds they are not at home with reverence. It is also because they carry reverence [seriousness] too far in dealing with things. This is what is meant by "Respectfulness, not in accord with what is rite, becomes laborious bustle. . . ." Rites are not a body of ceremonies but natural principles *(tzu-jan ti tao-li)*. Because one is only respectful, without practicing natural principles, he is not at home with himself *(tzu-tsai)*. One must be respectful and yet at ease.[17] Now the reason why one must be right in appearance and correct in speech is not merely to attain goodness for himself and see what others will say. It is because according to the Principle of Nature *(t'ien-li)*, he should be so [i.e., it is both natural and proper to be so]. Basically there should be no selfish ideas but only being in accord with principle.[18]

The relevance of this to "learning for one's self" as opposed to "learning for the sake of others" need not be elaborated here. This is a familiar problem of the spiritual life in other religious and ethical traditions: i.e., how to balance or reconcile moral effort with religious awe and acceptance.[19] In Ch'eng I's case it is complicated by the built-in ambiguity in his use of the term *ching*, meaning both "reverent" and "serious." As understood in the Ch'eng-Chu school it was meant to combine moral effort and religious acceptance in a way that was "natural" for a man of conscience.

For Chu Hsi too *tzu-te* had significance in relation to both finding the Way and practicing it in given contexts. In the *Mean* (14) the term is used in this sense in a passage which describes the Way of the Noble Man *(chün-tzu)* as applicable to and practicable in all life situations.

> The noble man accords with h s station in life and does not desire to go beyond it. In [or, according with] a position of wealth and honor, he does what is proper to a position of wealth and honor. In a poor and low position, he does what is proper to a poor and low position. Situated among barbarians, he does what is proper among barbarians. In a situation of sorrow and difficulty, he does what is proper in sorrow and difficulty. The noble man can find himself in no situation in which he is not himself.[20]

Sung commentators cited by Chu Hsi speak of *tzu-te* (here rendered by Legge as "being oneself" or finding [the Way] oneself") as a state of being so centered in the universal Tao that one finds within one all the resources needed to deal appropriately with any situation; one is so in tune with the Tao that one can act naturally in any place or time in perfect accordance with it. All one has need of can be found within one's own mind-and-heart.[21] In the context of the *Mean*, "accepting one's station in life and not wishing to go beyond it" is the natural condition of one centered in the Way, i.e., of one who has attained the Mean; and "acting naturally in any place or time" corresponds to what is said in the

Mencius about one who has "gotten it himself" being one who "can find its source wherever he turns."

Thus, despite the inherent "mistiness" of the subject, as Legge would have it, there is a consistency in the treatment of it in these two prime classical sources for its Neo-Confucian usage; so much so indeed that Legge is compelled to yield on his interpretation of *tzu-te* as the appropriation of something external to one and to translate it here as "no situation in which he is not himself," i.e., "being himself." And in Chu's summation of the significance of the *Mean* as a whole, he says:

> Tzu-ssu relates the ideas that had been handed down to him as the basis of his discourse. First he explains that the Way originally derives from Heaven and cannot be altered. Its substance inheres in the self and cannot be departed from. Next it sets forth the essentials of preserving and nourishing this [substance in the mind] and of practicing self-examination. Finally, it expresses the ultimate achievement of sagely and spiritual men in the transforming power of their virtue. In this Tzu-ssu wished for the learner to look within and get it [the substance of the Way] for himself.[22]

From this it is understandable that Chu's "repossessing or reconstituting of the Way" *(tao-t'ung)* should reflect the Ch'eng brothers' view of "getting it oneself," as well as Ch'en Ch'ang-fang's linkage of the sages' learning of the mind-and-heart to "getting it oneself." Wing-tsit Chan, in discussing how Chu arrived at his concept of *tao-t'ung*, notes Ch'eng I's central role, saying of him, "Ch'eng's main point was that his brother found the Confucian Way, meaning the teachings of Confucius and Mencius, in surviving Classics himself. Like most Neo-Confucianists, his emphasis was on 'acquiring for oneself' *(tzu-te)*."

In the same vein but in a quite different area of Chu's thought, Richard Lynn cites *tzu-te* among the qualities Chu Hsi appreciated in great poetry, along with others emphasizing naturalness, freedom, and spontaneity.[23] Indeed, to many Neo-Confucians, as well as modern readers of Sung poetry, *tzu-te* conveys a sense of spiritual joy and exaltation from having attained a kind of mystical union of the self with Heaven-and-Earth and all things. Ch'eng Hao is especially remembered for his poem translated by Professor Chan under the title "Composed Casually on an Autumn Day":

> With leisure everything is relaxed
> When I awake the sun shining through the eastern window is
>   already red
> All things viewed in tranquility are at ease with themselves.
> The delightful spirit in the four seasons I share with all.
> Tao penetrates through the physical limits of heaven-and-earth.
> My thoughts enter into the changing atmosphere of wind
>   and cloud.
> When one's heart is not dissipated by wealth and honor and one
>   is happy with poverty and low station,
> When one reaches this point, one is a hero.[24]

Professor Chan adds the comment that among poems by Neo-Confucians "This is surely the most popular and most often quoted. Chu Hsi saw in this poem that Ch'eng Hao understood principle or Tao to be in all things and necessary. It may be added that at the same time Ch'eng Hao was intimately involved in all changing events in both nature and human society. The distinction between self and things is forgotten. All things merge into one and are at ease, and joy is shared by all."

What Professor Chan has translated above as "at ease with themselves" is *tzu-te* in the sense of self-fulfillment and contentment described by Mencius above. In the seventh line one's heart not being dissipated and one's being happy with poverty and low station, refer to Mencius' conception of the "great man" *(ta-jen)* (3B:2). Finally in the last line is affirmed the kind of achievement that constitutes being a true hero in Neo-Confucian terms, as Ch'eng Hao had explained elsewhere in his *Collected Writings*.[25] The great appeal of this poem then, and its powerful influence on later thought, lay in the joining of these three conceptions—self-fulfillment in harmony with the universe *(tzu-te)*, true human greatness *(ta-jen)* achieved through dedication to principle, and the two together constituting the real hero *(hao-chieh)*. Since the "great man" or mature human being as described by Mencius took upon himself the responsibility for the Way, Heaven-and-earth and all things, and in this poem also was seen as completely attuned to nature, all of the basic elements in the Neo-Confucian conception of the individual were marvelously fused in Ch'eng Hao's eight lines: the solidarity with man and nature, the moral commitment, the affective/aesthetic rapport, and the spiritual exaltation. These evoked a deep response in the thought and writings of later Neo-Confucians.

"GETTING IT" AS A SCHOLAR

Thus far I have discussed "getting it oneself" as a concept of self-realization or self-transformation in relation to the Way as a whole. In such a broad perspective "learning for the sake of oneself" was not to be understood as simply the preoccupation of the learned man or literatus. Learning in the larger and deeper sense had the kind of ultimate meaning and value we usually associate with religion. It involved pursuit of the Way as the Neo-Confucians often understood it when they recalled the saying in the *Analects* of Confucius: "Hearing the Way in the morning, one can die content in the evening"(4:8).

There is, as we have seen, a sense of *wen*, "learning" or "culture," which comes close to this ultimate significance of the Way or Tao. Here *wen* stands for the highest values of the culture, for human civilization as carrying out the Way and the will of Heaven. Confucius had talked of his own mission in the world as bound up with "this culture" *(ssu-wen)*, and many Neo-Confucians likewise took it as their personal responsibility in life to make the Way manifest in the world through "this culture."[26] In this way they affirmed their conviction that human fulfillment cannot be achieved except through the distinctive cultural activities of the human species, in contrast to such teachings as Taoism and Ch'an Buddhism which sought religious fulfillment in ways that went beyond or transcended all cultural formulations.

We should remember that this cultural activity arose in the context of human life as a whole and had almost a cosmic dimension insofar as Confucians believed it to be a crucial creative contribution of man to the workings of Heaven-and-earth. Yet more than one meaning attached to the term "culture" *(wen)*, and this created a problem with respect to the human need for setting priorities among different forms of cultural activity. Confucius addressed this problem when, in the *Analects*, he spoke of one's primary moral obligations to others as having a greater claim on one's self-cultivation than the embellishments of polite letters:

> A youth, when at home, should be filial, and abroad, respectful to his elders. He should be earnest and truthful. He should overflow with love for all and cultivate the friendship of the good. When he has time and opportunity after the performance of these things, he should employ them in the study of polite letters *(wen)*.[27]

Here Confucius is speaking of the training of the young, and in recognizing the primary claims of the basic moral relations over the adornments of literary studies, he does not preclude the possibility of a greater involvement in scholarship at a later stage in life. Nevertheless, even at that later stage there would remain a question as to how a balance might be maintained between moral and intellectual self-cultivation, lest literary refinement and scholarly inquiry engulf moral cultivation and lead to the attenuation or enervation of the will.

To some extent every major religious tradition faces this problem, regardless of how high or low it rates cultural activity on its scale of values. As a "tradition," it must depend for the conveying of its message on some means of cultural transmission. Even fundamentalists with their distrust of, if not actual hostility toward, the more sophisticated forms of culture, cannot avoid this problem.

Insofar as their fundamentalism usually holds to some "literal" reading of scripture, it cannot be free of texts and some manner of textual interpretation.

From this point of view, we may say that "learning for one's self" as the substantive pursuit of the Neo-Confucian was not only revealed through his functional roles in society *(yung)* but in how he related to his tradition, to his culture *(wen)*, and, increasingly, to the Way *(tao)* as representing the highest or most basic values of that culture. It may well be that in all major ethico-religious traditions some relation to the scriptures is important to the process of self-discovery and self-definition, and that St. Augustine's *tolle lege* ("take up and read") or, by contrast, the Zen master's tearing up of the scriptures, are paradigmatic acts of almost universal significance. Nevertheless, there has probably been no other traditional so clearly committed to scholarship as the Confucian, and in the absence of sacerdotal, pastoral, or monastic activities, it was book learning and literary activity which became for the Confucian even more central tasks than for the Christian, Jew, Muslim, Hindu, or Buddhist. Accordingly, it is in this cultural context that we must look for the defining characteristics of Neo-Confucian personhood or individualism.[28]

In China, as in East Asia generally, the Confucians have been most commonly referred to as *ju*, which, whatever one's view may be as to the origins of the term, has in later ages most often been understood as representing scholarly or literary, rather than priestly or monastic, functions. In the standard dynastic histories Confucians have most often been classed as *ju*, and it was only in the *History of the Sung Dynasty*, written during the high tide of Neo-Confucian evangelism in the Yüan dynasty, that a term with stronger religious connotations, *tao-hsüeh*, (Learning of the Way) was applied to those who took a more metaphysical or ideological stance.[29]

To recognize this special scholarly orientation of the Confucians is not simply to take into account the particular ground on which this teaching had taken its stand, but also to acknowledge the limitation which often accompanied it, for to the extent that Confucians pursued a particular cultural vocation, or sought to achieve credentials which would qualify them as especially learned, they also set themselves somewhat apart from others and limited their own appeal as potential bearers of a "religious" message to the common man. Indeed, recalling how St. Paul boasted of being a fool, and made light of the wisdom of learned men, one might see such scholarly qualifications, from the religious standpoint, as a disadvantage and almost a disqualification.[30] Confucians, who professed to be a learned elite upholding high cultural standards, risked prejudicing their larger educative function by distancing themselves from uneducated masses who might be better appealed to through myth, ritual, and the popular religious imagination than through the more rational, scholarly methods of the Confucians. In the end this could not but have an effect even on the Confucians' avowed aim of winning "the hearts and minds of the people," which they insisted on as a primary responsibility of rulers.

To suggest that, in the larger view of history, this might have been a handicap to the Confucians as bearers of a universal message is not to deny their cultural achievements but only to identify these more precisely. For if that message was universal enough to exert a powerful attraction on the educated elites of East Asia as a whole, whatever the diversity of their social and cultural backgrounds, it remains true that for anyone to "get" this message entailed some special preparation. Access to Neo-Confucian discourse was not easily gained, and in no age, whether medieval or modern, could the basic texts of Neo-Confucianism be understood without a considerable training. Even though Chu Hsi, as an educator, had in mind meeting the educational needs of all the people, the texts he prepared for this purpose, such as the *Elementary Learning* and *Reflections on Things at Hand*, presupposed a fair knowledge of the classics, history, and philosophy. Even Chu Hsi's *Classified Conversations*, though making much use of vernacular speech, represented a continuing dialogue among cognoscenti, which required reformulation in simpler, sometimes more abridged forms and even vernacular translation, if it was to be understood by any but the most cultivated of audiences. This inherent problem of Neo-Confucian discourse must be taken into account if we are not to misjudge the context in which "getting it oneself" could have some meaning and relevance.

In the writings and conversations of the Ch'eng brothers and Chu Hsi the relation between the self and the Way as revealed in traditional texts is a central topic of discussion. Generally speaking, equal emphasis is put on 1) the need to learn the Way through the classics and histories, and 2) the importance of some personal engagement and live interaction with the mind of the Sages revealed therein. One of these without the other will not do. Ch'eng I and Chu were quite methodical in their approach to the subject, and Chu, in his *Questions on the Mean (Chung-yung huo-wen)* left a succinct statement of the procedure to be followed. It pertains to the same passage referred to in his "Articles of the Academy of the White Deer Grotto"; namely, the order among "studying, inquiring, thinking, sifting, and practicing":

> After one has studied extensively, he can have the principles of all things before him. He can therefore examine them and compare them to get the right questions to ask. Then, as he inquires carefully, his teachers and friends will wholeheartedly engage in give-and-take with him, and he will begin to think. As he thinks carefully his thoughts will be refined and free from impurities. Thus there is something in it he can make his own *(yu so tzu-te)*. He can sift what he has acquired. As he sifts clearly, he can make his decisions without making a mistake. He can therefore be free from doubts and put his thoughts into action. As he practices earnestly, all that he has achieved from studying, inquiring, thinking and sifting will become concrete demonstrations and will no longer remain empty words.[31]

The same theme is repeated many times by Ch'eng I. He says: "Students must find things out for themselves *(tzu-te)*. The Six Classics are vast and extensive. At first it is difficult to understand them completely. As students find their own way, each establishes his own gate, and then returns home to conduct his inquiries himself."[32]

In the learning process a problem could arise too if the teacher did not take into account the need for the young to find their own way into the classics, rather than accept the ready-made interpretations of others: "Explaining books orally is certainly not the intention of the ancients, for it would make people superficial. A student should think deeply and accumulate his thought, cultivating himself in a leisurely way so that he may find it himself *(tzu-te).* Today a book may be explained in just one day. This is merely to teach people to be superficial."[33]

Study of the classics must be an intensely personal experience if it is to fulfill the purpose of learning the Way, which demands of the individual that he himself activate or advance the Way:

> The classics are vehicles of the Way. To recite the words and explain the meanings of the terms without attaining the Way is to render them useless dregs. . . . I hope you will seek the Way through the classics. If you make more and more effort, some day you will see something lofty before you. Unconsciously you will start dancing with your hands and your feet. Then even without further effort you will not be able to keep yourself from going on.[34]

Here, and in numerous other passages from Ch'eng I's writings, the affective aspects of the learning process are greatly stressed. One should be moved by learning and not left unaffected. It is true that Ch'eng I also sanctioned the practice of quiet-sitting as a means of achieving tranquility, composure, or "reverence" (as he would most prefer to put it). But the aim here was to quiet down or curb only selfish desires, while directing active emotions toward unselfish ends. The reverent man would not be lifeless and unfeeling; on a basic level he would be experiencing the "self-enjoyment" *(tzu ch'ieh)* that goes with "making the intention sincere" *(Great Learning VI)*; on a higher level his affective nature would be fully engaged in the pursuit of sagehood. Study of the classics, then, if approached without ulterior motives or self-seeking expectations, should be inspirational and uplifting. It should induce a conversion experience, a natural exhilaration of the spirit over the prospect of being able to improve and transform oneself into a sage, a worthy, or a noble man. Thus, Ch'eng I says of reading the *Analects:* "If, after having studied it, one is still the same person as before, he has not really studied it."[35] And again, disapprovingly, "There are people who have read the *Analects* without anything happening to them. There are others who having read the book, love it. And there are those who, having read it, unconsciously dance with their hands and feet."[36]

To achieve this latter result one must approach study of the classics through the spirit and the affections as well as the intellect. One must "taste" or "savor" the essential flavor of the texts and assimilate the nourishment which true wisdom provides to the mind-and-heart.[37] Necessary though it is to understand the meaning of the words in the text, if one tries to explain classics like the *Analects* and *Mencius* literally, he will not get the full meaning, which often goes beyond the spoken word.[38] To apprehend and appreciate this, deep thought and reflection are necessary. Yet at the same time one should try to formulate his own understanding in words because the process of articulating one's thoughts in words helps to clarify them. "Whenever in our effort at thinking we come to something that cannot be expressed in words, we must think it over carefully and sift it again and again."[39]

READING AND SELF-RENEWAL

If these passages still seem inordinately preoccupied with a kind of learning narrowly focused on the classics, Chu Hsi was not unaware of the criticism which this drew from thinkers like Lu Hsiang-shan, who decried Chu's seemingly excessive involvement in the externals of classical scholarship and asserted instead the primacy of the moral nature within. Lu saw "respect for the moral nature" *(tsun te-hsing)* as "the first thing to be established" *(hsien li yü ch'i ta).*[40]

If study of the classics were so essential to self-cultivation, Lu asked how the ancient sages could have found the Way before the classics were written.[41] Chu Hsi acknowledged that there was an early stage of preliterate civilization in which virtue could be attained without recourse to book-learning:

> Tzu-lu [in *Analects* 11:24] did not say that one could govern even if he were not learned, but only that learning did not necessarily require the study of books. In ancient times when there was as yet no literature the learner of course had no books to read, and those of average ability or better of course got it themselves [i.e., found the Way in themselves *(tzu-te che)*] without having recourse to reading books. But once the sages and worthies had produced the classics, the Way conveyed by them was most explicit and even a sage like Confucius could not dispense with them in his pursuit of learning.[42]

Since it was generally accepted that Confucius had studied the classics and attained sagehood, the reading of the classics was not what created difficulties for those seeking the Way, but rather the faulty manner in which the reading was done in more recent times.

> In reading one cannot seek for moral principles simply by looking at the written page. One should reflect, look for the truth within oneself, and find its application and corroboration there. [But] from the Ch'in and Han dynasties on down, no one has talked about this. They have just directed their attention to volumes of texts and have not tried to gain understanding through self-application. They do not yet see that it is only when we take what the sages have said therein and apply it to ourselves that we can really "get it."[43]

For Chu Hsi the proper method for study of the classics was not essentially different from that of which Confucius had spoken in *Analects* 2:11 as learning from the past in order to understand the present: "Cherishing the old and understanding the new, one can be a teacher of men." Cherishing the old as one studies the classics involves, in one sense, learning what is external to one, while understanding the new involves grasping moral principles within one. Only by understanding the new as grasping principle within the self can one "get it oneself," says Chu, and respond creatively to every situation one encounters, as the teacher must be able to do.[44]

Here Chu Hsi interprets this famous dictum from Confucius' *Analects* in terms drawn from the discussion of "getting it oneself" and the methods of intellectual self-cultivation set forth in both *Mencius* and the *Mean*.

In another passage he further explains how "learning for one's self" is linked to Mencius' "getting it oneself" and the methods of intellectual self-cultivation set forth in both *Mencius* and the *Mean*:

> If one truly sets his mind on learning for one's self, even though he must strictly uphold all the rules and regulations in his manifest conduct of affairs, vigorously grasp and preserve what he has achieved and make continued progress day-by-day, month-by-month, not permitting any retreat, his effort will be just what Mencius called "steeping oneself in the Way." The term "steep" refers to the prolonged cultivation effort of "accumulating," while the expression "the Way" does not refer to anything apart from manifest daily affairs. Because of such cultivation efforts, inner and outer will become as one, the subtle workings of the mind and nature will be preserved, and the biases of his physical nature will be completely transformed. As for the conclusion "when he gets it in himself he will be at ease with it and can draw deeply upon it," how could it mean that he would leave behind the outer and turn inward, despise the shallow and pursue the deep, and dispense with the concrete efforts of learning, critical thinking, and conscientious practice, and devote himself to the subtlety of his mind and nature by some other means?[45]

Elsewhere Chu draws on the familiar language of the *Great Learning* to explain how the same learning process can reach the depths of the Way within oneself and, by learning from the principles enunciated in the classics, correct the corrupt tendencies that have arisen from specious learning and effete literary pursuits.

What the ancients studied was nothing but the clarifying of the moral nature, the renewing of the people and resting in the highest good. The virtue they so sought and the goodness they rested in—how could it have been something they would have to find outside? It was enough to know that these lay within oneself and could be preserved by reverence. The reason why they [nevertheless] spoke of reading books was that the principles of Heaven and Earth, Yin-yang and things and affairs, and the Way of cultivating self, serving parents, regulating the family, extending this to the state, and bringing peace to the world—to say nothing of the words and deeds of the sages, the successes and failures of past and present, the names and numbers for rites and music, and on down to such matters as the sources of food and money, military and penal affairs, and legal institutions— are all within our sphere and cannot but be matters for differentiation and discrimination. If one did not study the texts in which these are recorded and deeply immerse oneself in them, in order to get at their causes, one would have no means of manifesting the virtuous nature, perfecting its substance and functioning, or resting precisely at the point of highest good.

But after the sages' learning was no longer transmitted, those who wished to become scholar-officials, no longer knowing the original basis of learning and having nothing but books to read, sought to study only literary forms, textual exegesis, and how to memorize and recite in order to fish for fame and emoluments. Thus the more books there were, the more obscure principles became, and the harder scholars labored at it the more they lost their minds. The more elegant became their theories, the more lacking they were in virtuous deeds and practical achievements that could match those of the ancients. But it is not the fault of the books. It is that the readers do not know the basis of learning or the ground on which to practice it.[46]

Thus, while affirming that the principles of the Way are inherent within the self, Chu feels it necessary to explain how they could have become obscured by a corrupt culture. In another passage Chu probes more deeply into the sources of this corruption and recognizes that they can only exert such a pernicious influence because of a conflict within the self between the "mind of the Way" and the selfish desires that arise in the "human mind," which alienate him not only from others but from his true self. But to deal with this deleterious effect of culture on man, interior self-cultivation alone is not enough; the culture itself must be dealt with. Inner and outer can only be reconciled through the right combination of cultural rectification and true self-cultivation:

> Having a human body one is bound to have a mind-and-heart, and in the mind-and-heart there are bound to be principles. With humaneness, rightness, riteness and wisdom as substance, and the senses of commiseration, good and evil, deference and respect, right and wrong as function, all humans have this [nature], and it is not something that has to be sought outside oneself. But the reason why the sages did not let one learn by simply listening and looking, or seeking within one's own mind, but insisted further on the uses of poetry, the instituting of rites and the perfecting of music, as well as why they spoke of broad learning, thorough inquiry, careful reflection, clear discrimination and conscientious action, was because, while principles lie within our minds-and-hearts, they may be obscured by the selfishness of the desire for things in the physical endowment and one cannot perceive them. Although learning is external, it is all concerned with the realization of principle through a process of fusion, thorough interpenetration and "getting it oneself."
>
> Primordially there was no differentiation between inner and outer [principles] or refined and coarse [natures], but with the change in times and the decline into vulgarity, scholars did not understand how to study. In their picking and reading of books, they did not go beyond self-display and mutual contentiousness,

seeking to advance their own interests and gain lucrative rewards, while those who did give some thought to learning for one's self, believed that one could go straight to one's own heart-and-mind and find there all that was needed, without having to look anywhere else. Thus they fell into the deviant views of Buddhist and Taoist emptiness, and did not examine into the correctness of moral principles or the details of methodical procedure. When, happily perhaps, they have understood that principles inhered within the self and that learning could not but be concerned with them, if still they did not understand proper order and procedure, they singlemindedly followed whatever suited their own natural inclination, and in their haste to make judgments or in the shallowness of their opinions they often failed in the end to achieve a thorough fusing and interpenetration [of principle within and without.][47]

Of particular importance here is the balance Chu strikes between self-introspection and formal learning. Although the original nature is good, the actual condition of man is such that he cannot rely simply on free self-expression to perfect that original virtue. He must make an effort, through a conscious commitment of the moral will, to associate himself with what is right and good in the classics, in others, and in the world. Only so can one bring the inner structure of one's own being into proper alignment with principles in the world and overcome the estrangement of self and other, which is the source of selfishness in man.

At this point Chu makes clear the difference between his holistic view of what is natural to man and the "deviant views" of Buddhists and Taoists who take the self and subjectivity as absolutes, so that moral effort and objective learning are deemed unnecessary and unnatural. It is only through the proper exercise of the moral will and the correct use of man's learning powers that one can overcome the disparity between good intentions and flawed conduct, and so arrive at the state of non-disparity between self and others, or inner and outer, which is the highest good.

If the goal is this state of non-disparity, which Chu speaks of as transcending all dualities, the means to its achievement cannot be similarly intangible but must rely on the most rigorous and well-defined of methods. Insofar as this entails for the scholar a definite procedure for the study of the written record—classics, histories, rituals, and institutions—Chu provided a detailed reading method. I have discussed the significance of this reading method in an essay on "Chu Hsi's Aims as an Educator."[48]

Here I limit myself to just one aspect of that method which sometimes gives rise to misunderstanding. This is the practice of reading the classics aloud, over and over. Often this is understood as mechanical recitation and treated as rote-learning, which no doubt it could become. But as we have seen in the preceding quotations from Ch'eng I, he thought of it more as chanting or singing to oneself, renewing one's nature and revivifying the principles within through contact with the principles in the classics. Far from being a process of interiorizing teachings imposed from outside, or of conforming oneself to external models, this kind of soulful, inspirational reading was restorative of self.

No doubt there was an element of discipline and routine in it. Chu Hsi tells how as a youth he recited or chanted the *Great Learning* and the *Mean* to himself ten times every morning. Yet it was not a mindless exercise: "Generally in the reading of the text one should recite it intensively so that the words all seem to come from one's own mouth, and then one should continue by reflecting carefully on it until the ideas all seem to come from one's own mind-and-heart. Only then does one really 'get it.' "[49]

Although effort is required to recite in this way, and Chu reiterates often the need for this kind of repetition,[50] no particular virtue attaches to the number of recitations, nor is there any set goal or limit prescribed for them. How much recitation is appropriate depends simply on when the student comes to feel that he has "gotten it." The only criterion Chu can offer is the achievement of a sense of thoroughgoing, integral, and comprehensive understanding *(kuan-t'ung)*, in which all consciousness of the distinction between self and other is overcome.[51] "Recite many times in order to become one with it," says Chu. "The ancients too read and recited several times in order to achieve integral comprehension *(kuan-t'ung)*."[52]

The expression "integral comprehension" *(kuan-t'ung)* is best known from Chu Hsi's special note on "the investigation of things and extension of knowledge" *(ko-wu chih-chih)* in his commentary on the opening lines of *Great Learning*. Here "knowledge" or "knowing" *(chih)* is to be understood in the sense of the knowing faculty no less than of the things and affairs to be known, learned, or understood. Chu Hsi is careful in describing this process to use language that avoids any implication that the mind is simply assimilating something from outside. It is a process which begins with the mind already in possession of "all the principles with which one responds to the myriad things and affairs," so that true learning means bringing about the "full functioning" of the "mind's substance," to the point where the principles of the Way already within one are fully employed or activated in relation to the principles in things and affairs.[53]

This is an affective exercise, involving the sense of sympathy and compassion as well as cognitive learning, so that the result is an empathetic entering into and identification with principle that overcomes all distinction between inner and outer, self and other. Hence the conception of the "whole substance and great functioning" of the mind-and-heart is explained in a manner fully consistent with Mencius' account of "getting it" that is also a self-realization.[54]

Learning so understood as both active and reflective, affective as well as cognitive, also had both its critical and creative sides. It called on the scholar to doubt and to question received tradition as the prerequisite for giving full assent and active implementation to his understanding of the Way. Ch'eng I said, "The student must first of all know how to doubt"[55] and Chang Tsai also asserted the need to take a fresh approach to things: "Whenever there is any doubt about moral principles, one should wipe out his old views so new ideas will come."[56] Chu Hsi called this a "wonderful method," cited it in his methodological discussions with Lü Tsu-ch'ien, and quoted it in *Things at Hand*.[57] Morohashi Tetsuji, in his monumental study of the Sung school, also cited this skeptical method as a hallmark of the Neo-Confucian approach to learning.[58]

This questioning attitude toward received tradition was a major feature of Sung learning as a whole. A skeptical attitude toward the "classical" learning of the Han and T'ang underlay the Sung scholars' wholesale reinterpretation and reformulation of the classics.[59] It was also a notable feature of Sung historical studies from Ouyang Hsiu (1007–1072) down to Ma Tuan-lin (1254–1325).[60] Further, as the more extrovert outlook of the Northern Sung turned inward and dissatisfaction with the immediate past and present became increasingly directed toward self-awareness and self-reform as the precondition for social reform, this questioning attitude and critical method became deeply embedded in the new Ch'eng-Chu tradition of self-cultivation. Influential texts of the new movement like *Things at Hand (Chin ssu-lu)* and the Four Books as formulated by Chu Hsi gave explicit encouragement to this self-conscious, critical attitude[61] and concretely exemplified that spirit at work in classical studies. Thus, later scholars who studied these texts would find their attention drawn to the self-conscious mind and its autonomous operations. In the view of Ch'eng I and Chu Hsi, nothing would substitute for the individual's inner reflection on the scriptures and reevaluation of it in the silence of his own mind.

No less importantly, along with this questioning attitude went a positive and creative approach which drew something new from its reassessment of the old. True, the established convention called for scholars to follow the example of Confucius, who had professed to be a transmitter rather than a creator. In such a tradition complete originality would have been seen as a dubious merit. Nevertheless, while making no claims for themselves, Ch'eng I and Chu Hsi freely credited other Sung scholars with making their own distinctive contributions.

Ch'eng I greatly admired Chang Tsai's *Western Inscription* with its eloquent expression of a Confucian natural mysticism, affirming man's kinship with all creation. Praising its purity and sublimity, his older brother Ch'eng Hao had said it was unmatched by any other teaching since the Ch'in and Han, and Ch'eng I went further to say that it revealed what earlier sages had never taught. As an original contribution he likened it in importance to Mencius' doctrines of the goodness of human nature and the nourishing of the dynamic power within the self which reaches out to all creation.[62]

Chu Hsi, in his turn, credited Ch'eng I with "discovering" *(fa-ming)* the doctrine of the physical nature of man, which he regarded as a major contribution to the Confucian school. "With his disclosure of the doctrine of the physical nature, none of the other theories of human nature would hold water."[63]

Chu also gave credit to Ch'eng I for his new interpretation of the *Book of Changes.* Modern scholars have seen this interpretation as an unwarranted construction of Ch'eng's own devising, and Chu himself acknowledged that it was not in accord with the original meaning of the *Changes,* but this did not deter him from affirming its high value.[64] Similarly, Chu considered Ch'eng I to have developed a Confucian doctrine and discipline of the mind, in response to Buddhism, where nothing of the sort had existed before.[65] And in the generation after Chu Hsi his follower Chen Te-hsiu credited Ch'eng Hao with developing the philosophy of principle out of his own brilliance of mind, where the classics themselves had barely mentioned it in an obscure passage of the *Record of Rites.*[66]

Small wonder then that Ming and Ch'ing critics would look back on this as a revolutionary period in scholarly thought. "Classical scholarship," said the editors of the *Imperial Library Catalogue,* "as it came down from the Han, underwent a complete change in the Sung."[67] And the Ming writer Chu Yün-ming (1461–1527) castigated the Ch'eng-Chu school for its claim to have rediscovered the true meaning of the classics lost in the Han and T'ang, and for having set themselves up as the private custodians of a supposedly new revelation, without acknowledging their actual indebtedness to Han and T'ang scholarship.[68]

From these examples and others given in *The Liberal Tradition,* it can be seen that the Ch'eng-Chu school and especially Chu Hsi saw tradition as dynamic rather than static, a living growth and not a fixed monument to the past. It consisted not only of truths revealed in the classics but also things brought to light *(fa-ming)* by individual Sung scholars without whose contributions the Way would have been lost in obscurity. This view of the Way cannot be equated with the notion of progress underlying modern Western liberalism, but neither can it be dismissed as a basis for affirming the value of individual creativity.

Later scholars, especially in the eighteenth, nineteenth and early twentieth centuries, tended to view the Sung learning historically and critically, and had little sympathy with the liberties taken by Neo-Confucians in reinterpreting the classics. In their view the new constructions of the Sung masters only adulterated the supposedly pure legacy of Confucius and Mencius. But in the Sung a purely critical or skeptical approach would not have sufficed. The Ch'eng brothers and Chu Hsi, in an age of renewal and reconstruction, had larger needs and purposes in mind. To doubt and to adopt the questioning attitude was only the starting point, not the end, of scholarly inquiry. Repeatedly they expressed their belief in a method which would lead to some personal or social result—not perhaps to a conclusion that was final and fixed forever, but to one which would give one a goal in life and enable one to make one's own contribution to the advancement of the Way. We have seen this already in Ch'eng I's explanation of the learning process. In the passage cited earlier from Chang Tsai, he does not stop simply at "wiping out old ideas" but says that "new ideas will come." "Moreover, one should seek the help of friends. Each day one discusses things with friends, each day one's ideas will become different. One must discuss things and deliberate like this every day. In time one will naturally feel that one has advanced." [69]

In this passage and in others cited earlier the individual was seen to make his personal contribution in the context of a thoughtful interaction with the classics and in a free exchange with colleagues.

Thus the individual's distinctive contribution was recognized and encouraged, yet it was not for the sake of novelty or innovation, or because being different was valued in itself, but because the individual was expected to develop his own talent and offer his own share to the common scholarly enterprise. A delicate balance was to be maintained between self and tradition, individuality and collegiality.

With these qualifications then, we may be entitled to speak of a kind of individualism expressing itself in the cultural activities of the Neo-Confucian scholar. As such it reflected the special status and functions of the scholar-official class, the general affluence of the times, the influence of a religious atmosphere pervaded by Buddhist preoccupation with the problem of self, and the interaction of these with a humanistic tradition that attached special importance to the cultural and political roles of the educated man.

4. Individualism and Holism

If self-fulfillment for the Neo-Confucian meant a personal realization of the Way, the Way itself partook of both unity and diversity. Functionally speaking, it could take the several forms of the "Way of the Teacher," "Way of the Ruler," "Way of the Emperors and Kings," "Way of the Minister," "Way of the Parent," etc., which have been cited as the principal roles of the Neo-Confucian.[1]

Still, these functional roles, and their appropriate "ways" do not completely define the selfhood or personhood of the individual, which is more than the sum of its functional parts. It is sagehood, the working model of self-cultivation, that represents the integrating ideal of selfhood in the Ch'eng-Chu system and the Way of the Sage is the process by which the individual realizes in his own life the values of the Way. By achieving a unique personalization of it he fulfills at once, as Chu Hsi puts it, both "the whole substance" of his nature and its "great functioning" in the world.

To some extent this Way could be conceptualized and described. The Sung masters attempted to do this out of the conviction that the reality of sagehood was comprehensible in rational terms—up to a point. Neo-Confucians stopped short of a complete definition, recognizing that the perfection of virtue was not a fixed quantity but, in the form of human love and creativity, opened out indefinitely onto a larger vista of reality which had to be conceived holistically. As Chu Hsi said of *jen* (humanity, humaneness): "This principle cannot easily be conveyed in words. If a fixed definition is given to it, then violence might be done to its all-encompassing nature."[2]

Man's place in this larger and also deeper universe was presented by Chu Hsi in the first chapter of *Reflections on Things at Hand* (*Chin-ssu lu*), entitled "The Substance of the Way" ("*Tao t'i*"), as well as in his comments on earlier Confucian teachings related to the metaphysical or spiritual aspects of the Way. As his title *Chin-ssu lu* implied, the Way was something near at hand, simple and ordinary. Hence Chu had mixed feelings about putting the metaphysical aspect up front in chapter one. He did so, however, in order to provide a philosophical framework for the pursuit of sagehood—one which set forth his own philosophical assumptions in contrast to those of Buddhism and Taoism.

Confucius's saying, "Hearing the Way in the morning, one can die content in the evening" (*Analects*, 4:8), suggested to Neo-Confucians a religious or mystical conception of the Way and of self-identification with it as the ultimate in human fulfillment. Other passages in the *Analects*, cryptic in themselves and often uncertain of interpretation, were cited as expressing the essential quality of the Way under its numinous aspect. One example, frequently mentioned, is the characterization of the Way as the inexhaustible and unceasing stream of life. Ch'eng I quotes Confucius (*Analects*, 9:16):

Confucius, standing by a stream, said: "It passes on like this." He meant that the nature of the Way is like this. Here we must find out for ourselves. Chang I [a student of Ch'eng I] said, "This means infinity." The teacher said, "Of course it means infinity, but how can this single idea of infinity tell everything about the passing stream?"[3]

The reality Ch'eng I speaks of here is something to be experienced for oneself; it cannot be defined even in an expression like "infinity," though "infinity" is the word insofar as words will go. A similar conception underlay Chu Hsi's choice of the opening lines of Chou Tun-i's *Diagram of the Supreme Ultimate Explained (T'ai-chi-t'u shuo)* as the first principle to be asserted in *Reflections on Things at Hand*: "Non-finite and yet the Supreme Ultimate" *(wu-chi erh t'ai-chi)*.[4] Thus, he characterized the ultimate reality principle as non-finite and open-ended while at the same time fixed and definite as a normative principle or direction, like the North Star.

The significance of this characterization derives from the Neo-Confucian encounter with Taoism and Buddhism, in which the former sought to reaffirm the fundamental reality of enduring human values against the Taoist teaching of nothingness *(wu)* and the Buddhist doctrine of emptiness *(k'ung)*. Yet, in reasserting the Supreme Ultimate *(t'ai-chi)* from the *Book of Changes* as the first principle of being, Chu Hsi felt the need to take into account the Taoist view of change and the Buddhist law of impermanence. Simply to assert immutable principles would not do, unless one could also establish their simultaneous immanence in and transcendence of the world of change.[5] To say that the ultimate reality principle was "non-finite," "limitless," and "indeterminate" meant that it was not itself a thing subject to change. Thus, Chu Hsi said that *wu-chi* meant absence of "shape and form," of "sound or smell," "direction," or "position."[6] To speak of principle as the Supreme Ultimate gave it a definite moral significance, while speaking of it as non-finite or indeterminate would preclude its being identified with any given thing.[7]

Modern writers have tended, for a variety of reasons, to focus on Ch'eng-Chu thought as a philosophy of principle and on the

Supreme Ultimate as the quintessence of principle. But little has been said about *wu-chi,* an equally fundamental aspect of reality for Chu Hsi. One form taken by the former line of interpretation has been to see man and the human order as completely defined by a hierarchical structure of immanent natural laws, so that man's nature is bounded by rigid moral norms, rationalistically conceived, to support the claims of the established order on the individual. Thus, Neo-Confucianism has been described as having a "closed character."[8] Self-cultivation is viewed essentially as a process of bringing oneself into conformity with established norms, and Neo-Confucian teaching is seen as lending itself to, if not enlisting in, the ideological service of authoritarian regimes.

Important as rational and moral principle was to the Ch'eng-Chu school, it is wrong to disregard the nonfinite, formless, and indefinable aspect of *wu-chi* as if this were only a minor concession to Taoism or an eclectic element of no intrinsic significance for Chu's philosophy. There was nothing adventitious about this conception, arrived at in the mature development of Chu's thought. It was discussed by him at length and strongly defended against pointed opposition.[9] In Chu's debate with Lu Hsiang-shan it was a central issue. Lu saw *wu-chi* as a throwback to Taoism and therefore incompatible with true Confucian teaching. Chu responded that *wu-chi* should not be taken as Taoist nothingness, a first principle out of which existent things emerged.[10] *Wu-chi* and *t'ai-chi* were inseparable aspects, not successive stages, of being.[11] They were correlative aspects of a Way that was in one sense indeterminate and yet in another sense the supreme value and ultimate end of all things.[12]

Although Chu asserted this dichotomy as a cosmological principle governing all creation, for him as for Chou Tun-i, its primary significance lay in its application to man and the cultivation of sagehood. In man the Supreme Ultimate was the principle of perfection in the mind-and-heart, sometimes projected as the ideal of sagehood toward which self-cultivation was directed by the practice of "abiding in reverence and fathoming principle."[13] Yet, the closer one came to attaining the fullness of virtue—exemplified in the sage as sincerity or integrity *(ch'eng)* and asserted for all men as the "highest good" *(chih-shan)* for each—the more open-ended the process was seen to be and the less bounded the self. This is the meaning of Ch'eng I's assertion about the expansiveness of the self that comes with self-mastery: "If one can conquer self, his mind will become broad and generous and his body will become enlarged and be at ease." It is also why Chu Hsi refused to define "humanity" *(jen)* in words lest it seem to set a limit on man's identifying with the infinite mind of Heaven-and-earth.[14]

When in his *Questions Concerning the Great Learning (Ta-hsüeh huo-wen)* Chu Hsi discusses the "highest good" in the *Great Learning (Ta-hsüeh)* as the goal of universal self-cultivation, he speaks of the reality of *wu-chi* manifesting itself in the utmost refinement and spirituality of the creative process, by which yin-yang and the five agents combine in man, and he receives as his endowment from heaven all of the inherent principles (i.e., the inner structure or patterns constitutive of things as they are and should be) which will be applicable to daily human affairs.[15] The quintessence of these principles as the Supreme Ultimate or Norm is also infinite and inexpressible, but since one cannot help giving it a name, it is called "the highest good."[16] Attainment of this "highest good" comes through experiencing the Supreme Ultimate as "one undifferentiated Unity."[17] In the "square inch" of man's mind there is this empty spirituality which contains all principles. It is the wondrous, endlessly creative center of the human mind-and-heart; it is what distinguishes man from beast in the higher reach and refinement of his spirituality and what enables man, through the attainment of the highest good or Supreme Ultimate, to join Heaven-and-earth in the work of creation.[18]

Much of Chu Hsi's discussion of human nature and the mind must be understood in the light of these two fundamental characteristics of all reality. Thus, human nature *(hsing)*, which unifies all of the principles that make man what he should be, is, meta-physically speaking, the Supreme Ultimate *(t'ai-chi)* in each individual. Its particularity is defined in terms of a person's lot, or share in life *(fen)*, which determines the specific conditions under which this perfection is to be achieved and the functions through which the utmost degree of sincerity or integrity *(ch'eng)* is to be made manifest. Its universality involves participation in a process that is as limitless and indefinable *(wu-chi)* as the creative love which unites heaven, earth, and all things. In a letter responding to a question concerning his important lecture at the Jade Mountain, Chu said: "The nature is the substance of the undifferentiated Supreme Ultimate. Fundamentally, it cannot be spoken of in discrete terms, but it contains all principles including the four great constitutive virtues, which, if they are to be given names, are humaneness, rightness, riteness, and wisdom."[19]

In this passage Chu Hsi, while offering a definite method for the cultivation of this nature, describes the culmination of the process in terms suggestive of the inexpressible. For example—and it became a celebrated example in the Ch'eng-Chu school—Chu attached a special note to his commentary on the "investigation of things and extension of knowledge" in *Sentences and Phrases of the Great Learning (Ta-hsüeh chang-chu),* and he elaborated further on this theme in his *Questions and Answers on the Great Learning.* First, the commentary based on Ch'eng I:

> The foregoing fifth chapter of the commentary explained the meaning of "investigation of things and the extension of knowledge," but it is now lost. I have ventured to draw upon the ideas of Master Ch'eng [I] to supply it. That the "extension of knowledge consists in the investigation of things" means that, wishing to extend one's knowledge, one must fathom the principles in each thing or affair as it presents itself to us. The spiritual intelligence of man always seeks to know, and the things and affairs of this world all have their principles. But if there are principles yet unfathomed, man's knowledge is incomplete. Therefore the *Great Learning*, at the outset of its instruction, insists that the student, in regard to the things and affairs of the

world, proceed from what he already knows of their principles and fathom them to their utmost limit. After exerting himself for a long time, one day he will experience a breakthrough to integral comprehension. Then there will be nothing in the multiplicity of things external or internal, fine or coarse, that is beyond one's reach, and nothing in the whole substance and great functioning of the mind that will not be fully clarified. This is what is meant by the investigation of things, the extension of knowledge.[20]

Now for Chu's further explanation in the *Questions on the Great Learning:*

In the pursuit of learning what one studies is nothing but the mind and principles. Though the mind is the master of this one person, its empty, spiritual substance can command all the principles under heaven, and though the principles are dispersed in things, their operation [or function], in all its subtlety and refinement, does not lie beyond this one man's mind. Initially there is no distinction to be made between internal or external [principles], fine or coarse [natures], but if one is unaware of the spirituality of the mind-and-heart and thus is unable to preserve it, obscurations and vexations will prevent one from fathoming the fine subtlety of the principles. Unable to understand their fine subtlety and having no way to fathom them, one would be prevented by partiality, narrow-mindedness, and obstinacy from fully exercising the whole substance of the mind-and-heart. . . .

Thus the sage provided instruction so that man would become aware of this spiritual intelligence in the silence of his own mind and preserve it in dignity [of demeanor] and single-minded composure [quiescent unity] as the basis for his fathoming of principle; and [it was also] so that man would understand the subtlety of principles, fathom them through scholarly study and discussion, and accomplish the work of fully exercising the mind, so that the broad and narrow interpenetrate one another and action and quiescence sustain one another. From the start making no distinction between internal or external [principles], fine or coarse [natures], but with the persistent and genuine accumulation of effort, one will achieve a breakthrough to integral comprehension, and having come to understand all things in their undifferentiated unity, in the end there will be no distinctions of internal or external, fine or coarse, to speak of.

Nowadays people want to oversimplify the matter and wrap it up in mystery so as to make it seem like a profound and impenetrable doctrine of some very special sort. They would have scholars misdirect their minds to something outside words and letters, saying that only in this manner can the Way be apprehended. This is all attributable to the seductive and misleading doctrines of Buddhism in recent times, and it would be a great error to let this be put forward to the detriment of the ancients' real learning of "clarifying virtue" (i.e., manifesting the moral nature) and "renewing the people."[21]

The direct meaning and significance of these passages may be summed up as: (1) the need to study things and affairs in order to understand their principles; (2) a belief in the intelligibility of principle; (3) the characterization of the mind as "empty and spiritual" (in the sense of unlimited receptivity and permeability) while at the same time replete with principle (in the sense of the mind and things being similarly structured so that there is a natural affinity between them); (4) the view of the cumulative nature of learning and the increasing coherence of principles as pursued both extensively in things and intensively within the self; (5) the culmination of this learning in a comprehensive understanding of things in their undifferentiated unity or wholeness *(kuan-t'ung),* which eventually dawns on one (i.e., an understanding which is not necessarily an exhaustive knowledge of things in their particularity but which brings a fusion of cognitive awareness and affective response, overcoming the dichotomy of self and other, inner and outer, etc.); (6) the view that this holistic understanding, though it goes beyond words, is not to be confused with a Buddhist enlightenment which transcends morality and reason; and (7) the conviction that growth in learning leads to the fullest possible manifestation of the "whole substance and great functioning" of man's nature and of individual selfhood or personhood.

Admittedly, the text is not without its ambiguities, and these led to controversy among later Neo-Confucians. How extensive did the search for an exhaustive knowledge of the principles in things need to be? For some later critics, this seemed to require a lifetime of prolonged study, as if scholarly achievement had become a prerequisite to achieving sagehood. Chu undoubtedly believed that study and investigation were lifelong pursuits, yet here he is talking about a certain stage in the pursuit of learning when one's understanding finally brings a sense of being at home with oneself and the world. Chu does not actually stipulate that this sense of wholeness and fulfillment requires a mastery of all the principles in things; it is more likely that what he has in mind is a process of learning, both cognitive and affective, which brings one's capacity for empathetic understanding to the point where nothing in the world seems alien to one.

Presumably, this deep sense of being at home with oneself and things, of overcoming the dichotomy between self and other, inner and outer, also meant understanding one's own role and destiny in a manner similar to Confucius' "learning the imperative of heaven" *(t'ien-ming)* at the age of fifty. This is now seen in Chu Hsi's terms under the two aspects of understanding the reason for why things are as they are *(so-i-jan chih ku)* and the principle of how things should be *(so-tang-jan chih tse)*. Since each individual has his own principle and Supreme Ultimate, his integrated comprehension of the wholeness of things would include an insight into heaven's imperative under both these aspects as the basis of his individuality in relation to the Way as a whole.[22] Moreover, being established through the conjunction of man's heavenly nature (principle) with his physical nature, like the principle inherent in each seed of grain, this particularity of the individual would be recognized as a compound of the physical and emotional nature with the moral and rational. It was not just an abstract norm.[23]

As a succinct statement of Chu Hsi's mature views on the method and goal of self-cultivation, and one which appeared prominently in a basic text of the Neo-Confucian school—the first among the Four Books in the new curriculum—the special note in Chu's commentary on the *Great Learning* had extraordinary importance and influence. The further attention that Chu gave to it in *Questions on the Great Learning* not only amplified the rather terse language of the *Sentences and Phrases* and expanded its significance, but also demonstrated that this idea was no mere afterthought or casual comment of Chu's. Rather it came as the culmination of a long development in his thinking about the central concepts in Sung philosophy.

This philosophical dialogue goes back almost to the start of his intellectual and spiritual quest in colloquy with his teacher Li T'ung (1093–1163). It transpired in fulfillment of his father's injunction to Chu that he should pursue "learning for one's self," something which Chu said he only seriously began under the tutelage of Li T'ung.[24] Chu Hsi's *Responses of Yen-p'ing (Yen-p'ing ta-wen)* records his conversations and correspondence with Li in the years from 1157 to 1162. In the immediate background of this exchange is Chu's youthful fascination with Ch'an Buddhism, and in the direct foreground of the discussions are issues arising from the Buddhist-Confucian encounter. They are issues which significantly affect our understanding of Chu Hsi's holism as well as the alternatives he considered before arriving at his final position. Though we cannot review here the whole sorting-out process he went through, neither can we bypass it completely if we are to grasp the significance of Chu's holistic conception of self-fulfillment as compared to others proposed at that time.

The key terms in which this holism is discussed came down to Li T'ung and Chu Hsi from the Ch'eng brothers (Ch'eng I taught the teacher of the teacher of Li T'ung) and their uncle Chang Tsai (1020–1077). One of these expressions was Ch'eng's "unity of principle and diversity of its particularizations" *(li-i fen-shu).* Another was Ch'eng Hao's doctrine of the "humaneness which forms one body with Heaven-and-earth and all things" *(t'ien-ti wan-wu i-t'i chih jen),*[25] also spoken of by him holistically as "totally forming the same body [substance] with things" *(hun-jan yü wu t'ung-t'i).*[26] Still another formulation was Chang Tsai's description of man, set forth in his "Western Inscription" ("Hsi-ming"), as sharing in the same substance and having a fundamental affinity with Heaven-and-earth and all things. Chu drew upon these conceptions while also qualifying them in important respects. Together they provide the context for Chu's enigmatic expression "a breakthrough to integral comprehension" *(huo-jan kuan-t'ung),* which is the culmination of the learning process and the fulfillment of self-cultivation as described in Chu's commentaries above.

As Li T'ung explained to Chu the significance of the "unity of principle and diversity of its particularizations," he took issue with the idea of principle or substance as separable from practice or function. Some persons held that there was no essential difference in principle between Confucianism and Buddhism, since Confucian "humaneness' *(jen)* could be equated with Buddhist "compassion" *(tz'u).* According to this view, the only significant difference between the two teachings lay in the functional aspect—i.e., Buddhism's lack of a practical program such as Confucianism offered for dealing with the needs of human society. Li, however, and Chu following him, contended that the difference in practice also pointed to a difference in principle. One could not expect Confucian practice to follow from Buddhist principle, nor could one accept as true principle what did not lead to Confucian ethical practice. Hence, there could be no dichotomizing, as in Buddhism, of principle and practice to represent two different orders of reality, principle real and undifferentiated, practice less real because it pertained to the world of differentiation and discrimination.[27] To substantiate principle, one must realize one's humanity in the midst of practice, i.e., by coming to terms with one's individual lot *(fen)* or station in life and its differentiated duties, thus fulfilling one's own particular nature as well as joining oneself to the creative principle underlying all things. This is what was meant by realizing the unity of principle and the diversity of its particularizations.[28] It was also what distinguished Confucianism as "real or practical learning" from the "empty learning" of Buddhism, which viewed the world of human action as a qualified reality in comparison to the essential truth of Buddhist emptiness. In this way the reality of the individual was affirmed along with the unity of principle, so that self-realization involved no loss of individuality through absorption into the whole. In the end true individuality merged with, rather than being submerged in, holistic unity.

Li T'ung was willing to concede neither the Buddhist bifurcation of reality on two levels of truth nor the need for transcendental enlightenment as the precondition for coping with the world. For him, on the contrary, true self-realization and spiritual freedom were to be attained in the performance of the moral task.[29] To describe the characteristic spirit of the sage, Li borrowed an expression from Huang T'ing-chien's (1045–1105)[30] portrayal of Chou Tun-i as having achieved a state of mind that was "free, pure, and unobstructed *[sa-lo]* like a breeze on a sunny day or the clear moon."[31] This characterization later was included by Chu Hsi in his presentation of the "Dispositions [or Characteristics] of the Sages and Worthies" in *Reflections on Things at Hand.*[32] Chu also expressed his admiration for like qualities in Li T'ung, who had overcome his own wayward disposition to achieve a lofty state of mind, serenity of soul, and unfathomable profundity. It was a freedom of spirit attained by liberating oneself from all selfishness, obstinacy, and rigidity. In this state one's mind was completely impartial and open to reality. Principle inherent in one's nature could then express itself freely and clearly, with no selfish obstructions.[33]

As Li is quoted in the *Responses of Yen-p'ing:*

If in encountering things and affairs one can have not one iota of selfish obstinacy or rigidity, then that is to be "free, pure, and unobstructed." In other words, this is to be large-minded, open, and fair. It is to be completely one with principle and the Way. If in encountering things one is not to enter into them completely [it means that] in one's mind-and-heart, one has not freed oneself from all trace of partiality, or in other words that one is still obstinate and rigid. None of this will do.[34]

Elsewhere Li likened this state of mind to the "spirit at day-break" spoken of by Mencius, a spirit nourished by the restorative influence of the night *(Mencius, 6A:8)*. He also explained that it was a state of mind in which one naturally followed principle and the latter imposed no restraint. Indeed, if one felt any constraint, said Li, he would know he was not proceeding on the right course.[35]

Achieving this state in which the mind and principle had become one was not something to be accomplished in one stroke or by a headlong effort. It required constant attentiveness to one matter or affair after another, in the manner of Ch'eng I's "holding to reverence" *(chih-ching)* or "abiding in reverence" *(chü-ching)*. The mind should be allowed to dwell on each matter until principle in the mind and the principle in things became completely fused.[36] "If you go from one thing to another without really comprehending each in turn, it is of no use." After a long while this cumulative exercise would produce a natural sense of ease and freedom in the mind-and-heart.[37]

Chu Hsi saw this method of Li's in the light of Ch'eng I's practice of the investigation of things and the fathoming of principle *(ko-wu ch'iung-li)*. In the *Reflections on Things at Hand*, he quoted Ch'eng I as saying "When the mind is at ease, it naturally perceives principle."[38] And again, "One must investigate one item today and another tomorrow. When one has accumulated much knowledge, he will naturally achieve a thorough understanding like a sudden release."[39] This is similar to Chu Hsi's own account of the investigation of things culminating in a breakthrough to integral comprehension and a sense of total clarity, as set forth in his commentary on the *Great Learning* and elaborated in the *Questions on the Great Learning*. His final view, as expressed in the latter text, summed up a lifetime of study and reflection on the Neo-Confucian kōan Li T'ung had passed on to him and Cheng I's teachings had helped him solve.[40]

As a form of praxis in self-cultivation Li T'ung strongly recommended quiet-sitting *(ching-tso)*, which he also described as "sitting in silence and clearing the mind" *(mo-tso ch'eng-hsin)*.[41] Influenced though it was by Ch'an Buddhism's "sitting in meditation" *(tso-ch'an)*, this practice had been adapted to Neo-Confucian purposes and conformed to its own lifestyle.[42] Li believed that quiet-sitting would settle the mind and leave it with the transparency of still water, in which heaven's principle and one's own moral stance in relation to a given matter would emerge clearly.[43]

> The way of learning does not lie in too many words. It is just sitting silently, clearing the mind, and experiencing heavenly principle. Then even the slightest sign of selfish desire will not go undetected or unchecked. . . .
>
> Generally speaking, if one has doubts as to how to proceed, one should sit silently and look within oneself. Then one's moral obligations are sure to be revealed clearly, heavenly principle is sure to be observed and one can detect the point at which one's effort should be applied in daily affairs.[44]

For Li T'ung, this introspective practice was intended as a spiritual discipline to nourish the mind and keep it in a constant state of attentiveness, mindfulness, or readiness for action in daily life. While it focused on the unmanifest state of the mind-and-heart, before the activation and articulation of the feelings, it was not understood as opposed to rational discourse or scholarly learning. Li T'ung rejected the notion of "sudden enlightenment" in Ch'an Buddhism, with its transcendence of discursive knowledge. When Chu came to Li after his experiments with Ch'an, Li directed him to study the Confucian classics, which would engage him in rational discourse concerning the moral life. The kind of insight or enlightenment sought by Confucius should not be limited to words, but neither could it dispense with them. "Holding to reverence" through quiet-sitting went hand-in-hand with book learning, i.e., study of the classics.[45] Thus, the deep personal experience of truth, as taught by Li, should be of the wondrousness or mystery which is at the very heart of discursive knowledge itself. In other words, it should help one to understand the wonder of creation in the most ordinary things and to recognize in the numinous aspect of things something of enduring value, rather than the momentary reflection of an emptiness about which nothing can finally be predicated. Here the magic of the word expresses the wondrous functioning *(miao-yung)* of substantial Confucian principle, as contrasted to the "mysterious being" *(miao-yu)*, which arises from Emptiness but which, in Ch'an Buddhism, one should not try to capture in words *(pu-li wen-tzu)*.

Combining as it did objective observation and personal intuition, this method could produce a kind of enlightenment *(chüeh-wu)*, but Li T'ung preferred to express it as "finding the Way in oneself through personal experience" *(t'i-jen tzu-te)*.[46] Though Chu Hsi also spoke of "finding the Way in oneself" and of "personal realization," in the passages cited above from his commentaries, he preferred to express it in terms of achieving the "whole substance and great functioning" of the mind. The reasons for this are better understood if we look at the alternative formulations which Chu considered before arriving at his final position.

Chu had some reservations about the method of quiet-sitting precisely because it smacked too much of quietism, and because as a means of "nourishing principle in the mind" it seemed to concentrate on substance (i.e., the mind in its quiescent state) at the possible expense of function—a concern he felt even over Ch'eng's emphasis on the unity of principle.[47] Chu sought a formulation that would better express Li's own insistence on the need to combine the "unity of principle" with the "diversity of its [functional] particularizations."

Among the theories which Chu evaluated in this connection was Ch'eng Hao's "humaneness which forms one body with heaven-and-earth and all things."[48] Properly understood, this was a doctrine to which Chu could give his blessing, and with that it remained one of the most influential Neo-Confucian concepts down into modern times.[49] But without some qualification, it could easily be misinterpreted as putting primary stress on the sense of man's unity with the universe at the expense of the differentiated functions through which man's humaneness must in fact be realized. That is, a subjective experience or mystical feeling of oneness with the universe could become the counterfeit of a true holistic self-realization through moral effort and practical action. For Chu Hsi, a genuine holism could only mean the simultaneous realization of the "whole substance and great functioning" of human nature because the humaneness which forms "one body with heaven, earth, and all things" cannot be simply a subjective experience of undifferentiated unity—it must also express itself in loving actions of a particular sort.

Similar problems were involved in the extensive discussions of the Ch'eng brothers, Li T'ung, and Chu Hsi over the meaning and significance of the "Western Inscription" of Chang Tsai. The brevity of this text is out of all proportion to the wide attention it has commanded and the enormous influence it has exerted. As the succinct expression of a quintessentially Chinese mysticism of the human order, it appealed almost immediately to the humanistic religiosity of the Confucians and quickly became established as a classic statement of Neo-Confucian holism, being included in innumerable anthologies from Chu Hsi's *Reflections on Things at Hand* and the official Ming *Compendium on Human Nature and Principle (Hsing-li ta-chüan)* of 1415 to the Ch'ing dynasty's *Essential Ideas Concerning Human Nature and Principle* (Hsing-li ching-i) of 1715, to name only a few.

The essential spirit of the work may be conveyed in a few lines:

Heaven is my father and Earth is my mother, and even such a small creature as I find an intimate place in their midst.

Therefore that which fills the universe I regard as my body and that which directs the universe I consider as my nature.

All people are my brothers and sisters, and all things are my companions.

The great ruler [the emperor] is the eldest son of my parents [Heaven and Earth], and the great ministers are his stewards. Respect the aged—this is the way to treat them as elders should be treated. Show deep love toward the orphaned and the weak—this is the way to treat them as the young should be treated. The sage identifies his character with that of Heaven and Earth, and the worthy is the most outstanding man. Even those who are tired, infirm, crippled, or sick; those who have no brothers or children, wives or husbands, are all my brothers who are in distress and have no one to turn to.

When the time comes, to keep himself from harm—this is the care of a son. To rejoice in Heaven and to have no anxiety—this is filial piety at its purest.

He who disobeys [the Principle of Nature] violates virtue. He who destroys humanity is a robber. He who promotes evil lacks [moral] capacity. But he who puts his moral nature into practice and brings his physical existence into complete fulfillment can match [Heaven and Earth].

One who knows the principles of transformation will skillfully carry forward the undertakings [of Heaven and Earth], and one who penetrates spirit to the highest degree will skillfully carry out their will. . . .

Wealth, honor, blessing, and benefits are meant for the enrichment of my life, while poverty, humble station, and sorrow are meant to help me to fulfillment.

In life I follow and serve [Heaven and Earth]. In death I will be at peace.[50]

Critical discussion of the meaning of the text has tended to concede its importance as a basic affirmation of man's creative role in the universe, while seeking to amend it in one direction or another. Recent exceptions to this have been critics who see it as expressing a paternalistic philosophy readily exploitable by the traditional ruling elite, though Shimada Kenji has shown that in fact it was most often invoked by idealistic reformers and revolutionaries, not by defenders of the status quo.[51] This question need not concern us here, but insofar as Neo-Confucian holism had a vital connection with Sung-Ming individualism, certain points in the "Western Inscription" are worth noting: (1) the strong affirmation of human life as grounded in the creative power of Heaven-and-earth, and human love as an expression of that creative energy; (2) the sense of unity with the cosmos and continuity with all life; (3) the positive view of individual life in the context of the family and community, offering the prospect of a self-fulfillment that includes, but goes beyond, the meeting of one's social obligations; (4) the value of worldly goods and meaningfulness of human experience as contributing to self-fulfillment over a lifetime; and (5) the priority given to filial piety over loyalty to the emperor and the stress on self-respect and self-preservation as a filial duty.

From this it is plain what a high value Chang Tsai set on the individual self and its potential for creative communion with Heaven-and-earth. Questions arose almost immediately, however, over his emphasis on man's oneness with the universe and all things—to the neglect, some thought, of the performance of those specific duties which alone could give practical realization to man's humanity. It was objected that Chang preached a doctrine of universal love hardly different from Mo Tzu's or from Buddhist compassion, both of which were undifferentiated with respect to the priorities and form of ethical action appropriate to specific human relationships. Against this, the Ch'engs, Li T'ung, and Chu Hsi point to some of the specific duties referred to by Chang and asserted that, on the contrary, the "Western Inscription" served uniquely to express the proper relation between substance and function, unity in principle and diversity in particular applications.[52] Nevertheless, Chu Hsi saw a need in this discussion for greater clarity as to the relation between humanity (humaneness) and love, substance and function, the unity of principle and the diversity of its particularizations.

Ch'eng I had already raised this issue in his discussions of humanity with his students, and Chu quoted him in *Reflections on Things at Hand* in a way which expressed the irreducibly individual, and at the same time holistic, character of its realization:

> It is up to you gentlemen to think for yourselves and personally realize what humanity is. Because Mencius said: "The feeling of commiseration is what we call humanity" [6A:6] later scholars have therefore considered love to be humanity. But love is feeling, whereas humanity is the nature. How can love be taken exclusively as humanity? Mencius said that the feeling of commiseration is the beginning of humanity. Since it is called the beginning of humanity, it should not be called humanity itself.[53]

In his "Treatise on Humanity" (*Jen shuo*) and his "Lecture at the Jade Mountain" (*Yü-shan chiang-i*), Chu developed the distinction between humanity as the principle (substance) of love and love as the functioning of humanity. Confusion of the two led, at one extreme, to the identification of human nature or humanity with raw emotion or a diffuse humanitarian sentimentality, and, at the other, to a kind of undifferentiated consciousness which denied the value distinctions so vital to the practice of genuine humaneness. To avoid these pitfalls, Chu would ground human love in a larger cosmic principle, the life-giving energy and creature-loving mind-and-heart of heaven-and-earth, while also subordinating it to the higher end of perfecting human nature to attain the Supreme Ultimate. At the same time he would confirm as function the concrete reality of the love expressed in the mind-and-heart of man and given specific, practical application in human society. In Chu Hsi's words:

> In the teachings [of Confucius], it is said, "Conquer self and restore riteness." This means that if we can overcome and eliminate selfishness and return to the Principle of Nature [*t'ien-li*, Principle of Heaven], then the substance of this mind [that is, *jen*], will be present everywhere and its function will always be operative. It is also said, "Be respectful in private life, be serious in handling affairs, and be loyal in dealing with others." These are also ways to preserve this mind. Again, it is said, "Be filial in serving parents," "Be respectful in serving elder brothers," and "Be loving in dealing with all things." These are ways to put this mind into practice.
>
> Furthermore, to talk about *jen* in general terms of the self and things as "one body" may lead one to be vague, confused, neglectful, and make no effort to be vigilant. The bad effect—and there has been such—may be to consider other things as oneself. [On the other hand] to talk about love exclusively in terms of consciousness [function] will lead people to be nervous, impatient, and devoid of any quality of depth. The bad effect—and there has been such—may be to take desire in itself as principle. In one case, the mind is forgetful [and careless]. In the other case there is an artifiical effort to get results. Both are wrong.[54]

Here Chu argues against a concept of the self and things as forming one body if it means an identification so vague and a compassion so diffuse that one fails realistically to meet the concrete needs of the self and things in their own particularity, as in the case of the Bodhisattva's sacrificing himself to feed the starving tiger, a gesture so extravagant and unrealistic as to be meaningless.[55] This is to put undue emphasis on substance to the neglect of function. On the other hand, if one pursues consciousness—"using the mind to pursue the mind"—without regard to the larger vision that should guide the emotion of love, it can lead to an impatience for getting immediate results that is detrimental to one's true emotional and moral development. This is to put undue emphasis on function (immediate utility) at the expense of the "whole substance" (the perfecting of one's humaneness).

In his commentary on the "extension of knowledge" in the *Great Learning*, Chu had described cognitive learning as the initial stage in a process of self-cultivation that should lead to the realization of the "whole substance and great functioning" of man's nature. By "whole substance" he meant "humanity," seen in the larger dimensions of man's oneness with heaven, earth, and all things and also as the directive principle which gave ultimate meaning and significance to human life. By "great functioning" he meant the exercise of the full range of human faculties—intellectual, moral, emotional, and spiritual—which could participate in the creative work of heaven-and-earth, especially in meeting the needs of human society.

When in the *Questions on the Great Learning* Chu speaks of the mind as "empty and spiritual yet replete with principle," he alludes to the non-finite and limitless *(wu-chi)* aspect of the unity of the Supreme Ultimate, which is also the "highest good" to be realized in man on the basis of the "unity of principle and diversity of its particularizations." "The highest good," in the language of the *Great Learning*, represents the Supreme Ultimate in each individual as defined by his own share in heaven's endowment, his station and duties in life, and the circumstances which condition his actions. It is what is most appropriate for him in the context of these givens.[56] As for the "Supreme Ultimate," which is the rough equivalent of the "highest good" in the language of the *Changes* and Chou Tun-i, Professor Chan has summed up Chu Hsi's view as follows:

According to him, the Great Ultimate is at once the one principle and the sum total of all principles. At the same time, since everything has principle, everything has the Great Ultimate in it. Consequently, the Great Ultimate involves all things as a whole and at the same time every individual thing involves the

Great Ultimate. In other words, the universe is a macrocosm while everything is a microcosm. In a sense the pattern was hinted [at] by Chou Tun-i in his *T'ung-shu [Comprehending the Changes]* where he said, "The many are [ultimately] one and the one is actually differentiated in the many. The one and the many each has its own correct state of being. The great and the small each has its definite function."[57]

When Chu describes the culmination of the learning process as a "breakthrough to comprehensive understanding," he expresses the idea of an enlightenment that comprehends both the unity and diversity, the infinity and ultimacy, of principle in the mind and things. This implies an understanding of the total functioning of the substance of the mind in all its dimensions and faculties—an "enlightenment" that includes the cognitive and affective aspects of the mind-and-heart, yet goes beyond them in the same sense that Chu intended when he spoke of humanity as the guiding principle of love.

This, then, was the ideal of self-cultivation for Chu Hsi, which would define the kind of individual fulfillment he envisaged for man. It is also "finding the Way in oneself" in the deeper sense of *tzu-te* spoken of in Chu's summing up of the significance of the teaching of the *Mean*, which, he says, "speaks of the meritorious achievements and transforming influence of the sages and spiritual men in the highest degree. It was Tzu-ssu's desire that the learner should search within himself and find it [the Way] within himself."[58] For Chu, too, it represented the final fruit, even if it could not be a "definitive" result, of his lifelong search to achieve "learning for one's self."

The doctrine of the "whole substance and great functioning" of man's nature, in the terms it is expressed here, remains true to Chu's conception of the Supreme Ultimate as a nature that is both formed and yet-to-be formed, possessing in man an essential goodness that is still to be perfected. Among the various tendencies in Sung Neo-Confucian thought it was the Ch'eng-Chu school that particularly insisted on the goodness of human nature. This was a goodness which implied man's freedom to choose the path of self-improvement and self-perfection, to transform his actual nature so as to achieve, or at least approximate, sagehood. Understood as yet-unformed and, indeed, limitless *(wu-chi)*, that nature contained within it the possibility of achieving self-transcendence as well as self-fulfillment. Accepting the limits imposed by what was given (one's lot, station, condition, and disposition as "decreed" by heaven), and while still living within the form of things, one could by the exercise of that freedom pass beyond the limits of the given. In this sense Chu was affirming both the inherent dignity of the person and his inalienable freedom to opt for a self-fulfillment yet to be discovered within himself.

If this sounds rather too free-wheeling for "orthodoxy," it must immediately be said that Chu tried to hedge it around with safe-guards, conscious of the dangers that attended such a sense of freedom—the danger of self-delusion which may arise from failure fully to exercise one's cognitive faculties in relation to knowable facts and principles; the danger of being carried away by vague mystical feelings not substantiated in actual conduct or experience; and the danger, on the other hand, of pursuing immediate utility without due regard for the nature of oneself and things, and so on. The balance Chu sought to achieve through self-cultivation was a precarious one, as he himself implied in his discussion of the human mind as unstable and the mind of the Way as barely perceptible. Holism could easily become its own worst enemy if its component parts were not kept in line with the Way. So embracing was Chu's synthesis that later scholars—including Wang Yang-ming himself—could find some warrant there for views much in contrast to other emphases in Chu's thought.

Chu Hsi's system has long been recognized as the great synthe-sis of the philosophical speculation and dialogue carried on in the Sung. Here we can see that it also serves as the practical synthesis of the methods for attaining sagehood or enlightenment discussed in that time. In the words "integral comprehension" *(kuan-t'ung)*,

Chu Hsi's description of individual fulfillment expresses one of the highest ideals of Sung thought and scholarship. To penetrate, comprehend, and coordinate the full range of knowledge, and to bring it into a unity, was the aim of several major works of the period: Chou Tun-i's *Comprehending the Changes (T'ung shu);* the *Comprehensive Mirror for Aid in Government (Tzu-chih t'ung-chien)* of Ssu-ma Kuang, the *Comprehensive Treatises (T'ung-chih)* of Cheng Ch'iao (1140–1162); and in the late Sung, the *Comprehensive Inquiry into Literary Remains (Wen-hsien t'ung-k'ao)* of Ma Tuan-lin (1254–1325). The "comprehensiveness' *(t'ung)* spoken of in these titles reflects the prevailing ideal of broad and comprehensive scholarship *(po-hsüeh)* that Chu Hsi tried to harmonize with the Confucian ideal of integrated learning, the "one thread running through it all" *(i-kuan)* spoken of in the *Analects.*

Whether succeeding ages could sustain this magisterial view of learning would be a real question, but that it challenged them to achieve such an ideal of individual fulfillment is attested by the successive generations of scholars and thinkers who set themselves to this task in Yüan, Ming, and Ch'ing China, Yi-dynasty Korea, and Tokugawa Japan.

As it came from the hands of Chu Hsi, the Neo-Confucian "learning for one's self" rearticulated a perennial Confucian personalism, marked now by individualistic tendencies typical of the Sung period. That is, it expressed a more expansive view of the self responding to new opportunities and challenges. In the more complex society of the Sung, the literatus had to articulate a new sense of himself vis-à-vis the demands these times made upon him—the demand for loyalty to a state grown increasingly autocratic and bureaucratic; the conflicting claims of partisan politics; the need for functional specialization in many areas of life; the relative priority of book learning and moral cultivation in the face of a daunting proliferation of scholarly literature; and—to cite just one more challenge to his social conscience—the moral vacuum left by Ch'an Buddhism in the wake of its drive for a transmoral liberation.

To call this simply "Neo-Confucian individualism" would be to risk misunderstanding: it would seem to exaggerate the special features of the Sung "self" and to remove it from the social matrix and historical continuum in which the Confucian concept of person-hood is embedded. To view it, on the other hand, simply as an exhumed "personalism" of the classical variety, reaffirmed in a traditionalistic manner, might be to ignore the specific qualities of Sung life and culture, qualities which encouraged a new sense of human creativity and individual autonomy. The Sung environment produced imaginative reinterpretations of the classics and histories and new views of the nature, substance, and functioning of the self, which, though coined in the continuing dialogue with Buddhism and Taoism, produced a heightened sense of the human potential—moral, intellectual, aesthetic, and spiritual—to be realized through the effort of self-cultivation.

If what is "new," or "partly new," in these Neo-Confucian theories reflects the changed circumstances in which the Sung lit-eratus performed the political, scholarly, and literary functions of his class, it is also true that the continuing quest for self-fulfillment, the aspiration for a learning which went beyond all worldly gain or social function, generated a dynamic spirituality and forms of self-expression quite unprecedented in past tradition. Indeed, this radi-cal testing of the limits of the self eventually evoked the censure of more traditional scholars, faithful above all to the original core of Confucian teaching, and led them to repudiate the grandiose con-ceptions of the self envisioned by Sung thinkers. The intensity of this reaction in seventeenth- and eighteenth-century China and Japan is, however, a measure of the challenge which Neo-Confucian individualism was seen to offer to established values and institu-tions. There was here a potential for radical activism which re-mained one aspect, though until now largely a neglected one,[59] of the Neo-Confucian legacy to modern times.

If we review this development in terms of "individualism" and "holism" and consider these two terms to be represented in Con-fucian thinking by the "self" and the "Way," it is evident that for Chu Hsi, as for his tradition, these were properly seen as complementary conceptions, not opposed values. One's moral nature, according to the *Mean (Chung-yung)*, comes from heaven and is ordained toward a perfection specifically defined by the lot or share *(fen)* in life also granted by heaven—that is, by the working out of one's own destiny in the circumstances decreed by heaven. Thus, a distinctive fulfillment for each individual is ordained for him as his own Supreme Ultimate, the highest good uniquely defined within the limits of his own lot in life. Whether this should be likened to what is called the "unique value" or "dignity" of the individual in the West may be a semantic question, but there can be no doubt that Chu Hsi saw the individual as partaking of the supreme value of the Way in his own concrete particularity, or that Chu Hsi assigned man a high dignity by virtue of his role in the creative process of heaven-and-earth.

In these terms, the more profound one's participation in the Way of heaven-and-earth, the more deeply rooted one's own individuality becomes. This allows for nonconformity to prevailing social or political trends, but not unconformity to the Way. On this basis, then, holism may be seen as implicit in the Confucian sense of individuality.

On the social level the same is true. In terms of the "Three Guiding Principles" *(san kang-ling)* of the *Great Learning* as explained by Chu Hsi, the ordering of human society starts with self-cultivation, but true cultivation of one's nature, one's humanity, implies the extension of this process to all mankind by assisting everyone to achieve self-perfection. For the ruler and those who participate in rulership it becomes their duty—part of their own self-cultivation—to provide the means for others' achievement of self-perfection. To the extent, then, that fulfillment of the highest good/Supreme Ultimate in each person corresponds to what one might call the development of his own individuality or personhood, the extension of this principle to all men as the precondition for "ordering the state and pacifying the world" amounts to recognizing the need for a more generalized individual*ism* and not just the valuing of individuality in certain persons or the members of a certain class.[60]

In this sense, Chu Hsi's teaching may be seen as approaching a doctrine of individualism. In another sense, the hierarchical social arrangements which Chu saw as necessary to the maintenance of order among men—and without which no individual entitlements could be incorporated into an institutional structure—would no doubt appear to modern egalitarians as imposing severe limits on the realization of many individuals' full potentialities. Many Neo-Confucians accepted the inevitability of such limitations, while others saw in heaven's principles *(t'ien-li)* the basis for a pushing-back of these limits and in heaven's unfailing creativity *(sheng-sheng)* the prospect of richer opportunities for individual fulfillment.[61] These were to be pursued further by Neo-Confucians of the Yüan and Ming.

5. *Learning for One's Self in the Yüan and Early Ming*

As the Learning of the Way was passed on from Chu Hsi to his followers in the late Sung and Yüan periods (thirteenth and fourteenth centuries), the cult of moral heroism expressed in "taking responsibility [for the Way] oneself" *(tzu-jen)* went hand-in-hand with the "Succession to or Repossession of the Way" *(tao-t'ung)*. This is seen in the account by Wei Liao-weng (1178–1237) of his colleague Chen Te-hsiu (1178–1235), who in the early thirteenth century was cast in the same mold as the Ch'eng brothers and Chu Hsi after the suppression of the latter's works and his virtual martyrdom as a heretic. Chen appeared in this dark hour, Wei said, and "single-handedly took upon himself the responsibility" for the Way *(tzu-jen yü tao)*, propounding and disseminating it so that, with the proscription [against Chu Hsi] lifted, true learning could be manifested throughout the land.[1]

Leading Neo-Confucians of the Yüan period, who inherited this same conception of the repossession of the Way, felt called upon to undertake a similar responsibility for the defense or advancement of the Way, making a commitment which often set the inner-directed individual apart from his age. Hsü Heng (1209–1283) was described as taking up Chu Hsi's mission, in the aftermath of the Mongol conquest, by gathering together his texts and teachings, and vigorously propounding the Way in plain language the new rulers could comprehend.[2] To him and another great Neo-Confucian of the age, Liu Yin (1249–93), were attributed quite different understandings of what their responsibility for the Way demanded of them—Hsü believed that it obliged him to accept office under the Mongols in order to advance the Way, while Liu felt that he must decline such service in order to preserve the integrity of the Way—yet they were equally impressed by the example of the great Sung Neo-Confucians in setting a high standard of individual dedication to the Way.[3] Liu was greatly inspired by the Ch'eng brothers and credited them with being "instrumental in helping us to understand the Heavenly truth and to appropriate fully the meaning of the principle in things."[4] As Tu Wei-ming has put it, "Liu's enthusiasm for unusually courageous persons was more than a reflection of his adventurist spirit as a young man. His poems and essays clearly indicate that he was continuously impressed by them, and that he believed their idiosyncratic modes of behavior have a universal appeal."[5] One of Liu's heroes was Chu Hsi's teacher, Li T'ung (1093–1163), whom he admired for the same qualities of purity and integrity Chu had described in his *Responses of Yen-p'ing (Yen-p'ing ta-wen)*, which also stressed "getting it oneself" *(tzu-te)*. Liu, known for his own independence of mind, was also completely devoted to Chu Hsi and the Sung Learning. In the conventional view these two qualities might seem antithetical, yet in Liu's mind—and that of other Neo-Confucians—the Sung masters commanded respect for their own integrity and perseverance in the pursuit of sagehood, so that it was precisely in emulating them that Liu and others could achieve their own independence. Tu says that:

Despite Liu's whole-hearted devotion to Chu Hsi, and, for that matter, to Sung Learning in general, he was absolutely serious about maintaining an independent mind as the ultimate judge of relevance and value. He not only confidently remarked that a thousand years of "divinational wisdom" really resides in the human mind, but insisted that one's "innate knowledge" *(liang-chih)* must not be swayed by opinions from outside, even if they are as authoritative as the teachings of the Sung masters.[6]

From this we may well conclude that it was not "despite" Chu Hsi, but on his very authority, that Liu exercised his independent judgment.

These two masters in the Yüan period, Hsü Heng and Liu Yin, differed among themselves on several issues but to each of them "getting it oneself" was a fundamental tenet, usually expressed in relation to the Learning of the Way as found in the classics. Hsü Heng said one should take the original text of a classic and read it over and over until he "gets something for himself." Only if one has read it over many times and failed to get some real meaning for himself should he consult the commentaries. In fact, much as he admired Chu Hsi and the Sung masters, it was only when all else failed that Hsü Heng would recommend consulting their more recent interpretations.[7]

Hsü Heng was known as a Neo-Confucian teacher at court who constantly talked about Chu Hsi's Four Books, giving them priority over the Six Classics. Liu Yin, on the other hand, thought this was getting things backwards:

In the learning of the three dynasties down to the Ch'in, the Six Classics, *Analects* and *Mencius* were the major texts. Since the epochal change [in the Ch'in], customs have steadily deteriorated; scholars have accommodated themselves to the new age and no longer exert themselves to learn. . . . Men today give priority to the *Analects* and *Mencius*, without realizing that the *Analects* and *Mencius* are the end product of the sages' and worthies' teachings. Contrary to the well-known principles of "broad learning" and "detailed explanation," they talk now of reducing things only to essentials. What the sages and worthies thought of as the final conclusion is now taken as the beginning of learning; instead of explaining the full details, they speak about the bare essentials. Isn't this reversing things and running off in the wrong direction? . . . Indeed one cannot dispense with a phrase-by-phrase reading of the texts, but should read them carefully and not force interpretations upon them. Let your mind wander through them while you chant and hum them to yourself; let the words sink deeply into your breast. Even if all is not clear to you, this will suffice to guide you into making your first entry into learning. . . . Then, having finished the *Six Classics*, you can reflect upon it as it applies to you, and get it for yourself.[8]

Of this judgment—reaffirming Chu Hsi's view of sequence, effort, and process in "getting it oneself"—the leading Neo-Confucian classicist of the early fourteenth century, Wu Ch'eng (1249–1333), is another outstanding example, for he too accepted Chu Hsi's view of the repossession of the Way and was moved by the example of the Sung masters in carrying forward the Way of the Sages, while yet he maintained his own independence from state orthodoxy.[9]

Yü Chi, in his account of Wu Ch'eng's conduct of life, speaks in terms similar to Liu Yin's of Wu's study of the classics and "getting it for himself."[10] Despite his early captivation with the Four Books, Wu gave greater attention to the Five Classics as his thought and scholarship matured. Partly this reflected his own growing disagreement with the direction of government policy in educational matters and civil service recruitment, which he, like Liu Yin, believed put too much emphasis on memorization and recitation of the Four Books at the expense of a deep experience of the Way through study of the classics as a whole. Wu lived through a crucial phase in Chinese history, when the Four Books became the basis of the new curriculum and the civil service examinations assumed the form they were to have throughout the late Imperial dynasties. Wu's rejection of the new system as a misappropriation of the true Learning of the Way was to be echoed by many Neo-Confucian scholars later for whom the official system seemed a travesty of "learning for oneself" and "getting it oneself."[11]

Sometimes this reaction of Wu's to over-emphasis on the Four Books, and the fact that he made no studies of the Four Books himself, is taken as a sign of his growing disenchantment with the Ch'eng-Chu learning and his veering toward Lu Hsiang-shan. However Wu's primary engagement in textual studies of the classics followed the main line of Chu Hsi scholarship, not the anti-scholasticism of Lu Hsiang-shan.[12] For Wu the key issue was to preserve the proper balance between objective investigation and subjective interpretation in the study of the classics, pursuing principle as found in the texts but also having an inner experience of it as expressed in "getting it oneself." It was in defense of this true learning, not in protest against Neo-Confucian classicism, that Wu attacked those who loud-mouthed the Four Books. They were, as he had said earlier, "criminals against the Four Books."[13]

To Wu "getting it oneself" had a profound significance and was a matter of deep conviction. There were, he says, three senses of the word "tzu" to be considered.

There is the *tzu* of "by or from oneself" *(so yu chih tzu)* as in "self-authentication" *(tzu-ch'eng)* and self-enlightenment *(tzu-ming)*; there is the *tzu* of "likening oneself" *(so yu chih tzu)* as in "self-examination" *(tzu-hsing)* and "self-accusation" *(tzu-sung)*; there is the *tzu* of self-so, natural, or spontaneous *(tzu-jan)*, as in self-transformation *(tzu-hua)* or "self-reformation" *(tzu-cheng)*. When Mencius speaks of "getting it oneself" he means to get it naturally. How is this? Principles in the world cannot be sought out by pressing in their pursuit; affairs cannot be dealt with in a headlong and heedless manner. If you apply yourself, exert yourself, for some time and let the getting come naturally, it will be all right.

"Getting it" refers to the effect on one, the experience, and not to what is achieved. It is not that one does not believe in the achievement [but] it is hard to express. Thus when one speaks of just going along with the Way, "with the Way" means following along its course and progressing gradually. The noble man certainly wishes to reach deeply within himself [as Mencius said]. How can he expect in just one leap suddenly to reach deep within himself? He must proceed gradually and wait upon it to develop in time. Thinking on it, thinking again and yet again, so as to extend his knowledge, all at once he will achieve a breakthrough to integral comprehension *(huo-jan kuan-t'ung)*. Working at it, working at it again and yet again, so as to perfect his conduct, eventually he will experience a sense of freedom and untrammeled harmony. At this point can he explain what he has experienced in getting it? Moreover, in advance of his making the effort and applying himself, can he add any thought or exertion?[14]

When Wu speaks of the gradual method and sustained effort of the learning process culminating in an experience of "integral comprehension" or achieving a state of untrammeled harmony in action, he is following Chu Hsi's own characterization of the climax to the learning process, as found in the latter's commentaries on the *Great Learning*, his commentary on "getting it oneself," and his dialogues with Li T'ung. Elsewhere Wu, again in the borrowed language of Chu Hsi's commentary, speaks of it as "resting in the highest good," a state in which one experiences the interrelatedness of all being and all principles, a communion inexpressible in words.[15]

This experience of naturalness refers not only to an illumination of the mind-and-heart but to a sense of freedom in actions undertaken on behalf of one's fellow man, a largeness of spirit unbounded by selfishness.[16] In his youth Wu had been powerfully attracted to this moral and spiritual ideal as exemplified in Chu's characterizations of the Sung masters and in Chu's account of their heroic repossession of the Way.[17] In fact Wu had wondered if his own times did not call for someone like himself to take up this heroic role. The world, he says, thinks of "heroes" as men capable of impressive military feats, great drinking capacity, and extraordinary poetic gifts, like Ts'ao Ts'ao and the bold spirits of the Chin period. But these types glorified themselves and turned their backs on human society.

Who then can really be considered heroes *(hao-chieh chih shih)?* The kind Chu Hsi spoke of as exceedingly able and wise, who surpassed others in being able to transcend their times and rise above the common herd. In the Warring States Period the age had been dominated by utilitarian trends; it was flooded by the likes of Yang Chu and Mo Tzu who misled the world, hoodwinked the people, and blocked the way to humaneness and rightness. In those days Confucius' followers had almost disappeared, but there was Mencius who, coming into the world at that time and springing up in its midst, refused to chase after utility or be misled by Yang and Mo, but made up his mind to study Confucius and . . . in the end succeeded to the tradition coming down from Confucius. For the Warring States period to have had only Mencius was like a deserted land having one sole human being. Was he not then a real hero? . . .

After the death of Mencius for more than a thousand years, from the Ch'in through the Five Dynasties, scholars were sunk in the routines of vulgar pedantry and seduced by the strange doctrines of Taoism and Buddhism [with the partial exception of Han Yü noted in the original text]. . . . Then in our dynasty Heaven brought forth civilized rule and a succession of extraordinary men—Chou Tun-i, the Ch'eng brothers, Chang Tsai, and Shao Yung—who all appeared at that time. This culture [of Confucius] had long been in a state of decay, when Master Chou, all by himself, was able to rise up out of the gloom and silently perceive this way across a thousand years. Next, the two Ch'engs alone were able to follow the teaching of Master Chou, and Master Chang alone was able to befriend the Ch'engs. . . . As for Master Shao, again all by himself, he was able silently to perceive the transformations of Heaven-and-Earth and pursue to the utmost the subtleties of sign and number. . . . If they had not indeed been heroic men, would they have been able to do this?

Nevertheless, those in the school of the Ch'engs and Chang were not able to carry on their Way. Only after the removal [of the Sung] to the South, one hundred years after the passing of the Ch'eng's and Chang, was Master Chu in Fukien able to complete the great synthesis of the masters. Thus Master Chu was the great hero following the period of the revival. Now, since the passing of Master Chu another hundred years have passed, and who is there to take the responsibility upon himself *(tzu-jen)* for carrying on Master Chu's tradition?[18]

Although Wu later relegated this and other youthful writings to an appendix at the end of his Collected Works, unwilling to stand by some of the immature views expressed therein, the key elements for us—the mythos of the heroic champion of the Way as one who takes responsibility for it himself and stands as a lone individual against the decadent times—remained major themes in Yü Chi's account of Wu's life and potent symbols for later Neo-Confucians.[19]

Recently Professor Ch'ien Mu, in his *Chinese National Character in Historical Perspective,* has argued that the Chinese tradition has given only a subordinate role to the kind of individualism expressed in the cult of the hero *(hao-chieh chih shih),* which he identifies also with Western individualism, and instead has attached a high value to a more modest leadership role in harmonizing discordant elements.[20] It is significant that he identifies the cult of the hero in China with a tradition of individualism, but no less significant that his view of it is one generally in accord with the popular conception with which Wu Ch'eng and Yü Chi take direct issue. For them the real hero and presumably the true individual would be the one exemplified by the great figures in the periodic repossession of the Way. From this it would seem that there was in Neo-Confucianism a tradition central to its conception of orthodoxy which expressed a kind of individualism, converging in certain aspects upon the popular conception of the hero but differing from it in others. This, I think, Professor Ch'ien might be willing to concede was not wholly foreign to China.[21]

By the same token, however, we are reminded that Wu Ch'eng's Neo-Confucian heroism, as a product of the educated elite, could easily slide into the other sort, so that the special focus on the individual, instead of highlighting his service to the people and advancement of the Way, became a vehicle of romantic self-glorification (or when frustrated, self-pity), celebrated mostly in poetry and drink. The heroic vocation then could range the spectrum from the most self-sacrificing martyrdom to a "getting it for oneself" hardly distinguishable from aesthetic self-indulgence.

In the early Ming these concepts found expression in two figures whom Huang Tsung-hsi saw as ushering in the distinctive Ming phase in the development of Neo-Confucianism as a more active and dynamic version of the Way—Wu Yü-pi (1392–1469) and his pupil Ch'en Hsien-chang (1428–1500). Wu in particular stressed the importance of individual moral struggle:

The ultimate in sagehood was reached by Yao and Shun, the Duke of Chou and Confucius, and nothing more could be added to this; yet even they could not be satisfied with their capabilities or be the least bit negligent in attending to the mind-and-heart.

Later heroic scholars *(ying-hsiung chih shih)* and those who stood above others, aspired to the capabilities of Yao, Shun, the Duke of Chou, and Confucius, and wished to take the mind-and-heart of Yao, Shun, the Duke of Chou, and Confucius as their own mind-and-heart. In all their thoughts and actions they kept the several sages constantly before their eyes.[22]

If the sage served as the ideal self and model for the individual, the role for Wu Yü-pi was Mencius' "great man" *(ta jen)*[23] or *(ta-chang-fu)*,[24] who represented the individual as moral hero.[25] Here the "great man" stands in relation to the sage as the bodhisattva had stood to the Buddha in the Mahayana dispensation. With Chu Hsi's doctrine of man's inherent moral nature supplanting in Neo-Confucianism the earlier belief in the universality of the Buddha-nature, so dramatized in the *Lotus Sutra,* it was the "great man" who assisted other men to fulfill this inherent potentiality for sagehood in a manner similar to the bodhisattva's helping of men to attain Buddhahood in the *Lotus.* For Chu Hsi the "great man" was the man truly adult and mature, ready to play a fully human part in a larger world.[26] In its larger dimensions this corresponded to Mencius' description of the "great man" as *ta-chang-fu* (3B:2):

> He who dwells in the wide house of the world, stands in the correct station of the world, and walks in the great path of the world; he who when successful practices virtue along with the people, and when disappointed, still practices it alone; he who is above the power of riches and honors to corrupt, of poverty and mean condition to turn away from principle, of power and force to bend—he may be called a great man.

In the Sung, Ch'eng Hao had dilated upon this in one of his poems: "When one's heart is not dissipated by wealth and honor and one is happy with poverty and low station; when one reaches this point, he is a hero."[27] As Hsü Heng later explained it, following Chu Hsi's commentary on the opening lines of the *Great Learning,* the "great man," having clarified the lucent virtue of his mind-and-heart" in accordance with the teaching of the *Great Learning,* "extended this mind-and-heart to the common people, so that each could rid himself of any blemish and clarify his own mind-and-heart." In this way the "great man" would, by "loving the people," achieve the *Great Learning's* aim of "renewing the people."[28]

It is not surprising then that this cluster of concepts should again be invoked by Wu's pupil, Lou Liang (1422–91), who was later to inspire Wang Yang-ming's heroic quest for sagehood, when he said in his biographical account of Wu:

> After the death of Chu Hsi for several generations there was no "repossession of the Way" *(tao-t'ung [wu] ch'uan)* until the Master roused himself to follow in the footsteps of those who had gone long before him, and took the opportunity to assume personal responsibility for the Way. Though removed in time, he carried on the learning of the Lo and Min schools [i.e., the Ch'engs and Chu Hsi] which had been broken off. He is truly a hero for endless ages.[29]

To Wu Yü-pi, who refused office but led a dedicated life as a teacher, this heroic ideal, with its sense of individual moral responsibility *(tzu-jen)* for imparting the Way to other men,[30] was also intimately linked to the idea of "getting [the Way] oneself" *(tzu-te)*. After studying Chu Hsi's version of the Four Books and finding therein a deep personal meaning for himself, Wu wrote in a letter of 1421 to an instructor in a local school: "The mundane world may indeed forsake me but I am able to help myself. The mundane world may laugh at me, but I am able to get [the Way] for myself. In intimate association with the sages and worthies, why should I need to worry about those others?"[31]

Inspiring though the words of the Sages were and reassuring their example, the heroic individual had to find the Way for and in himself. The Four Books might point to it, but could not deliver it. "The problem is that people do not know how to 'turn inward and find all things in themselves,' " Wu wrote, citing Mencius' words (2A:7). "Thus books remain just books, and I remain just myself [as if there were no active repossession of the Way]. If the books one reads just pertain to the mouth-and-ear [i.e., do not become truly a part of oneself], it is a great waste."[32] It was for such reasons as this and because of the sense of joy and contentment from thus "finding oneself," that Wu named his study "The Pavilion for Getting It Oneself" *(tzu-te t'ing)*.[33]

Wu's pupil, Ch'en Hsien-chang, pursued this line of thought much further. Indeed "getting it oneself" *(tzu-te)* became a dominant theme in Ch'en's thought.[34] Deeply impressed by Wu Yü-pi's personal example of heroic dedication to the Way,[35] Ch'en also took to heart what Wu said about the following of models seen as external to oneself. He wrote:

> Men should learn from the sages and worthies but in the final analysis one must dispense with learning from others. If the Way is pursued with a mind to emulating others, then I fear it will prove difficult to make a match between oneself and one's model in all the details of life, and one would end up abandoning the effort. But if the Way cannot be a matter of emulating sages and worthies, you might question whether one would still wish to pursue this learning [to become a sage]. Reflecting on this, however, one can see that such a view is inadmissible. Even in ancient times, before there were any sages and worthies, it would have devolved on oneself to make this effort and still cannot be otherwise. This is what is meant by "learning to get it oneself" *(tzu-te chih hsüeh).*[36]

Ch'en went on to develop this concept in ways that went beyond anything found in Ch'eng-Chu tradition, but we do well not to assume that Ch'en's thought represents too radical a break with the past. Chu Hsi himself had offered similar admonitions against setting up the sages as too precise a model for oneself. In his *Classified Conversations (Chu Tzu yü-lei),* someone is reported to have asked why, if indeed one's aim was to become a sage, Ch'eng I had cautioned against "setting up a model for oneself." Chu responded:

> Of course a student should regard a sage as his teacher, but what need is there to set up a target (or standard)? As soon as one sets up a target, his mind will be calculating and deliberating as to when he will become a sage and what it will be like. . . . Although we now say we must learn to become sages, we must

keep on making an effort from the start. If every day we compare ourselves with others this way and that, it will not do.[37]

Original though Ch'en was in his own way, he owed much to the example and teachings of the aforementioned Li T'ung, of whom Chu Hsi had written in his *Responses of Yen-p'ing (Yen-p'ing ta-wen)*. Some of Ch'en's characteristic doctrines—such as "getting it oneself," the practice of reverence through quiet-sitting, the joys of spiritual freedom, and "learning for the sake of one's self"—came down from the Ch'eng brothers and Shao Yung through Li T'ung. Concerning "learning for one's own sake" Ch'en wrote in 1482:

> Confucius said, "The learning of the ancients was for their own sake; the learning of men today is for the sake of [gaining] others' [approval]." Master Ch'eng [I] said "Those who served in office in ancient times did so for the sake of other men; those who serve in office today do so for their own sakes."[38] Learning should be pursued so as to enable one to serve; service should be performed so that one can manifest the fruits of learning. [These should go together] like front and back, form and shadow.
>
> The sage kings and ministers of old, in their edicts, plans, and instructions, promulgated what would enable men to be of service [to others]; could it ever have been with the idea that one should serve one's own interest? What Yen Tzu, Tseng Tzu, Tzu-ssu, Mencius, Chou Tun-i, the Ch'engs, Chang Tsai, and Chu Hsi imparted in their writings was what would be fruitful as learning; could it ever have been with the idea that this should be for the sake of [gaining] others' [approval]? These gentlemen each shone in his own way, but put in one another's position, would they not have been capable of responding in the same manner?
>
> Since ancient times however it has not been so among those who have ruled the dynasties. They have felt no need to promote education and cultivate talent. From the Han onward what was sought in the schools was to recruit officials and there have been

few famous men who did not come up through the schools. Hence the important thing in maintaining schools has been the recruitment of officials. The essence of learning, however, is that it should be for one's self. Without this the famous men of old would have lacked the means to perfect their virtue.[39]

Ch'en was certainly not wrong in seeing China's rulers as motivated by the desire to use schools for the recruitment of officials. This was as true of the Ming founder as of any. Yet this fact should not keep us from recognizing the larger educational effort in the Ming period and its effect on the extension of learning. With the prominence given to the *Great Learning* as the first among the Four Books in the basic Ming curriculum, and with Chu Hsi's preface to it proclaiming the idea of universal schooling,[40] a certain democratization of learning took place through both state and local schools, as Neo-Confucians undertook the responsibility of the "great man" in "extending the mind-and-heart of the *Great Learning* to all men," as Hsü Heng had put it, aiming to assist them in the self-perfecting of their moral natures.

In a sense the popularization of Chu's teachings had already begun with the use of the vernacular in Chu's conversations with his students, as recorded in his *Classified Conversations.*[41] Hsü Heng and Wu Ch'eng, the leading Neo-Confucian teachers of the Yüan period, had, in their lectures on the Four Books from the classics mat, rendered this teaching into the vernacular so as to make it accessible to those who lacked training in classical Chinese,[42] including Mongol rulers and their Central Asian aides. In the Ming this process was furthered on the local level by the lectures and discussions conducted among community compact groups, a practice Wang Yang-ming himself encouraged and his followers in the T'ai-chou school widely popularized.[43] Accompanying this was a growth in the number of local academies which were set up in the wake of Wang Yang-ming's teaching efforts, as his voluntaristic philosophy stimulated an interest in popular education and a greater sense of responsibility among literati to provide for this.[44]

Ch'en's leading disciple, Chan Jo-shui (Kan-ch'uan, 1466–1560), though a major thinker in his own right, has been better known as a foil for the more daring and brilliant Wang Yang-ming, a slightly younger colleague with whom Chan carried on a dialogue and correspondence over philosophical issues. Their differences centered mainly on the "investigation of things" *(ko-wu)*, the central issue in the continuing debate generated from within the Ch'eng-Chu school over the nature of learning and the implications of this for self-cultivation.

Chan understood well the importance in Ch'eng-Chu thought of "getting it oneself." He knew too that this had been a major theme of his teacher Ch'en Hsien-chang. Though he had reservations about Ch'en's emphasis on quiescence and quiet-sitting, as perhaps leaning toward Ch'an Buddhisrı and Taoism, he readily accepted the basic Neo-Confucian assum ptions of Ch'en concerning naturalness or spontaneity *(tzu-jan)* aıid the autonomy of the individual as expressed in "getting it oneself." The question was how that autonomy and spontaneity were to be understood in the context of Neo-Confucian holism: i.e., in terms of the "humaneness that forms one body with Heaven and Earth and the myriad things."

Chan's solution emphasized Mencius' teaching that the humane man should "neither forget" *(wu-wang)* moral principles and qualitative distinctions (as the Taoists would have it), "nor try to abet" *(wu-chu)* the natural course of things by any self-interested action. The moral life should be a conscious, reflective one, but also disinterested. It should be a spontaneous expression of one's moral nature, responding creatively to life's situations without any preconceptions or predetermination to impose one's own will on the outcome. To do this one had to understand the nature and workings of Heaven's principle *(t'ien-li)*, but such principles were dynamic *(sheng-li)*, not static—alive in the mind as well as in things. Hence learning to live with the natural course of things, while being true to one's own moral nature, meant for Chan "personally realizing or experiencing Heaven's [moral] principle wherever one may be *(sui-ch'u t'i-jen t'ien-li)*."

Wang Yang-ming's interpretation of "the extension of knowledge *(chih-chih)* as the "extension of innate knowing," translated the investigation of things *(ko-wu)* into "rectifying one's own intention." This, to Chan, internalized and over-simplified the practice of virtue at the expense of objective learning and moral effort. To "extend innate knowing" might become too subjective and willful a way of carrying into action one's good intentions. Therefore Chan preferred to express the idea of combining knowledge and action by interpreting *ko-wu* as "to reach or arrive at the principle in things and affairs." Here "to reach" or "arrive" has the connotations of the mind-and-heart coming into congruence with the principles in things and affairs so that there is no longer any distinction in principle between self and other. It is no accident that Chan here employs the word *tsao*, "create," in the special sense of "to reach," "arrive," 'fathom," for it was Mencius who had used *tsao* in the same sense when he discussed "getting it oneself" as teaching or meeting the Way deep within oneself, a "getting" that was also a finding of something already in one's possession. It was a convergence which obviated either self-assertion, on the one hand, or loss of selfhood on the other.

In a letter to Wang Yang-ming, Chan put it as follows:

> *Ko* means *chih* (to reach, arrive) as in [the Book of Documents] "went to the temple of the Accomplished Ancestor" ["Canon of Shun"] and the "prince of Miao arrived" *(Ta Yü mo)*. . . .[45] *Wu* (object, thing, affair) refers to Heaven's Principle, or in other words to the actuality of things. It is *wu* as in "Shun's clearly understanding the multitude of things" *(Mencius* 4B:19), which is to say, the Way. *Ko* has the meaning of *tsao-i* (to reach, attain, fathom) and so *ko-wu* means "to fathom the Way."

> Knowing and doing go together. Broad learning, judicious inquiry, thorough pondering, careful discrimination, and earnest practice [as in the *Mean*] are all means of fathoming the Way. The reading of books, befriending teachers and colleagues, and social intercourse—all of these involve the personal realization

of Heaven's principle, as appropriate to the time and place, as well as the nurturing of it; and all contribute to one's fathoming of the Way. Making one's intention sincere, cultivating one's person, rectifying one's mind-and-heart, each and all go together, and all constitute one effort, not two separate things [knowing and doing]. The effort of making the intentions sincere, rectifying the mind, and cultivating the person in the latter portion of the *[Great Learning]* text, are all applications of this same process, not separate stages. This then is what is meant by "resting in the highest good."

This is why I have said of "resting in the highest good" that "manifesting the moral nature" and "loving the people" find their completion therein. Only in this [reaching] can one say that knowing has arrived. If one seeks for it in secondary sense-knowledge, can one say that knowing has arrived? "For knowing to arrive" is what Confucius referred to as "hearing the Way" [in the morning, one can die content in the evening] (*Analects* 4:8).

Thus the interpretation of self-cultivation in terms of *ko-wu*, as was done in the latter part of the *[Great Learning]* text, is confirmed. Consequently, it is enough for us colleagues simply to engage in the practice of "arriving at [the Way in] things" and affairs *(ko-wu)* throughout each day, to the end of our lives. [In *Mencius* 4B:14] "reaching deeply for the Way" [within oneself] means reaching or arriving at [the principles] in things and affairs *(ko-wu)*. "Getting hold of it in oneself" means that one's knowing arrives. "Being at ease with it, trusting it deeply and meeting its source" [as in the same passage from Mencius] corresponds to "cultivating the self, regulating the family, ordering the state, and pacifying the world."[46]

With his emphasis on "naturalness," "getting it oneself," and "personally realizing Heaven's principle wherever one may be," Chan Jo-shui naturally eschewed any rigid, formulaic approach to truth or codification of conduct. On the other hand, part of experiencing Heaven's principle was learning from others, from books, and especially from the classics, for one encountered and experienced principle in all these forms and made it part of one's realization of the Way. Hence, Chan often (as in the passage above) criticized Wang Yang-ming for his seeming deprecation of book-learning and minimizing of the steps in the learning process which Chu Hsi had stressed in his "Articles of the White Deer Grotto Academy."

Yet it remained a problem just how far one could go in formulating or expressing truth in words. In a discussion of this question in Chan's recorded dialogues, there is the following colloquy:

A friend asked, "When Ming-tao [Ch'eng Hao] spoke of Heaven's Principle, he said he had learned it from personal experience. Now I see that whenever our friends talk about anything, they speak of Heaven's principle. It seems to me that when Teacher [Chan] instructed us, he asked that we observe Heaven's principle as something to be personally experienced by everyone, not as something to be written about and pictured for everyone to see." Ch'ung responded: "Indeed, indeed. How could Heaven's principle have a defined form? It is just in the equilibrium of the unmanifest (a priori) state, and how could the equilibrium have a defined form? People need only pay attention to seeking the state of equilibrium and uprightness [correctness] in the mind. Personally to experience [this principle] and modulate this mind so as to be constantly in accord with equilibrium and uprightness— this is finding Heaven's principle wherever one may be. What the "Announcement of K'ang" speaks of as seeking and meeting the central virtue is like this.[47] Here *ch'iu* is taken to mean "matching" or "meeting" as well as "seeking." It is to seek and get it oneself. No one else can intervene. Once one has perceived and gotten it, one still cannot describe or picture it for others to see. Nevertheless, speaking in terms of praxis [one's effort to practice], one certainly cannot conceal it from others.

[The teacher said:] Simply to speak of Heaven's principle as self-experienced is not the end of the matter. From what point can we begin talking about Heaven's principle? What can be spoken of is only the beginning of the road. If one is not even to talk about the beginning of the road, how can there be any personal experience? Not to speak of it at all means, I fear, not to have any method of achieving personal experience. It is like someone who has never walked on the road at all having no [way to ask] questions. What you have said about the mind seeking equilibrium and uprightness is fine. But one should also try to reach and fulfill Heaven's principle, which is also attaining equilibrium and uprightness. There are some who do not reach and fulfill Heaven's principle, like the Buddhists who would have no dependence or attachments and just let the mind burst forth [in any direction], but how could they ever reach and fulfill Heaven's principle? [48]

It is in the very nature of the human mind-and-heart, the "humane heart," to want to express itself, to communicate, and to use language for this purpose. It is true that words can only be suggestive, not definitive, and that one's deepest personal understanding of principle always goes beyond rational definition. Nevertheless speech is, Chan says, "the sound of the human heart"; It is a necessary means of pointing out the Way, which Chan says his teacher, Ch'en Hsien-chang, did most effectively through his poetry. [49]

Dialogue and discussion were important for pointing the Way to others but also for confirming one's own experience of the Way; one's own learning needed to be checked against that of others if it was not to fall into subjective errors. As Chan explained in a letter to Wang Yang-ming contesting his interpretation of *ko-wu* as "rectifying one's intentions" rather than as the investigation of things (or, as Chan would have it, "arriving at principle") this makes the subjective consciousness the sole authority. It encourages one to be opinionated, stubborn, and dogmatic in asserting the correctness of one's views. In ancient times Yang Chu and Mo Tzu, according to

Chan, did not realize the error of their ways because they were narrow-minded and made no effort to learn from others. Mencius also criticized Po I for this, as well as Yang and Mo. In contrast to Confucius, who never tired of learning from others and modestly inquired of others' views before expressing his own, the former "made no effort to engage in the 'discussion of learning' *(wu chiang-hsüeh chih kung)*, lacked substance or orderly priorities, and had no subtlety of understanding or reasoning."[50]

For his own part, Chan saw no incompatibility between "getting it oneself" and learning from others. His view of *ko-wu* as "arriving at principle," he says, was something he "first 'got by himself,' but then on inquiring further into the writings of Master Ch'eng, [I found that] it accorded with what I had gotten before—one and the same."[51] On this point perhaps there was no necessary disagreement between Chan and Wang. The latter recognized that Chan did not favor externalized knowledge, but put the highest priority on "getting it oneself," to such an extent indeed that he was unjustifiably accused of Ch'an Buddhist heresy.[52] Yang-ming also agreed with Chan that *tzu-te* was of the essence of the Sage's learning. Chan, on the other hand, was well aware that Yang-ming engaged most actively in "learning by discussion" *(chiang-hsüeh)*. Yet Chan astutely observed that if the investigation of things *(ko-wu)* were interpreted as "rectifying one's intentions," and "extending knowledge *(chih-chih)* were taken as "asserting one's right intention," much latitude existed for subjectivism and dogmatism, in which case discussion could lapse into lecturing or preaching to others, or perhaps lapse altogether, leaving none of the dialogue necessary to confirm one's own hold on truth.[53] Meanwhile Chan himself was most active in promoting such scholarly discussion and in opening up many schools and academies in the places where he lectured.[54] This, as we shall see, became an increasingly crucial issue in the later development of Neo-Confucian thought as between those whose Learning for One's Self remained within the domain of open public discussion or discursive learning and those who sought to go beyond it.

6. Wang Yang-ming: Sagehood and the Self

Among several new trends in the mid-Ming period Wang Yang-ming's teaching was to have the most explosive effect on the Neo-Confucian movement. His views on the mind-and-heart—quickly recognized as strikingly new—dynamized the conception of the self, sagehood, and the individual as nothing had before, and came to dominate the intellectual scene during the sixteenth century almost as if they represented a new orthodoxy.

Wang Yang-ming himself thought of these conceptions as fully orthodox because he understood his own mission in the world against the background of Chu Hsi's concept of the repossession of the Way (tao-t'ung) and the deep sense of personal responsibility for the Way which is characteristic of the Great Man. In his *Inquiry on the Great Learning (Ta-hsüeh wen)*, written toward the end of his life, Wang commented on Chu's characterization of the *Great*

Learning as the "learning of the great man," stressing the cosmic dimensions of the great man's sense of responsibility.

> The great man regards Heaven, Earth, and the myriad things as one body [with himself]. He regards the world as one family and the state as one person. . . . Thus the learning of the great man consists entirely in getting rid of the obscuration of selfish desires by his own efforts to make manifest his lucent virtue, so as to restore the condition of forming one body with Heaven, Earth, and the myriad things. . . . To manifest lucent virtue [i.e., the moral nature *(ming-te)*] is to bring about the substance of form- ing one body with Heaven, Earth and the myriad things, whereas loving the people is to put into universal operation the function of forming one body. Hence manifesting lucent virtue consists in loving the people and loving the people is the way to manifest lucent virtue.[1]

Here Wang's activist spirit and dynamic conception of the Way is shown in his emphasis on "loving the people," rather than simply "renewing" their original moral nature, as with Chu Hsi. Yet this only intensifies the sense of active moral responsibility which the "great man" must bear, a responsibility Wang agonizes over in another passage:

> Whenever I think of people's degeneration and difficulties I pity them and have a pain in my heart. I overlook my own unworthi- ness and wish to save them by this teaching. And I do not know the limits of my ability. When people see me trying to do this, they join one another in ridiculing, insulting, and cursing me, regarding me as insane. . . . Of course there are cases when people see their fathers, sons, or brothers falling into a deep abyss and getting drowned. They cry, crawl, go naked and bare- footed, stumble and fall. They hang onto dangerous cliffs and go down to save them. Some gentlemen who see them behave like this . . . consider them insane because they cry, stumble, and fall as they do. Now to stand aside and make no attempt to save the

drowning, while mocking those who do, is possible only for strangers who have no natural feelings of kinship, but even then they will be considered to have no sense of pity and to be no longer human beings. In the case of a father, son, or brother, because of love he will surely feel an ache in his head and a pain in his heart, run desperately until he has lost his breath, and crawl to save them. He will even risk drowning himself. How much less will he worry about whether people believe him or not?[2]

The agony for Wang is further intensified by the conflict between his respect for Chu Hsi and his conviction that he must be true to the Way as he has found it himself. Though he has his differences of interpretation from Chu, he must make the Way manifest in the same manner as the Ch'eng brothers earlier, who had repossessed and revealed it in the form of principles common and open to all.[3]

The fact is that in my own mind-and-heart I cannot bear to contradict Master Chu, but I cannot help contradicting him because the Way is what it is and the Way will not be fully evident if I do not correct him. . . . The Way is public and belongs to the world, and learning is public and belongs to the world. They are not the private possessions of Master Chu or even Confucius. They are open to all, and to discuss them openly is the only way.[4]

Being true to himself and to his humane responsibility may lead the moral hero to suffer isolation and loneliness, but Wang knows from Chu Hsi's account of the repossession of the Way *(tao-t'ung)* that this has been the lot of the "great man" from Confucius down to the Sung masters.[5] It is only with this reassuring thought that he dares to take up the Way of Confucius as his own responsibility.[6] This, and the conviction that the truth will surely emerge in discussing matters with others, give him the confidence that differences can be overcome and all men brought into a grand unity *(ta-t'ung)*.⁷

From this we may see how in Wang Yang-ming the concepts of "repossessing the Way," the great man's taking of personal responsibility, his "finding the Way in himself," and his correlative belief in the value of self-expression shared in dialogue with others, carry forward some of the grand themes of the Neo-Confucian discourse.

The key, however, to Wang's near-revolution in the Sage Learning that came down to him through the Ch'eng-Chu school was his reformulation of the Learning of the Mind-and-Heart, especially as represented by the message and method of the mind *(hsin-fa)*. This is revealed in his preface to the *Collected Writings of Hsiang-shan* (1520) written for the first reprinting since 1212 of Lu's collected works:

> The sage Learning is the learning of the mind-and-heart. As it was handed on from one to another by Yao, Shun, and Yü, it was said: "The human mind is precarious; the mind of the Way is subtle. Be discriminating and single-minded. Hold fast the Mean." This is the source of the learning of the mind. The "Mean" refers to the mind of the Way. When the mind of the Way, being refined [discriminating] and single, is referred to as "humaneness," it is what we call the "Mean." The learning of Confucius and Mencius, which urged the pursuit of humaneness, carried on the transmission of the Sages' refinement and single-ness. Nevertheless a prevalent evil at that time was found among those who insisted on seeking this outside the mind. Thus the question arose with Tzu-kung as to whether Confucius' learning consisted in acquiring much cognitive knowledge [*Analects* 6:28]. So Confucius told him how to take what is near at hand [in oneself] as a gauge of the feelings of others, which meant having them seek within their own minds. Then in Mencius' time Mo Tzu spoke of humaneness as going so far as to wear the hair off one's scalp and heels [on others' behalf] while the likes of Kao Tzu talked about "humaneness being within and righteousness

being without [the mind]," which did grave harm to the learning of the mind-and-heart.[8]

Despite Mencius' efforts, Wang goes on to explain, the Way of the Sage-Kings declined and a utilitarian view came to prevail which identified principle with selfish gain and in effect disconnected it from the moral mind of Heaven's imperative. With this "the mind and principle became two separate things and the learning of refinement and singleness [unity] was lost." Scholars occupied themselves with the external pursuit of the principles in things without realizing that there is truly no difference between the principles in the mind and the principles in things. Likewise the Buddhist and Taoist teachings of emptiness dispensed with the moral constants which should govern human relations, again not realizing that the mind and principle are inseparable and that moral constants cannot be dispensed with.

Finally, in the Sung, Chou Tun-i and the Ch'eng brothers tried to rediscover the essential meaning of Confucius and Yen Yüan, and with such doctrines as the "Non-finite and yet Supreme Ultimate"; "stabilizing the mind with humaneness and rightness"; "the mean and correctness"; "putting quiescence first"; "stability in both action and quiescence"; "neither external nor internal" and "neither following nor going forward to meet events" (referring to *Chuang Tzu*, 21, 7:32), they came close to the original idea of refinement and singleness. "After this," Wang says, "came Lu Hsiang-shan, who, though not the equal of the two Ch'engs for purity of character and equability of disposition, nevertheless was able, through his simplicity and directness of mind, to connect up with the transmission from Mencius." Indeed, "his insistence that learning must be sought in the mind was singleness of mind itself. It is for this reason that I have adjudged the learning of Hsiang-shan to be the learning of Mencius."[9]

Seeing Lu, and not Chu Hsi, as the true heir to Mencius and the Way, Wang goes on to defend Lu against the charge of lapsing into Ch'an Buddhism—an issue which, however, need not detain us here. It should suffice to note the parallel between Wang's account of the Learning of Mind and Chu's presentation of the Succession to the Way in his Preface to the *Mean*, consistent with earlier identification of this text with the Learning of the Mind-and-Heart. Where Wang differs in his account is his insistence on the unity, stability, and quiescence of the mind, in contrast to Chu's earlier emphasis on the fallibility of the human mind and the subtlety of the Mind of the Way. Reflecting this difference, according to Wang, Lu's method was direct and simple; Chu's was burdened (as Wang now saw it) by the need for caution and objective investigation. The basis for Wang's endorsement of Lu's approach is not only his acceptance of the idea that the mind and principle are inseparable—which Chu himself had said—but his view of them as indeed identical. Wang expressed this idea unequivocally in a memoir of 1524; when he said that the constant unvarying Way was "endowed in man as his nature and, as the master of his person, was called the mind. The mind is the nature, Heaven's Imperative, the One, pervading man and things, reaching out to the Four Seas, and filling Heaven-and-earth." [10]

It is important to recognize here two equally important points. Wang accepts the received Ch'eng-Chu teaching as a "learning of the Mind" and speaks of it as earlier Neo-Confucians do in terms of the message and method of the mind. Wang also affirms that it is no less a teaching concerning principle—indeed the equation of mind and principle is what this is all about. Thus the dichotomy of mind versus principle, or *hsin hsüeh* versus *li-hsueh*, is not at issue here. How one understands both as vital to self-cultivation (i.e., Learning for One's Self) *is* the issue.

In a later adversion to the same theme, when Wang wrote a memoir on the reconstruction of the Shan-yin prefectural school (1524), he took no issue with Chu's distinction between the human mind and the mind of the Way. The real problem lay elsewhere:

The Sages' learning is the "Learning of the Mind and Heart." It is learning which seeks fully to employ the mind-and-heart.

What Yao, Shun, and Yü passed on from one to the other was "The human mind is precarious; the mind of the Way is subtle. Be discriminating and singleminded. Hold fast the Mean." The "mind of the Way" refers to what [in the *Mean*] "follows the nature . . ." It is unmixed with the human, has no sound or smell, and is manifested with the utmost subtlety. It is the source of sincerity. The mind of man is mixed with the human and thus becomes prone to err. It has the potential for unnaturalness and insincerity. When one sees an infant about to fall into a well and feels a compassionate impulse [to rescue it], that is [an instance of] the Way guiding human nature. If that impulse becomes confused by thought of gaining the approbation of parents or a reputation in the community, that is the human mind. . . .

To be single-minded is to be one with the mind of the Way; to be discriminating is to be concerned lest the mind of the Way should lose that oneness and possibly become divided from the human mind. Always to be centered on the Mean and to be unceasingly one with the mind of the Way is to "hold fast the Mean." If it is one with the mind of the Way, the mind will always be kept on center, and in its expressed state there will be no disharmony. Thus, following the mind of the Way, its expression in a parent-child relationship is always affectionate; as expressed in the ruler-minister relationship it is always right; expressed in the relationship of husband-wife, senior-junior, friend and friend, it is always respectful of gender differences, always respectful of precedence, always respectful of fidelity to friends. . . .

Shun had Hsieh as minister of education see to instruction in these moral relationships and teach people the Universal Way.[11] At that time people were all noble men and could all be entrusted with the responsibilities of noble rank. There was no instruction but this instruction, and no learning but this learning. With the passing of the sages, however, the learning of the mind-and-heart became obscured, human conduct unnaturally strove for fame and profit; those who pursued the learning of textual exegesis, memorization and recitation, and literary embellishments arose together in confusion and profusion. Fragmentation and divisiveness flourished apace. Month by month and year by year, one scholar copied from another, each confirming the other's mistakes. Thus day by day the human mind became more swollen with self-importance and could no longer perceive the subtlety of the mind of the Way. . . . How then is the learning of the mind to be clarified? . . . The learning of the sage seeks fully to employ the mind-and-heart so as to form one body with Heaven-and-earth and all things . . . for in this learning there is no distinction between self and other, internal or external; the mind is one with Heaven-and-earth and all things. Ch'an learning, however, arises from self-interest and expediency, and cannot avoid division into internal and external This then is the reason for the difference between the two. Today those who pursue the learning of the mind and nature while not treating human relations as external to one or leaving out things and affairs, but who rather concentrate on preserving the mind and make it their business to nourish the nature, certainly represent the learning of refinement and singleness in the Sages' school.[12]

In this memoir Wang sees the method of "refinement and singleness" as a means of preserving the mind of the Way, originally and essentially one with Heaven, Earth, and all things. As something already complete within the mind, it requires nothing external to it but only unmixed, unobstructed expression of its human feelings—its natural empathy for all things. There is no place then for principles to be studied as if these were objects of investigation, no room for the nature, as Heaven's principle in man, to be learned or assimilated from outside. All one needs in the learning of the mind is single-minded attention to the unity of the mind and principle, the oneness of man with Heaven and earth and all things. For Wang this is a unity one starts with and expands upon, in contrast to Chu Hsi, who in his note on the investigation of things in the *Great Learning*, speaks of the gradual accumulation of principles until finally one achieves a breakthrough to integral comprehension (as seen in chapter 4).

Wang's new interpretation of the Learning of the Mind-and-Heart, based on his revision of the Tradition of the Way, immediately preceded his enunciation of the doctrine of innate knowing *(liang-chih)* and was followed by his important "Inquiry on the Great Learning" *(Ta-hsüeh wen)* in 1527. To a disciple of Wang, such as Ch'ien Te-hung, the editor of his *Literary Records (Wen-lu)*, the "Inquiry on the Great Learning" was seen as conveying the essence of Wang's mature teaching.[13] Wing-tsit Chan has called it "Wang Yang-ming's most important writing, for it embodies his basic teachings and represents his final conclusions."[14]

As the title implies, the *Inquiry* deals with central questions in the text of the *Great Learning*, but also as Ch'ien Te-hung points out in a prefatory note, it presents the starting point and basic premises of Wang's teaching as drawn from both the *Mean* and the *Great Learning*.[15] Chu had explained the *Great Learning's* "manifesting lucent virtue" in terms of the original endowments of Heaven's nature (principle) in the mind, to be nourished and cultivated by methodical practice of intellectual inquiry, the refining of value distinctions, and the exercise of moral restraints—lest the human mind, precariously perched between selfish and unselfish desires, should stray from correct principles as represented by the mind of the Way. Wang's alternative view was that "lucent virtue," instead of being a mind of the Way at odds with the human mind, consisted essentially in the cardinal virtue of humaneness, as expressed in a feeling of oneness with Heaven-and-earth and all things. Cultivation of this virtue, then, should consist essentially of encouraging the free and full expression of that empathetic feeling without the intervention of any ratiocination or calculation involving self/other or subject/object distinctions. In this Wang placed a prime value on the feeling of love for, or oneness with, all creation and on the natural integrity of the mind, as opposed to a mind divided against itself by the counterposing of the human mind to the mind of the Way (i.e., the nature).

The original pure mind Wang identified with the "highest good" of the *Great Learning,* regarding it not as a perfection beyond one, to be reached or achieved, but as an inherent perfection within, to be uncovered, released, and extended to others. He says:

> As the highest good emanates and reveals itself, we will consider right as right and wrong as wrong. Things of greater or less importance and situations of grave or light character will be responded to as they act upon us. In all our changes and movements, we will stick to no particular point, but possess in ourselves the mean that is perfectly natural. This is the ultimate of the normal nature of man and the principle of things. There can be no consideration of adding to or subtracting anything from it —such a suggestion reveals selfish ideas and shallow cunning, and cannot be said to be the highest good. Naturally, how can anyone who does not watch over himself carefully when alone, and who lacks refined discrimination and singleness of mind, attain to such a state of perfection? Later generations fail to realize that the highest good is inherent in their own minds, but exercise their selfish ideas and cunning and grope for it outside their minds, believing that every event and every object has its own peculiar definite principle.[16]

In this passage we see how Wang incorporates into his doctrine of the mind the language of the Ch'eng-Chu method of the mind —the method of refined discrimination and singleness and holding fast to the Mean—and focuses it on the unity of principle rather than on the diversity of principles in events and things. Thereby he sets a higher priority on primary intuition, or undifferentiated sensibility, than on acquired learning or secondary rational and moral judgments. In the same way, Wang places a prime emphasis on the substantial unity of innate knowing, rather than on the different steps in the *Great Learning*'s method of self-cultivation. He says:

> While the specification of tasks can be expressed in terms of a graded sequence of priorities, in substance they constitute a sin-

gle unity and in reality there is no distinction of a graded sequence to be made; yet, while there is no such distinction to be
made, in respect to function and its refinements [discrimination]
(wei-wei), these cannot be left wanting in the slightest degree.
This is why the *[Great Learning's]* doctrine of investigation,
extension, being sincere, and rectifying can be taken as a correct
exposition of the transmission from Yao and Shun and evinces
the mind of Confucius.[17]

Here, in his conclusion to the *Inquiry*, Wang makes a point of
casting his basic argument concerning the method of the *Great
Learning* in the language of the sixteen-word formula from Chu's
preface to the *Mean*, and of identifying it as the true transmission
of the mind of the sages. Moreover, Ch'ien Te-hung, in his comment following Wang's *Inquiry*, stresses the same point when he
says: "The teaching of the *Great Learning* had, after Mencius,
found no worthy transmitter for more than a thousand years, but
with this exposition in terms of innate knowing *(liang-chih)*, it was
restored to full clarity of understanding as if one day had encom-
passed all of time past."[18] Ch'ien thus completed the thought
implicit in Wang's finale—that Wang's doctrine of innate knowing
represented the new dispensation of the tradition of the Way and
succession to the mind of the sages.

It was this new learning, as encapsulated in the doctrine of innate
knowing *(liang-chih)* and "extending innate knowing," that trans-
formed the Sage learning, understood as "learning to be a Sage"
and made it far more accessible to Everyman, to a degree that Chu
Hsi had hoped for but in ways he had not conceived. Wang thereby
opened the way to a kind of "popular" movement involving a
greater potential participation of ordinary men in the fulfillment of
Neo-Confucian ideals.

It was possible so to popularize the notion of sagehood only
because Wang had internalized or subjectivized it. "How can the
signs of sagehood be recognized? . . . If one clearly perceives one's
own innate knowing, then one recognizes that the signs of sagehood

do not exist in the sage but in oneself."[19] And the way to achieve sagehood was not to set up some idealized image far beyond one, as many scholars had done, "seeking to know what they cannot know and do what they cannot do."[20] It was to stop relying on external standards, to become completely identified with the principle of Nature (or Heaven) within oneself and thus become self-sustaining.[21]

This subjective approach opened up almost unlimited possibilities for the individual's attainment of sagehood, with the means of its attainment so available, within ready reach of the common man. It would be the mission of the Wang Yang-ming school to take this message far beyond the usual scholarly audience, now that book-learning was no longer a prime qualification. But this outreach to the common man also carried with it a certain limit or qualification on the individualism it might engender. In fact Wang's holistic approach—so evident in the doctrine of "humaneness forming one body with heaven, earth, and all things"—stressed what was shared and common to all, not what was unique and different in each individual. Indeed, its common character was almost Wang's fundamental article of faith; individual differences were important for him, but the uniqueness of the individual is not something Wang sets in opposition to common humanity, any more than would one, accepting the doctrine of the "unity of principle and diversity of its particularizations," see these as antithetical.

An immediate consequence of this fact, so far as Wang's own outlook is concerned, is that the achievement of his own goal involved no radical social reforms. He sought to free the individual from within, not to set him against anything without. There was no question of breaking away from social obligations or restrictions, nor any consciousness of the kinds of conflict between the individual and society often found in modern individualism. Moreover, the principles and affairs which he discussed in relation to innate knowledge were the traditional moral virtues and concerns expressed in Mencius' formulation of the Four Beginnings: the sense of sympathy or commiseration, of shame, of deference to others, of right and wrong (2A:6). Each of these presupposed some interrelationship or interplay between the self and others. Wang Yang-ming accepted without question the contextual character of Confucian ethics whereby these virtues were linked concretely to existential human relationships.[22] We find him illustrating the principle of innate knowledge again and again with reference to the virtue of filial piety, and we know that a crucial experience in his own development had been his discovery, when he tried to practice a kind of Taoist-Buddhist meditation, that to detach himself from his parents would be inhuman and would amount to destroying his own nature.[23]

As a result Wang Yang-ming seems to have assumed that the traditional Confucian relationships would remain intact. Innate knowledge would only confirm them, revivify them with the spontaneity of freely given assent, and assure them of selfless commitment on the part of the individual. Perhaps nowhere is this traditional character of Wang's social ideal so apparent as in the vision of the Golden Age described in his famous essay "Pulling Up the Roots and Stopping Up the Source":

> The mind of a sage regards Heaven, Earth, and all things as one body. He looks upon all people of the world, whether inside or outside his family, or whether far or near, but all with blood and breath, as his brothers and children. He wants to make them secure, preserve, educate, and nourish all of them, so as to fulfill his desire of forming one body with all things. Now the mind of everybody is at first not different from that of the sage. Only because it is obstructed by selfishness and blocked by human desires, what was originally great becomes small and what was originally penetrating becomes obstructed.[24]

Concerned over this, says Wang, the sage sought to teach people how to overcome their selfishness. On its practical side this teaching was expressed in the terms of Mencius:

> Between parent and child there should be affection, between ruler and minister there should be rightness, between husband and

wife there should be differentiation of function, between old and young there should be a proper order, and between friends there should be trust—that is all. (3A:4)

In the time of Yao, Shun, and the Three Dynasties, teachers taught and students studied only this. At that time *people did not have different opinions, nor did families have different practices.* (Emphasis mine.)[25]

This was possible, Wang says, because "there was no pursuit after the knowledge of seeing and hearing [i.e., sense-knowledge or secondary knowledge] to confuse them, no memorization and recitation to hinder them, no writing of flowery compositions to indulge in, and no chasing after success and profit." Thus everyone was content with his own station in life, whether as farmer, artisan, or merchant. "Those who served also desired only to be united with their superiors in one mind and one character to bring peace to the people. [They were] all diligent in their various occupations, so as mutually to sustain and support the life of one another without any desire for exalted position or strife for external things."[26]

From this we see clearly that Wang's social ideal is based on moral self-reformation, not on any radical change in the traditional social relationships. It strongly emphasizes a community of interests as opposed to individual differences. Like so many other Confucian reformers, however, he invokes the past in order to censure the present. In the lines just quoted the source of all evil in the world is identified in terms of the characteristic problems of his own age, and Wang goes on at much greater length in this essay to vent his moral indignation over these evils: people's involvement in and dependence on external knowledge and received opinion (i.e., the competition for official positions and emoluments, which lead the individual to think and do what will gain the approval of others rather than what his own conscience approves).

If we looked no further than this, Wang might seem a hopeless traditionalist and idealist, completely out of joint with civilization and his own times and naively addicted to moralistic solutions of complex cultural problems. His social views would also seem greatly to vitiate any promise of distinctive individualism growing out of the doctrine of innate knowing. Indeed, if Wang had simply found a direct way to introspect the common human nature within, it might have opened the way to an experience of a universal principle within—the same in all men of every age and place, throughout all time and space, as Lu Hsiang-shan had been wont to put it—but the results would probably not have been much different for Wang than for Lu. From this Wang's teaching might well have evaporated in a diffuse, amorphous, ethical mysticism. As it was, however, Wang's whole outlook and method remained deeply imbued with certain educational values of the Chu Hsi school—before all, the initial assumption that learning is for one's "self"; that this means making and shaping a "self" through the process of "getting it oneself," a deeply personal thing for each individual but reaching out to others; that each person is a unique compound—a singular unity—of moral principles and psycho-physical constituents, whose education should lead both to the self-development of singular individuals and the renewal of the people as a whole; and that effective social organization—as in the community compacts Wang, following Chu's example, tried to set up in areas he "pacified"— depends on eliciting the voluntary cooperation of such individuals. More particularly, however, Wang's active commitment is to teaching and scholarly discussion (i.e., to carrying on the tradition of discursive learning *(chiang-hsüeh)* among Neo-Confucians. This, in the end, is what enables him both to achieve fulfillment as a Confucian and to give practical expression to his belief that self-improvement and social improvement go together.

If Wang has little to say about the reform of social organization, he has much to say about educational reform. His own greatest talent may well have been that of a teacher, rather than a philosopher, scholar, or official. Perhaps no other figure in Chinese history except for Confucius and Chu Hsi has had such an influence as a teacher in terms of the number of his students, the schools established by him and by them and the wide effect of this teaching on the thinking of the time. It is in this sphere, then, that Wang's brand of personalism, verging on a new individualism, manifested itself most clearly and authentically.

The significance of this was expressed by the late Ming follower of Wang, Chiao Hung, who in discussing "Learning for One's Self," "learning to be human" and "getting it one's self," said:

> The learning of Confucius and Mencius, when it reached Sung scholars, became obscured. I-ch'uan (Ch'eng I) and Yüan-hui (Chu Hsi) had scholars exert their efforts in searching out the principles in things, and the person (body and mind) of the individual self *(tzu-chi i-p'ien)* was left aside as something unworthy of discussion. Then Master Yang-ming revealed to scholars the teaching of innate knowing; he deserves great credit for showing how to find it in ourselves . . .[27]

From a Sung perspective it was only because Ch'eng I and Chu Hsi had given such priority to "Learning for One's Self," that it remained such an issue for later Neo-Confucians like Wang and Chiao Hung to deal with. From Chiao's perspective in the late Ming, however, it was the over-intellectualization and emphasis on scholarly inquiry, implicit in Chu Hsi's view of the investigation of things as prerequisite to integral comprehension, that needed to be corrected by giving priority to the unity of mind and principle in innate knowing.

"Learning," Wang said, "must be for one's self."[28] That is, there must be no self-deception, no learning simply to please others. As a teacher himself he was careful always to respect this basic principle, demonstrating a primary concern for the self-development of the person. His *Instructions for Practical Living (Ch'uan-hsi lu)*, which are in large part dialogues with students, reveal an active interest in what others have learned for themselves and what results they have achieved by their own efforts.[29] Unless we understand this, for instance, the following encounter might strike us as having a surprising, if not comic, twist to it.

Ou-yang Ch'ung-i said, "Sir, your principle of the extension of knowledge expresses all that is excellent and deep. As we see it, one cannot go any further."

The teacher said, "Why speak of it so lightly? Make a further effort for another half year and see how it is. Then make an effort for another year and see how it is. The longer one makes an effort, the more different it will become. This is something difficult to explain in words."[30]

What would seem to have been the most whole-hearted praise cannot by Wang be accepted as a genuine compliment. It implies that the student has received from his master the full and final answer, which only shows that he has understood nothing. "Why speak of it so lightly" means "Don't think it's that easy." For Wang everything depends on continuing thought, effort, and reflection. The truth, since it is not an object or a statement, cannot be summed up in a formula but must be experienced in an intensely personal way.

Later Huang Tsung-hsi, following the same line of thought and practice as Wang, would recall in his *Case Studies of Ming Confucians (Ming-ju hsüeh-an)*, an anecdote concerning Chu Hsi that illustrated the same idea:

In learning we accept as truth what each person has found and illumined for himself. . . .

Hu Chi-sui[31] studied under Chu Hsi, who made him read *Mencius*. One day Chu asked him in reference to 6A:7 about what is common to human nature. Hu gave his own understanding of the matter, which Chu thought was incorrect, saying that Hu studied the text carelessly, without reflecting upon it. Thereupon Hu thought about it so hard that he became ill. Only then would Chu explain it to him. This shows that the scholars of old did not transmit their teachings in a routine manner, but wanted students to get it for themselves *(tzu-te chih)*.[32]

The original anecdote is found in the *Recorded Conversations* of Lu Hsiang-shan, where it has a different point.[33] Lu wondered why

Chu would put Hu to such toil and anguish over such a small matter. For Lu everything should be easy and simple, reduced to the least common denominator; for Chu, Wang Yang-ming, and presumably Huang Tsung-hsi, the struggle was necessary in learning for one's self because it was particular to the making of that self; this was not just something obvious to all.

There are here, one might suspect, strong overtones of Ch'an training, which it would be idle to deny since so much conscious reference is made to Ch'an in the *Instructions*. But if there are indeed similarities to Ch'an in the irreducibly personal method, the insistence on a life-and-death earnestness in the seeker, and the ineffability of ultimate truth, there is also a significant difference. Learning for Wang is not directed toward a special experience of "enlightenment." Such things may occur but are incidental. Learning for him is a simple day-to-day and life-long process. "Here is our innate knowing today. We should extend it to the utmost according to what we know today. As our innate knowing is further developed tomorrow, we should extend it to the utmost according to what we know then.[34]

Moreover, Wang refuses to set himself up as an authority or as one who sets his seal on another. Truth emerges in action, discussion, and constant self-criticism. Indeed, the insistence on authority in both patriarchal Ch'an and traditional Confucianism is called into question in a most fundamental way. The title of the *Ch'uan-hsi lu* suggests the passing on of a method of practice, not a received revelation or an inherited body of doctrine. If we render it as "Instructions," we must remember that it carries none of the traditional connotations of indoctrination. Otherwise we could not appreciate the extent to which general discussion as a means of arriving at truth became the most important feature of education in the Wang Yang-ming school.

The most radical challenge to authority was, of course, posed by the doctrine of innate knowing itself. If Ch'en Hsien-chang had already declared his independence of intellectual authority, it was Wang who made it fully explicit:

If words are examined in the mind and found to be wrong, although they have come from the mouth of Confucius, I dare not accept them as correct. How much less those from people inferior to Confucius! If words are examined in the mind and found to be correct, although they have come from the mouth of ordinary people, I dare not regard them as wrong. How much less those of Confucius![35]

At this point, however, we must remind ourselves that Wang's confidence in trusting one's own mind as the ultimate authority rests squarely on his faith that all men's minds reflect and express a common standard of truth. Thus we recall him saying, as above:

The Way is public and belongs to the whole world, and the doctrine is also public and belongs to the whole world. They are not the private properties of Master Chu [Hsi] or even Confucius. They are open to all and the only proper way to discuss them is to do so openly.[36]

There is perhaps no more striking example than this of Wang's basically Confucian—and we might even say Chinese—outlook: for all his emphasis on individual effort and personal intuition of truth, he retains a faith in the fundamental rationality of man; and for all his insistence on discovering right and wrong for oneself, it does not occur to him that there could be any essential conflict between subjective and objective morality, or that genuine introspection could lead to anything other than the affirmation of clear and common moral standards.

Ch'an, though a distinctively Chinese form of Buddhism, nevertheless was true to its Indian and Taoist origins in seeking truth beyond the moral sphere and in withdrawing from the arena of rational debate in order to achieve it. Wang, on the other hand, not only challenges authority in public (as indeed the *kōan* or "public case" did) but goes on to reestablish it in public discourse.

Here is the underlying reason why Wang Yang-ming's Confucianism could have had such a quickening effect on the thought of those times and such an explosive impact on all levels of Ming society and culture—its tremendous moral dynamism, its enormous confidence in man, and its faith that life could be dealt with by opening people up to one another from within. This is also why Ch'an Buddhism, though it maintained a silent presence throughout the age, depended upon the vitality of Wang's teaching for a momentary reinvigoration of its own intellectual life during a long period of decline.[37]

Without Wang's passionate faith in humanity, and in the Heavenly principle implanted within man, his teaching might have been as lifeless and moribund, culturally speaking, as Ch'an at that time. With this faith in the underlying unity of man, however, Wang Yang-ming was also able to accept the diversity manifested in the development of his individual students. Wang's strength as a teacher, and his weakness as a philosopher (from the analytic point of view), lies in his seemingly deliberate cultivation of ambiguities which could be explored by his own students and clarified by their own experience.[38] Had he not allowed these ambiguities to stand, there might have been far less discussion and debate within his school, less room for individual and regional differentiation, and perhaps no such ranges of opinion as justified making distinctions between right, center, and left.[39] Nor could we have found so many remarkable personalities, so many striking individuals, among his followers.

7. Wang Chi and the Freedom of Innate Knowing

Wang Chi (1498–1583), one of Wang Yang-ming's closest and most devoted followers, was from the same region of Chekiang and from a similar scholar-official background. He early attached himself to Yang-ming and soon became known as a disciple of great brilliance and promise. After pursuing an official career with modest success, beset by the usual disappointments and frustrations, he left it in order to take up the life of a teacher. For over forty years he lectured at academies and lecture halls throughout North, East, and South China, attracting large audiences and many students, as well as much criticism for his highly original and, some said, unorthodox views. His influence went far beyond his own school. Thus he stands as one of the most important and controversial figures among the large number of able individuals attracted to Wang Yang-ming's teaching.[1]

That so many thinkers could play their own distinctive role in spreading Wang Yang-ming's ideas suggests how adaptable these were to individual needs and temperaments. Wang Chi, in particular, opened up new and challenging prospects for the development of Yang-ming's thought. As an articulate exponent of Yang-ming's innate knowing, he interpreted it as a dynamic principle, both transcendent and immanent in the mind, in a way that greatly heightened its significance for the spiritual freedom of the individual. Subsequent developments would show that he opened a large door for the creative interaction of Neo-Confucianism and other religious tendencies in late Ming China and Tokugawa Japan.

Wang Chi's view of Yang-ming's "Four Dicta," strenuously challenged in his own day and much discussed since, characterized the essence of innate knowing as beyond good and evil. "There is neither good nor evil in the original substance of the mind."[2] By this he meant that the faculty of judging good and evil had to be free of any preconceptions or predeterminations if it was to do its work. Here Wang Chi was equally concerned that innate knowing should be both firmly grounded in the common mind of man and susceptible of striking exemplification in heroic figures like Wang Yang-ming, who could help others to realize their potential for sagehood. Yang-ming's sageliness and his demonstration of the power of innate knowing, according to Wang Chi, were especially shown in his selflessness, his lack of any egoistic attachment to preconceived ideas, and his largeness of spirit in dealing with others. This magnanimity was characteristic of Mencius' "great man"; it suggested that the individual was most fully human who was most receptive to others and open to new experience.

Wang Chi's thought is largely centered on this question of how one activates the dynamic power of the mind to the full exercise of its natural freedom, unencumbered by formal dogmas, acquired prejudices, habitual routines, or self-serving rationalizations that cannot stand up to the reflected light of innate knowing. In this respect he is true to one of the deepest strains in Neo-Confucianism and to the underlying assumption of its voluntaristic individualism, the principle of naturalism *(tzu-jan)*. He was also true to the basic

Neo-Confucian belief in natural learning as "getting it oneself" *(tzu-te)*. Although Wang Chi preferred to express this in terms of Yang-ming's "innate knowing," he did not insist on this formulation as the only way of putting it. When asked his view of a prominent alternative to Yang-ming's teaching, as formulated by Chan Jo-shui (1466–1560) in terms of "Heaven's principle," he refused to get entangled in terminological disputations over the similarities and differences between Wang and Chan Jo-shui. He responded to his questioner:

> You should not be seeking out similarities and differences but only seeking to get the Way for yourself. If it is "innate knowing" you are talking about, then you should really try yourself to work out that knowing, but if it is "Heaven's principle" [as Chan Jo-shui speaks of it], then you should really try to reach that principle [within the self, using Mencius' language in describing *tzu-te*].
>
> In "getting it oneself," the mind is one. If you speak of it in terms of a natural awakening *(tzu-jan chih ming-chüeh)*, it is called "innate knowing." If you speak of it in terms of natural principles, it is "Heaven's principle." Whether it is "innate knowing" or "Heaven's principle," how could one allow it to be two separate things?[3]

THE THREE TEACHINGS AND LEARNING FOR ONE'S SELF

Similarly there is no inherent rightness or authority vested in any teaching. The only, but still essential, criterion of the validity of a teaching is whether it satisfies the requirements of innate knowing in "getting it oneself."

> There is only the slightest difference between our Confucian way and Buddhism and Taoism, yet it lies precisely in this: that they [the Buddhists and Taoists] are obsessed with the after-traces of [the self's] involvement with things and identify with what is

evanescent, rather than basing themselves on innate knowing as the means of finding what must be gotten for oneself.[4]

Elsewhere Wang Chi explains how it is that all men have this firmly rooted inner standard to guide them. It is based on the central Neo-Confucian conception of the underlying empathy among all things which unites them in one spiritual substance:

> When men are given life in this world they all equally receive a common nature and there is no distinction among them as to Confucian, Taoist, or Buddhist. Innate knowing is the spirituality of that nature, in respect to which Heaven-and-earth and all things are of one substance. It embraces what is most essential in the Three Teachings without being bound to their canonical forms or getting involved in their rationalizations. Emptiness and substantiality co-exist without falling into [Taoist] nothingness; passivity and responsiveness abet each other without falling into [Buddhist] extinction. Whatever accords with the common people's sense of good and evil, and does not depart from an empathetic response to others, meets the test of the sages.
>
> If someone studies Taoism or Buddhism and yet is able to satisfy the criterion of "returning to one's true nature," without getting lost in wild and perverse ways, then he is a Taoist or Buddhist Confucian. If someone is a Confucian, and yet makes selfish use of his learning and cannot keep to normal standards in common dealings, then he is no less deviationist or unorthodox for being labeled a Confucian.[5]

It is this original nature, this primordial affinity among all things, to which innate knowing, as the highest consciousness or spirituality of that nature, gives expression. It is the shared basis of the "Three Teachings," but as the positive affinity or empathy among all things its most authentic expression is found in the Neo-Confucian doctrine of the "humaneness that forms one body with Heaven,

Earth, and all things."[6] As we have seen, this was also the key point in Wang Yang-ming's "Inquiry on the Great Learning."

"Innate knowing," Wang Chi says, "does not detach itself from an empathetic response to things and human relations. It is the real, practical learning that is primordial to the uniting of all things in one body. Buddhism's 'illumining the Mind and seeing one's nature' may be understood as manifesting lucent virtue, but it is solely concerned with self-awakening and self-confirmation. It is disconnected from any empathetic response and mutual affection for the people. It regards the self and the world as a delusion and sees all things as ultimately reverting to silent extinction, so it has no basis on which to order the state and the world."[7]

Innate knowing was also, according to Wang Chi, the true original learning handed down from the ancient sages, the message and method of the mind-and-heart *(hsin-fa)* as it came from Yao and Shun,[8] and was, according to Wang Chi, repossessed by Shao Yung in the Sung as the "method of the mind in its a priori state" *(hsien-t'ien chih hsin-fa)*, the "learning anterior to Heaven," which for Wang Chi is innate knowing.[9] Some people, Wang says, have the mistaken notion that this learning or discipline of the mind was only a latter-day importation from Buddhism, not realizing that it had been the essence of sagely learning from the beginning and only got lost after the time of Confucius and Mencius. This he often refers to as the "lost (lit. 'cut-off') learning of the thousand sages" *(ch'ien-sheng chih chüeh-hsüeh)*, thereby conveying the sense of both its high antiquity and abrupt discontinuity.[10]

If anything more were needed to show that Wang Chi is still heir to the *tao-t'ung* view of Confucian tradition propounded by Chu Hsi and the School of the Way, it is shown by Wang's acceptance of the idea that only in the Sung was this lost learning rediscovered. At this point, however, it is Chou Tun-i, not the Ch'eng brothers or Chu Hsi, who serves as Wang's highest patriarchal authority, the great hero and sage of the Way refound in the Sung. After Chou's time, and following another long lapse of the

Way into obscurity, Wang Yang-ming is the next great hero worthy of the highest encomiums. In effect, what Wang Chi gives us is Wang Yang-ming's teaching interpreted in the special light of Chou Tun-i:

> The learning of the sages in all times past is the learning of the mind-and-heart. The Supreme Ultimate is the ultimate of the mind-and-heart. Actuality and nothingness arise in alternation with one another; motion and quiescence are correlated with one another. From the non-finite to the Supreme Ultimate, from yin-yang and the five powers to the myriad things, proceeding from nothingness to actuality—this is what is called procession in sequence *(shun).* From the myriad things back to the five powers and yin-yang, from the Supreme Ultimate to the non-finite—returning from actuality to nothingness—this is what is called reversion [to the original state]. First a sequence; then a reversion. This is the key to creation, production, and completion. But since the transmission of the sages' learning was lost, the meaning of the Ultimate in the mind-and-heart became obscured. Han scholars took "actuality" as the standard. Everything, from humaneness, rightness, the Way, virtue, rites, music, systems, and statutes, was given canonical form, to be preserved exactly as if it were the Ultimate [absolute norm] *(t'ai-chi).* Since they did not even realize that the Supreme Ultimate is based in the Non-finite [nothingness], how could they even make sense of "actuality" [determinate being]?
>
> The learning of the Buddhists takes emptiness as the standard. Humaneness and rightness are for them mere illusions; rites and music are just encumbrances. Statutes, laws, and systems can all be left aside, while everything comes back to silent extinction. "Nothingness" could be absolutized as if it were Ultimate Nothingness. Since they did not know about the "Non-finite and then the Supreme Ultimate," how could they even make sense of Nothingness?

One [the Han Confucians] got stuck in old ruts, understanding procession in sequence but not reversion [destruction]. The other [Buddhists] got lost in Emptiness; they understood reversion but did not know about procession in sequence. Cramped and uptight, each from their own fixations, they had no way of appreciating the fullness of the Ultimate of the mind-and-heart.

This distortion of learning had long persisted when Chou Tun-i arose after a thousand years silently [i.e., without being told] to grasp the original truth and clearly perceive the errors of these two. He constructed his Diagram and set forth the meaning of the "Non-finite and then the Supreme Ultimate" to remedy the situation. Some said he had gotten the secret untransmitted for a thousand years and that it was worthy of credence. Others said that from the most ancient time there had never been any talk of the Supreme Ultimate before Confucius spoke of it [supposedly in the Great Appendix to the *Changes*] not realizing that Chi Tzu had passed it on when he spoke about the field measures of the Sovereign Ultimate [referred to in the "Hung fan" of the *Book of Documents*]. The Sovereign Ultimate has the same meaning as the Supreme Ultimate, but it was only Confucius who picked it up and developed it. [Others said] Confucius never spoke of the Non-finite [*wu-chi*] and yet Master Chou spoke of it. They don't realize that the *I-ching* speaks of the Supreme Ultimate and the Changes as having no fixed substance. "Having no fixed substance" is the same in meaning as "Non-finite." [Chou] spoke of "stabilizing the mind in equilibrium and correctness, humaneness and rightness, and giving primacy to quiescence."[11] Thus he explained to men the essentials of practice. To stabilize the mind with equilibrium and correctness, humaneness and rightness, is the Supreme Ultimate, and to give primacy to quiescence is what is called the Non-finite. Thus he spoke of "setting up the human ultimate." Quiescence is the substance of the mind. The quiescence of "giving primacy to quiescence" actually combines activity and inactivity. A later scholar [Chu Hsi] spoke of humaneness as the action of *yang* and rightness as the quiescence of *yin,* and of equilibrium and correctness as coordinating them.[12] This is an error. The Sage based it all on quiescence. . . .

Several hundred years after Master Chou, our teacher Yangming proclaimed the teaching of innate knowing in order to awaken the world, and the meaning of the Ultimate in the mind-and-heart again became clear to the world. Still and unmoving—such is the substance of innate knowing: responding and then penetrating to the end—such is the functioning of innate knowing. Ever still, ever responding; "forgetting" both stillness and response—such is the ultimate norm of innate knowing. Innate knowing knows right and knows wrong, but really there is no [fixed] right and wrong. Actuality out of the midst of nothingness; nothingness in the midst of actuality—this is the essence of the great Change. Therefore when Chou talks about "establishing the Way of Heaven," he speaks of yin and yang as ultimates of Heaven. When he speaks of establishing the Way of Earth, he speaks of softness and hardness as ultimates of Earth. And when he speaks of establishing the Way of Man, he speaks of humaneness and rightness as the ultimates of man. Man is the mind-and-heart of Heaven and Earth, the finest expression of yin-yang and the five powers, the master of the myriad things. Extend innate knowing and the three ultimates [of Heaven, Earth, and Man] are established, inviolable among Heaven, Earth, and all things.

When Master Chou pursued the learning of sagehood, he made oneness [singleness of mind] the essential thing, desirelessness the major element, and reducing the desires the method. The key to it was the subtle refinement of a single thought. Desirelessness is carrying it out naturally; this is the learning of the sage. Reducing the desires is the endeavor to carry it out. The noble man practices this and things go well for him. Those who have many desires ruin themselves, abandon themselves, not knowing how to carry it out. The small man flouts this and things go wrong.

Thus, apart from innate knowing there is no true knowledge; apart from practicing innate knowing, there is no true pursuit of learning.[13]

Here Wang Chi interprets Chou's *wu-chi* as the ground of Infinite Nothingness out of which existent things emerge and to which they revert. In his interpretation of Chou Tun-i's doctrine of the Supreme Ultimate, he has to deal with an ambiguity in the original *wu-chi erh t'ai-chi*, which may be understood either as Non-finite and *yet* the Supreme Ultimate [i.e., as a concomitant condition] or as "*The* Non-finite [indeterminate] and *then* the Supreme Ultimate." He resolves this in favor of the latter, as a process of sequential procession into determinate actuality, alternating with retrocession or reversion to the original state, which he also identifies with undifferentiated unity and with quiescence. That is, he gives priority to the Non-finite, the undifferentiated, the quiescent state.

Chu Hsi had specifically ruled out taking *wu-chi* as a separate state prior to the emergence of things, or as the original source of things, and instead explained *wu-chi* as the non-finite or indeterminate aspect of present reality.[14]

Although Wang Chi criticizes the Taoists and Buddhists for emphasizing nothingness and emptiness at the expense of actuality, when he speaks of "quiescence as the substance of the mind," and of "giving primacy to quiescence," as well as of the sage reducing everything to quiescence, he leans to a more quietistic interpretation than Chu Hsi would allow (though it is not without some basis in Chou's original). Further, he takes specific issue with Chu Hsi's emphasis on equilibrium (centrality) and correctness as what must control and coordinate the alternating phases of action and quiescence, insisting instead that "the sage based everything on quiescence."[15]

In giving Chou Tun-i's concept a more Taoistic reading, Wang Chi also opted for a more mystical holism which he would often describe in Taoistic terms of emptiness *(hsü)* or nothingness *(wu)*, and as we see in the preceding passage he speaks of "forgetting" (i.e., letting go, rising above) action and quiescence, and all such dichotomies, in terms very reminiscent of Chuang Tzu. Wang Chi did not see this as lapsing into Taoism but rather as assimilating a Taoist perspective into a larger Confucian view. Thus the Non-finite *(wu-chi)* comprehends both nothingness and actuality; emptiness *(hsü)* is a mirror-like receptivity assimilated into the unitary operation of innate knowing; desirelessness *(wu-yü)* is an altruistic attitude appropriated to the humaneness which is one in substance with all things; "doing nothing" *(wu-wei)* is acting naturally in accordance with the spontaneous dictates of innate knowing and without any selfish rationalization or predisposition; "knowing nothing" *(wu-chih)* and "thinking nothing" *(wu-ssu)* are a knowing and thinking which impose no preconceived order or constraint upon the free operation of innate knowing, etc.[16]

In his drive to assert the utmost metaphysical freedom for innate knowing and to overcome the limits of any cultural conditioning or ingrained habits of thought, Wang Chi makes full use of the vocabulary of both Buddhism and Taoism in describing this state. Thus, for instance:

> Innate knowing knows right and knows wrong, but really there is no [inherent] right and wrong. Nothingness is the basis for all that is. . . .[17]
>
> The learning of the noble man takes enlightenment as his only role and guide.[18]
>
> . . . Only Yen Hui was able to express the distilled essence of the Sages . . . but we, millennia and centuries later, have failed to understand this kōan propounded long ago [by Yen Hui]. . . .[19]
>
> Hsiang-shan trusted in his own original mind. All his life he tried to put into practice just one saying: [Mencius] "First set up the greater part of one's nature" as if it were a kōan for him. Although he gained access to the Way by following these words, there was much that he got for himself *(tzu-te)*.[20]

If anyone should object that this is facile syncretism, playing fast and loose with terms ripped out of their original contexts, Wang Chi would probably not disagree. The important thing for him is not the provenance of ideas or concepts but whether one can make good use of them in finding the Way for one's self—"it is not whether you got it from Chu Hsi or Wang Yang-ming but whether you can rest satisfied with it in your own mind." [21] "Learning starts with understanding one's own nature and destiny, silently [inwardly] cultivating oneself and attesting to it oneself. Thereupon to set up one's own school and defend its ideas is to wrap one's ideas in a protective shell. It is not real learning for one's self *(wei-chi chih hsüeh)*." [22]

Creative use of the past, not slavish adherence to established forms, was the vital thing to Wang Chi—an ability to see the underlying unities amidst diverse experiences. For this, self-understanding had to claim priority over classical learning. Thus Wang Chi was fond of quoting Lu Hsiang-shan to the effect that "The Six Classics are commentaries on me; it is not for me to comment on the Six Classics." [23] Wang Chi did not mean to rule out study of the classics, just to put it in proper perspective:

> Although books are only dregs and leavings [from the past], the sages and worthies from of old have relied on them as a means of transmitting what could be expressed of their minds-and-hearts. What's wrong then with reading them? To get stuck in books, however, and not "get it" in your own mind-and-heart—this is "letting the Lotus Sutra turn you" [instead of you turning the Lotus] [24] and falling into the defect of rootlessness. [25]

This shows how Wang Chi recognized that a basic principle of the spiritual life in Buddhism applied no less to the Confucian—it was more fundamentally an aspect of human spirituality than it was an exclusive sectarian property.

For Wang Chi being "rooted" meant being fully established in the exercise of innate knowing as the substance of one's nature.

"Innate knowing is the pivot of the Classics and rule of the Way. If the classics are clearly understood [in relation to one's self], there is no need for commentary. If the Way is clearly understood [in oneself], there is no need to depend on the classics. A former scholar [Lu Hsiang-shan] said: 'The Six Classics are all commentaries on me.' This was not just empty talk!"[26]

In Ming Neo-Confucianism as it had developed in the Ch'eng-Chu school, learning was carried on in two principal ways thought to be complementary in the process of self-cultivation. One was book learning centered on the Classics. The other was quiet-sitting as a contemplative discipline and form of self-scrutiny.[27] One looked outward on the world; the other inward on the self. Given Wang Chi's stress on the autonomy of self, and his readiness to make use of concepts and practices from Buddhism and Taoism one might expect him to be well-disposed to so self-centered a form of spiritual praxis as quiet-sitting. Yet it was even more true of him than of Wang Yang-ming that he resisted dependence on any formal routine for the exercise of innate knowing. When questioned about the endorsement of quiet-sitting by the Ch'eng brothers, Wang felt no embarrassment over acknowledging that this was a practice not found in classical Confucianism and only borrowed from Taoism and Buddhism. It was, he said, a concession warranted by the corrupt state of men's minds under the stultifying influence of Han Confucian formalism. Quiet-sitting was not, however, the most dynamic way to practice innate knowing, nor was it necessary to the understanding of innate knowing, while the latter was indeed indispensable to the effective practice of quiet-sitting.[28]

In other words, Wang Chi rejected any formalized practice, whether scholarly or contemplative, which might impede the active, spontaneous exercise of innate knowing, while he could have no objection to such practices when pursued in the light of innate knowing. Any unexamined or unquestioning routine was inimical to the life of the mind. "The true learner values questioning. If he does not ask questions about what he sees and has doubts about, then he is not pursuing the way which seeks truly to benefit the self."[29]

If this sounds like a skeptical method, it is indeed, but linked in Wang Chi's mind to a mystical view of innate knowing as bridging the sacred and profane, the divine and the mundane:

The innate knowing of the mind-and-heart partakes of the holy, the sagely. It is the spirituality of the nature, supremely empty and divine, utmost nothingness and transforming power. Requiring neither study nor deliberation, as the Heavenly it is what comes naturally. At the lowest level it can be readily understood by even ignorant men and women; in its highest reaches it goes beyond the comprehension of even sages and worthies, so that they liken it to the sun or moon shining in the heavens. . . . It can match Heaven-and-earth, span the four seasons, reach down to a thousand generations. It is active cultivation and ready enlightenment. Gotten for one-self, it owes nothing to externals, while the key to it lies in no more than a fleeting moment of thought.[30]

At times Wang Chi describes the practice of innate knowing in terms redolent of popular theisms and even strikingly reminiscent of devotional religions which teach "living in the presence of God." The commitment to the Way of the sages is no less a holy vocation for being directed to self-knowledge and calling for faith or trust in one's self. "The commitment to self-knowledge means to do without selfish calculation, premeditation, or disputation, and just to stand in the sight of the Lord-on-High to the end of one's days."[31] Elsewhere, in terms recalling the Book of Odes' facing or answering to the spirits of Heaven-and-earth[32] he specifically endorses this kind of religiosity as preferable to a slavish adherence to sacred texts. "If we can always face the Lord-on-High, then we need have no dependence on books."[33]

The studies of Professor Yamashita Ryūji have particularly emphasized the significance of Wang Chi's religious orientation and the relation of his thought to theistic currents in East Asia during the sixteenth and seventeenth centuries. Wang Chi was influential on the thought of Nakae Tōju (1608–48), the so-called founder of the Wang Yang-ming school in Japan, who blended the Neo-Confucian philosophy of mind with a Shinto devotionalism.[34] Other Neo-Confucian activists in late Tokugawa Japan, who combined a kind of religious messianism with the cult of the heroic individual, were also inspired by Wang Chi.[35] Moreover, there was an atmosphere of religious revival in the spread of the Wang Yang-ming movement itself in sixteenth-century China.

This poses a question as to whether a movement of thought like the Wang Yang-ming school, which stimulated many new currents of moral reform and religious syncretism, had the potential for outgrowing or breaking down some of Neo-Confucianism's elitist character as a product of the scholar-official class. It is a question best addressed in connection with Wang Ken, whom we take up next. But it is not without some pertinence to Wang Chi as well, since his thought is the most mystical in its manner of expression and yet also the most radically individualistic vis-à-vis tradition. Could the religious impulse in Wang Chi have led to an evangelism and communitarianism which would extend his radical individualism in the direction of social equality or an egalitarian program?

On this point, I think, the answer might be "yes" to equality as a generalized value but "no" to any program or active advocacy of it. Wang Chi seems not to have envisioned any new community other than the totality of individuals freely exercising their innate knowledge. His preoccupation is still with the individual's "getting it," and hardly at all with his taking upon himself any well-defined responsibilities toward society other than the familiar one of self-cultivation in the basic virtues as a model for universal emulation.[36] The only social role Wang discusses at any length is that of teacher, but the teacher's function, like that of the bodhisattva, is to enlighten others, liberate their minds, and not to reform the social order. One can see how his mystical message and religious enthusiasm might well mean all things to all men, but not how they could give defined form and discipline to an educational program or to the structuring of individual rights. Like others of his school Wang Chi believed strongly in the value of "lecturing and discussion" as a means of promoting general enlightenment, and he practices this with genuine dedication, as many of his writings testify.[37] Yet, however humanitarian his aims were as a Neo-Confucian "forming one body with Heaven-and-earth and all things," there would have been available in his system no shared body of public discourse as a vehicle for social advocacy, only a limitless effusion of moral enthusiasm, spiritual freedom, and mystical liberation, which might in the practical order still not escape the social confines of elitism. Since Wang Chi had propagated the idea that "good knowing as beyond good and evil" was a teaching for those of superior intelligence, there would be some grounds for suspecting, not that Wang Chi himself believed in the need for an intellectual elite, but that his esoteric interpretation of innate knowledge might lend itself to the idea that intellectual autonomy and spiritual freedom were more likely to be enjoyed by the few than shared by the many.

8. Wang Ken and His School: The Common Man as Sage

Probably none of the influential followers of Wang Yang-ming exemplifies as well as does Wang Ken (1483?–1540),[1] both in his person and in his thought, the potential for an egalitarian individualism within this school—that is, for an individualism most nearly resembling that of the modern West. Claims might be made for others as being more faithful to other basic teachings of Wang Yang-ming or to the main line of Confucian tradition, but it is Wang Ken who carries forward most vigorously the idea of the common man as sage.

What distinguishes Wang Ken from the start is that he began life as the son of a salt maker and never sought or attained the status of a Confucian scholar-official. A man of tremendous energy and vitality, he seemed to draw strength and self-confidence as if through a taproot striking deep into the soil of China. Wang Yang-ming apparently appreciated this rugged quality of Wang Ken, when later he suggested that the latter change his name from Yin (silver), to Ken for "stubborn strength" (symbolized by a mountain, but phonetically related to *ken* for "root").[2]

A native of T'ai-chou, in modern Kiangsu Province, Wang Ken had only five years of instruction at the village school before economic necessity forced him, at the age of eleven, to leave it and assist his father in the family business. Later, on repeated business trips to Shantung Province, he carried copies of the *Analects* of Confucius, the *Classic of Filial Piety*, and the *Great Learning* in his sleeve, and discussed them with anyone he could find who might aid his understanding. His determination to become a sage was aroused, it is said, when he visited the shrine of Confucius at Ch'ü-fu and realized that the immortal Sage himself had been, after all, just a man.[3]

By the age of twenty-one he had become established as an independent salt dealer, and prospered enough so that he could devote more time to self-study. He developed the practice of shutting himself up in a room for quiet-sitting, meditating in silence day and night for long periods of time in a manner reminiscent of Ch'en Hsien-chang, by then not an uncommon method of seeking "enlightenment." In an age marked by a heightening of the mystical spirit and a widespread belief in dreams and visions, it is not extraordinary that Wang Ken's spiritual awakening should have followed a dream in which he saw the heavens falling and people fleeing in panic. Answering their cries for help, he stood forth, pushed up the heavens, and restored order among the heavenly bodies. People were overjoyed and thanked him profusely. When Ken awoke, bathed in perspiration, he suddenly had his enlightenment, described in terms of an experience of being united with all things through his humanity *(jen)* and of finding the universe within himself.[4] Here again the resemblance to both Ch'en Hsien-chang and Wang Yang-ming is obvious. Though he has not yet come directly under the influence of any teacher, he seems to breathe the same spiritual atmosphere as they, and spontaneously to manifest similar ideas and experience.

What is of special interest in Wang Ken is the sense of mission which arose from this experience. He felt a vocation to become a teacher to mankind. But since he had had little formal education, his approach to learning was highly individual, and emphasized personal spirituality and activity as opposed to scholarly study. The classics he used simply to document his own experience. As he put it, "One should use the classics to prove one's own enlightenment, and use one's own enlightenment to interpret the classics."[5] In his daily life he combined teaching with solitary study and meditation, the active with the contemplative life. And, as if to confirm the contemporary theory that activity arises from quiescence, from the depths of Wang Ken's subjectivity arose dynamic ideas, dramatically expressed in his own actions.

As an example, at the age of thirty-seven, not long before he met Wang Yang-ming, Wang Ken's reading of *Mencius* and his reflections on the true meaning of sagehood in one's daily life produced a startling thought. "Mencius says, 'Can one speak the words of [the sage-king] Yao, and perform the actions of Yao and yet not wear the clothing of Yao?'" Whereupon, following some prescriptions found in the *Book of Rites*, he made himself a long cotton gown, a special hat and girdle to wear, and a ceremonial tablet to carry around with him.[6] Above his door he inscribed the declaration: "My teaching comes down through [the sages] Fu-hsi, Shen-nung, the Yellow Emperor, Yao, Shun, the Great Yü, Kings T'ang, Wen, and Wu, the Duke of Chou, and Confucius. To anyone who earnestly seeks it, whether he be young or old, high or low, wise or ignorant, I shall pass it on."[7] Many people laughed at this, but some were moved by Wang Ken's sense of active concern to make the ancient Way live in the present, and, ignoring the ridicule of others, took up the cause.

Involved here is something more than just a quaint and quixotic gesture on the part of an eccentric old scholar. Wang Ken is not in his dotage, not even much of a scholar, and not really an antiquarian. Like Wang Yang-ming he is struggling to discover, to work out for himself, the meaning of sagehood for his own time, to bring the conception of the sage down from the lofty heights and out of the remote past directly into the foreground of his own life. Wang Ken lacks the self-consciousness of Wang Yang-ming, and is not so tortured by doubt, but he undergoes something of the same tension that made Yang-ming cry out:

> Whenever I think of people's degeneration and difficulties I pity them and have a pain in my heart. I overlook my own unworthiness and wish to save them by this teaching. And I do not know the limits of my ability. When people see me trying to do this, they join one another in ridiculing, insulting, and cursing me, regarding me as insane. . . . Alas! The minds of all people are the same as mine. There *are* people who are insane. How can I not be so? There *are* people who have lost their minds. How can I not lose mine?[8]

Wang Ken, though not the kind to experience such agonies, undoubtedly expects to be similarly misunderstood, if not thought quite mad. Yet there is a difference. Yang-ming found it trouble enough to be natural and humane; Wang Ken's eccentricities are of another sort. They reflect not only a difference in temperament from Wang Yang-ming—a deliberate self-dramatization—but a conflict which the latter never had to face. Wang Ken, after all, is a commoner, the uneducated son of a salt merchant; Yang-ming, a distinguished scholar-official and the son of a distinguished scholar-official. For Yang-ming to discover sagehood in his contemporaries meant ignoring the accidents of birth and status, stripping away the cultural and social adornments of the Confucian, and finding the essential moral man. For Wang Ken, however, the question is not whether "he will take off his clothing" to save mankind, but what clothing to put on; not whether he should "take the Way of Confucius upon himself,"[9] (already answered in his fateful dream) but the next question to follow: how shall the commoner fulfill that mission in a world where Confucian virtue is everywhere identified with membership in the ruling class? He refuses to accept the superiority of the scholar-official, to ape the manners and dress of the so-called gentry, or even to acknowledge a debt to centuries of learned Confucians. Instead, he boldly clothes himself in the garments of the primordial sage, and though it may appear to the conventionally minded a sign of eccentricity, for Wang Ken it is enough that at least it not be taken as a sign of affectation. Symbolically the simple cotton gown of Yao signifies the common man's direct access to sagehood, Ken's unwillingness to yield this responsibility to any official elite, and his life-long adherence to the status of commoner.

WHEN SAGES MEET

Wang Ken was already thirty-eight, and well-established in his own thinking, before he met Wang Yang-ming. He had been living intensely in his own small world while scholars and officials from all over that region flocked to hear the brilliant governor of Kiangsi lecture on innate knowledge. Then a friend, more in touch with scholarly thought than he, remarked to Wang Ken how similar his ideas were to the famous Wang Yang-ming's. "Is that so?" he said, and then went on with characteristic forthrightness: "But you say Mr. Wang teaches 'innate knowledge' while I teach 'the investigation of things.' If they are indeed similar, then Mr. Wang is Heaven's gift to the world and later generations. But if they differ, then Heaven is giving me to Mr. Wang!"[10]

If their ideas correspond, in other words, they share the same high mission; but to the extent that they differ each may have something to learn from the other.[11] With this remarkable combination of conviction, self-confidence, and, at the same time, humility in pursuit of the Way, Wang Ken, dressed in his outlandish gown, set off to meet the governor. But having entered the latter's courtyard, he stopped at the middle gate and stood erect, holding aloft his tablet and refusing to come in as a mere client, until Wang himself came out and escorted him in. When that was done he strode in and took the seat of honor. Only after some debate did Wang Ken acknowledge Wang Yang-ming' superiority and move down to a lower seat, signifying his readiness to become the latter's pupil. "He is so simple and direct. I cannot equal him." [12] But even then, reflecting upon the day's debate that night, Wang Ken found himself not wholly convinced. He went back the next morning and said, "I gave in too easily," resuming the seat of honor. Far from being offended, Yang-ming was delighted to find a man who would not yield assent too readily. But after further debate, Ken surrendered completely and made his submission as a disciple. Later Yang-ming told his disciples, "When I captured [the rebel Chu] Ch'en-hao, I was not a bit moved, but today I was moved by this man." [13]

Wang Ken was never wholly tamed, however, nor would Yang-ming have had it so—except perhaps once. Ken's active disposition made him restless to carry the true way to all men. He returned home, built himself a cart like the one Confucius allegedly used when he traveled to the courts of feudal princes, and went off to Peking. There his dress, his cart, and his somewhat pig-like appearance attracted much attention and great crowds came to hear him. Many people became convinced of his deep sincerity and were drawn to his ideas. In ruling circles, however, he was looked on either as a joke or else as a potential troublemaker. Some of Wang Yang-ming's disciples at court found it embarrassing. They urged him to leave, which he eventually did, but only after the Master himself ordered Ken out. [14]

On his return Yang-ming showed his displeasure by refusing to see him for three days. Contrite, Ken waited by his gate and, when Wang Yang-ming came to see a guest off, tried to make apologies. The Teacher would not listen, but as he turned to go back inside, Ken followed and cried out bitterly, "Confucius would not have carried things to such an extreme!" (quoting *Mencius* 5B;10), a telling reproach from someone charged with extremism. Yang-ming relented, helped him to his feet, and took him in. [15]

Accounts differ as to how much of a change this worked in Ken, [16] but it is less of a problem when one recognizes that stubbornness and humility were complementary aspects of his personality. He seems to have settled down to a less spectacular role while Yang-ming remained alive, but thereafter resumed an active life as a teacher in his own school and had wide influence.

WANG KEN'S CELEBRATION OF SELF

Before visiting Wang Yang-ming, Wang Ken had described his own teaching as "the investigation of things," but recognized that his interpretation of it was similar to Yang-ming's "innate knowledge." The similarity lies in the fact that "investigation of things" means for both essentially the "rectification of affairs." In other words, the starting point of all self-cultivation as formulated in the *Great Learning* should be the application of one's own moral sense to all things, matters, actions, and events, so that they are made to conform to one's own sense of right and wrong, shame and deference, etc., and are thus "rectified."[17]

If there is a significant difference between the two, it is that Wang's "innate knowledge" stresses man's moral awareness whereas Ken's places more stress on the self as the active center of things. Simply stated, Ken's view was that the self and society were one continuum, with the self as the root or base and society as the branch or superstructure.

> If in one's conduct of life there is any shortcoming, one should look for the fault within himself. To reflect on oneself is the fundamental method for the rectification of things. Therefore, the desire to regulate the family, order the state, and pacify the world [as in the *Great Learning*] rests upon making the self secure *(an-shen)*. The *Book of Changes* says: "If the self is secure, then the empire and state can be preserved."[18] But if the self is not secure, the root is not established.[19]
>
> To make the self secure, one must love and respect the self, and one who does this cannot but love and respect others. If I can love and respect others, others will love and respect me. If a family can practice love and self-respect, then the family will be

regulated. If a state can practice love and self-respect, then the state will be regulated, and if all under Heaven can practice love and self-respect, then all under Heaven will be at peace. Therefore, if others do not love me, I should realize that it is not particularly because of others' inhumanity but because of my own, and if others do not respect me, it is not particularly that others are disrespectful but that I am.[20]

This, according to Huang Tsung-hsi, is what was called the "Huai-nan [method of the] investigation of things," so-called because Huai-nan is the classical name for Wang Ken's home region.[21] It is a recurrent theme in Ken's recorded conversations and writings[22] and rests on two cardinal Confucian principles: that reciprocity is the basis of all social relations, and that higher forms of social organization depend on the self-cultivation of individuals in the lower forms and ultimately on the individual himself.

On the other hand, there is implicit here a subtle shift of emphasis and of context. When the *Book of Changes* speaks of the preservation of the state being dependent on the security of the individual it is speaking to the "gentleman" who is a member of the ruling class, if not the ruler himself. Wang Ken, however, is actualizing the theoretical potential in this principle, and broadening its significance to include the common individual as well as the traditional Confucian "gentleman" or "noble man." His intent is clearly to alter the balance in the reciprocal equations of Confucian politics and social relations, that is, to make the welfare and security of the individual the *sine qua non* in every case. Thus, starting from the premise of the individual's moral responsibility, and proceeding by a disarmingly simple reductionism of a type which appealed to Confucians, he established the welfare of the individual—not just the common man en masse—as the primary basis of the social order.

We must be careful not to exaggerate this shift. It keeps the individual well within the bounds of Confucian reciprocity and social responsibility. But within that context it does allow new possibilities for a fuller development of the conception of the individual. One of these is revealed in Wang Ken's brief essay entitled "Clear Wisdom and Self-preservation" *(Ming-che pao-shen lun),*[23] from which the following passage is drawn: (The reader is asked to bear with Wang Ken's simple style and repetitious argumentation, which reflect both his own homespun character and his desire to communicate to the simplest people.)

Clear wisdom is innate knowledge. To clarify wisdom and preserve the self is innate knowledge and innate ability. It is what is called "To know without deliberating and to know how without learning how."[24] All men possess these faculties. The sage and I are the same. Those who know how to preserve the self will love the self like a treasure. If I can love the self, I cannot but love other men; if I can love other men, they will surely love me; and if they love me, my self will be preserved. . . . If I respect my self, I dare not but respect other men; if I respect other men, they will surely respect me; and if they respect me, my self is preserved. If I respect my self, I dare not be rude to other men; if I am not rude to others, they will not be rude to me; and if they are not rude to me, then my self is preserved. . . . This is humanity! This is the Way whereby all things become one body!

If by this means I regulate the family, then I can love the whole family; and if I love that family, they will love me; and if they love me, my self is preserved. If by this means I rule a state, I can love the whole state; if I love that state, the state will love me; and if the state loves me, my self is preserved. Only when my self is preserved can I preserve the state. If by this means I pacify all under Heaven, I can love all under Heaven; and if I can love all under Heaven, then all who have blood and breath cannot but respect their kin, and if they all respect their kin, then my self is preserved. Only if my self is preserved can I preserve all under Heaven. This is Humanity! This is [the Mean's] unceasing Sincerity! This is [Confucius'] Way which threads through all things!

The reason men cannot fulfill it is because of the partiality which arises from their physical endowment and material desires, and this is also what makes them differ from the sage. Only when they differ from the sage do they need education. What kind of education? Education in clear wisdom and self-preservation—that is all.

If I only know how to preserve my self and do not know to love other men, then I will surely seek only to satisfy my self, pursue my own selfish gain, and harm others, whereupon they will retaliate and my self can no longer be preserved. . . . If I only know how to love others and do not know how to love my self, then it will come to my body being cooked alive or the flesh being sliced off my own thighs, or to throwing away my life and killing my self, and then my self cannot be preserved. And if my self cannot be preserved, with what shall I preserve my prince and father?[25]

When Wang Ken speaks of "my body being cooked alive or the flesh being sliced off my own thighs, throwing my life away," etc., he alludes to extravagant gestures of self-sacrifice, and protests against a highly idealized view of the self which called for heroic self-denial and an almost religious dedication to one's ruler or parents, so contrary to man's natural instinct for self-preservation.[26] His quarrel is not at all with loyalty or filial piety; he himself was known for his exemplary filiality and devotion to his father.[27] Rather he reminds his Confucian brethren of the true meaning of filial piety: that one's duty to Heaven and one's parents, from whom one receives life, is to nourish, preserve, and reproduce that life in its most fundamental biological form.[28]

Here then we observe a difference between Wang Ken and Wang Yang-ming which has important implications for those who follow them. Wang Ken's conception of the self is strongly physical—the bodily self or person *(shen)*. Wang Yang-ming's emphasis in innate knowledge is on the mind *(hsin)*, especially the identity of mind with principle or nature. Nature for Wang Ken is the physical self

—not excluding, of course, the mind, which was understood as of one substance with the body and which most often has the sense of "heart." Hence the terms "School of the Mind" or "Subjective Idealism" frequently used to designate the Wang Yang-ming school can be applied to Wang Ken and his followers only with substantial qualification.[29] Liu Tsung-chou, later "revisionist" within the Yang-ming school, noted the crucial difference between Wang Ken and Yang-ming on this point, and asked whether it did not portend the abandonment of mind control and of the restraining influence of the mind over the bodily desires.[30]

SELF-MASTERY AND SELF-ENJOYMENT

In the passage above, Wang Ken does refer to material desires as giving rise to selfishness, a typically Neo-Confucian view, but he sees this tendency as essentially unnatural and remediable through nothing more than education in "clear wisdom and self-preservation," that is, by the exercise of innate knowing through and for the self. The easy optimism with which he regards such selfishness in man springs from his identification of human nature *(hsing)* with natural spontaneity *(tzu-jan)*.[31] Action in accordance with nature is in direct response to innate knowing, which, as we have seen, is "knowing without deliberation." It draws upon the unlimited creative power of nature. The only need is to see that one's actions are uninhibited by artificial restraints or devices *(wei)*.

Here Wang Ken uses the language of Taoism, but in a context that still suggests important Confucian overtones. Take, for instance, his equation of the Way (Tao) and self. These are fundamentally one. "To respect the self and not respect the Way is not [truly] to respect the self. To respect the Way and not respect the self is not [truly] to respect the Way. To respect both the Way and the self is the Highest Good."[32] But if one suspects a lapse here into a kind of quietism or passive acceptance of Nature, in Wang Ken the goal is seen as dynamic self-mastery, and approximates Ch'en Hsien-chang's aim of making the whole universe dependent on oneself, rather than oneself dependent on the universe.[33] The aim of all study should be precisely that "Heaven and earth and all things should be dependent on the self, rather than the self dependent on Heaven and earth and all things. Any other way than this is the 'way of the concubine' " [spoken of by Mencius].[34]

The "way of the concubine" is the way of dependence on others and loss of integrity. Instead of such a passive, feminine role in the world, the sage takes an active, masterful role. Being true to the Way means for him fulfilling the mission of the Confucian sage, who remakes his world to conform to the Way of moral and political order. "The sages put the world in order by means of this Way." And what is most worthy of respect in the self is man's capacity to "enlarge the Way" by putting it into effect in his life and in the world.[35] For this reason the Confucian sage does not hide himself, but comes out into the world and makes his principles plain. Does this mean, then, that the Way can be fulfilled only by ruling, by taking office in the government? Not at all. Confucius did it by cultivating his self and by teaching. The sage serves as "teacher to the ruler," as "teacher to all generations."[36] For him or for anyone else to compromise his self and his Way by taking office in questionable circumstances is again the "way of the concubine."[37]

If there is Taoist influence here, it is expressed in terms of the natural spontaneity and creative power of the Way manifesting itself through the individual, while the Confucian element is expressed in terms of that Way serving the needs of man. Wang Ken's activism draws heavily on both. He is alive with the spontaneous joy of the Tao and finds that joy in learning. Thus his paean to the "Enjoyment of Learning":

> The human heart naturally enjoys itself
> But one binds oneself by selfish desires.
> When a selfish desire makes its appearance,
> Innate knowing is still self-conscious,

And once there is consciousness of it, the selfish desire
    forthwith disappears,
So that the heart returns to its former joy.
Joy is the enjoyment of this learning:
Learning is to learn this joy.
Without this joy it is not true learning;
Without this learning it is not true joy.
Enjoy and then learn,
Learn and then enjoy.
To enjoy is to learn, to learn is to enjoy.
Ah! among the joys of this world what compares to learning!
What learning in the world compares to this joy![38]

Wang Ken is not the first Chinese thinker to find joy in life. This is a common theme among his predecessors, from Confucius and Chuang Tzu down through the Sung masters to Ch'en Hsien-chang and Wang Yang-ming.[39] But he is the first to express such rapturous joy in learning—that is, learning of a kind that is available to all and not just the secret delight of the scholar. Wang Ken's joy arises from the fact that learning is so simple and easy. It does not require any erudition or intellectual exertion; it is the operation of ordinary intelligence in everyday life, which should be effortless. Joy is spontaneous when one does not rely on one's own strength, but lets nature, innate knowing, the Way be manifested freely through the self.[40]

THE COMMON MAN AND THE GRAND UNITY

During his mature years as a teacher Wang Ken laid special emphasis on making the Way answer to the everyday needs of the people *(pai-hsing jih-yung).*[41] The substance of man's heavenly nature is manifested in people's ordinary desires and wants; there is nothing mysterious or transcendental about it. Just follow the way of "ignorant men and women" *(yü-fu yü-fu),*[42] who, without education, go about their daily tasks.[43] The sage, like the ordinary man, must be concerned with what nourishes people's bodies and hearts. "What is nearest at hand," he says, echoing Ch'en Hsien-chang, "is divine."[44]

In recent years Wang Ken has attracted special attention from left-wing writers who have not unnaturally stressed the "popular" aspects of Wang Ken's character and teaching, his great concern for the needs of the poor, and his general antipathy toward those in power who failed to provide for these needs.[45] There can be no doubt that these points have a real basis in Wang Ken's thought, and that his school has historical significance as a kind of "protest movement" against the "establishment" (whether that be defined as "feudal" or bureaucratic). It is a school that engenders widespread popular interest and support, not just another current of scholarly thought.

Nevertheless, noticeably lacking in Wang Ken's writing or in what has been recorded of him is any indication that he has a significant social or economic program, or any sign that he ever discussed the people's problems in other than the most immediate personal terms.[46] He shares Wang Yang-ming's vision of the primitive ideal of Grand Unity, which is thoroughly traditional, and bases it on the principle of "all things forming one body," which is so fundamental to Ming thought, but he is extremely vague as to how this is to be achieved except through the accumulation of individual actions performed in that spirit. One may argue that the paucity of sources renders any speculation as to his social and economic views inconclusive.[47] Still, such evidence as there is indicates that the main thrust of his teaching keeps to the predominant Neo-Confucian emphasis on dealing with social problems primarily as they relate to the self, and insofar as Wang Ken adds a new dimension to such discussion, it is to liberate the potentialities of the individual and satisfy his immediate needs, rather than to deal with the complex problems of a mature society.

THE NEW HEROISM

Wang Ken's egalitarian tendencies and his concern for the practical needs of the common man, like those of the early reformer Mo Tzu, are expressed in an idealistic vision of a society based on love, which evokes a kind of religious enthusiasm. His activist temperament and his conviction that man can master his own destiny also recall Mo Tzu's "antifatalism" and the dynamic quality which infused the latter's popular reformist movement. On the other hand, among the many differences which could be pointed to is the absence in Wang Ken of Mo Tzu's self-denying asceticism and puritanism. The *Chuang Tzu* had commented that this quality in Mo Tzu's teaching had called for a life of strenuous exertion and heroic self-sacrifice.[48] Wang Ken too calls for heroism, but without self-sacrifice.

In Wang Ken's "Ode to the Loach and Eel,"[49] which is a kind of parable—indeed, almost a Confucian *jataka* tale—the loach saves the life of a floundering eel, but seeks no credit or thanks for it.[50] His is a spontaneous act of generosity, prompted by the suffering of a fellow-being but not tainted by self-importance or vainglory and not vitiated by the kind of pity which demeans its object. The observer of this scene asks himself where such humaneness and detachment can be found among men, and recalls the type of "great man" or "hero" spoken of by Mencius:

> He who dwells in the wide house of the world, stands in the correct station of the world, and walks in the great path of the world; he who, when successful, practices virtue along with the people, and, when disappointed, practices it alone; he who is above the power of riches and honors to corrupt, of poverty and mean condition to make swerve from principle, and of power and force to make bend—he may be called a great man![51]

Applying this concept to his own time, Wang Ken sees the "great man" *(ta-chang-fu)* as one who ranges widely over the land, helping people in distress, but doing so in a spirit of spontaneous self-fulfillment. Wang Yang-ming, after picturing the ideal society and contrasting with it the corrupt state of his own, almost despaired of setting things right. But—

> Fortunately the principle of nature lies within the human mind and can never be obliterated; the light of innate knowing shines through all ages. When they hear what I have to say about pulling up the roots and stopping up the source [of evil], some men will surely be touched and pained, and will rise up in indignation, like a river that cannot be held in check. To whom shall I look if not to heroic leaders *(hao-chieh chih shih)* who will rise up without further delay?[52]

To his followers Wang Yang-ming himself was a heroic leader, but the quality in him that most impressed them was his combination of active commitment and personal detachment.[53] For Wang Ken the "great man" will manifest these qualities in the spontaneous joy with which he fulfills his human responsibilities, in his outgoing love for mankind and his ceaseless action in the world. He will be a Neo-Confucian Vimalakīrti, a layman who has achieved transcendent wisdom within the secular world, but also a kind of sage-savior whose activity within that world expresses the fullness of his humanity.[54] As Shimada has aptly put it, Wang Ken's "great man" is one who "acts according to the nature of his inner self, whose absolute subjectivity is at once the basis of his perfect freedom and unlimited joy, and of his outgoing desire to rescue others from their sufferings.[55]

If we think of Wang Ken as representing a new moral heroism inspired by Wang Yang-ming, it is, of course, only a new phase or revamped version of an earlier heroism. Wang Ken believed that each individual had his own role in the struggle to advance the Way, but he saw his vocation as almost a timeless one. From the start he had identified himself with Confucius, and at the end of his life he composed a song for Lo Hung-hsien (1504–1564) called "The Learning of Great Realization" *(Ta-ch'eng hsüeh-ko)* in which he refers to Confucius and Mencius as heroic figures who were able truly to exercise and exemplify innate knowing to the highest degree; then he asks, who now will stand forth to take personal responsibility for the Way?[56]

Contemporaries and followers of Wang Ken clearly saw him and Wang Yang-ming as carrying on the Confucian Way in much the same terms as Chu Hsi had spoken of the revival of that learning in the Sung. Without specifically referring to it as the "orthodox tradition" *(tao-t'ung),* contemporary eulogistic or commemorative accounts of Wang Ken place him in the familiar Neo-Confucian pantheon, invoking all of the elements of the prophetic or heroic mythology associated with the *tao-t'ung.* Thus Wang Ken is spoken of as manifesting heroic qualities in his efforts to carry on the teaching of Yao and Shun, the Duke of Chou and Confucius, the Great Learning and the Mean, referring to this sagely "learning" in the terms of Chu Hsi's prefaces to the latter (but without attribution) as the learning of "refinement and oneness," and "holding fast to the Mean," i.e., the original Neo-Confucian learning of the Mind-and-Heart as taught in the School of the Way *(tao-hsüeh).*[57] Another commemorative piece sees Wang as a latter-day exponent of the Message and Method of the Mind-and-Heart handed down from Yao, Shun, Yü, and Kings Wen and Wu of the Chou to the Ch'eng brothers in the Sung, identifying the sources of the orthodox discipline of the mind in the same way Chu Hsi had done.[58] In other accounts the prophetic elements in this conception of *tao-t'ung* are evoked to underscore the role of the inspired individual whose understanding of the Way and response to it show both deep insight and a strong sense of individual responsibility. After recounting how the Great Way declined, first with the passing of Confucius and Mencius, and then again after the demise of Chou Tun-i and the Ch'eng brothers, Wang Yang-ming is portrayed as the hero who appeared in the Southeast to reclaim the "learning that had been cut off" *(chüeh-hsüeh)* after it had become obscured by the pedantry of conventional scholars and the abusive exploitation of the classics for examination purposes. Then among those heroic spirits who responded to Yang-ming's teaching was Wang Ken, who:

> rose as a commoner to take responsibility for the Way *(i-tao tzu-jen)*, accept Yang-ming as his teacher, and without any thought of personal fame or gain, work untiringly so that later students could get for themselves *(tzu-te)* the true tradition of innate knowing. . . . Yang-ming's teaching spread throughout the land and the Master's [Wang Ken's] was also far-reaching in influence, carrying on the tradition bequeathed from Chou [Tun-i] and the Ch'engs. . . . In those days there were many scholars who took up the Way, but who else was as exemplary in his faith as the Master? There were many too who studied under the Teacher [Yang-ming], but who else got [the Way] for himself as the Master was able to "get it" from Yang-ming? There were many who excelled in the Way, but who else so quickened men's spirits that they came in such great numbers to hear his teaching?[59]

This same sense of personal responsibility and individual initiative is testified to by one of Wang Ken's most prominent followers, Keng Ting-hsiang. After paying tribute to Wang Yang-ming's teaching for giving a great stimulus to learning and for inspiring many men to take personal responsibility for the Way *(tzu-jen)*, he said of Wang Ken that, although there were many who had taken up the Way following Wang Yang-ming, there was none who had such influence as Wang Ken in spreading the teaching far and wide. This, says Keng, was because he based his method so squarely on the self or person *(shen)* that every man could confirm it in his own experience, and thus the model could be emulated throughout the land and transmitted to later generations.[60]

LEARNING GOTTEN FOR ONESELF

What distinguishes these stereotypical accounts of the heroic repossession of the Way from earlier versions is the heavier emphasis on innate knowing as the essence of the Learning of the Mind-and-Heart and as the philosophical basis for "getting it [the Way] oneself." Wang Ken's thought and scholarship have been characterized by Shimada Kenji as "Learning gotten for oneself" *(tzu-te chih hsüeh).*[61] The most obvious meaning of the term here is that Wang Ken was largely self-educated. Indeed, some accounts outdo themselves to embellish this characterization by describing him as a poor lad of humble peasant origins, who taught himself how to read and only at the rather late age of thirty *(sui)*, studied the Four Books for the first time, and experienced a kind of illumination.[62] Since this is juxtaposed to the rather precious and effete scholarship of the learned exegetes of the day, we may have here a bit of populist myth-making in the vein of the Platform Sutra's depiction of the Sixth Patriarch of Ch'an Buddhism as a poor uneducated lad who became self-enlightened and put to shame more learned monks. Be that as it may, the "myth" served well to dramatize a central feature in Wang Ken's thought—that the common man could "get it for himself" with only a little help from his friends.

This point is particularly emphasized in the biography of Wang Ken by his student Hsü Yüeh.[63] The opening lines invoke the conception of the Way and human nature presented in the first passage of the *Mean (Chung-yung)*. This doctrine, Hsü says in the familiar language of Chu Hsi's commentary, was passed down from the sage-kings Yao and Shun to Confucius and Mencius as a means of educating the people so that they could govern themselves. The key to this process was for the individual to activate in his daily life that consciousness by which he might "reach into his original mind *(tzu-te ch'i pen-hsin)*" *(I-chi,* 4:6b), get the Way for himself, and realize it in the world of action. In the Three Dynasties of old the sage-kings were able fully to exhaust the potential in this mind by practicing the doctrine of "self-correction [as a basis] for others' correcting of themselves *(cheng-chi erh wu cheng)*" *(I-chi,* 4:6b). But by the time of Confucius this had survived only as a way of teaching, not a way of government, and though some scholars got something of the Way they were not able to unlock the gate by which all men might open their minds-and-hearts to Heaven's Imperative. Later it was the rare exception like Chou Tun-i, who, according to Ch'eng Hao (using the words of Mencius), "could reach deeply within and get the Way for himself *(shen-tsao erh tzu-te chih)"* (*I-chi*, 4:7a). Still later it was left for Wang Yang-ming to break through the confusion of empty, obscurantist talk and again "reach the Way deeply within himself *(shen-tsao ssu-tao)"* (*I-chi*, 4:7a). For Wang Ken too the essential thing in his practice of filial piety and reverential respect was to experience the Way deeply within himself and "get it for himself" (*I-chi*, 4:7b). "Getting it oneself" was indeed the starting point for everyone's self-cultivation and, because it overcame the dichotomy between the internal and external, self and others, and thus served as the key to achieving love and harmony within the household and community *(I-chi*, 4:7a). Similarly, establishing the self *(li-shen)* was seen as the underlying basis of governance, and maintaining self-respect *(tzu-tsun)* as the prerequisite for all learning.[64]

This was no less true of Wang Ken's more limited pursuit of the Way through the study of the classics. As his "Life Chronology" *(Nien-p'u)* recorded it, "whenever he lectured on the classics he brought out what he had 'gotten for himself' *(tzu-te)* and did not stick to the standard commentaries."[65] He was never satisfied with his reading until he could relate it to his own experience and, in those terms, explain difficult points fully. The Six Classics and Four Books, he is recorded to have said in the *Record of his Conversations (Yü-lu)*, only confirm what in essence one must learn for oneself. It is on this basis that one can understand what Confucius meant when he spoke of comprehending past and present, old and new, in relation to one another *(wen-ku chih-hsin)*, i.e., through a process of empathetic identification of oneself with others.[66] According to Keng Ting-hsiang, from his early years Wang Ken did not engage much in classical studies, but rather "reached deeply within his own mind-and-heart and got it for himself *(tzu-te)*, saying the Classics and Books were just footnotes to the substance of one's own mind-and-heart."[67] And in another tribute to Wang

Ken his approach to the Classics was described as "When the Classics themselves are made plain, there is no need for commentaries. The Six Classics and Four Books confirm what is in my mind-and-heart. [Master Hsin-chai] upheld the classics but brought it back down to the mind."[68]

There is one further respect in which Wang Ken fulfilled to an extraordinary degree the implications of the concept of "getting it oneself." We have already noted earlier that in Mencius and even more in Chuang Tzu, "getting it oneself" had the connotation of getting deep joy and satisfaction out of learning the Way. Here the affective side of learning was stressed over the cognitive. In Wang Ken this is apparent in his paean to the joy of learning translated above. A contemporary testimonial to Wang describes this ode to joy and Wang's later ode to the Learning of Great Realization as being expressive of what Wang Ken "got for himself in the depths of his own bosom" *(ch'u hsiung-chung so tzu-te chih).*[69]

Kasuga Senan, a late Tokugawa Neo-Confucian who admired Wang Ken's heroic qualities and inspirational teachings, has a marginal comment on the "Joy of Learning" in his Japanese edition of Wang Ken's works, pointing out that "earlier scholars" (the usual form of reference to Sung Neo-Confucians) had taught that one should seek out what Confucius and his disciple Yen Hui had delighted in. Undoubtedly, Senan refers to such Sung masters as the Ch'eng brothers, Shao Yung, Li T'ung, and Chu Hsi, who had all cited Yen Tzu as a model of the joy and contentment which derives from learning the Way. To these names one could add, most notably, Wu Yü-pi and Ch'en Hsien-chang in the early Ming.

Though Senan makes this connection with "earlier scholars," it is possible that Wang Ken (ostensibly "uneducated") owes no direct debt to them, and that what we have here is a case of spontaneous response to his reading of the Four Books, conditioned perhaps by a cultural climate in the sixteenth century notable for its romantic exuberance. In any case, Keng Ting-hsiang, among others, observes that when Wang Ken first read the *Analects* he was particularly struck by Yen Tzu's dedication to the pursuit of humaneness and his delight in learning.[70] In the *Analects* (6:2) Confucius had said Yen Tzu loved learning more than anyone else, and Mencius had said: "Yen Tzu, in a disordered age, dwelt in a mean narrow lane, having his single cup of rice and his single gourd dish of water; other men could not have endured the distress but Yen Tzu did not let it affect his joy. Confucius praised him."[71] It is thus not implausible when we read in a preface to Wang Ken's works, that the latter was seen as a direct successor to Yen Tzu in this sense, namely that Wang Ken's reading of the Four Books evoked a deep response from within his own being and aroused the same love of learning.[72]

Yet we cannot, despite Wang's disclaimers concerning the uses of commentary, rule out the pervasive influence of Chu Hsi's interpretations so embedded in the available editions of the Four Books, through which Wang had already developed definite views on key issues before he met Wang Yang-ming. In other words, his self-education had brought him to a position quite similar to Yang-ming's before he had received formal instruction or become associated with any school. Thus what he had presumably "gotten for himself" coincided remarkably with the trend of thought articulated so effectively by Yang-ming, though it was expressed by Wang Ken in terms still reminiscent of Chu Hsi's "investigation of things"—i.e., what was called the "Huai-nan [method of the] investigation of things." We recall however that the "investigation of things" had also been a main concern of Yang-ming—a problem amounting almost to a kōan for him—until he found a resolution of it in terms of Mencius' "innate knowing" *(liang-chih)*. This leads to the strong suspicion that Chu Hsi's *problematik*, as formulated so lucidly in his commentaries on the Four Books and especially on the *Great Learning*, was still very much working in the minds of sixteenth-century thinkers and suggesting similar options to them, even in what they "got for themselves."

THE GREAT MAN AND LEARNING FOR ONE'S SELF

The point at which Wang Ken's "investigation of things" converges on Wang Yang-ming's is his interpretation of the extension of knowledge as "self-knowledge," which corresponds roughly to Yang-ming's "innate knowledge." For Wang Ken extending this self-knowledge is primarily understood as a likening of oneself to others —an extending of one's self-awareness to others in consideration of their feelings and needs. The "things" *(wu)* being investigated or rectified are conceived of mostly as "others," as in the expression Wang Ken was so fond of: "Rectify oneself and others *(wu)* will become rectified *(cheng chi erh wu cheng)*."[73] Again the idea is that self-knowledge is the basis of all learning, because within the self lies the root and center of all things human—the nature which one shares with others. Thus Keng Ting-hsiang sums up the essence of Wang Ken's teaching as "investigating things to know the root *(ko-wu chih-pen)* and awaken the moral nature *(wu hsing)*."[74] The terminology is Chu Hsi's but the dominant emphasis in this "investigation of things" is not intellectual but moral and spiritual.

Only if the self is honored can there be communion with the Way.[75] Implicit in this honoring of self, however, is the honoring of others. Hence "getting [the Way] oneself *(tzu-te)*" and "taking responsibility [for the Way and others *(tzu-jen)]*" are inseparably linked, and the hero or great man combines both in himself. Yet this basic sense of mutuality or responsiveness to others should not be taken as mere love for others or fellow-feeling. Wang Ken is aware of the dangers of sentimentality at this point, and presses relentlessly for self-examination and self-correction as the indispensable method for fulfilling one's responsibility to self and others. Men, he says, may think they are pursuing the way of love for all men and then find themselves looking for faults in others rather than in themselves. If so, they are not pursuing the Way of the Great Man or of Learning for one's self. "In the noble man, 'learning for one's self' means disciplining oneself unceasingly while ceasing to find fault with others."[76]

Wang Ken has been considered by some to be the very embodiment of Chang Tsai's *Western Inscription,* with its spirit of overflowing love for all men[77] and this is certainly true of his strong sense of "the humaneness which forms one body with Heaven-and-earth and all things." Yet, for all the empathy and affectivity celebrated in his teachings, Wang Ken never fell into the swamp of sentimentality which Chu Hsi had seen as a possible danger attending Chang Tsai's effusive idealism. It was this danger which, in part, prompted Chu Hsi to insist on the equal importance of substance and function, that is, a profound conception of human nature in its fullest dimensions as the guiding principle for action, matched by practical efforts fully to realize that human potential. On either side of this central conception lay the contrasting aberrations of quietism and utilitarianism. Wang Ken refers to the same point in a letter to a friend whose views are expressed in language that sounds somewhat Buddhistic but comes from Chu Hsi's commentary on the opening passage of the *Great Learning:*

> Your letter speaks of the empty spirit which is free and unobstructed. This refers to the substance of the Way. To be refined and subtle in [the conduct of] things and affairs refers to the practice (function) of the Way. Substance and practice have one source. To try to know substance without learning practice will lead inevitably to a delight in quiescence and distaste for action, which lapses into a dangerous simplism. To try to learn practice without understanding substance [i.e., man's nature] will lead inevitably to disintegration and fragmentation of the self [among utilitarian functions].[78]

This is why Wang Ken spoke of "working at one's humanity" *(mien-jen)* as directly implicated in both the Way of the Great Man and Learning for One's Self.

THE WAY OF THE TEACHER

Yet it is also the reason why the path of the hero may prove a lonely one. However much he seeks to understand others, they may not understand him or comprehend the vision that inspires him. Thus people laughed at Wang Ken for his deep sense of vocation and lofty ambition to become a teacher to all men of any age, any social status, or any level of education. Nevertheless this rejection, it is said, only caused him to redouble his efforts to take such a responsibility upon himself.[79] As an individual who sometimes had to stand apart from others, he identified himself with the sages and great men of the past. "Yao and Shun," he said, "had outdone themselves in taking upon themselves responsibility for the sufferings of the people. In this one could see their essential humaneness. . . . One can also see that the learning of Yao and Shun, King Wen and Confucius was the same. In their rank and functions they differed, some standing higher and others lower, but they were one in setting their hearts on the service of Heaven-and-earth and in devoting themselves to the livelihood of the people."[80]

Wang Ken was sustained in his mission by his faith in the Way, confidence in himself, and conviction that underlying all differences of opinion lay the essential unity of truth. Practically speaking he could adopt a pluralistic view with regard to individual differences of opinion because of his faith in the ultimate oneness of truth:

In learning there are no fundamental [ultimate] differences, but depending on what each man sees each differs from the other. Take, for example, a man who has a personal name and a literary name. There are some who know his personal name but not his literary name, so they will insist on the personal name as correct and the literary name as incorrect. There will be others who know the literary name but not the personal name; they will insist on the literary name as correct and the personal name as incorrect. Thus each thinks what he himself has seen is correct and what others have seen is incorrect. But once one knows the man, and knows both his personal name and literary name, one recognizes that what he himself has seen is correct and what others have seen is also correct. Then all at once the doubt is resolved![81]

It is the function of the Great Man to assist people in their attainment of self-awareness and mutual understanding through the extension of innate-knowing, which Wang Ken likens to Confucius' "knowing what you know and knowing what you don't know."[82] It is as plain as that. Innate knowing deals with everything in its proper place and time, without any preconception, calculation, or superimposition. "It is a way that is utterly simple and utterly easy. However, one must have wise teachers and good friends to help one in practicing it lest one make mistakes. Thus I say that the Way and rightness come to us through teachers and friends *(tao-i yu shih-yu yu chih)*." Without this help one may fail to hold up a high standard of conduct for himself and not be attentive to regular self-examination; one may sequester himself in the mountains, seeking a tranquility beyond human happiness and developing a distaste for action in the world of men.[83]

The Way of the Teacher is thus a duty, a responsibility to one's fellow man, undertaken in the spirit of the "humaneness which forms one body with Heaven-and-earth and all things."[84]

For Wang Ken it is also a public service which justifies his refusal to accept political office, on the ground that teaching is the most basic of social responsibilities. He says, in the words of Chou Tun-i: "When the Way of the Teacher is established, good men abound; and when good men abound, the court is correct; and when the court is correct, the world is well-ordered."[85]

When a friend and former student under Wang Yang-ming reconstructed the An-ting Academy, dedicated to his famous fellow townsman of T'ai-chou, Hu Yüan (993–1059), Wang Ken was invited to lecture there. Besides paying tribute to Hu Yüan as "a teacher for all ages," he noted how his friend had followed Yang-ming's teaching of innate knowing by accepting his personal responsibility to advance "this culture" in such a tangible way as to reconstruct this academy. After invoking again Chou Tun-i's encomium of the Way of the Teacher, he says:

The Way of Heaven and Earth knows no difference between past and present; from of old there have been dedicated men anxious to hear the Way. As Confucius said: "Hearing the Way in the morning, one can die content in the evening." What more needs to be said than this? For no age lacks men of dedication, but if they do not have intelligent teachers and good friends to rouse their energies or restrain and guide their enthusiasms, they will fail to attain the Mean . . .[86]

For teaching to have the desired effect it could not be mere indoctrination. The lecturing was understood to be of a kind that involved the student personally. It was talking things out with others, learning through discussion. "In learning there is no understanding without discussion."[87] "Teachers and friends help one to clarify one's own thinking by talking things out. Being true to oneself and becoming a genuine person depend on this."[88] Indeed "Among the tasks to be undertaken to bring order to the world none comes before 'learning by discussion' as a means of stimulating men's talents."[89] For the noble man this is a matter of personal obligation, as for the sages it had been a responsibility to the Way, but for Wang Ken it is not all that serious a business or that much of a struggle. As Confucius had said there was great "joy in having friends come from afar" to share their learning and aid in each other's cultivation. This is a joy, says Wang Ken, that shares in the joy of Heaven-and-earth and brings great peace and harmony to the world.[90]

Although Wang Ken's investigation of things had a different meaning from Chu Hsi's, in important respects his aims and methods as a teacher were in line with those of Chu Hsi. One suspects, in fact, that his basic orientation was much influenced by his early reading of the *Great Learning* and by Chu Hsi's interpretation of "clarifying" and "manifesting" the moral nature *(ming-ming te)* as a means of renewing the people.[91] As we have seen earlier, this was Chu's basic political doctrine: to engage in self-cultivation, as well as to aid in others' self-cultivation, so as to achieve good government through universal self-discipline and thus "rest in the highest good" for all. Wang Ken believes the same. He says "the way of the noble man is to govern men through men (or according to the man)," i.e., through individual and mutual self-correction in which the starting point is one's self.

"It is to reform the man and rest with that. But as long as there is anything unreformed, how can one rest? If my discussion and exploration [of a matter] is unclear, then I am to blame; if the approach is untimely, then I am also to blame for that. If I see a fault in someone and cannot forgive it, the fault is mine. If I forgive it but cannot help him to correct it, the fault is mine. To wish others *(wu)* to reform without first reforming myself is not the Way of the Great Man. Thus to be true to myself is not just to fulfill myself but it is to fulfill others. To fulfill myself is to be humane; to fulfill others is wisdom. It is the virtue of the moral nature. It is the Way which combines inner and outer (self and others)."[92]

The significance of this for Neo-Confucian individualism is two-fold. In the first place, it means that lecturing and discussion, talking things out and working things out with one's fellow men, is an indispensable part of one's own self-development. Hence Wang Ken's extraordinarily self-centered approach still remains within the bounds of Confucian personalism and holism. At the same time it means that Wang Ken's valuing of self is something that carries with it the extending of this value to others; it is not claimed for oneself alone. Hence there could be some basis here, in the concept of the moral nature and the natural principles inherent in it, for asserting the inherent rights of individuals on a universal ground and in a public philosophy.

The importance of this is underscored by the evangelistic zeal with which Wang Ken carried his message to the people, to the ordinary, uneducated persons *(yü-fu, yü-fu)* who are constantly in his mind and frequently referred to in his writings. Wang Ken's was an elitist doctrine only in the sense that it appealed to moral heroes; otherwise it was an egalitarian social gospel to be spread by those heroes through popular education.

Wang Ken was not a social revolutionary, but his efforts, following up the implications of Chu Hsi's and Wang Yang-ming's teachings, probably did more to reach a larger public audience than anyone since Hsü Heng in the Yüan had done. To be sure the Ming founder, Chu Yüan-chang, had tried to promote universal schooling, but the close link between schooling and official recruitment tended to vitiate this effort by orienting education too much toward entry into the governing elite, while Wang Ken explicitly disavowed and personally renounced any such intention, emphasizing instead general education for the ordinary man. In this respect, he may well stand as the preeminent example of a Neo-Confucian who, spurning political power, believed that the main action lay in bringing the benefits of education to every man. By comparison, though Li Chih later carried the implications of this teaching for the individual to more radical conclusions, and with greater intellectual brilliance, his failure to match Wang Ken's active social commitment could be seen as a handicap to the wider extension of that individualism.

THE T'AI-CHOU SCHOOL AS A POPULAR MOVEMENT

From Wang Ken's teachings and personal example his school (named T'ai-chou from his home town) drew remarkable vitality, and was able to exert a wide influence on sixteenth-century China. That it has been called the "left" or radical wing of the Wang Yang-ming school reflects both its popular character and the revolutionary nature of its ideas. Thus his school is the only one which can claim such a large number of commoners, including a woodcutter, a potter, a stonemason, an agricultural laborer, clerks, merchants, and so on.[93] A foremost student of social mobility in this period credits Wang Ken and his son with "carrying the intellectual torch to the masses. . . . Never before and never afterward, in traditional

China, were so many people willing to accept their fellow men for their intrinsic worth or did they approach more closely the true Confucian ideal that 'in education there should be no class distinctions.' "[94]

Such a development could not have come about, of course, simply through the force of Wang Ken's ideas alone, or even those of the Wang Yang-ming school as a whole. Other factors contributed. Economic affluence had prepared the ground by raising the general level of subsistence and enabling more people to participate in the cultural life of the nation. The lower Yangtze valley area, in which T'ai-chou was situated, had for several centuries been a major area for economic production and commercial activity.[95] In the Sung and Yüan (as reported by Marco Polo) it was already the center of a flourishing culture, which allowed for the pursuit of individual interests, the satisfaction of individual tastes, and the expression of individuality in art and literature.[96] Though confined originally to a relative minority in the bureaucratic gentry, the base for this cultural activity had widened to include segments of the middle classes. In the Sung and Ming, for instance, the spread of high culture is shown in the existence of literary societies which sponsored the writing and printing of poetry in the classical *shih* form by merchants and artisans.[97] The reverse process is seen in the adoption by the literati (not wholly legitimized) of forms which developed in the market places and amusement centers—especially the popular drama and fiction which grew out of popular story-telling.[98]

This combination of economic strength and cultural activity was particularly marked in the lower Yangtze valley during the sixteenth and seventeenth centuries. Yang-chou, the prefecture in which T'ai-chou was situated, was a leading center of the salt industry, and the great Yang-chou salt merchants were munificent patrons of both classical and popular culture.[99] Nanking, across the Yangtze, was described by the Jesuit Matteo Ricci as far outdoing Peking or any other capital city in size, wealth, and splendor.[100] Nearby Soochow could also lay a claim to being the true economic and cultural capital of China. At the end of the sixteenth century it had a population of well over two million, paid one tenth of the total taxes collected in the empire—an amount equivalent to that paid by the whole province of Szechuan.[101] Indeed, Ricci spoke of it as a city

> known for its wealth and splendor, for its numerous population and for about everything that makes a city grand. . . . When the Tartars were expelled and the kingdom taken over by the ancestor of the present reigning monarch, this city of Succu [Soochow] was stubbornly defended by its chiefs and up to today a tremendous tax is still levied on it as a rebellion city. . . . The whole province followed the capital city in opposition to the King, and even now it is heavily guarded, as the fear of rebellion from this quarter is greater than from anywhere else in the kingdom.[102]

This affluence and independence, however, were not associated with a single economic or social class. Increasing social fluidity was accompanied by strong political and cultural crosscurrents. The sixteenth and early seventeenth centuries saw the apogee of upward mobility from the merchant families into the bureaucracy. Among these families, as Wang Tao-k'un said, "trade and studies alternated with each other."[103] Some old gentry families could survive only by going into business, while others, more fortunate in maintaining their position in the official class, participated in the culture of the non-official classes as sponsors of theatrical performances and collectors on a large scale of works of popular fiction and drama.[104]

In such circumstances the T'ai-chou school reflected a growing confusion of class roles and concepts. For all its "radical" or "progressive" character, it cannot be identified with the rise of one class such as the merchant or the "commoner." No doubt the growth of commerce and the economic strength of the middle classes contributed to the self-confidence and optimism that is characteristic of T'ai-chou thought, but on the whole this school defies description as a "bourgeois" or "middle-class" phenomenon, much less a movement of the lower classes (and we remember, of course, that from the traditional or formal standpoint merchants were regarded not as in the middle but as at the lowest end of the social scale). Significant though the T'ai-chou school is as a movement led by a commoner to awaken the masses, in its membership as a whole the official class or bureaucratic gentry played a major role. Of twenty-five thinkers and teachers discussed by Huang Tsung-hsi in relation to the T'ai-chou school, seventeen had a clear connection with officialdom, and no less than eleven had won the advanced civil service *(chin-shih)* degree.[105] In several cases it was the protection afforded by persons in high places that enabled the more radical activists to escape or hold off official persecution.[106] Though some of these officials may well have originated from families of nonofficials, taken as a whole the official majority in the movement probably represents a typical cross-section of the educated elite at that time.

As Kuei Yu-kuang (1507–71) observed, "the status distinctions among scholars, peasants, and merchants have become blurred."[107] In such a situation the infusion of new blood and the raw energy of men like Wang Ken is probably less significant as an expression of rising class consciousness than as a bold attempt to grapple with a common human problem: the search for identity at a time when traditional roles have been obscured by rapid change and new energies can no longer be channeled along established lines.

In the T'ai-chou school itself personal relationships crossed traditional class lines, intellectual associations crossed political lines, and educational work crossed religious lines. While the penetration of the movement to the lower levels of society is significant, as contrasted to the type of individuality cultivated almost entirely within the upper class of the Sung period,[108] its broad extension to all levels of society and to many areas of life is of more fundamental importance than its class character. That is, of importance not only to society but the role of Confucianism in it. For with its primary engagement in education, and what might be called proselytizing and propaganda, in the T'ai-chou school Confucianism for the first time became heavily involved in the sphere traditionally occupied by the popular religions.

Huang Tsung-hsi, no admirer of the T'ai-chou school as a whole, says that, owing to the activities of Wang Ken and Wang Chi, the teachings of Wang Yang-ming "spread like the wind over all the land."[109] True to his self-declared mission as a teacher to the world, Ken traveled widely and stirred up discussion wherever he went. On his homemade touring car he had written that he would "travel to the mountains and forests in order to meet recluses and into the towns and villages in order to mix with ignorant commoners."[110] One of these uneducated commoners, the potter Han Chen, after his "conversion" and a period of study with Wang Ken's brother, took up the mission of spreading the new gospel among ordinary folk, and developed a large following among peasants, artisans, and merchants. After the fall harvest he would gather people together for lectures and discussion. When he had finished in one town he moved on to another. A regular feature of these gatherings was group singing: "With some chanting and others responding, their voices resounded like waves over the countryside." The atmosphere of a religious revival prevailed, and Han Chen personally exemplified a kind of religious dedication to the cause. When at these meetings the talk turned toward partisan politics and personalities, he would ask, "With life so short, how can you spend time gossiping?" And when the discussion became too pedantically involved with the niceties of classical scholarship, he would ask if those so engaged thought they were on a scholarly lecture platform.[111]

Hou Wai-lu's researches, drawing on the writings, records, and letters of Wang Ken's disciples, indicate that as the movement spread in all directions it developed a kind of organization on the local and regional levels, with a corps of able and dedicated leaders helping in the planning, scheduling, and conducting of public meetings. The whole community participated: scholars, officials, Buddhists and Taoists, monks and laymen. The leaders were often men of outstanding reputation or influence, but a more important qualification was the receipt of a personal transmission of the true teaching from Wang Ken or his authorized successors. Wang attached great importance to a man's demonstrating a total dedication to the fulfillment of the Sage's teaching. Along with his public lecturing he had a more private communication through which he confided his deeper understanding of the Way only to those who were ready for it. [112]

Thus an esoteric quality and religious aura surround the legitimate transmission in this school and for the same essential reason as in Ch'an Buddhism: instead of the truth being defined in a set of doctrines it was seen as a living Way and a highly personal experience, culminating in a personal encounter between master and disciple which recognized the personality, capabilities, and insights of the individual. Hence in the very laicizing of Confucianism by the Wang Yang-ming school we find a new mystique of the secular order, discovering the divine (as Wang Ken had put it) in what is most commonplace and what is most intimately human. [113]

Huang Tsung-hsi had said of Wang Ken that, while he did not match Wang Chi in dialectical subtlety, there was no one more successful than he in awakening people to the living truth within them and to the Way as something answering to the everyday needs of man. [114] Among the persons upon whom his earnest teaching made a deep impression was Yüan Huang (1533–1606), whose father had been an intimate acquaintance of both Wang Chi and Wang Ken and had traveled a great distance to attend the latter's funeral. [115] Yüan Huang's forebears had been professional Taoists for generations, and at one point he was overcome by a deep pessimism and fatalism when the prophecies of a Taoist wizard convinced him that he could never achieve the *chin-shih* degree and would die without a male heir. Subsequently Yüan was roused from this hopelessness and became persuaded that man, through moral action and the accumulation of meritorious deeds, could become the master of his own destiny. When eventually he succeeded in the examinations and also became the father of a boy, Yüan was confirmed in a mission to preach the value of moral effort as a means to personal success in life. He did this through his popular "morality books" *(shan-shu)* and "ledgers of merit and demerit" *(kung-kuo ko)*, which were widely printed and sold, not only in China but even in Japan.[116]

Yüan's immediate conversion from fatalism was achieved by a Buddhist monk, Yün-ku, but, having been a student of Wang Chi, Yüan expressed his philosophy of mastering one's own destiny through moral action in the language of the Wang Yang-ming school.[117] Also, while the morality books were of a type used earlier in popular Taoism, Professor Tadao Sakai has emphasized a significant difference in their employment by Yüan. In the earlier case reward and retribution were seen as meted out by the gods, and many superstitious practices were encouraged as means of winning divine favor. In Yüan Huang's case the system of moral reward and retribution was self-enforcing, a kind of ethical science. The good deeds prescribed pertained to the ordinary conduct of life, and the promised recompense answered to people's ordinary needs.[118] Though a somewhat mechanical system, with too quantitative an approach to the value of ethical acts, it nevertheless strengthened the confidence of the ordinary man that he could cope with the challenges and crises of life.

Another important proponent of the system of merits and demerits was the great Ch'an monk Chu-hung (1535–1615), who helped to revive the declining fortunes of Buddhism at this time by his synthesis of Pure Land and Ch'an Buddhism.[119] In this way he allied the most popular form of devotional Buddhism with the more austere Meditation school. Through Chu-hung's efforts the Ledgers of Merit and Demerit for the first time became widely used as a means of moral reform among Buddhists.[120] In this case the direct influence of the T'ai-chou school might be difficult to prove, but Chu-hung had many associations with this school and indirectly its emphasis on the moral potentialities of the individual must have encouraged the belief, which Chu-hung's ledgers presupposed, that man could affect not only his karmic destiny in the afterlife but also his status and welfare in this life.[121] This tended to give lay

Buddhism a more practical and humanized character, no doubt reflecting the new faith in man which Wang Yang-ming and his followers encouraged.

From a deeper ethical standpoint it would be hard to reconcile this system with the disinterested morality of either Wang Yang-ming and Wang Ken or the loftier forms of Buddhism, but from the historical standpoint it represents something more than just another case of religious syncretism.[122] It is a concrete expression of the trend toward secularization of traditional teachings and the definition of an ethical common denominator in the midst of social and cultural change. To this extent it might have helped to widen the base for the growth of individualism.

The vitality of the T'ai-chou school is shown in the wide range of thinkers and personalities it produced.[123] Though it has been referred to as the "left wing" and as the "Wild Ch'an" movement within the Wang Yang-ming school, this is only because its more radical and extreme tendencies have readily attracted attention. The less spectacular side of the school shows a greater diversity and complexity of thought. Of those who were activists not all were radicals, and of those who turned toward Ch'an some were quite conservative in politics and morals.[124] A full study of individualistic philosophies in the late Ming would require far more extensive treatment of the available alternatives, not only within the Wang Yang-ming school as a whole, but even within the T'ai-chou school itself.

Nevertheless, among these diverse individualisms some tended in an esoteric or mystical direction, and offered little hope of establishing a more positive and widely extended individualism in Chinese society as a whole. Their adherents may have asserted their own independence or autonomy but not necessarily that of others. The radical wing at least was identified with a kind of social reformism which might conceivably have led to fundamental changes in the situation of the Chinese individual generally. Some recent writers in China and Japan have also considered it a real hope in sixteenth-century China for an indigenously generated force toward modernization.[125] I cannot enter into all aspects of this larger problem, but the question of individualism, since it arises naturally in Ming thought, is one way of approaching the larger issue from within the Chinese tradition.

HO HSIN-YIN: THE HERO AND THE NATURAL MAN

The sixteenth-century historian Wang Shih-chen (1526–90) said that the popular lecturers of the Wang Yang-ming school:

> flourished and spread throughout the land in the Chia-ching [1522–1567] and Lung-ch'ing [1567–1572] periods. What led finally to their great excesses was that they used their lecturing to serve the cult of heroism, and used the cult of heroism to indulge their unrestrained selfishness. Their arts had basically nothing to them that might rouse men to action, and lacking any real conviction or concern they joined in beating the drums, blowing their horns, and flapping their wings, drawing crowds together and flashing here and there, until they came near to causing a disaster like the Yellow Turban and Five Pecks of Grain [movements at the end of the second century A.D.]. Now the change from Wang Yang-ming to T'ai-chou [Wang Ken] had not yet done too great damage, but with the change from T'ai-chou to Yen Chün[126] everything rotted apart and it could not be put together again.[127]

Wang Shih-chen had great contempt for Yen Chün as an illiterate with little real knowledge of the classics, who was so fond of his own ideas that he did not hesitate to misconstrue the classical texts in support of them. "He believed," Wang says, "that man's appetite for wealth and sex all sprang from his true nature" and should not be repressed.[128] Wang then goes on to make many charges of licentiousness and sedition against Yen and other members of his following, especially Ho Hsin-yin (1517–1579).[129] Huang Tsung-hsi, writing a couple of generations later in his preface to the T'ai-chou school in the *Ming-ju hsüeh-an*, says that most of the wild stories about Yen and Ho derive from Wang Shih-chen's partisan and one-sided accounts which are not to be trusted. Nevertheless, Huang himself shared the general feeling against the leaders of this movement as having brought the Wang Yang-ming school to disgrace and undermined public morality. His discussion of them is confined to the preface; he gives neither formal biographies of them nor excerpts from their writings. "After T'ai-chou his followers wanted to seize the dragon's tail with their bare hands [i.e., seize hold of life and truth without any help from past teachings]. As transmitted to Yen Chün and Ho Hsin-yin, it reached the point where they could no longer be restrained by traditional morality."[130]

According to Huang, Yen Chün had received the teaching of Wang Ken from Hsü Yüeh, who followed Ken's "Way of Self-respect."

> Yen believed that man's mind was an unfathomable store of mysterious creativity and that his nature was like a transparent pearl, originally without flaw or stain. What need was there for "caution" and "apprehension" whenever one saw or heard something? In ordinary times one should simply follow wherever one's nature leads, trusting its spontaneity—this is what one calls the Way. Only if one should on occasion go to excess is it necessary to exercise "caution" or "self-watchfulness" or "apprehension" in order to correct such excess. All of the knowledge, principles, and norms of earlier Confucians suffice only to obstruct the Way.[131]

Huang also says that Yen followed the way of the *yu-hsia*, imperfectly translated as "knight-errant,"[132] a free spirit and daredevil who would risk anything to help a friend in distress or a sufferer from injustice. He and Ho Hsin-yin were both known for their extraordinary heroism in devotion to their friends. When Chao Chen-chi (1508–1576), a fellow student under Hsü Yüeh who became a grand secretary, was sent in official disgrace to a remote post for his outspokenness at court, Yen insisted on accompanying him, an act of loyalty which Chao is said to have appreciated deeply during his hour of trial. Also, when his teacher Hsü Yüeh died in battle in Yünnan (ironically as a result of his own imprudence) Yen went to search for his remains and bring them back for burial.[133] Keng Ting-hsiang, a younger friend of Ho Hsin-yin, said of Yen Chün that his "teaching was Confucian but his actions were those of a 'hero' or 'knight-errant' *(hsia)*."[134]

The description might well apply to Ho Hsin-yin[135] himself, whose abilities, Huang says, far exceeded those of Yen. In 1546 he won first place in the Kiangsi provincial examinations and was considered a person of great promise, but after learning the teaching of Wang Ken from Yen Chün, he gave up all thought of an official career[136] and set out on an independent course, paying little respect to the views and counsels of the established scholars in his home town. Taking as his basis the teaching of the *Great Learning* that the ordering of the state depended on the regulation of the family, he conceived a new type of organization for his own clan which would have made it a self-sufficient, autonomous community. Through this organization, centering around a so-called Collective Harmony Hall *(Chü-ho t'ang)*, he attempted to regulate clan life in the strictest detail. There were to be two leadership groups, one supervising the educational and cultural affairs of the clan, and the other its economic and social welfare. All clan affairs, including the rituals of capping, marriage, funerals, care of the aged, the collection of taxes, and the performance of labor service, were to be handled on a cooperative and egalitarian basis. Schooling was to be provided for the sons of all in the class, irrespective of wealth or status. They would live together at school, carrying on a cooperative life and submitting to the same discipline. This meant, in effect, pioneering a kind of public education on the local level.[137]

Ho ran into difficulty trying to maintain the autonomy of his utopian community, however. When special taxes were imposed by local officials, he remonstrated against them and so antagonized the authorities that he was arrested and imprisoned. Only through the intervention of powerful friends did he escape banishment.[138] Thereafter he taught and lectured widely throughout the country and attracted a great following. He had many friends in officialdom, and enjoyed their hospitality for long periods. During a stay in Peking he became involved in a conspiracy to unseat the powerful and corrupt grand secretary Yen Sung, which succeeded in its object but resulted in Ho's becoming a hated and hunted man after his part in the plot became known. Yen Sung's party sought vengeance.[139] As a consequence Ho led a kind of nomadic existence for the rest of his life, taking refuge with his official friends and patrons wherever they happened to be, and having no fixed abode. His difficulties were increased by his having once antagonized Chang Chü-cheng, who subsequently became all-powerful at court. During a brief personal encounter he had bluntly challenged Chang's understanding of the real import of the *Great Learning*.[140] Moreover, as a leading exponent of public lecturing and a champion of the freedom of teaching and discussion, Ho was closely identified with the independent academies where such discussion was carried on, and on this account too he was at odds with Chang, who later ordered the suppression of the academies. Ho's fugitive life came to an end at the age of sixty-two when he was arrested and subsequently died at the hands of jailers in Wu-ch'ang who probably thought his elimination would ingratiate them with Chang Chü-cheng.[141]

FROM DESIRELESSNESS TO DESIREFULNESS

Ho's life was an exemplification of his philosophy. Following Yen Chün, he believed that self-expression was more important than self-restraint. Above all he valued a man's vital spirit or force *(i-ch'i)*. Every man is endowed with this spirit—ideas and feelings and a natural passion to manifest these in his life. This is his share of the living Way, and it is precisely through his active self-assertion that the creative power of the Way asserts itself. All things in Heaven and earth, all beings from the sage to the least of men thus have the Way working in and through them.[142] Ho went so far as to reinterpret a famous passage in the *Analects*, wherein, according to the traditional reading, Confucius had seemed to be a model of self-effacing moderation: "There were four things from which the Master was entirely free. He had no foregone conclusions, no arbitrary predeterminations, no obstinacy, and no egoism." (*Analects* 9:4)

According to Ho's interpretation the passage really meant that Confucius would have nothing to do with nonegoism, noninsistence, nonobstinacy, and having-no-ideas-of-one's-own. These attitudes represented the passivity of Lao Tzu, and Confucius rejected such Taoistic quietism as incompatible with his own activism in behalf of mankind. "He did away with these [attitudes] lest they harm the Way."[143]

From this we can see how Wang Yang-ming's conception of man's nature as an active principle within the mind and Wang Ken's emphasis on the physical as well as moral self have developed to the point where Ho is ready to liberate man from traditional forms of self-repression. In Wang Yang-ming innate knowledge had been opposed not only to external knowledge and influence but also to selfish desires. Ho Hsin-yin still recognizes selfishness as a problem, but he refuses to identify it with man's desires. Indeed, he strongly affirms the validity of the so-called material desires. Sense appetites have their basis in the inborn nature of man, and are to be nurtured and satisfied rather than denied and suppressed.[144] Further, he is prepared to dispute the authority of Chou Tun-i, the great patriarch of Neo-Confucian philosophy, on the validity of Chou's "desirelessness" (*wu-yü*), which he implies is a Taoistic intrusion into Confucian thought.[145] It is not possible for the mind-and-heart of man to be without desires, for even the wish to be without desires is a desire. On the other hand, if one recognizes that in any case it becomes a question of choosing among desires rather than attempting to eradicate them, it will suffice for the preservation of man's mind-and-heart if only the desires are reduced. He cites Mencius:

I like fish and I also like bear paws. If I cannot have the two together, I will let the fish go and take the bear paws. Life too I like and also rightness, but if I cannot have the two together, I will let life go and choose rightness. . . . There are cases when men by a certain course might preserve life and yet do not take that course, or when by certain things they might avoid danger and yet will not do them. Therefore men have that which they like more than life and that which they dislike more than death. (6A:10)

"To love fish and love bear-paws," says Ho, "are desires. To do without the fish and take the bear-paws is to reduce one's desires. To love life and love rightness are desires. To give up life and choose rightness is to restrict one's desires. But can one reduce and reduce to the point of nothingness and still preserve one's mind-and-heart?"[146] Thus, man's emotional desires and sense appetites, like his moral or spiritual aspirations, are rooted in his inborn nature. Without them he would dwindle to nothing. As undeniable expressions of the natural self, they cannot be left unnurtured, and even when subordinated to man's higher instincts, the sacrifice must serve the whole self, not some diminished self. Self-denial through a reduction of desires can be justified only as a means of self-fulfillment through identification with others.

Neo-Confucianism in the Sung had rejected the skeptical Buddhist view of the essential self as beyond all predication, and insisted that an understanding of one's rational, moral nature was precisely the means whereby one could achieve unity with Heaven and earth and all things. This was the first step in reaffirming the Confucian view of the natural man as essentially moral man. Chu Hsi, however, had distinguished between two components of the self: the essential moral nature and the physical, psychic, and emotional disposition of each individual which might obscure, distort, or unbalance the rational, moral nature unless kept under strict control. This dichotomy and tension Wang Yang-ming had tried to overcome by identifying the moral nature not as an abstract ideal but as a living principle within the actual self. And the T'ai-chou school, especially as represented by Wang Ken and Ho Hsin-yin, completed the process by broadening the allowance made in the conception of the natural man for the expression—rather than repression—of the drives and appetites that constitute the most dynamic element in his actual nature.

THE INDIVIDUAL AND THE COMMUNITY

To live in this world meant for Ho Hsin-yin what it had for Confucius: to be a man among men. And if to be a man, in his times, called for heroism, it was because only a hero could rectify the injustices and master the disorder which prevented other men from achieving self-fulfillment. One of Ho's arguments for the validity of human desires came from Mencius' urging the rulers of his time to take the people's desires as their own—that is, to provide for the satisfaction of their material wants.[147] From this we can see that he viewed the problem of self-satisfaction and self-fulfillment in a clear relation to that of others. Whatever extremity of means he might resort to as "hero" and master of his own destiny, he was not asserting his radical independence of society. Indeed, as in the case of Wang Yang-ming and Wang Ken, self for him meant primarily the common self of mankind, and only secondarily the individual as distinct from others.[148] Perhaps what most distinguishes his thought from that of other thinkers of the T'ai-chou school is his passionate concern for the common welfare, as well as his attempt to redefine man's relation to other men.

The virtues of humanity and rightness had most often been defined within Confucianism in terms of some such definite relationship to others—in the family, the community, or the state. Ho argued for the broadest possible conception of these virtues. "Humanity regards all as one's own kind. . . . The kinship between father and son is not the only kinship; kinship extends to all worthy of one's kindness—to all creatures that have blood and breath." Similarly, rightness regards all as worthy of respect. It is not respect just for the ruler, but for all who have blood and breath. Thus, he argued, one should enlarge one's dwelling to include the whole world.

At first sight this might appear to be only a reiteration and rephrasing of the common Neo-Confucian theme: that "the humane man forms one body with Heaven and earth and all things." But for Ho this familiar phrase is no mere pious platitude or vague humanitarian sentiment. Nor can it be the basis of a purely interior illumination in which he attains a sense of oneness with the universe as did many other Ming thinkers. His experience of life makes him more conscious than most men of the individual's inescapable dependence on others. At the same time his vision of a larger world is strongly conditioned by his awareness of the individual's need to find security in some community. It is impossible to maintain oneself otherwise. Most people achieve some measure of security through family or clan, class or profession. But what about the man who is neither peasant, merchant, artisan, nor official—especially the scholar who is unwilling to find his security in serving the state?[149] A wanderer himself much of his life, Ho knew what it meant to "dwell in a wider world," but also what it could mean to stand exposed to the world, facing alone the power of the state.

Ho first attempted to find that security in his autonomous clan community—a rather typical Chinese utopia of a kind which appeals to both Confucian decentralist thinking and the yearning for a totally ordered life.[150] It failed, and though we know little of its internal weaknesses, in any case the community could not withstand pressure from the local and central government. The cooperative, collective, and egalitarian features of this scheme have appealed to some modern writers,[151] but it is likely that Ho himself came to recognize its limitations in his situation. He seems to have made no further efforts to establish such communities elsewhere, and his main efforts at social and political reform were increasingly directed toward the scholarly community and the schools.

It is significant, however, that Ho thought of the wider commu-

nity or collectivity not so much in terms of the highest level of
generality or abstraction as in terms of an enlarged family system.
He recognized the need for transcending the pettiness of traditional
family loyalties, but wished to preserve and extend the basic values
of the kinship system rather than dissolve them. His favorite
expression for the group or collectivity was the "family" or
"household" *(chia)*, while the individual members or components
of any higher-level organization were referred to as "selves" *(shen)*.[152]
In this he not only attempted creatively to adapt the kind of Confucian thinking found in the *Great Learning* to the needs of sixteenth-century Chinese society; he also foreshadowed one of the
most typical Chinese responses to the challenge of modernization:
the drive to adapt the kinship system itself to serve new functions,
instead of yielding to the trend toward ever more rational and
impersonal systems of organization.[153]

Ho believed that the narrow limits of the self and family could
best be overcome through the relationship among friends, understood, as one might expect in the Ming context, as friendship
among scholars with a common social commitment. Within this
sphere the ultimate relation was between teacher and student, friends
in the pursuit of truth and in the education and leading of men. To
stress such a deep bond was only natural for the Confucian; it
corresponded to the actual facts of his life as an intellectual whose
closest personal relations were with other scholars. But Ho goes
further than this. In a society where the scholar is so dependent on
the state, he sees a need for the scholars to organize in some kind
of association that gives them collective strength, and not just
personal intimacy.[154] They must be able to complement and, if
necessary, check the ruling power; they must support one another
as scholars, thinkers, and teachers so that the work of Confucius
can go on:

The fulfillment of the Way starts with the relationship of ruler
and minister on the highest level and ends with the relationship
of friend and friend on the lowest. If there is intercourse between

highest and lowest, then the way of parent and child, older and younger brother, husband and wife can be unified between them and achieve fulfillment. Though these latter relations are essential to fulfillment of the Way, they cannot unify all under Heaven. Only through the [cooperation of] ruler and minister can the heroes of the land be gathered together in order to establish humanity as the basis of instruction and have all under Heaven naturally return to it.[155]

For this reason Ho makes a distinction between two types of sages, corresponding to a differentiation in function within society. Earlier the Confucian model had been the sage-king, combining intellectual and political functions, and the model Confucian had accordingly been both scholar and official. In the Sung some differentiation in such functions was implied in the Learning of the Emperors *(ti-hsüeh),* which argued the need for rulers to be advised by wise scholars with a knowledge of both the classics and history. Ho distinguishes between Kings Yao and Shun as model rulers and Confucius as model teacher. They serve distinct but complementary functions. On occasion Ho even suggests that the latter may be more fundamental, since without the work of Confucius the true way of ruler and minister would have been lost.[156] Moreover, in his own day Ho felt it urgent that men of ability commit themselves to teaching and spreading the great Way, foregoing government service, as Confucius had, because education contributed more importantly to government than did official service in the bureaucracy.[157] Beyond this, he argued also for the necessity of scholarly associations and independent schools so that the Way could be discussed and spread even when the ruling power opposed it. By far his longest surviving work is an essay in defense of free lecturing and discussion in the schools.[158]

Li Chih, an admirer of Ho, said that of the five Confucian relations Ho discarded four and kept only the relation between friend and friend.[159] The life Ho led, apart from his family and in opposition to the ruling power, no doubt strengthened this impression among his contemporaries. Others, less sympathetic than Li, accused Ho of heterodoxy, of resorting to magic (the plot against Yen Sung involved a Taoist adept who tricked the emperor), of utilitarianism (using questionable means to benefit his friends), and even of lapsing into Ch'anism.[160] This is not the place to evaluate such charges, which may well have some basis in his actual conduct and his belief in uninhibited self-assertion.[161] But Ho protested his own orthodoxy and compared the charges of heterodoxy against himself to the persecution of Chu Hsi in the Sung.[162] Like other T'ai-chou members he had frequent associations with Buddhists and Taoists, and was ready to enlist anyone in his cause, but with him this reflected no tendency to equate the "Three Teachings as One."[163] For him Confucius' teaching, which affirmed self and human relations, was clearly superior to that of Lao Tzu or the Buddha, who set them aside. Likewise he rejected all forms of quietism. He had no use for those who forsook the world and he criticized so-called scholars-in-retirement who took no active part in the common struggle.[164]

So far as Ho's thought is concerned, there is ample evidence that it kept within the essential Confucian tradition. In any case, as an example of individualistic thought in the Ming, it represents a significant attempt to redefine the place of the individual in Confucian terms. Having recognized the new potentialities of the individual, as well as the new demands of society upon him, Ho was forced to question whether either the family system or bureaucratic officialdom was an adequate instrument for the reform of society, the defense of the individual, or the perpetuation of Confucian values. The family was too weak and limited, as the inability of his own clan organization to contend with centralized power had demonstrated. Officialdom had lost its soul in the scramble for power. Unless some independent platform could be established, where the "brave and talented men of the land" might carry on free discussion, Confucian protests could not be heard and there would be no limit to the despotism of a totalitarian power structure—totalitarian in the sense, not that everything was controlled in detail from the top, but that in the absence of any alternative center of power or protection the insecurity of ordinary men would make them susceptible to even the imagined wishes of those in power, as Ho's jailers thought they might win favor with Chang Chü-cheng.

Ho Hsin-yin failed, perhaps as much from his own audacity as from the inherent weakness of his personal position, but his proposed solution was not totally lacking in realism. He sensed that in Ming society there was only one hope for establishing a vital Confucianism in the existing order: in the indispensable function of education, which even the bureaucracy and China's dynastic rulers had need of. And he pursued this with all of the courage and conviction of Wang Yang-ming's hero or Wang Ken's Great Man. In this respect he represents the climax of the Confucian activism and humanitarianism generated within the Wang Yang-ming school, which peaked at a crucial juncture in the development of its individualism, about to diverge now along several different, and sometimes opposing lines.

9. *Li Chih: Arch-Individualist*

The tide of individualistic thought in the late Ming reached its height with Li Chih (1527–1602),[1] who has been both condemned and acclaimed as the greatest heretic and iconoclast in China's history. He is in any case one of the most brilliant and complex figures in Chinese thought and literature.

Li was born and raised in the Chin-chiang district of the port city of Ch'üan-chou, Fukien Province. In earlier times Ch'üan-chou had been a center of foreign trade, with a somewhat cosmopolitan character. Li's forebears had been active in this trade, one of them traveling to Iran.[2] They were members of a Chinese Muslim community, and Li's wife too may have been a Muslim.[3] Some writers have seen special significance in Li's associations with a minority religious community and a non-Chinese value system, as well as in the commercial background of his family.[4] But in his voluminous writings Li makes no mention of Islam.[5] Moreover, his family, by virtue of their talents as interpreters and knowledge of foreign trade, had been drawn into official life—a not unnatural course for merchants in China, who considered themselves truly successful only when they had gained acceptance into the ranks of scholar-officials. This must have meant a closer identification with Confucian values, and no doubt a weakening in their adherence to Islam.[6]

The commercial atmosphere of Ch'üan-chou is vividly recalled in Li's writing by his frequent use of the language of the market place and by his aggressive, hard-driving mentality. But Ch'üan-chou's foreign trade had been largely cut off by the Ming seclusion policy; what survived was mostly illicit or severely regulated—trade of a kind that had the nefarious connotations of smuggling, the black market, official collusion, and squeeze. Its spirit could hardly have been that of the self-confident bourgeois, the expansive builder of a new world, but must rather have reflected a deep sense of frustration, ambivalence, and, probably, guilt.[7] This, it seems, is the characteristic spirit of Li Chih, whether it mirrors his Ch'üan-chou background, his mixed ancestral heritage, or the larger contradictions of life and thought in Ming China which he was to experience.

Li was given a classical Confucian training but, as he said later, he was a skeptic from his youth, repelled by anything or anyone—Confucian, Buddhist, or Taoist—identified with an organized creed.[8] He felt a great revulsion, too, against the kind of mechanical learning required for the examinations to enter an official career, and though he managed to overcome his scruples and pass the provincial examinations in 1552, he did not go on to the higher examinations at the capital.[9] Financial difficulties may have combined with personal aversion in this decision, but, whatever the reason, his failure to achieve the *chin-shih* degree tended to limit his opportunities for official advancement. Such an attitude on Li's part hardly demonstrates a completely uncompromising independence, but it does suggest a recognizable pattern of alienation among members of the educated class in Ming and Ch'ing China, typified by the sensitive, highly intelligent child of a well-to-do family on the decline, who feels a fundamental conflict between his own individuality or intellectual integrity and what he must do in order to succeed in the world and discharge his family responsibilities.[10] Something of the same conflict, however, was widely felt in the sixteenth century by scholars of varying background and temperament, and Li's own subsequent development suggests important differences, as we shall see, from Wang Yang-ming, Wang Ken, and Ho Hsin-yin.

After his qualifying examination Li spent almost thirty years in the status of an official, going from one routine assignment to another, interrupted by periods of mourning for his father and grandfather and by periods in which he waited for reassignment. Though a somewhat frustrating life, marked by frequent conflict with his superiors, it was not without considerable leisure in which he could pursue his own studies. Assignments in Peking and Nanking gave him opportunities to meet with other scholars, in and out of office. He did an enormous amount of reading and his intellectual proclivities were greatly strengthened, but a profound spiritual unrest was at work within him. As he put it, he yearned to "hear the Way,"[11] borrowing the phrase from Confucius: "Hearing the Way in the morning, one could die content in the evening" *(Analects* 4:8). In other words, he too was searching for something worth living and dying for.

Thus through five years at the Board of Rites in Peking, Li's mind was little occupied with official duties but rather "sunk deep in the Way."[12] In the course of these years, he formed close associations with others who shared his serious interests, including members of the Wang Yang-ming school who introduced him to the teachings of Wang Yang-ming, Wang Chi, and the T'ai-chou school. "They told me the teachings of Master Lung-hsi (Wang Chi) and showed me the writings of Master Yang-ming. Thus I learned that the True Man who has attained the Way is deathless, and that he is one with the True Buddha and the True [Taoist] Immortal. Though an obstinate person, I could not but believe."[13]

One of these friends, Hsü Yung-chien,[14] participated in the public lecture meetings of Chao Chen-chi,[15] a leader of the T'ai-chou school, but Li had a strong antipathy to such meetings and would not go. Hsü therefore gave him a copy of the Diamond Sutra, one of the key texts of the Prajñāpāramitā philosophy of Buddhism. He said, "This is the learning that leads to deathlessness. Will you refuse to consider that too?" This, it is said, proved a turning point in Li's thinking.[16]

What kind of turning point? Li was nearly forty by this time. His personality and many of his attitudes must already have been well formed, and these experiences perhaps only confirmed the direction in which he was already headed. It is noteworthy, for instance, that they are intellectual experiences—spiritually significant but not described in deeply emotional or mystical terms, as was the case with Wang Yang-ming and Wang Ken. The feeling of oneness attained by Li is of the oneness of Truth, the identity of the Three Teachings. It shows the influence of Wang Chi in particular, and an attitude in which the moral demands of the left wing yield to a more transcendental faith. Does this then leave Li Chih without the sense of mission that emerged from Yang-ming's and Wang Ken's experiences? We shall see.

Li's next long assignment was in Nanking, where he had close associations with other T'ai-chou members, notably the Keng brothers, Ting-hsiang[17] and Ting-li,[18] and Chiao Hung.[19] The latter became perhaps Li's closest friend, soul mate, and sworn brother. He was a distinguished scholar and historian, with a fine library and, like Li, a sharp, critical mind combined with a broad tolerance for the Three Teachings. In such company Li's thinking and studies were greatly stimulated, and when in 1578 he was reassigned to serve as a prefect in remote Yunnan, it was a great hardship for him to leave Nanking.

But if this brought on a personal crisis for him, such as Wang Yang-ming had experienced in the border region of Kweichou, for Li its resolution was of a different sort. Reduced to his essential self, Wang had discovered his moral identity with the uneducated or uncivilized men around him. His sympathies were enlarged, his effectiveness in dealing with men enhanced, and his mission of social and political action confirmed. For Li Chih, on the other hand, it brought a further withdrawal from the world, not into inactivity, but into an independent life of study and contemplation. At the end of his three-year term he resigned from official service.[20]

Without returning home, Li went to stay with the Keng brothers at Huang-an, in northeast Hu-kuang Province (modern Hupei). He preferred life as a house guest and family tutor to the social responsibilities and involvements that awaited him in Ch'üan-chou.[21] But a strain eventually developed in his intellectual and personal relations with Keng Ting-hsiang, partly owing to Li's belief that Keng, an influential official, had not done all he could to save Ho Hsin-yin. Li moved out and took up residence in the Buddhist temple of Chih-fo yüan, at a lakeside retreat in the same county. He sent his wife and children home to Fukien, and, when a few years later he took the Buddhist tonsure, it signified as much as anything else his determination to make a complete break with family cares and social obligations.[22] Though not without some sympathy for his wife, he regretted that she was not more intellectually compatible, and in any case he wished to pursue his own interests unencumbered. Indeed, the expense he went to earlier in providing a suitable burial ground for his parents and grandparents is in striking contrast with his rather indifferent treatment of his immediate family.[23]

Li gave many different reasons for his decision to shave off his hair and become a monk, some of them perhaps only half serious and some apparently dubious rationalizations.[24] The most plausible is simply that he wished to escape the control of others and achieve a degree of personal freedom not possible for the layman. There can be no doubt of his serious interest in Buddhism, but he was as individualistic in this respect as in all others. In fact his desire "to be an individual" *(ch'eng i-ko-jen)* is given by Li as intimately involved in his decision to become a "monk."[25] Officially he was not a licensed monk, nor did he keep the monastic discipline. Instead he pursued even more intensively his scholarly interests. His friend and admirer Yüan Chung-tao has described in detail his life in the temple, his devotion to his books, to his writing, and to a select group of friends with whom he kept up active intellectual relations. Yüan conceded that no one could hope to take Li as a master to follow, both because of his extreme idiosyncrasies and fastidiousness and because of a capacity for scholarship no one else could match.[26]

Two years after becoming a "monk," in 1590, he published his *Fen-shu* (A book to burn), the title of which acknowledged the dangerousness of its contents. It was a collection of letters, essays, prefaces, poems, etc., expressing his repudiation of conventional morality and much of Neo-Confucian philosophy, his belief in the essential identity of the Three Teachings, and his revolutionary views on history, literature, and a wide range of other subjects. He expected the book to be condemned as heresy and it was. But despite attacks upon it and mounting pressure against him, Li persisted in his course. He became even freer in his conduct, and though the charges of social and sexual misconduct made against him are undoubtedly exaggerated, he did not hesitate to relieve his intense scholarly efforts with pleasant diversions in and out of the temple.[27] Aware of the risks, and prepared for the most extreme persecution, he went ahead with the preparation of his voluminous study of Chinese history, the *Ts'ang-shu* (A book to be hidden away),[28] which challenged many long-accepted Confucian views of history. After its publication in 1600 a mob incited by local authorities burned down his residence at the temple, and he spent the remaining few years of his life taking refuge in the home of friend after friend in different places. Finally, in 1602, a memorial at the court in Peking charged him with a long list of offenses, and an edict was issued ordering his arrest and the burning of his books. In prison in Peking he made his last protest, committing suicide by slashing his throat.

INNOCENCE AND INTELLIGENCE

Li Chih was a passionate man, and he knew it. He had violent hatreds and unbounded enthusiasms. He said of himself that:

> His nature was narrow, his manner arrogant, his speech coarse, his mind mad, his conduct rash and imprudent. He did not mix much with others but in personal contacts could be warm and friendly. Toward others he was critical of their faults and little impressed with their good points: those he did not like he would have nothing to do with except wish them ill to his dying day.[29]

But if, in this self-characterization, he belligerently asserts his absolute independence of others, he was nonetheless a hero-worshiper. To him Wang Yang-ming and Wang Chi were sages, and Wang Ken was a hero followed by other heroes of the T'ai-chou school: Hsü Yüeh, Yen Chün, Chao Chen-chi, Lo Ju-fang, and—greatest of them all—Ho Hsin-yin, the martyr to the Way, who was a "scholar for the whole world, a scholar for all ages."[30]

Li thus paid full tribute to those who inspired him, and there is no question of his debt to them: he clearly draws upon and carries forward some of the main ideas and tendencies generated within the Wang Yang-ming school.[31] On the other hand, since many of his attitudes must have been well formed by the time he came under their influence, the individuality of his thought is no less significant than his identification with any school. He does things with others' ideas which they had not done.

The first piece in Li's first published work, A Book to Burn, gives us a clue to this in a passage with a typically ironic touch:

> Under Heaven there is no man in whom consciousness does not arise, no thing in which consciousness does not arise, no moment in which consciousness does not arise. Though some may be unconscious of it themselves, they can always be made conscious of it. It is only such things as earth, wood, tiles, and stones, which cannot be made conscious of it because they are unfeeling

and cannot be communicated with, and there are also the wise and the foolish, who though not incapable of being made conscious of it, are difficult to communicate with precisely because they do have feelings. Excluding these two types, then even the different animals, in the depths of their suffering, can be reached and made conscious.[32]

Some scholars see this as essentially a reformulation of Wang Yang-ming's innate knowledge, or have pointed to the classical source in the *Mean* (20) of the term used by Li, *sheng-chih*, where it means "the knowledge one is born with."[33] In the *Mean* it signifies an awareness of human obligations, as innate knowledge does for Wang Yang-ming. But the *chih* here is the most generalized sort of consciousness, shared with other animate and even inanimate beings. It has no specific human or moral character. It is consciousness in the Buddhist sense, applicable to all sentient beings. This is clear from the continuation of the same passage, where Li says that the beings "can be made conscious, can be apprised of the way to Buddhahood." "Those in whom consciousness has arisen are Buddhas; those in whom it has not are not yet Buddhas."[34]

This, then, is innate knowledge as mediated to Li through Wang Chi, and we recall that Li's introduction to the latter was simultaneous with his introduction to the Diamond Sutra. Innate knowledge as the transcendental perfection of Wang Chi was also, for Li, the Great Perfect Wisdom of the Prajñāpāramitā: "All men possess the mirror of Great Perfect Wisdom *(ta-yüan-ching chih)*, which is the lucent virtue [of the Great Learning] shining within. It is one with Heaven above and Earth beneath, and with thousands of sages and worthies in between. They do not have more of it nor I less."[35]

In this apparent convergence of Confucian and Buddhist concepts, innate knowledge appears not in its moral aspect but in its universal and egalitarian aspect, which then combines with the undifferentiated consciousness of Mahāyāna Buddhism. One might interpret this process as showing the influence of Buddhist egalitarianism on Confucianism, but the interaction is mutual. In discussing the relative merits of Ch'an meditation and the invocation of Amitābha as a means of salvation, Li disputes the view of some Ch'anists that the former is higher and the latter lower, and he uses a typically Neo-Confucian argument: "As heaven, earth, and I have the same root, who is superior to me? As all things form one body with me, who is not as good as I?"[36] From the process of equation and interaction, then, we should observe what actual meaning "equality" can have in this new and somewhat confusing context. Is Li able to derive from it a more profound and universal humanism?

One active ingredient in Li's thinking is the notion of Yen Chün and Ho Hsin-yin (in whom it has no Buddhistic connotations) that man's nature is originally pure and one should follow wherever it spontaneously leads. Li develops its implications in his celebrated essay on the "Childlike Mind" *(T'ung-hsin).*[37] The childlike mind, he says, is originally pure, but it can be lost if received opinions come in through the senses and are allowed to dominate it. The greatest harm results when moral doctrines are imposed upon it, and the mind loses its capacity to judge for itself. This comes mainly from reading books and learning "moral principles."[38]

Once people's minds have been given over to received opinions and moral principles, what they have to say is all about these things, and not what would naturally come from their childlike minds. No matter how clever the words, what have they to do with oneself? What else can there be but phony men speaking phony words, doing phony things, writing phony writings? Once the men become phonies, everything becomes phony. Thereafter if one speaks phony talk to the phonies, the phonies are pleased; if one does phony things as the phonies do, the phonies are pleased; and if one discourses with the phonies through phony writings, the phonies are pleased. Everything is phony, and everyone is pleased.[39]

Moreover, says Li, the phonies have seen to it that the best in literature was destroyed.

This was because the best in literature always came from the childlike mind, and if the childlike mind continued to exist in this way, moral principles would not be practiced, received impressions would not stand up, and the writing of any age, any man, any form, any style, and any language would all be accepted as literature.[40]

From this Li proceeds to argue against adherence to classical literary canons, and in favor of accepting the literature of every age as having its own value. Further to establish his point, he even calls into question the authenticity of the Confucian Classics as authoritative sources of the Sage's teachings. Indeed, one may say without exaggeration that Li Chih anticipates in the sixteenth century the criticisms of the classical Confucian tradition which erupted in the twentieth century during the so-called New Culture movement. Like the modern reformers Li contributed significantly to the promotion of a contemporary vernacular literature in his own day, especially through his editing of *The Water Margin (Shui-hu-chuan)*.[41]

While arguing for a more spontaneous and less moralistic or rationalistic literature, however, Li is not necessarily anti-intellectual in his attitude. It was frequently charged against the T'ai-chou school and the so-called Wild Ch'an movement that they neglected book learning and scholarship. To some extent this may have been true. Ch'an itself is anti-intellectual to the extent that its spiritual training demands a thorough process of intellectual demolition and cultural de-conditioning. And though Li described himself as a skeptic from his youth, it is not unlikely that Ch'an irreverence toward scripture contributed to his debunking of the Confucian Classics. Still, even in the monastery Li devoted himself to scholarship, not Ch'an training. Moreover, what makes his attitude unorthodox or "wild" even as Ch'an Buddhism is his positive endorsement of the literature of the emotions, of a heroic and passionate approach to life. Thus, for him *The Water Margin* and similar works of vernacular fiction were justified, not merely as harmless diversions but as exemplifications of heroic virtue in the common man and, indeed, as serious works of importance even to government.[42]

Li makes no pretense that the ancient sages did without books. Others might be corrupted by book learning, but the sages, "even when they did read many books, did so in such a way as not to lose their childlike minds."[43] Nor does Li's attack on artificiality involve a wholesale repudiation of culture. He does not pine nostalgically for a primitive, uncomplicated past, nor does he see all art, artifice, and technology as alien to man. Art and inspiration in the genuine sense are complementary.[44] And even rites or riteness *(li)* has its natural place. The criterion is whether or not it is a spontaneous expression of inner feelings.

> What comes forth from within may be called riteness; what comes from without is not. What comes without studying, deliberation, premeditation, effort, intellection, or knowledge is called riteness; what comes through the eyes and ears, deliberation and calculation; what involves talk first and action later, or is based on some comparison with others, is not riteness.[45]

A NEW LOOK AT HUMAN RELATIONS

It is from this standpoint that Li undertakes a reevaluation of human relations and human morality. We have seen his comment on Ho Hsin-yin that "of the five human relations [as defined in Confucian tradition] he abandoned all but one—the relation of friend and friend." But Li proceeds to a more fundamental reexamination of all five relations than had been attempted by anyone before, and against the background of social change in the sixteenth century we can appreciate how he anticipated the modern dilemma of Confucianism: how can a moral philosophy based essentially on human relations survive in a world of rapid social change and mobility?

Many of Li's writings reflect his critical attitude on this question, but one devoted solely to an extensive treatment of it is the *Ch'u-t'an chi*. Significantly, its general introduction discusses the primacy of the husband-wife relationship in an unusually abstract manner for Li, and has a philosophical importance transcending the concrete relationship. In effect, Li argues that the genesis of all human life—indeed of all life—depends upon the male-female relationship; all other relations derive from this because procreation is their precondition. On the moral level Li thus disputes the usual primacy given to the parent-child or ruler-subject relation which tend to exemplify a patriarchal or a paternalistic system, and stresses a relationship of equality or complementarity. Further, on the basis of the irreducibility of the male and female principles represented by yin and yang, Li denies the existence of any first principle at all. Most particularly he rejects any monism based on the Neo-Confucian concepts of the Supreme Ultimate *(t'ai-chi)* or principle *(li)*.[46]

Two things stand out here. One is Li's attack on the rationalistic-moralistic mentality of the Neo-Confucians as represented by the concept of "principle." He seems to sense that male dominance in society is linked to the whole system of moral principles embodying that mentality. On the other hand, he is not wholly antirationalist. For him the intuitive mentality, represented by the female, is complementary to the rational mentality, as represented by the male, but—in a separate letter discussing male-female equality—he insists that the difference between the sexes is only one of degree, and that each possesses both types of intelligence, which each should be allowed to develop.[47]

The second point is the manner in which Li makes a philosophical issue of the question in his general introduction. Taking the contents of the *Ch'u-t'an chi* as a whole, little space is actually devoted to the husband-wife relationship (four chapters or *chüan*) and only ten altogether to the three relationships within the family, whereas the remaining two relations—between teachers and friends, and rulers and ministers—occupy twenty chapters. If, then, he has less practical interest in the familial relations than in the broader social ones, it seems clear that his interest in the male-female relations is of another sort. In fact, his final argument goes beyond both Neo-Confucian morality and metaphysics and any possible alternative to them. "I speak only of the duality of male and female, not of the 'One' or of 'Principle.' And if I speak not of the One, how much less would I speak of Nothingness; and if not of Nothingness, how much less of No-Nothingness."[48] In other words, beyond the cosmogonic dualism of male and female nothing whatever can be predicated, and Li therefore feels no urge to construct a new metaphysics of his own. Though it has definite overtones of Chuang Tzu and the Madhyamika dialectic of negation, this attitude also may be linked to the rising antimetaphysical temper of the sixteenth and seventeenth centuries.

Generally speaking, in his discussion of human relationships Li attached the greatest importance to the relation of friendship, which for him tended to supersede all others. In other words, when speaking about Ho Hsin-yin in this regard, he was also speaking for himself. At the same time, however, there is a noticeable disillusionment even with the possibilities of true friendship. The fate of Ho himself, abandoned by his friends, is much in Li's mind. Moreover, a true, like-minded friend, though dearer than a kinsman, is extremely rare. Confucius searched all over and found only one, Yen Hui.[49] And if in the end the relation of friendship cannot be depended upon, the individual is thrown back entirely on his own resources. Li is therefore compelled to probe more deeply into the whole basis of human nature and the nature of the individual. How could one still hold to Confucius' ideal: to be a man among men?

THE IMPORTANCE OF SELF-INTEREST

Li Chih's discussion of human nature is premised on the uniqueness of the individual and the necessity above all for being oneself. "Each human Heaven gives birth to has his own individual function and he does not need to learn this from Confucius. If he did need to learn it from Confucius, then in all the ages before Confucius could no one have achieved real humanity?"[50] Indeed, even Confucius had not taught people to study Confucius, but had taught them to look within themselves. Not surprisingly "learning for one's self" is a key issue for him:

> Confucius never taught people to study Confucius. If he had taught them to study Confucius, why is it that when Yen Yüan asked about humaneness, Confucius answered that one achieves humaneness in and through one's self, not through others? Why is it that Confucius said, "In ancient times learning was for one's self [not for the sake of others]," and said "The noble man seeks it in himself"? Because it was from the self, his followers did not need to ask Confucius about humaneness. Because it was for one's self, his teaching of others was based on his own self-study. This is learning that does without either self or others [i.e., as a preconceived dichotomy].
>
> Because it is selfless, it starts with overcoming [a false sense of] self; because it is without [regard to the self's impressing] others, its teaching aims only at motivating others.[51]

The reason learning cannot be for the sake of others, or to gain their acceptance, is that while all humans have common elementary needs, every human being differs in his individual constitution and capacities, and one cannot serve as a model for others, nor can the view of one be taken as the standard for others. "What others consider right and wrong can never serve as a standard for me. Never from the start have I taken as right and wrong for myself what the world thinks right and wrong."[52]

To others Li's stubborn independence seemed the most willful egotism and he was urged to have a greater respect for the feelings and opinions of others, to follow the example of the sage-king Shun, who was said to have "given up his own view and followed that of others," thus ruling according to the wishes of his people.[53] But to Li this makes little sense. How can one yield one's own opinion to that of others? In the final analysis, even if one yields, it must represent what one chooses to do and depends on knowing what one really wants. Yielding by itself solves nothing. If, whenever there was a conflict of wills or opinions, the rule were always to yield, everyone would have to accept the opposing opinion and the conflict would remain unresolved. Thus a solution can be found only by transcending the dichotomy of self and other, through a deeper understanding of what is common to the self and others. "Not to know oneself and yet to speak of yielding one's opinion to others, not to know others and yet speak of following them—is it any wonder that each holds to his opinion and will not yield, is stubborn and will not follow?"[54]

Another common idea among Neo-Confucians was "having no mind [of one's own]."[55] This notion came from Ch'eng Hao, and meant achieving a state of mind in which one has no self-conscious intent or ulterior motive in doing good. For Li this is the worst sort of self-deception. "Self-interest is the mind-and-heart of human beings, who must be self-interested so that what is in their minds can be made known. If there is no self-interest, there is no mind."[56] Even to desire rectitude is a matter of self-interest. Thus the Way is made manifest through the desires of individuals to achieve something for themselves. "If I do not seek to achieve anything for myself, how and when will the Way be made manifest?"[57]

Li goes on further to develop Wang Ken's idea that the people's daily needs are the very substance of the Way. When Shun inquired into the desires of the people as a basis for his rule, he learned about:

Their desire for goods, for sexual satisfaction, for study, for personal advancement, for the accumulation of wealth; their seeking out of the proper geomantic factors *(feng-shui)* that will bring blessings to their children—all the things which are productive and sustain life in the world, everything that is loved and practiced in common by the people, and what they know and say in common.[58]

In this Li finds a new basis for human relations: "To wear clothing and eat food—these are the principles of human relations.

Without them there are no human relations. . . . The scholar should learn only what is real and unreal in respect to these relations, and not impose other principles of human relations on top of them."[59]

The essential thing in social relations is to let people satisfy their own desires, to let them find their own natural place in the world.

> People have always found their own natural place [when left alone]. If they do not it is only because they are harassed by those who are greedy and aggressive and harmed by humanitarians *(jen-che)*. The humanitarians worry about everyone finding his place in the world, and so they have virtue and rites to correct people's minds, and the state with its punishments to fetter their limbs. Then people begin to lose their place in a big way![60]

THE INDIVIDUAL IN HISTORY

Li devoted the last years of his life to the massive study called *Ts'ang-shu* (A book to be hidden away), in which he attempted a reevaluation of historical personages whom he thought Confucian historians had misjudged because of their moralistic biases. Or, to put it more accurately, whom he thought that earlier historians had failed really to judge.

> For over eleven hundred years there have been no real judgments of right and wrong. Could there, then, have been no right and wrong among men? [No], it was because they all accepted what they thought to be Confucius' judgments as to right and wrong, and never had any right or wrong of their own. . . . Now the conflict of right and wrong is like the passing of the years and the seasons, or the alternation of night and day, which cannot be reduced to one. Yesterday's right is today's wrong. Today's wrong is right again tomorrow. Even if Confucius reappeared today, there is no way of knowing how he would judge right and wrong.

So how can we arbitrarily judge everything as if there were a fixed standard?[61]

Just as in the case of literature each age has its own characteristics, so in history each age has its own conditions and needs. The achievement of the individual must be judged in each context. Although Li has his own view of the pattern of history, moving in cycles of roughness and refinement somewhat similar to those of the Arab historian Ibn Khaldun, it serves mainly to differentiate the kind of "morality" appropriate to each age. Nothing is so vain as trying to preach frugality in an age of luxury, or expecting cultural refinements and gentlemanly conduct in a desperate and disordered age.[62]

What standards, then, can be applied to such different situations? Basically it is a question of how one applies ordinary intelligence to provide for the security and material welfare of the people. In a letter to a friend Li says, "My book is [intended] for the achieving of peace and order throughout the ages."[63] To accomplish this, different talents and capabilities must be employed for different purposes: there is no single model for all of the wise and virtuous ministers. Weak rulers and strong have different needs; the former require strong ministers, the latter able and talented ones. Some ages call for strong, activist policies, others for the laissez-faire approach. But always there must be a realistic attention to the uses of power. This Confucian ministers have been largely incapable of, mainly because they have neglected military affairs and considered it a virtue to confine themselves to civil administration and the polite arts. Though committed to the business of government, they are largely unfit to govern. "Again and again, though they have the capability of doing something, they are unwilling to exert their full efforts to achieve it, so worried are they lest others suspect them of seeking wealth, power, fame, or gain for themselves."[64]

In A Book To Be Hidden Away, despite the perverse delight Li Chih gets from exposing the failures of Confucian moralism, he is still very much the moralist himself, judging men in history. Some people have questioned whether Li can be considered a philosopher in the usual sense, and histories of Chinese philosophy barely mention him, if at all. But if he forswears metaphysics and moral philosophy, he nevertheless writes as a moralist and critic.

Carson Chang describes Li as "primarily a literary man,"[65] and yet we find that he left no literary work of great distinction. This makes it all the more significant that so much of Li's writing should be in a historical vein. Whether he would qualify strictly as an historian is another question, but Li obviously still shares the Confucian belief that history provides the ultimate ground for verifying essential truths. Thus, for him the written record and the right kind of book learning are of real importance. There is, as we have already indicated, much more of the scholar and intellectual in him than in earlier thinkers of his school, who had virtually set aside scholarly study and cultural pursuits in order to assert the primacy of moral man and the demands of humanitarian activism.

Li is still heir to Wang Yang-ming and the ground has been prepared for him by the subjectivistic and pragmatic tendencies in the new School of the Mind. Moreover, he is to some degree still moved by its spirit of activism in the pursuit of human welfare. But new and different uses have been found by him for the rationalistic criticism which his predecessors had directed at the cultural man. By this time the undermining of tradition has gone so far that even traditional morality can be called into question. All the moral values which Wang Yang-ming had so easily assumed were written on the heart of the essential man can now be reexamined in the light of reason and history. If culture must submit to moral judgement, so must morality submit to historical judgment.

Thus the scholarship which not long before had been deprecated by some within the Wang Yang-ming school has reappeared to haunt those who believed that morality could dispense with culture. This, in fact, is what makes Li Chih so dangerous a revolutionary. Though he was attacked for turning to Ch'an Buddhism, had he really disappeared into the silence of Ch'an meditation, Confucians would have had little to worry about from him. It was precisely his scholarship and his extensive use of history that made Li a more formidable antagonist, and at the same time a seemingly more traitorous and treacherous one, than any ordinary bonze could have been.

THE FAILURE OF HUMANITARIANISM

If Li Chih is a "realist," however, one still could not mistake him for a dispassionate scholar or objective historian. He is too embittered and vindictive for that. Indeed it is here that he seems almost a classic case of alienation from his whole society and culture. That he is disillusioned with official life is not surprising, nor is his questioning of received tradition. What really strikes us is his disillusionment even with the kind of moralism and humanitarianism that has emerged from the Wang Yang-ming school.

Li did not believe that morality could be taught. "Confucius, in his teaching of men, taught them only to seek humanity [within themselves]. If they sought it and failed to achieve it, that was that —nothing more could be said."[66] As regards the various virtues, these too could only develop naturally and spontaneously. It was all a matter of self-confidence and self-fulfillment *(tzu-ch'eng)*. But now those who promote "lecturing" or "learning by discussion" *(chiang-hsüeh)* "think they can teach filiality, brotherliness, loyalty, and good faith by talking about them. This can only do great harm to people's natures."[67]

It is easy to agree with Li's view that virtue cannot be taught, being largely a matter of self-motivation and self-development. But when he says, "If they sought [humanity] and failed to achieve it, that was that, nothing more need be said," one wonders about such a laissez-faire attitude as an approach to education. Wang Chi had said, in explaining "neither good nor evil," that this view applied to those of superior capability, naturally enlightened, whose learning was on a non-discursive level. Its implication of higher and lower orders of learning, however, is fraught with problems. Does this suggest a kind of natural elitism, directed toward a higher, esoteric knowledge, in which case it would diverge from the general egalitarian spirit of Wang Yang-ming's teaching? Does it direct learning toward a kind of private enlightenment, not only individual and voluntaristic but individualistic and idiosyncratic? How is this reconciled with Yang-ming's emphasis on the open and public character of learning, and on the responsibility of the Great Man to help educate his fellows? Wang Chi himself was an extraordinarily dedicated teacher, active in the academies into his eighties. But Li Chih had his own ideas about how to exercise the full freedom of an innate knowledge beyond good and evil. He is convinced that no amount of instruction would serve most people as well as the use of their own native intelligence. Thus, for instance, he insists that people's basic instinct for survival will serve them best in most crisis situations, and nothing the ruler can do by way of moral example or instruction will win the hearts of the people, or inspire confidence, so much as the confidence engendered by having sufficient food and arms to defend themselves with. Hence he belittles the thought found in *Analects* 12:7 that, without food and arms, people might still have confidence in the ruler.[68]

Li still had great admiration for some of the individual members of the T'ai-chou school, like Lo Ju-fang, who went out among the people but did not "preach" to them.[69] But, as we have seen, he had a strong aversion from the start to the kind of group philosophical discussion developed within the Wang Yang-ming school, and refused to attend such meetings. He showed great inner resistance to any moral pressure or any effort to "organize" him. It was apparent, too, that for him scholarship and book learning in private took priority over public discussion. But on top of this Li developed a disgust with anything that took the form of a "school," of a teacher with a following, of a group that wants to organize for political action. Undoubtedly, his own experience with Keng Ting-hsiang had much to do with this, as well as his bitterness over the fate of Ho Hsin-yin. In his eulogy and lament for the latter he castigated the "lecturers" *(chiang-hsüeh che)* for their failure to lift a finger to save Ho, and one of their great leaders, Keng, he charges with the worst hypocrisy.[70]

In Li's scathing attacks on these "hypocrites" one can see what has become of the grand humanitarian slogans of Wang Yang-ming and Wang Ken.

> If there is something to be gained by it and they want to take charge of public affairs, then the "lecturers" will cite the saying that "all things are one body" [and it is their duty to serve mankind]; if they stand to lose by it, however, and they wish to avoid blame and censure, then they invoke the saying "The clearest wisdom is self-preservation" [in order to withdraw from threatening danger].[71]

Or again:

> In ordinary times when there is peace, they only know how to bow and salute one another, or else they sit the day long in an upright posture [practicing quiet-sitting] like a clay image, thinking that if they can suppress all stray thoughts they will become sages and worthies. The more cunning among them participate in the meetings to discuss innate knowledge, secretly hoping to gain some recognition and win high office. But when a crisis comes, they look at each other pale and speechless, try to shift the blame to one another, and save themselves on the pretext that "the clearest wisdom is self-preservation." Consequently, if the state employs only this type of scholar, when an emergency arises it has no one of any use in the situation.[72]

Of their activities as teachers, he says the "lecturers" gather crowds of followers and take in students:

> to enhance their own name and fame and make themselves rich and honored, not realizing that Confucius never sought wealth or honors or to surround himself with disciples. . . . But the teachers of today—one day out of office and their disciples abandon them; one day without funds and their followers scatter.[73]

Again and again Li mocks the moralistic pretensions of those who preach the Way but have "their hearts set on high office and the acquisition of wealth."[74] He compares them with a type of literary man whom he considers equally "phony"—the so-called mountain-men *(shan-jen)* who affect the independence and eccentricity of artists and poets who live alone in the midst of nature.

> Those who consider themselves sages today are no different from the mountain-men—it is all a matter of luck. If it is a man's luck that he can compose poetry he calls himself a "mountain-man"; if it is not and he cannot compose poetry and become a mountain-man, he calls himself a "sage." If it is a man's luck that he can lecture on "innate knowledge," he calls himself a "sage," but if it is not and he is unable to lecture on innate knowledge, he gives up being a sage and calls himself a "mountain-man." They turn around and reverse themselves in order to deceive the world and secure their own gain. They call themselves "mountain-men" but their hearts are those of the merchants. Their lips are full of the Way and virtue, but their ambition is to become "thieves of virtue" (*Analects* 17:13).
>
> Those who call themselves "mountain-men," if considered as merchants would not be worth one copper cash and without the protection of high officials would be despised among men. And how do I know that I am any better? Who knows but that I too have the heart of a merchant and have put on Buddhist robes just to deceive people and make use of the name?[75]

Whatever people may think, says Li, at least he will have had the satisfaction that, by becoming a "monk," he will have spared himself worry over the acquisition of wealth and the danger of losing it, the buying of lands and houses, getting the right geomantic factors, etc., which other people trouble themselves with.

That scholar-officials are worse than merchants and no better than cheats is a constant refrain in Li's writing. Outwardly they are sages, inwardly merchants. But the merchants in their business dealings could never compete with the scholar-officials, who are masters in the business of selling out dynasties, sacrificing rulers on the altar of the sage, and then carrying their heads into the market place.[76]

One might indeed believe that Li Chih has the "heart of a merchant" if some contemporary writers are right in saying that Li's satirizing of the scholar-officials shows a sympathy for the merchants and reflects a "rising bourgeois capitalist spirit."[77] That he has such a sympathy is quite evident, especially in a passage which has been cited from a letter of Li to Chiao Hung wherein he expresses his compassion for the merchant who "is burdened with heavy loads, runs great risks and braves many dangers, endures many humiliations from the tax officers and insults in the market place."[78] What Li describes here, however, has been the typical lot of the Chinese merchant throughout history, and Li goes on in the same passage[79] to make clear that the condition he describes is of a depressed, not a "rising," bourgeoisie. For all their pains, he says, the merchants' gain is slight. They have to curry favor and enter into collusion with high officials to make even a little profit. They are despised as "profit seekers," simply for seeking honest gain, while the scholars and poets, who are just as mercenary and less productive, sit with the high and mighty and thereby avoid all danger and harm.[80] Surely if this is the capitalism for which Li is cast as a spokesman, it is what Shimada has called, following Weber, "pariah capitalism."[81]

THE IDEALIST AND THE REALIST

What we actually face here is an unresolved conflict between Li's philosophy of self-interest and his remaining Confucian idealism. Though he accepts self-interest and the laws of the market place as governing the dealings of most men, true sagehood of the kind that Confucius represented is a different matter; it is a priceless commodity which can be obtained only by total self-dedication.[82] There is no room for self-seeking here, only for self-sacrifice. Thus commercialism or the profit motive are things to be decried, not accepted or endorsed, when found in the Confucian scholar-official or moralist. They are a betrayal of the high idealism of Confucius' "Noble man" or Mencius' "Great Man."

Truly the strain is beginning to show, in the humanitarianism of the T'ai-chou school, between its belief that every man is a ready-made sage and its ideal of the "great man" who serves the welfare of the common man while preserving a lofty detachment himself. At heart Li is still deeply moved by that ideal, yet he is also shocked by the discrepancy between the ideal and the actuality as revealed in the self-professed "sages" around him. The latter stand in obvious contradiction to both of these articles of the T'ai-chou faith. Sagehood is not all that easy to find or attain.

Whether Li is really conscious of this dilemma is difficult to say. Rather than face it, he prefers to denounce the "phony" sages as the source of all evil. How they have fallen into this state of utter depravity we are not told. In Li's sight they have become almost "non-men" or "non-people," but in the fundamentally Confucian sense that, not being humane, they have ceased to be human. As such, they are virtually deprived of any right to sympathy or the benefit of the doubt as to their intentions. Thus, to sustain his ever-narrowing but all the more intense idealism, to preserve his faith in the goodness of human nature so widely proclaimed by the T'ai-chou school in the face of the movement's moral degeneration, Li must attack and destroy the "hypocrites" who have betrayed the cause. But in destroying the "pharisees" with such demonic fury and savage wit, does not Li himself verge on a new phariseeism? It is a question Li asks of himself.

To answer it, or even to understand it better, we must first consider what happens to the common man at Li's hands. He becomes, really, two things. As one, he remains the naturally good man of Wang Ken and the rest, with emphasis on his biological self, his innate intelligence, and (with Li) his Buddha-consciousness. As the other, he is man subject to illusion, constantly falling victim to the hypocrites and moralists. It is only in some such terms that one may explain how every man can be a sage or possess the Buddha-nature, how "the streets are full of sages," and yet the sage turns out to be such a rare and lonely figure. Li says, "Confucius spoke of the noble man *(chün tzu)* being 'unsoured even though men take no note of him' *(Analects* 1:1). By men he means the common man. It is because the common man does not know me that I can be called a 'noble man.' If the common man knew me, I too would be a common man and no more."[83] The common man in this sense is obviously not the sage, but his direct antithesis. And elsewhere Li indicates that the noble man, like the Bodhisattva, has superior knowledge. Though all men have the capability for enlightenment, few attain it.[84]

Here Li's sharp differentiation of the noble man from the common man is quite striking, since in the context of the *Analects* it is more likely the ruler than the common man *(min)* who fails to recognize the noble man.

The susceptibility of the ordinary man to prevailing opinion and conventional conduct also explains why one cannot actually look for sages among them, but must look for heroes—men who are wild and impetuous and ready to break the bonds of convention. Confucius, he says, set a high value on true humanity; unable to find heroes, he was "unwilling to sell himself cheap."[85] As for the majority of men, Li comes to doubt that they are any better than beasts.[86] He cannot even call them dogs—that would be unfair to the dog, who like man possesses the Buddha-nature but unlike man is capable of some loyalty.

Against this background we may better understand the significance of Li's political views. With his admiration for political realists goes also his pessimism about the judgment of ordinary men in political matters. He retains his faith in the ordinary man's ability to take care of his own affairs, and from that standpoint the problem of government is simply to provide conditions in which the individual can take care of himself. But this responsibility Li is ready to leave to strong rulers, who will use power ruthlessly when necessary and in any case with utter realism and efficiency. Hence his great esteem for the Legalist statesmen and authoritarian rulers of the past; hence his description of the first emperor of the Ch'in —the bane of all Confucians for his totalitarian policies—as the "greatest emperor of all time" and of Emperor Wu of Han—who emphasized military power and strong state control over the economy—as "the greatest sage of all time."[87]

Thus, for all his radical individualism, Li extends the rights or functions of the individual into politics only insofar as a few exceptional individuals may display their rare talents in ruling over the masses. The latter, he agreed with Lao Tzu, are better off completely ignorant of state policy and innocently unaware of what the ruler is doing, except that he makes their lives secure and their bellies full. To Li the one thing most needful for this is military power, and after that, for the people to know only what will bring certain rewards and inescapable punishment.[88]

Given Li's historical relativism, one must allow for the fact that he will not commit himself to one type of rule in all circumstances. Further, if we grant that in the transcendent freedom of his enlightenment he remains forever uncommitted to any particular political system, one cannot call him a totalitarian. Yet it is evident that, while questioning the moral constants of traditional Confucianism, he is not unwilling to generalize rather broadly about the constant power factors in human society, and to see biological man as often best served by a powerful state.

Some have wondered how the gentle mysticism of Lao Tzu could have been appropriated so readily by the early Legalists and made to serve as a mystique of state power. Li Chih shows how tempting it is for the frustrated idealist, the believer in the natural goodness of man, to strike a bargain with the dictator, thinking that somehow the latter's realism will dispose of the messy human complications that prevent the fulfillment of his dream. Anarchism only needs a capable sponsor. And if Li's view of history does not enable him to envisage the "withering away of the state," his hatred and contempt of the moralists is enough to persuade him that in most ages the individual is better off with the despot than with the preacher or teacher.

THE MONK, THE MAN, AND THE MARTYR

For Li Chih as an individual, however, this still does not solve the problem. He himself will be no statesman or general. A sage, perhaps, but no sage-king. His destiny is to be a hero. And if he has forsworn moral philosophy, the hero nevertheless carries with him a heavy moral burden—the psychological cost of having broken with the establishment and turned his back on his own class, the ruling elite. Though emancipated from tradition, he is still the servitor of a Confucian conscience which demands justification and vindication before his enemies. As the hero who has cut himself off from all the sources of power and influence, and as the sage who will not compromise with a corrupt world, he has sought the sanctuary of a monastery and shaved his head. But whatever freedom he has found there has not released him from his own inner needs.

Most modern writers, hero-worshipers no less than Li, have been loath to speak about him as a Buddhist or a Confucian. To them, he is a completely emancipated individual who has risen above all sectarianism and achieved heroic stature in a wider world. He has taken what was best in the Three Teachings, their common human denominator and forged it into a philosophy for the modern man. As regards his "Buddhism" or "Confucianism" one need not probe too deeply into what, after all, he himself has discarded or transcended.

There is truth in this, as we have said: he was as individualistic in his "Buddhism" as in his "Confucianism." But if we assume that his becoming a "monk" is purely a matter of personal convenience and not at all a matter of conviction, we fail to reckon with the serious interest in Buddhism undeniably manifest in his writings. On the other hand, we must, if we take him as a genuine monk, confront the fact that he devoted his last years to scholarly work as if his salvation depended on it, and said that he was ready to be judged in history on the basis of his final work, *A Book To Be Hidden Away*, which is exclusively concerned with history and politics.[89] This in turn may seem to suggest that, after all, he was really more of a Confucian than anything else, a view which gains apparent support from the title of one of his essays: "The Three Teachings Converge in Confucianism."

Our concern here being with Li as an individualist who challenges the prevailing orthodoxy, we do not pursue the matter as a question of sectarian allegiance. The essay just mentioned, however, throws some light on the enigma of Li Chih himself. The Three Teachings are one, he says, because they all originate in the expectation of "hearing the Way." Confucius said that "if he could hear the Way in the morning, he could die content in the evening" (*Analects* 4:8). Being bent on this alone, and unready to die until he had heard it "he looked on wealth and rank as so much manure, and the Buddhist, as a snare and a trap through which man suffers a painful life and a painful death. The Three Teachings are thus one in their transcendence of the world and differ only in the degree of their contempt for it."[90]

The essential unity of the Three Teachings is then "their seeking for the Way in order to be delivered from this world, for only by escaping the world can they avoid the sufferings of wealth and rank."[91] Even in Confucius' time it was evident that most men, and even most of his disciples, could not match Confucius' dedication to the Way, and although Li goes on to detail the stages in the degeneration of the true teaching, it had been inevitable that the educated class would be corrupted by wealth and rank. There is nothing really strange in things having deteriorated to the point reached in his own time, when scholars "outwardly pursue the Way but inwardly seek wealth and rank, dress themselves in Confucian robes but act like dogs and swine."[92]

Now, however, it has reached the point where no one can escape contamination. To succeed in the professedly Confucian world one must study moral philosophy, and even those who have no desire for wealth and rank, if they want to achieve anything in the world, cannot help getting involved in it. Consequently, concludes Li, for those who sincerely wish to study the Way in order to learn the essence of Confucianism, Buddhism, and Taoism and thus be delivered from the world, there is no alternative but to shave their heads and become monks.[93]

From this it is evident that the real essence of the Three Teachings is the heroic vocation pursued in a world of hopeless corruption and suffering—a strange combination of Confucian commitment to life and Buddhist pessimism concerning the world. And Li's withdrawal to the monastery is more than a convenient escape from the contamination of the world. It is his last desperate effort to reconcile the contradiction between his "realism" and his "idealism," between his philosophy of self-interest and his search for something holy, between his sanctioning of self-interestedness and his condemnation of the self-seeking moralists, between his recognition of the legitimate self-interest of the common man, and his continued insistence on the rigorous demands of the heroic life for the Great Man or Noble Man as leader in the society. This was a conflict no longer so easily resolved in the over-arching ideal of the Sage for everyman.

There are indications that in the monastery Li is somehow aware of and reconciled to the absurdity of his position. As was commonly the case in Chinese temples, the image of Confucius was worshiped in Li's along with other deities and Buddhas, and he comments:

People all think Confucius a sage and so do I. They all think Lao Tzu and Buddha are heretics and so do I. But people don't really know what sagehood and heterodoxy are. They have just heard so much about them from their parents and teachers. Nor do their parents and teachers really know what sagehood and heterodoxy are; they just believe what they hear from the scholars and elders. And the scholars and elders don't know either, except that Confucius said something about these things. But his saying "Sagehood—of that I am not capable" [as quoted in *Mencius* 2A:2] they take as just an expression of modesty, and when he spoke of "studying strange teachings [as] harmful" (*Analects* 2:16) they interpret this as referring to Taoism and Buddhism.

The scholars and elders have memorized these things and

embroidered on them; parents and teachers have preserved and recited them, and children have blindly accepted them. . . . So today, though men have eyes, they do not use them. And what then about me? Do I dare use my eyes? I too follow the crowd and regard him as a sage . . . I too follow the crowd in doing him honor at Chih-fo yüan.[94]

We have here the same sense of irony and absurdity found in the *Journey to the West* (or *Monkey*) attributed to Wu Ch'eng-en, a contemporary of Li's who shares with him a fondness for the philosophy expressed in the Heart Sūtra.[95] But Wu's ironies and satire are most often gentle and compassionate. There is little of the bitterness and disillusionment that puts such a biting edge on Li's satire. Thus, if Li has achieved some self-transcendence in the monastery, at best he is still only a bodhisattva and not yet a Buddha. His Confucian karma has yet to spend itself; his scholarly genius has yet to vindicate the renegade's rejection of his own class and abandonment of his family. Moreover, as a bodhisattva who shows compassion for the world essentially through redemptive power of his enlightenment, he can now become a teacher to the world through his writings.

There is more than enough evidence in these writings to document his final view of life as a "sea of suffering,"[96] and at the same time his conviction that the hero can triumph over this through his own martyrdom. Li's sympathies are strongly elicited by those who sacrifice themselves for a cause. He would wish them to be more realistic sometimes and not sacrifice themselves uselessly; also, as in the case of Fang Hsiao-ju in the early Ming, he would insist on distinguishing between simple martyrdom and actual political accomplishment.[97] But he pays loving tribute to Fang among three Ming martyrs whose writings he collected in a special anthology entitled *San i-jen chi* (Works of Three Nonconformists). And in one of his essays he discusses five good ways to die, the best of which is to die a heroic death for a noble cause. It is a wasted death just to die at home in the bosom of one's family.[98] In death as in life there is nothing more worthwhile than to register one's protest and pour forth one's indignation against the evil in the world.[99] In one of his letters Li writes: "You can see that I have no fear of death, no fear of men, and that I have put no reliance in power and in influence. All men just have one death; you can't die twice!"[100]

LI CHIH AS A NEO-CONFUCIAN

Li Chih had many heroes, but for someone so often called a rebel or maverick himself, it is striking how many of his heroes come from the ranks of orthodox Neo-Confucians. Fang Hsiao-ju, much admired by Li among early Ming Confucians for resisting the usurpation of the Yung-lo emperor, was a follower of the Ch'eng-Chu school who lived up to the highest Neo-Confucian standards of ministerial integrity and loyalty to the legitimate sovereign. Admired for both his forthright criticism of the ruler and unflinching devotion to principle, Fang has been recognized as squarely in the orthodox tradition—an orthodox nonconformist, as it were.[101]

This same combination of individual integrity and conformity to principle, expressing itself in social or political nonconformity, is found in another early Ming figure, Wu Yü-pi, whom Li Chih also greatly respected.[102] Moreover, in *A Book To Be Hidden Away* and its sequel, historical figures presented in a favorable light include many considered orthodox Neo-Confucians. Listed, among others, are such personages as Chou Tun-i, Ch'eng Hao, Li T'ung, Chu Hsi, Chen Te-hsiu, Hsü Heng, Ou-yang Hsüan, Hsüeh Hsüan, and Hai Jui.[103]

More than just testifying to Li Chih's broad-mindedness as a historian, this catholicity of judgment shows the respect in which Li still holds certain values of the Neo-Confucian tradition. There is a place for them in his scheme of things, as shown for instance in the typology of the *Tsang-shu* and *Hsü ts'ang-shu* for "Ministers Distinguished in the Learning of Principle *(li-hsüeh ming-ch'en)*," "Ministers Distinguished for Loyalty and Integrity *(chung-chieh ming-ch'en)*," "Confucian Ministers of Worthy Accomplishments *(te-yeh ju-ch'en),"* etc.[104] We would be underestimating Li Chih's considerable learning, as well as the formative influence upon him of his earlier training, if we did not take into account these indications that Li Chih's critique of contemporary scholarship arises from deep reflection on the core values of Neo-Confucian tradition.

Evidence has already been given of Li Chih's devotion to the ideal of sagehood, so central to the Learning of the Way and to the orthodox Ch'eng-Chu school in particular. The religious intensity which Li brings to his pursuit of this ideal is itself characteristic of the "orthodox" School of the Way. Indeed, in the very moral passion and rigorism manifested in his criticism of the School of the Way Li shows how much of the prophetic zeal of this school still lives in him. From Li's point of view it is he who has remained true to the ideals which many *Tao-hsüeh* followers themselves have compromised, and it is they, not he, who have deviated in their conduct from true rectitude.

Li Chih's treatment of Chou Tun-i in *A Book To Be Hidden Away (Tsang-shu)* is indicative of his view of the "Way" *(Tao)* as primarily the Way to Sagehood. Li emphasizes the crucial influence of Chou on the Ch'eng brothers in teaching them to pursue "what Confucius and Yen Tzu loved to learn," i.e., the learning of sagehood, and he cites portrayals of Chou as the personification of sagely virtues, dwelling on his lofty and sterling character rather than on his contribution of philosophical concepts such as "Nonfinite and yet the Supreme Ultimate" *(wu-chi erh t'ai chi),* which goes unmentioned (as it does even in the account of the Transmission of the Way by Chu Hsi's premier disciple Huang Kan).[105] Moreover, Li cites the posthumous tribute to Chou for his key role in the revival of the Confucian Way—the first teacher after Mencius from whom one could gain full access to the Learning of Sagehood.[106] Since Chu Hsi himself had been the one who first canonized Chou Tun-i and enshrined him as the progenitor of the Sage Learning in the Sung, this view betrays the influence of Chu's conception of the Way as something much grander and more elevated than anything ordinary Confucian scholars before Chou could comprehend.

In this connection, though Li presents Chou as one who had repossessed the Way of Sagehood after the long lapse of time from Mencius, he does not refer here to *tao-t'ung* as the vehicle of orthodox tradition. Indeed he takes issue elsewhere with the view of *tao-t'ung* as a special transmission from one great mind to another. The reason for this is that he wishes to stress accessibility to the Way in and by the mind of every man. In other words he prefers to dwell on the intuitive and prophetic aspect of the original *tao-t'ung* concept, rather than on its scholastic or authoritarian character. He says:

> The Way is found in human beings like water in the earth. Human seeking for the Way is like digging into the earth for water. Thus water is always to be found in the earth and the Way is always to be found in human beings. Can one say then that there is such a thing as water not running [through the earth] or the Way not being carried on [among humans] . . .? To say that after Mencius the Way was no longer transmitted is truly a great falsehood, but once it had been asserted, Sung scholars could accept the notion that the masters—Chou, the Ch'engs, Chang Tsai, and Chu Hsi had a direct transmission from Mencius. From the Ch'in down through the Han, T'ang, and Sung over a thousand and some hundred years passed. If the earth had been without springs of water that long, everyone would have died of thirst, and similarly had humankind been unable to get the Way [for such a long time], then the Way of humankind would have been utterly lost; how then could humans have survived [without it] for so many generations?[107]

It was a great conceit on the part of Sung scholars, Li says, to think that somehow they were different from those who had gone before and failed to get the Way, and a great calumny against their predecessors to allege that they had failed to uphold the Way. Not only did this imply that the people of those days had no access to the Way but it also meant that the ministers of those times were lacking in the Way and the rulers of those times likewise. Thus summarily were the rulers and ministers of millennial ages convicted of failing to keep to the Way. Li had long wished to have the time to reexamine the record, he says, and to rectify this injustice, but only now in his old age had he had time for it—not enough to conduct a full-scale revision but enough at least to demonstrate that in fact the Way was not "cut off" for all those years.[108]

Li's point is not to deny that the Sung masters had personal insights and made their own contributions to the learning of the Way; it is simply that such insights are open to all and cannot be reserved exclusively to one school. They evince a basic human capability, rather than the special property of those possessed of, or possessive about, the orthodox tradition.

Another side of Li Chih, however, tells him that while the Way is available to all human beings and thus the attainment of sagehood is open to all, in the present corrupt state of the world true sages cannot in fact be found anywhere, and, as we have seen above, one must look instead for heroes. In a letter to Chiao Hung, he says:

> People are like water; the hero is like a big fish. If you wish to catch a big fish you have to look for a different kind [i.e., the right kind] of water and if you want to look for a hero you must look for an extraordinary person. This is a principle in accord with the nature of things.[109]

Thus, explains Li, a well may have water that is clear, sweet, and good for drinking, but if you want a fish the well is not the place to find it. You have to go out into the ocean where fresh water is not to be found but fish are. So too with heroes. If you try to find them among the goody-goodies in the village (as referred to in *Analects* 13:24), it is like trying to find fish in a well—it can't be done.

> Heroes are not the kind of people villagers like, and heroes are never produced among villagers. In the past as well as in the

present, it has been the heroes who became sages and worthies, and there has never been a case of someone who was not a hero becoming a sage or worthy. . . .

In my view anyone who is not a true hero will be unable to demonstrate the true resolve to become a sage or a worthy. How so? Because if he is a true hero, he will never fail to recognize another hero, and if he has the true resolve to become a sage or worthy, he will not fail to recognize the path to sagehood.[110]

Here again we see how great a strain has developed between the Neo-Confucian cult of the hero, and the egalitarianism which had brought the Way of the Sage within reach of the average human. If Li articulates this contradiction more clearly than most of his contemporaries, it is because, in his own way, he is trying harder than most to be true to the original impulse in Chu Hsi's teaching that "Learning to be a Sage" means "learning for the Sake of One's Self."

In his important letter to Keng Ting-hsiang, quoted above, Li says that "Each human being Heaven gives birth to has his own individual function and he does not need to learn this from Confucius." Chu Hsi himself had said something similar in discussing individuality in poetic expression: "I have always maintained that each and every thing under Heaven has its own distinct standard [way or pattern] *(t'ien-hsia wan-shih chieh yu i-ting chih fa).*"[111]

Li continues, as in the passage cited above concerning Confucius' answer to the question Yen Yüan asked about humaneness, the answer was, 'Does not the pursuit of humaneness come from within oneself?' *(Analects* 12:1), and also in 'The noble man seeks it in himself' *(Analects* 15:21).[112] It is not that one cannot learn from Confucius, but that, learning from Confucius, one knows this learning must be "for one's self." On this basis, as Li says in the same letter, one can "by following what is true of one's own nature, and then extending and expanding it to others, share it with all under Heaven—this is what is called the Way."[113]

The nature referred to here is the "virtuous nature" or moral nature *(te-hsing)*, which most Neo-Confucians, following the *Great Learning* (1) and the *Mean* (27) took as the starting point of self-cultivation. For Li Chih this virtuous nature has an absolute value, "worthy of the highest respect."[114] This does not mean that the pursuit of learning or the study of texts should be dispensed with, as earlier thinkers of the so-called Lu-Wang persuasion were sometimes alleged to do, since Li recognizes the complementarity of moral cultivation and scholarly study and refuses to accept any basic dichotomy here as between Chu Hsi and Lu Hsiang-shan. Literature is necessary as a means of communication so that "what should be most honored and respected can come to be loved and sought within the self."[115] The *Mean* itself is an example of such teaching concerning the virtuous nature. One cannot speak of "honoring the moral nature" without also pursuing the path of scholarly inquiry. Yet scholarly inquiry must always be confirmed within the self.[116] For this reason "the former sages and recent worthies all put the greatest stress on 'getting it oneself' . . . and scholars too should seek to benefit from the sages' and worthies' [teaching concerning] 'getting it oneself.' "[117]

"Getting it" or "finding the Way in oneself" was the primary consideration for Li Chih, as he explained in his discussion of the passage from the *Mean*, cited earlier, concerning the noble man's readiness to accept, and be himself in, whatever station, position, or situation he finds himself:

> The noble man accords with his station in life and does not desire to go beyond it.
>
> In [or according with] a position of wealth and honor he does what is proper to a position of wealth and honor. In a poor and low position, he does what is proper to a poor and low position. Situated among barbarians, he does what is proper among barbarians. In a situation of sorrow and difficulty, he does what is proper in sorrow and difficulty. The noble man can find himself in no situation in which he is not himself.[118]

Here, in what is translated as "being oneself," we have *tzu-te* in its several senses of "getting it oneself," "finding [the Way in] oneself," "being at ease or at home with oneself," etc. Li Chih refers to this passage often, and has this to say about *tzu-te* as representing a basic inner stability in one's life akin to an attitude of religious acceptance:

The reason the noble man does not seek to go beyond his station is that he can accept his station, and the reason he can accept his station is that there is no situation in which he is not himself [i.e., is not at home with himself]. If it were not for the satisfaction of finding [the Way in] himself, then if he disesteemed what he found within himself and esteemed what he saw without, he would always want to go beyond his present station. If you want to go beyond, how can you accept your station? Therefore the noble man has his heart set on finding [the Way in] himself.

Now finding myself in a poor and humble position, I accept it. Another time when I dwell in a position of wealth and honor, then in view of wealth and honor I likewise accept it, do what is proper in a position of wealth and honor, and accept these as nothing strange. If one accepts dwelling in China, the barbarian tribes do not enter into one's consciousness, but eventually if one goes and dwells in a barbarian land, one likewise accepts living among barbarians without being conscious of being a Chinese.

To be rich and honored, to be poor and humble, to be in sorrows and difficulties, to be among the barbarians—these are all human stations or situations. If you look on them as situations you can accept, you can be at ease in changing situations. Thinking in terms of "not wanting to go beyond one's station," there is always a "beyond," and not going beyond, one finds himself in no situation where he is not himself or has any thought of going beyond his station. Therefore the noble man wishes to find [the Way in] himself. If he can do so, wherever he dwells it is all right. Whether he dwells on high or dwells below,

whether he deals with his own situation or others' he understands them all.

Our Confucius taught humankind to accept their station so
that those who pursue learning should seek the benefit of the
sages' and worthies' finding [the Way in] oneself. If finding it
leads in different directions, what's the harm in that?[119]

This same passage from the *Mean* is discussed elsewhere by Li
in a context blending Buddhist transcendence of the world with a
Taoist naturalism:

Su [accepting or according with] means "empty." If I am rich
and honored but do not identify myself with [i.e., am detached
about] being rich and honored, then alone can my Way be practiced in a position of wealth and honor. If I am poor and in
humble station but do not identify myself with being poor and
humble, then alone can my way be carried on in a poor and
humble station. And it is the same with being among barbarians
or in sorrow and difficulty. This is why the noble man can get
into no situation where he cannot find [the Way in] himself.

The reason the Buddha sought to go beyond life and death
was so that the seriousness of life and death would not loom
large in one's mind. If life and death do not loom large in one's
mind, then wealth and honor, poverty and low station, living
among barbarians or in sorrow and distress are all the same to
him. This is [the reason] why the noble man finds himself in no
situation where he cannot be himself. The alternation of day and
night, the periods of the sun and moon, the rotation of the
seasons, the appearance and disappearance of the ghosts and
spirits, birth and death among men—these all occur in the natural course of things. The reason the Buddha sought to go beyond
life and death was to make clear their natural basis *(ming ch'i
tzu-jan chih ku).*[120]

Here "getting it" or finding [the Way in] oneself is spoken of as
an inner realization that combines Buddhist non-attachment or

"emptiness" with naturalistic realism. This enlightenment, transcending and yet accepting things as they are, achieves intellectual objectivity through spiritual detachment. In Li's discussion of man's basic need for food and clothing, cited earlier, he insists on these forms of physical dependence as the most fundamental of human relations. He also speaks of recognizing and accepting these facts of life as a perceiving of "true emptiness" *(chen-k'ung)*, and says that without this kind of discriminating insight into the true nature of things one can never arrive at the stage of "getting it oneself." This is the essential difference in Lu Hsiang-shan's distinction between learning that is plain and simple" *(chien-i)* (i.e., integrated and holistic) and learning that is calculated, analytic, and fragmented *(chih-li)* (i.e., allows the self to become dispersed in things, and in effect become dis-integrated).[121]

Allowing for the Buddhist ar d Taoist overtones here, the central concern is still for the integrity and wholeness of the self, a typically Neo-Confucian concern as expressed in the *Mean*'s "self-watchfulness" which allows of no doubleness or self-deception; or as found in the doctrine of "sincerity" apotheosized in the final portion of the *Mean*. It is also set forth in the *Great Learning*'s discussion of "making the intention sincere," which was also linked to "self-watchfulness": "To make the intention sincere means allowing of no self-deception, as when we hate a bad smell or love what is good-looking. This is called self-satisfaction. Therefore the noble man is watchful over his solitary self."[122]

In all of his thought Li Chih remains preoccupied with this problem of not deceiving oneself, of being true to the intuitive response of the inner self, and thus of achieving that deep inner satisfaction which was identified with "getting it oneself" or achieving self-realization in the Way.

These ideas were, of course, common property of the Wang Yang-ming school, but common because they trace back to a parentage in the School of the Way and its featured texts, the Four Books. Li Chih's thought too is deeply rooted in these texts, and nothing reveals him as a Neo-Confucian so much as his continual reversion to these themes, or his constant invocation of the *Mean* and *Great Learning* as his basic sources, accepting in effect the extraordinary status accorded them by Chu Hsi.

Li's quest for the sincerity and integrity of the sage, and his exposure of hypocrisy in pretenders to sagehood, mark him as a special student of the *Mean*. But like Wang Yang-ming and Wang Ken he is also much taken with the *Great Learning*, and his thought can be seen as especially focused on the question of how the more intellectual, political, and social problems of this key text are to be defined in terms of the *Mean*'s view of the self as Chu Hsi had interpreted it. Thus Li says of the *Great Learning* that it was intended by Confucius, not just as advice to Duke Ai (who, being the ruler of such a small state as Lu, was in no position to bring peace to all under Heaven), but was meant as a universal doctrine for rulers of later ages:

> I say Confucius was not advising Duke Ai alone but his own students and disciples, with a view to setting forth the correct teaching for all under Heaven and the rulers of all ages to come.
> . . . Now when we read what the *Great Learning* says about the Way to purify all under Heaven, it is indeed complete in itself. It is entirely based on self-questioning, self-answering, self-proclaiming, and self-confirming. He did not have to wait for his students and disciples to inquire [concerning his views on this] but just expressed them for himself. . . . The *Great Learning* says that the ancients wished to manifest lucent virtue to all under Heaven. I say that Confucius wished to manifest lucent virtue to all ages.[123]

"Lucent virtue" *(ming-te)* is for all Neo-Confucians after Chu Hsi the inherent virtuous nature *(te-hsing)* and what constitutes the natural goodness in human beings. (Though sometimes translatable as "the moral nature," *te-hsing* and *ming-te* represent for Li Chih an inherent power not exclusively bound up with conventional virtue—but this is a matter of translation and not an issue here.) For Chu Hsi this "manifesting of the lucent nature" had been the starting point of the process for bringing peace to the world, since, as human nature, it was the innate principle linking the basic reality of human life to the fundamental structure and process of the universe. Li Chih, as we have seen, has little use for Chu Hsi's "principle" *(li)*, but he fully accepts the view of human nature being one with Heaven and Earth [124] and he strongly reaffirms the *Great Learning*'s doctrines of innate virtue as the basis of any polity and of self-cultivation as the key to good government.

In Li Chih's case this constitutes no more than the most general recognition by him of the importance of individual motivation and cooperation without implying any need for popular participation in government. Its immediate application for him is to the recruitment of officials, for, he says (and here quite in line with the traditional wisdom), the basis of good government lies in the selection of men to serve the ruler, which in turn depends on the character of the "persons" so chosen, and this finally on their self-cultivation. [125] On what basis, Li then asks, should this self-cultivation proceed? On the basis of perfecting the virtue of humaneness, which is none other than "reflecting on oneself and looking for the fault within," as Confucius was said to have put it in the passage on finding one's proper station above (*Mean* 13). Two other essential steps in the process of self-cultivation are to "know men" and to "know Heaven," but one knows Heaven through what one knows of man, and man through what one understands of oneself through reflective self-cultivation—not, Li says, by looking outside the self. [126]

In discussing the Three Guiding Principles or Mainstays *(san kang-ling)* of the *Great Learning*, Li puts even more stress than Chu Hsi had on the priority of manifesting or clarifying "lucent virtue" or the virtuous nature. His view of it is influenced, of course, by Wang Yang-ming, but Li has distinct reservations concerning the humanitarian impulse expressed in "loving the people," which Wang and the T'ai-chou school had favored.

> Lucent virtue is the root; loving the people is the branch. Thus it is said [in the *Great Learning*] "Things have their root and their

> branches" and also "From the Son of Heaven down to the com-
> mon man, for all alike self-cultivation is the root." [But] if the
> moral nature is not manifested through cultivation of the self,
> the root is disordered, so how could one hope to set the branches
> in order. . . ?[127]

People who discuss these things today, says Li, set aside the manifesting of lucent virtue and go straight to the discussion of "loving the people." For Li, however, it is essential, before one engages in humanitarian activism on behalf of the people, to address first the need for "manifesting lucent virtue" in the light of "resting in the highest good."[128] In other words he links the first of the Three Guiding Principles directly to the third and assigns a lower priority to the second, namely "loving the people." In one sense this order of priorities corresponds to Chu Hsi's, for Chu too believed that self-cultivation and the manifesting of one's own virtuous nature were prerequisites to renewing the people, inasmuch as one could assist in the renewal of others only to the extent that one had progressed with one's own. In Li's case, however, "resting in the highest good" was understood in the transcendental sense of Wang Chi: as a value that goes beyond ordinary good and evil. Thus, the achievement of a trans-moral enlightenment and spiritual freedom in the pursuit of sagehood, as in Wang Chi, has a higher value than social reform.[129]

Given Li's priorities and his interpretation of the "highest good," one is left to wonder how great a departure this represents from the political priority Chu Hsi had assigned to self-cultivation. We have seen earlier that Chu spoke often of self-cultivation or self-disci-pline as the prime reliance for achieving the governance of men, and that this became a staple of Neo-Confucian political doctrine wherever the movement spread. Li still believes in "the governance of men through self-cultivation," and in his own way remains true to the underlying voluntarism of Ch'eng-Chu thought. Yet, one may ask, in his brand of individualism, does "self-cultivation" still imply "self-discipline," as it did for Ch'eng-Chu? This is a real question, not as easily or simply answered in the negative as critics of his libertarianism might assume.

More often than not Li prefers to express this idea in the slightly different terms of "the governance of man according to the man (or for a less "sexist" but more awkward rendering, of humankind according to the human being, or "through the human individual" *(i-jen chih jen).*[130] There is warrant for this in Chu Hsi's writings, for he was the one who first associated "governing men through self-cultivation *(hsiu-chi chih jen)* and self-government *(tzu-chih).*"[131] Wang Ken too had expressed himself in these terms (see chapter 8). There are extended discussions of this matter in Li's *Tao ku lu,* written at age seventy, which presents his mature interpretation of the Four Books and demonstrates his continuing preoccupation with these core texts of the Neo-Confucian canon. First the locus classicus in the *Mean* 13:

The Master said: "The Way is not far from man. If one pursues the Way and departs from man, it cannot be considered the Way."

In the *Book of Odes* it is said: "In hewing an axe handle, the pattern is not far off. We grasp one axe handle to hew the other; and yet if we look askance from one to the other they might seem far apart. Therefore the noble man governs men according to the man. Once they change, he goes no further. When one is true to himself *(chung)* and treats others likewise [practices reciprocity *(shu)*], he is not far from the Way. What he does not want done to himself, he does not do to others. . . ."[132]

Chu Hsi's commentary on the *Mean* explains this as follows:

The Way does no more than guide man's nature. It is what the common man can know and do. Thus it is never far from man. If in pursuing the Way one condemns what is lowly and close at hand and thinks it not worth doing, but instead feels he must do things that are lofty and remote and hard to practice, then it cannot be considered the Way. . . . If one governs man according to man, the Way by which man is what he is, is found

in each man's person. Fundamentally there is no difference between this man and that. Therefore the noble man's governing
of the man governs according to that man's way. If the man can
change, one goes no further and does not try to govern him any
more. One's reproof is limited to what a man could know and do,
and one does not ask him to pursue a Way that is beyond him.
To fulfill one's own mind-and-heart is being true to oneself. To
infer from oneself and apply it to others is reciprocity . . . not
doing to others what one would not wish done to oneself is a
matter actually of being true to oneself and treating others likewise [practicing reciprocity]. If one gauges others' hearts by one's
own, they are always the same. That the Way is not far from
man can be seen in this. That not departing from the Way is the
actuality of the Way is shown in treating others in accordance
with what one would not want done to oneself. It is, as Chang
Tsai said, loving others as one would love oneself is the fulfillment of humaneness.[133]

Li Chih's discussion of the matter is largely consonant with Chu
Hsi's interpretation, but attempts to pursue further "what is found
in each human being." First of all, Li explains that "governing
humans according to the human being should be premised on the
principle of 'honoring the virtuous nature *(tsun te-hsing)*' ". The
sage, he says, seeks nothing more than this: to act in accordance
with his own nature and rule in accordance with the people's natures, especially in keeping with what is really possible for a human
being.[134] He does not set up an ideal that is too lofty, but echoing
the *Mean* and Chu Hsi, Li says the Way is never far from the
human, and the sage and common humanity are, for these purposes
at least, basically the same. In one of the many passages discussing
this question, Li says:

Essentially the Way is not far removed from the human but to
be far removed from the human is [often] thought of as the
Way. Therefore one cannot speak of the Way, but one can know
that the human is the Way and the Way is human. There is no

Way apart from the human and no human being apart from the Way. Therefore the noble man governs human beings according to the human being and does not dare govern him according to his own preconceptions.

"According to the human being" means essentially to have each one be self-governing. If humans are self-controlled, they are restrained without the need for prohibitions. If one wishes to restrain them without allowing them to be self-governing, it is doing violence to them.

The reason for inability to govern humans according to the human being is the inability to infer from oneself and apply it to another. Therefore the Mean speaks of being true to oneself and treating others as oneself. . . .

It is "not doing to others what one does not wish done to oneself." "What you do not want" follows from the reality of being centered in one's own mind and heart. "Not doing to others" is inferring or projecting from one's own mind-and-heart. If one can do this then one can govern humans according to the human being. . . .

Being true to oneself and treating others as oneself are not the Way but can come close to the Way. Thus it is said [in the *Mean*] one will not be far from the Way. . . .

When one is open in finding fault with others but not open about one's own faults, a discrepancy arises between one's words and one's actions and one does not really know oneself. How much less is one able to infer from oneself and treat others as oneself?

. . . The sage's mind is one that reflects upon himself and finds fault with himself. From this, being true to himself and always considerate of others, he can naturally find himself in a position to treat others as himself.

If one can infer from oneself and extend it to others in order to carry into practice "making an earnest effort to empathize with others," then one is able oneself to "govern humans according to the human being" through a spontaneous and effortless transformation. But if there is such a thing as not being able to infer from oneself and extend it to others, it is because one does not know the Way to reflect on oneself and find the fault in oneself. . . .

If one speaks of "governing according to the human being" one cannot use detailed instructions, prohibitions, and restrictions to do it. Why does the sage speak of education as practicing the Way? The book of the *Mean* is all such teaching, lest men not understand that the Way is not apart from the human. If the human is not apart from the Way, and yet one thinks the Way is far beyond the human, then the more you practice such a Way the further you are from it, the more you try to govern humans [by such a Way] the greater the misgovernment.

Therefore I say the Way is not far beyond the human, and governing humans should be in accordance with the human being. But if you do not know the Way, in the end you cannot practice it and one who does not learn how to understand the human being will not be able to govern him.[135]

Here Li probes further into the meaning of "being true to oneself *(chung)*" and practicing reciprocity, emphasizing the difficulties of genuine introspection and the complications in treating others as oneself when others are different and would not appreciate being treated according to one's own likes and dislikes. There is no simple formula that can be applied in such cases except the need to be honest with oneself and to develop a sensitivity to the subtleties of the Way as it works in different persons:

Thus the sage is no different from others; it is just a matter of not deceiving oneself. The sages' ordering of the state and pacifying of the world are no different from this; it is just a matter of extending this principle of having no self-deception. Thus to have no self-deception is essential, and to make the intention sincere is fundamental. How important it is not to deceive oneself in what one learns from "solitary knowing!" How is it then that in the end humans cannot help deceiving themselves in the matter of self-knowledge? It comes from not knowing that this is the true reality of knowing. Thus when the *Great Learning* speaks of making the intention sincere, it makes extending one's knowledge [learning] the precondition. Extending one's knowledge: That says it all.[136]

From this one can see how Li accepts the principle of voluntarism, so central to Chu Hsi's own thought, and then relentlessly pursues the implications of the twin virtues of reciprocity and self-understanding, which had been the key to this Neo-Confucian teaching. In one sense Li still believes in the common human nature, rooted in undeniable appetites and elementary needs. On the other hand, individuals differ and one cannot assume that their likes and dislikes are the same. This is where one's self-knowledge and sincerity are put to the test—how to recognize that treating others as oneself, in the manner of Confucius' "not doing to others what you would not wish done to yourself," often means restraining oneself from doing to or for others what one would like for oneself. One must be humble and self-critical enough to recognize one's own faults and limitations, and not project on others feelings that are private or peculiar to oneself. One can do this only by being honest with oneself about one's own egoistic tendencies and self-interestedness, and, without projecting, rationalizing, or masking these private feelings as in the interest of others (i.e., representing a common good), granting the same feelings to others as being natural to all. Thus to be unselfish toward others truly means to gain deeper insight into the workings of self-interest, and to extol this self-awareness means, paradoxically, to recognize such self-interestedness as universal, thereby granting a larger place for so-called "human desires," "selfish desires" within the scope of natural or heavenly principles.[137]

To this extent then Li Chih can press outward on the limits of moral and social acceptability, while doing so in the name of that hallowed Neo-Confucian maxim: "Conquer the self and restore riteness *(k'o-chi fu-li)."* "Conquering the self" for him means having insight into one's own selfish conceptions, rationalizations, and prejudices; "restoring riteness" means accepting as a valid social standard customs which are based realistically on the facts of human behavior. Here, instead of challenging the authority of Confucius' dictim or Chu Hsi's interpretation, Li invests riteness with the norms of common custom and rejects a rigoristic, idealistic standard which would insist on rectifying customs and trying to change peoples' natures. Thus he popularizes the notion by identifying the rites and riteness of the sage with the needs of the common man rather than with the exacting standards of a moral elite (such as is represented by the distinction between the "noble man" *(chün-tzu)* and small man *(hsiao jen)*. [138]

Herein lies an issue of some significance depending upon how one understands the traditional Confucian *li:* i.e., whether in the sense of rites or riteness, and whether they/it are to be identified with upper-class standards or with human society generally. The idea of the rites meeting basic human needs and appetites goes all the way back to Hsün Tzu's chapter on Rites. Chu Hsi, for his part saw the classic rites as an aristocratic tradition of the Chou period which needed to be adapted to the changed, and more modest, circumstances of the Sung *shih-ta-fu,* as he did in his *Family Ritual (Chu tzu chia-li).* At the same time Chu, idealistically, upheld a high and exacting social standard for the noble man. Now Li Chih's emphasis on the lowest common denominator of a basic humanity carries to its logical and most radical conclusion the Ming trend toward a populist Confucianism, which stands in contrast to the earlier rigoristic "noblesse oblige" of the *chün-tzu* as the *Tao-hsüeh's* ideal for the Sung leadership elite *(shih-ta-fu).*

Yet something of that ideal survives in Li's self-denying conception of the hero, which shows up here in his interpretation of "conquering one's self and restoring riteness," wherein the self *(chi)* is called upon to be selfless *(wu chi)* in abandoning all preconceived standards or self-serving rationalizations and accept as "rite" the customs and desires of the common people, as Li claims the ancient sages did. [139] In other words, the self *(chi)* is to be selfless *(wu chi)* in recognizing the legitimate self-interest *(ssu)* of the common man as he expresses it naturally from within, not as something imposed on him from outside or above. Likewise "rites" or "riteness" are not a matter of conformity to something external to one, but of true "rites" being "natural rites," conforming to the instinctive desires of human beings.

Yet Li retains the basic Confucian sense of rites and riteness as something differentiated according to circumstances and particularized to the individual. Here the authority of the sage, as representing the highest consciousness of the individual, is invoked against the conventional standards of the educated elite. Thus when it comes to "self-conquest," in place of the moral effort of the noble man's self-discipline or even the active personal engagement of a Wang Ken, we get in Li Chih a higher stage of self-critical enlightenment à la Wang Chi, which primarily understands the self by knowing the Way within,[140] i.e., going beyond any preconceived "good" or "evil."

Whatever the concessions Li is ready to make elsewhere to Legalist "law" in the sense of systems, institutions, and their realistic uses, his preference is still for Confucian rites as a personalized guide to conduct rather than for the impersonality of universal laws. "Rites are the great root of all under Heaven."[141] At the same time Li's radically individualistic approach shows itself in his laissez-faire view of "riteness" as essentially indefinable, being based on a self-introspection that must vary with the person. Here the only universals he will acknowledge are the seemingly Taoist ones of doing what comes naturally *(tzu-jan)* or "doing nothing" *(wu-wei)* in the sense of doing nothing unnatural. As we have seen "doing nothing" for Li does not preclude a certain activism if the times warrant it; thus the Confucian sage-kings Shun and the great Yü had outstanding accomplishments in their own times, as did the first emperor of the Ch'in and the Emperor Wu of Han, each in accordance with the historical circumstances he faced.[142]

Li's criteria for "doing nothing," other than historical adaptability, do indeed have a Taoist ring. The sage ruler, he says, "does not look after things yet they are spontaneously ordered; he takes no action but naturally commands respect, does not speak yet receives credence, gives no rewards but people are spontaneously encouraged, vents no angry reproof yet his authority is made manifest; makes no display of himself and yet becomes a model for all; makes no manifest effort and yet accomplishes the transformation of the people."[143]

Li is aware that this kind of language will be interpreted as Taoistic or Ch'an Buddhist, and so he makes a point of characterizing this rule of the sage in terms used by the *Mean*. Echoing Wang Chi, he says, "This is what is called 'genuine reverence' (or 'sincere respectfulness,' *tu-kung*) which brings peace to all under Heaven (as it says in Chu Hsi's concluding commentary to the *Mean* 33).[144] It is no mystery (*hsüan*, i.e., not Taoism or Neo-Taoism). It is not Ch'an Buddhism. It is the language of our Confucius."[145] Thus he attributes to the classical Confucian tradition an attitude of reverence or piety which springs from a primordial source in the ancient religiosity underlying all three Teachings. As described in the metaphysical language of the *Mean* it represents the Confucian equivalent of "doing nothing," which for Li points to the common ground of a religious humanism in terms of which all traditions may be reevaluated and reconciled.

In a sense, this is what the Ch'engs and Chu Hsi had done in putting forth the Neo-Confucian doctrine of reverence *(ching)*, providing a Confucian interpretation for such Taoist concepts as "quiescence" *(ching)* or "naturalness" *(tzu jan)* or for a Buddhist concept like "having no mind" *(wu-hsin)*. Li, we have noted before, rejects the Neo-Confucian doctrine of "having no mind" as essentially unnatural, and brings this same critique to bear on the reinterpretation of "doing nothing," again drawing on the Taoist-sounding language of the *Mean*:

> The learning of the sage does nothing and yet all is accomplished *(wu-wei erh ch'eng)*.[146] But those who talk about "doing nothing" today, only speak of "not minding" (lit. "having no mind")

(wu-hsin). However, once you start talking about the mind-and-heart, how can you speak about "having no mind"? And when you start talking about "doing," how can you "do something" without having a mind [to do it]. If a peasant did not "mind" [what he was about], his fields would surely go to weeds. If the artisan did not mind [what he was about], his tools would surely get ruined. If the scholar did not mind [what he was about], his task would certainly be left undone. How is it possible "not to mind"?

Some explain this "not minding" as meaning not that one literally has "no mind" but that one has no selfish mind or intention. Now "self-interest" is "man's minding." Man must be self-interested if his mind is to be made known. If he were not self-interested, there would be no mind. It is like tending a field; there must first be some self-interest to obtain the autumn's harvest before one would go to the "effort of working the field." [147] Or like the husbandman, there must first be the self-interest to gain by "storing things up" [148] before one will go to the effort of husbandry. Or like the scholar, there must first be the desire for self-advancement before one will undertake to prepare for examinations.

Thus an officer who had no thought of gaining the emoluments of office would not be responsive to an invitation to serve. If he were to have no high rank, no amount of exhortation could persuade a man to come forth and serve. And even in the case of a sage like Confucius, if there were no office of Minister of Justice by which he shared in the business of governing he certainly would not have found even a day of service in the state of Lu tolerable. This is a natural principle, to which practice must conform. One cannot just engage in airy talk and groundless speculation. . . .

Confucius said "the humane man first faces the difficulties and only later thinks of the rewards [*Analects* 6:20]. He speaks of facing the difficulties first, after which one could expect some reward. He does not say there should be no seeking for reward at all, nothing aimed at, and all done thoughtlessly and without any consideration.

Thus if you wish to be true to moral principle, there must be some thought of gain. If there is no thought of gain, there can be no "being true." If the Way is to be made manifest, one's own success must thereby be accomplished. If there is no consideration of one's own success, how can the Way ever be made manifest? Now if someone says that in the learning of the Sage there is no self-interestedness, and thus no such aim could be allowed, how could anyone aim to achieve sagehood?[149]

In the end, Li argues, "doing nothing" cannot be mindless or disinterested, nor can it depend on whether one chooses to act or not. It depends rather on how the individual ruler or statesman uses his capabilities for dealing with the needs and circumstances of the times. The Emperor Wen of Han was no activist but his laissez-faire policies in the given circumstances laid the basis for the dynasty's prosperity; the Emperor Wu, an activist, by his military undertakings made China's borders secure for years to come. Some Confucians had grandiose ambitions to "do something" but overreached themselves and failed to accomplish a thing; other Confucians possessed great talents, but for fear of being thought selfish-minded or ambitious, failed to act resolutely and thus let their capabilities be wasted. Those who have been true to themselves and have not let themselves be confused by empty talk are the sages: they are the ones for whom "doing nothing" means doing what comes naturally to one in the circumstances, with one's given abilities.[150]

For Li, then, "doing nothing" and doing "what comes naturally" *(tzu jan)* are no longer just Taoist concepts, but in this rather special sense of Li's have become the keys to "governing humans according to the human being," i.e., according to the individual case. At the same time Li has redefined in these terms Chu Hsi's principle that self-cultivation (self-discipline) is the basis of good government *(hsiu-chi chih-jen)*, emphasizing self-expression rather than self-discipline. In that this interpretation still keeps to the voluntarism underlying Ch'eng-Chu thought, stressing the role of the individual in the relations of ruler and ruled, and in that it also allows scope for a certain activism *(yu-wei)* in accordance with the new conception of the natural *(tzu-jan)* in Sung-Ming thought,[151] Li's views of "doing nothing," and "governing men according to the human being" represent a further development of individualistic tendencies in Neo-Confucianism, and not just a relapse into Taoist quietism.

Similarly with Li's frequent emphasis on "rites" and "riteness." For Confucians, "rites" had always signified a formal order consonant with the principle of voluntarism and in contrast to a Legalist emphasis on the coercive enforcement of laws. Li Chih places himself squarely in this Confucian tradition and, in the passages translated above, renounces the use of laws and prohibitions. Thus "governing humans according to the human being" *(i-jen chih jen)* takes on the meaning of "governing according to the ways of man" as expressed in social traditions which embody the principle of live and let live—and again, not according to the likes or dislikes of idealistic reformers who would take it upon themselves to rectify popular customs.

Moreover, following through on the Neo-Confucian idea of "conquering the self and restoring riteness," Li again affirms the importance of the social order but rejects conventional decorum and leaves the individual free to judge according to his own lights. In this perspective Li's admiration for "legalist" type rulers can be seen as less an endorsement of the Legalist philosophy itself, than an expression of Li's penchant for heroic figures who exemplify the sage individual—one who is above all true to himself, finds the Way in himself, and as Mencius says, can draw deeply on its power in any situation.

Undoubtedly this gave Li himself a great sense of spiritual freedom and enlightenment, releasing extraordinary natural energies and critical powers. His was a brilliant display of "manifesting lucent virtue" intellectually, enabling his critical faculties to penetrate the pretensions of others to sagely wisdom or humanitarian virtue. In both scholarship and literature the gains were great, but the price was also high. For in so insisting upon the indefinability of truth, the emptiness of principle, and the utter spontaneity of action, Li offered no basis other than a laissez-faire approach—live and let live—on which to predicate a new human order. In this respect, by following Wang Chi's view of man's inherent nature as beyond good and evil, indeed beyond all predication, he left no substantial foundation upon which to build a structure of rights or entitlements for the individual. As Ray Huang has aptly put it, assessing the significance for Li Chih of Wang Chi's view of innate knowing as beyond good and evil: "Innate knowledge, which alone is real, transcends all physical characteristics, properties and inclinations. It is not non-being, yet it exists without a trace. When the argument had reached this point, the displacement of Confucian ethics by Buddhist metaphysics was apparent."[152] Just so, there could be no fulfillment in Li Chih of the Neo-Confucian educational imperative to "renew the people" through any defined social program.

For Li the ultimate value was sincerity, the natural expression of the inherent goodness in each individual. To the extent that its practice also led him to acknowledge and expose the natural "self-interestedness" of man, and to insist on honestly facing up to the evil in man, one can say that this "sincerity" involved him in the struggle for individual authenticity. Both of these impulses derived from the core of Neo-Confucian teaching, but went beyond the original optimistic formulation in the Ch'eng-Chu teaching and strove for a new realism.

Chu Hsi's realism and Li Chih's were of different sorts, but each of them had to cope with the evil and suffering in human life, and each experienced tragedy in his last days. Chu Hsi's final political defeat came not long before his death in official disgrace, and as a consequence of this we have a most revealing episode which may reflect some light on Li Chih.

Following his forced retirement from the court, Chu had worked on and completed his commentary on the *Elegies of Ch'u (Ch'u tz'u)*, an early work expressing the sorrows of Ch'u Yüan over the political injustice done him. This was not in the usual line of classical or philosophical studies Chu Hsi engaged in, and one of his disciples Yang Chi (1142–1213) took particular note of the fact that Chu, on hearing of the martyrdom in exile of the ex-premier Chao Ju-yü, under whom he had served, suddenly showed his students his commentary on the *Ch'u tz'u.* Deeply affected by Chao's death, Chu would not discuss it directly but preferred to let Ch'u Yüan and his own commentary speak for him. In the view of Yang Chi this was a most extraordinary step for Chu Hsi, who usually based his instruction on the Four Books, Five Classics, histories, and biographies, and rarely drew attention to poetry of the Ch'in-Han period. But in Chu's preface we find these words:

> Ch'u (Yüan)'s ambitions and actions may have exceeded the mean and cannot serve as a model, but they sprang from a sincere heart, loyal to his ruler and devoted to his country. As for his writings, although the meaning of his words may tend to be unrestrained and even demonic, and hatred and resentment so welled up in them that they are inappropriate to serve as moral teachings, nevertheless all of them are the products of the most honest sentiments of profound concern and sad worry, which he could not stop from feeling in spite of himself.[153]

One wonders if Chu Hsi, had he known Li Chih, would not have rendered a somewhat similar judgment on him. When Chu says that Chü Yüan would not serve as a model for others and yet one could not but feel deeply for his "sincere heart" and "loyal devotion," one might well imagine him expressing similar feelings for Li Chih's "sincerity"—his "honest sentiments of profound concern and sad worry, which he could not stop from feeling in spite of himself"—while at the same time he would have rejected Li's ideas as a sound basis for education, "inappropriate to serve as moral teachings."

CAUSE AND COUNTER-CAUSE

Modern writers have often seen Li Chih as suffering a kind of martyrdom for his convictions. To what cause then did he himself die a martyr? Some might say to the cause of intellectual freedom. If so, they are putting it in modern Western terms and not those of Li himself. He has lived and died for the Way, which for him meant no cause other than pursuit of the Way and self-realization. Clearly his cause implies the affirmation of his own integrity as an individual and his faith in the inherent worth of all human beings. Yet it remains doubtful that he means to assert the equal right of all individuals to express themselves freely. In an abstract way he does believe that humans should have the freedom to develop and express themselves with the least possible interference—Lao Tzu's freedom to be left alone. But in practice, as we have seen, he has no program leading to the general exercise of political freedom or public discussion, and he applauds strong rulers who have suppressed such discussion. As a believer in the economic survival of the fittest, he expects that inequalities will necessarily result from differences in people's capabilities and the weak will be compelled to submit to the strong.[154] In this light, then, we can say only that Li Chih died for his own convictions, and not necessarily in the cause of intellectual freedom for all.

The significance of Li's "martyrdom" must also be seen against the background of the times. Among recent writers the view has generally prevailed that Li's unconventionality and independence of mind inevitably made him the object of remorseless attack by the traditionalists, the ruling class ("feudalistic reactionaries" or entrenched bureaucrats, as you will), bigoted and hypocritical Confucianists—and so on down the list of those who could be identified with the "establishment" and whose vested interests were threatened by Li's revolutionary ideas. Moreover, his conduct "aroused a custom-loving and conformist society to rise up and vilify him."[155]

Alongside such views one would have to put the comment of Li's good friend and admirer Yüan Chung-tao, who, in a postface to a

1613 edition of Li's works, says: "When Cho-wu [Li Chih] was arrested, there was some suppression of his books, but within a few years they reappeared and circulated everywhere. In this one can see how far the liberality of our dynasty toward its scholars exceeds that of the Sung dynasty [which suppressed the works of Su Shih]."[156]

To the historian of the late Ming neither of these views adequately represents the reality. In Yüan's statement there is no doubt some calculated flattery. If the Ming had been as wholly liberal as he says, there would have been no need for him to say anything at all about the matter, and Li Chih, instead of meeting so dramatic an end, would have had to suffer the disappointment of dying a natural death in his own bed. But of the two views Yüan's is certainly much closer to the truth. The suppression of books in the late Ming was rarely so systematic and prolonged as to be fully effective, and in any case Li's works were quickly reprinted after his death. Yüan writes hardly more than a decade after Li's demise and already Li's books are widely available. Many writers testify to their enormous popularity with all segments of the literate population.[157] A number found their way to Japan and enjoyed a comparable popularity there. Indeed, so great was his reputation and popularity that his name was attached to many spurious works as a means of increasing sales.[158]

What really undid Li's reputation in the long run and deferred for centuries the recognition he so confidently expected history to bring, was in fact not the immediate smothering of his ideas and destruction of his books by pharisaical censors, but their powerful appeal to the taste for sensational and shocking literature among the sophisticated reading public of the late Ming. This taste obviously extended to the ruling classes, for they comprised the majority of literate persons. And if they delighted in Li's mordant wit and unsparing ridicule of the Confucians, his irreverence, disillusionment, and cynicism plainly reflected a deep deterioration of morale and inner crisis within the ruling class itself.[159]

It was therefore not the conventionalism or repressiveness of late Ming society which undid Li Chih, but its decadence in the eyes of the conquering Manchu dynasty, who did not wait long to proscribe Li's books and enforce the ban with far more ruthless efficiency than the Ming.[160] There is irony in this too, of course. For the Ch'ing not only were masters in the art of governing through attractive rewards and unhesitating punishments, but they followed up their military conquest with an administration that could hardly be matched for its success in promoting the people's material welfare while sapping or suppressing all resistance among the educated class. Li Chih would have found it hard to withhold his admiration.

But it would be misleading to imply that it was the Manchus who really disposed of Li and his ideas. The real counterattack was mounted by the scholars themselves, and among them men whose reputation for intellectual integrity and moral courage is not easily questioned. It is often said that Huang Tsung-hsi, Ku-Yen-wu, and Wang Fu-chih are the three leading thinkers and scholars of the early Ch'ing period. Huang's attitude toward Li we have already seen. Though probably the most objective of the early historians of Ming thought, and certainly the most sympathetic in his approach to it, his attitude toward Li is one of such profound hostility and resentment that he will not even dignify him with criticism.[161] Ku Yen-wu, on the other hand, devotes a section of his famous *Jih-chih lu* to Li and the corrupting influence of Ch'an and the left wing of the Wang Yang-ming school on public morality and the civil service in the late Ming. To him there had never been anyone in Chinese history so shameless and so audacious as Li in his rebellion against Confucian teaching.[162] Wang Fu-chih, though sharing many of Li's "progressive" views in philosophy, history, and politics, and notably his kind of quasi materialism, nevertheless reacted in horror to Li's seeming total abandonment of moral standards. He describes him as a man who has lost all conscience, and says that Li's *Book To Be Hidden Away* has done incalculable harm.[163]

None of these judgments can be dismissed as simply conventional or unthinking. Huang, Ku, and Wang had maintained their intellectual independence of the Ch'ing establishment, refusing to serve the new dynasty, and it is much more likely that their own views on Li influenced the official one rather than the other way around.[164] Moreover, Wang cut himself off from the world far more than did Li.[165] To him it is Li who took the conventional path, who "followed the crowd," "catered to human passions," and made no distinction between legitimate and illegitimate, noble and base desires.[166]

These judgments reflect, in fact, a reaction already fully apparent in the late Ming dynasty. If Li's writings were widely read in the early seventeenth century, there were important segments of the scholarly community who saw Li's influence as a great danger to the whole social and moral fabric of Chinese life. These were men who took an active role in the political life of the time, and are important not because of their identification with the "establishment," but because as reformers they spoke out vigorously and courageously against the political corruption at court as well as the moral decadence within the educated classes. I refer, of course, to the Tung-lin school and party, and to colleagues of theirs like Liu Tsung-chou, the teacher of Huang Tsung-hsi. Although they tended to be wary of the cult of "heroism," because they associated it with opportunism, they too were great enemies of cant, conventionalism, and hypocrisy.[167] Many of them paid with their lives in Ming prisons for the courage of their convictions, as did Huang's own father.[168]

Since these were men of great courage and fierce dedication, it is perhaps understandable that their judgment of Li Chih was no less moralistic than his was of others. It became a "cause" with them to subdue the heresy of Li's moral spontaneity. Shih Meng-lin wrote:

Today the leaders of "philosophical discussion" *(chiang-hsüeh)* and education generally direct scholars to "live in the present." This is most solid advice. But if you ask how, they say it is like eating when hungry or sleeping when tired; one does these things naturally and spontaneously, completely without exertion. . . . [However] to give rein to one's feelings and lusts—so interpreted, "living in the present" becomes a deep pit to ensnare people. . . .

When Li Cho-wu [Li Chih] discoursed in Nanking on the learning of the mind, all his directions to his pupils consisted of "living in the present" and "spontaneity." He said that every man is a ready-made sage. When anyone spoke about loyal, chaste, filial, or righteous people, he said that all this was artificial. . . . Students were pleased by this easy formula and flocked to him like mad. . . . Therefore, not to recognize that "living in the present" truly means for the student to take up the immediate moral task is to cast men into a deep pit.[169]

A similar view is expressed by Tsou Shan,[170] of the moderate wing of the Wang Yang-ming school. When asked about the great popularity of Li Chih, he explained that according to Li "the desires for wine, sex, money, and power do not block the road to Buddhahood. Who would not want to follow someone who sanctioned such things?"[171]

The official indictment against Li had accused him of, among other things, disporting himself with worthless fellows and lewd women in the temple, bathing with them in broad daylight, and corrupting nuns and the wives and daughters of the gentry, who slept there with him.[172] Some of the charges have been discredited, and others are no doubt exaggerated.[173] At his age Li could not have written so many books had he engaged in that much dissipation. Yet Li himself made no pretense of following monastic discipline, and might not have considered it a favor to be exonerated of the charge if it meant that he was prepared to abide by such standards. Yüan Chung-tao, in his sympathetic portrait of Li, says, "He had nothing much to do with music or women and little use for love and lust, and yet when his mood was so disposed and his affections aroused, he would enjoy to the fullest the company of some boy or girl amidst the flowers and the moonlight, as if to embellish his solitary existence."[174]

Li's attitude, then, was probably not too different from that of the Japanese monk Kenkō, who had a reputation as a "sensual monk" *(iro bōshi)*, and whose *Tsurezuregusa* expresses a similarly epicurean attitude toward sexual indulgence.[175] In any case Li's commentary on the Heart Sūtra shows that, in principle, he did believe as Tsou Shan said that the passions are no obstacle to Buddhahood, because they are in themselves empty. The enlightened one knows that the passions are no different from emptiness, and that there is no emptiness apart from the passions. Since he has no attachments, indulgence leaves on him no stain of sin. "There is no impurity in the passions, no purity in emptiness."[176] As a deep student of the Prajñāpāramitā literature, Li no doubt derives this view from Nāgārjuna's *Ta chih-t'u lun* (Treatise on the great perfect wisdom) which provides the scriptural basis for the doctrine that "Lustful desires are identical with the Way" *(yin-yü chi-shih tao)*,[177] from which developed the saying that "the passions are enlightenment" [or Buddhahood] *(fan-nao chi p'u-t'i)*.[178]

That Li Chih took the full freedom which such a doctrine might allow is indicated by the criticism of him which came even from within Buddhist circles. The monk Chu-hung, whose approach to the unity of the Three Teachings reflects the moral dynamism of the Wang Yang-ming school more than the affirmation of man's physical and appetitive nature,[179] has these things to say about Li:

> I respect Li Chih's superior talents and heroic spirit, but if I respect them I also have my regrets. For a man to have such great talents and spirit and yet not take the sages' teachings as a guide or traditional norms as a foundation, for him not to govern these powers with virtue and magnanimity or to restrain them with caution meant inevitably that his talk about "shocking the world in order to reform evil customs" would be only a matter of self-indulgence.[180]

Given the severity of Li's judgments on worthy men of the past, says Chu-hung, it was inevitable that "the fire he set should eventually burn him too."[181] "He did not keep to the hills and forests, but enjoyed himself in the towns and cities."[182] Li's unrestrained actions and wild talk violated the norms of Buddhism. "A monk should think of his obligation to the state and not flout its laws. . . . To kill such a criminal is not contrary to the precepts of Buddhism."[183]

Chu-hung's stern repudiation of Li Chih is almost matched by the Ts'ao-tung sect monk Yüan-hsien, who accused Li Chih of "pursuing the Way through the passions. He never failed to indulge his passions. No matter how wide his learning became, nor how broad his knowledge grew, his egotism only thrived the more."[184]

In the light of these statements Li Chih's "cause" and the reaction it evoked cannot be interpreted in relation to traditional Confucianism or Buddhism alone, or to established convention, or to the Ming-Ch'ing "establishment." The individualism of which he is the final and most radical expression arose as one tendency within the optimistic humanitarianism of the T'ai-chou school. It generated enthusiasm and energy from the fact that it appealed to common elements in the Three Teachings, and yet it also tended to generate a common reaction within at least two of them, Confucianism and Buddhism. The point of original convergence had been the goodness of human nature, a persistent belief of the Chinese[185] but intensified at this moment by the almost ecstatic view of this-worldly salvation which was such a powerful element in Ming thought. The exaltation of self and of the individual, based on the belief in every man's potentiality for sagehood, drew some of its plausibility from the Mahāyāna Buddhist idea of universal salvation, and more particularly from the Ch'an belief that the Buddha-nature is inherent in all beings. But in Li Chih we can see how the original moral basis of Confucian sagehood has undergone a sharp transformation, while the Buddhist awareness of egoism and selfish craving, which is the starting point of all its philosophy and discipline, no longer serves the same purpose. As the original T'ai-chou optimism concerning human nature evaporated under the stresses of actual life, Li Chih himself reflects disillusionment, but it is turned toward a new this-worldly enlightenment and liberation of the self. Within both the Confucian and the Buddhist communities, on the other hand, there is a strong reassertion of the need for discipline, the one calling for moral effort and civic action, the other, for a renewed insistence on the rooting out of egotism and the dispelling of a delusory sense of freedom.[186]

Thus within both Confucianism and Buddhism there is a noticeable effort to recover their former balance. But it is a static balance, not a dynamic one, and we are left to ponder whether the new humanitarianism and individualism of the Ming remained only a momentary enthusiasm, without any real substance, or might still in some way have contributed to the enlargement of the Chinese spirit.

THE LIMITATIONS OF LI CHIH'S INDIVIDUALISM

When Li Chih died he left no disciples or school to carry on his work or further any "cause." This was as he intended it. He did not wish to become a teacher, gather students, start a school, or organize a movement. And it was not just a matter of personal preference, but one of principle.[187] On the other hand, this would be another way of saying that his "cause" too was an individual one, and provided no ground for establishing within the society any wider basis for the exercise of individual freedom.

It may be argued that in any case the historical situation did not allow for such a thing. Individualism of the Western type is a product of a different historical development. In China the extreme weakness of the middle class, the nondevelopment of a vigorous capitalism, the absence of a church which fought for its rights against the state, or of competing religions which sought to defend the freedom of conscience against arbitrary authority; the lack of university centers of academic freedom, deriving from their original function as monastic sanctuaries; the want of a free press supported by an educated middle class—the list, of course, is almost endless of the elements lacking in China which contributed in some way to the rise of Western types of individualism.

Carson Chang, in attempting an even-handed judgment of Li Chih, balances his criticism of seventeenth-century China as a "custom-loving and conformist society" with the comment on Li Chih that "he had only himself to blame. His unconventionality could only have been tolerated in a country where fundamental rights were well-protected."[188] This, however, begs the question. What would one do who wished in China to establish such fundamental rights? Would not one run the same risks as Li Chih did in speaking out? Would he not be given the same advice that Li got from Keng Ting-hsiang: that it is imprudent to insist on one's views if they are unpopular? But on the other hand, so far as rights are concerned, may we not ask of Li Chih whether he had any intentions whatever in regard to "fundamental human rights"?

In view of all that has gone before, this is a question difficult to answer in the affirmative, and yet some aspects of it deserve to be considered. If we speak of "fundamental rights," some basis in law, custom, or institutions is implied, but whether Li's historical and moral relativism will allow him to establish a fundamental human basis for law, apart from the institutions that satisfy man's biological needs, is a real question.

Here Li's views are not only so unconventional, but in some fundamental ways so *radically individual,* that they do not lend themselves to characterization either in modern terms or even in the conventional terms of traditional thought. We have seen above that for all his admiration of strong rulers who sometimes employed so-called Legalist methods, in the final analysis Li did not put his reliance on laws but on something more like the traditional Confucian rites. These he saw as recognizing and nurturing individual variation and voluntarism, rites rooted in a primordial religiosity of fundamental respect for life and human creativity—something he saw as underlying and common to all Three Teachings.

Again, as we have seen, his resort at times to Taoist or Buddhist language for different ways of expressing this underlying religiosity—in such terms as "doing nothing" *(wu-wei)* or doing "what comes naturally" *(tzu-jan)*—was acknowledged by Li as a possible source of confusion. Thus he insists that it is really "no mystery" (i.e., not Taoism) nor "Ch'an Buddhism" [as some will suspect], but something best described "in the language of our Confucius." Translated, perhaps the closest one could come to it is "natural rites" or "human rites." But the concept remains so radically individual and laissez-faire that one wonders by what corporate or institutional means it could become embodied in human society.

To the extent that Li might turn in the direction of Buddhist "law," it may not offer much more hope for the assertion or defense of fundamental human rights. The principle of indeterminacy implicit in Mādhyamika Buddhism could not easily serve as a positive basis for law in the legal or constitutional sense.[189] When, above, he refused to stand on the idea of No-Nothingness, Li realized that it was only a transitory moment in the dialectics of negation, and not a double negative constituting an affirmative.

The traditional position of the Buddhist clergy, moreover, is exemplified by the monk Hui-yüan, who argued for the religious freedom of the monk and his independence of state authority precisely on the ground that the monastic life represents a *different* life from that of the ordinary citizen or householder. He claimed a special status for the monk, an immunity from the demands which the ruler might legitimately make upon the ordinary man. In other words, he defends the monk's right to leave the world, while acknowledging and confirming the ruler's complete authority over those who remain in it.[190]

That Hui-yüan's view remained the predominant, if not the "orthodox" view among Ming Buddhists, is indicated by the quotation from Yüan-hsien above (pp. 264–65), when he insists that the monk, in return for the special favor he enjoys in the pursuit of the religious life, is obliged to uphold the established laws and customs. By and large, therefore, the attitude of Ming Buddhists was neutral toward social problems, possibilities for legal reform, or the establishment of any new order within the world of men.[191]

Although there were exceptions, like the monk Ta-kuan who admired Li Chih and followed him in martyrdom, "the great mass of Buddhists shrank back into or persisted in an attitude of passivity and conformity."[192]

Li's individualism then did enable him to achieve a large measure of intellectual independence, to rise considerably above the traditional limits of his culture (above most of the cultural determinants of Buddhism as well as Confucianism) and to envisage a new world —one might almost say a modern world, except that it transcends not only the parochial limits of traditional culture but even the limits of a modernism perhaps too closely identified with one particular conception of law. Nevertheless, having stripped himself of all social or cultural support, he stands there naked and alone, without the means to create any new order or to protect himself from the old.

In the traditional Chinese context, however, we may consider all the more remarkable the achievement in the seventeenth century of Huang Tsung-hsi, who in his *Ming-i tai-fang lu* saw clearly that Chinese absolutism could never be restrained or individual freedom guaranteed without the establishment of fundamental law and the creation of independent centers for free discussion.[193] We cannot help asking how much the free thought and widespread skepticism of the late Ming contributed to this attempt at reconciling the age-old conflict between Legalist "law" and the Confucian respect for the human person, by challenging Huang to a more radical reexamination of tradition than even Li Chih had attempted.

Yet Huang Tsung-hsi's ideas, too, were suppressed by Manchu absolutism with the able assistance of Confucian scholars. To the extent that this repression arose partly in reaction to the "heresies" of Li Chih, and was justified by the necessity to reestablish traditional law, order, and morality,[194] the shock of Li Chih's challenge to tradition may have had a double effect. While some men were provoked to deeper thought, others reacted to the threat of moral and social anarchy in Li Chih's thought with renewed efforts and more drastic means to preserve the purity of Chinese tradition.

From this limited survey of the Wang Yang-ming school we may perhaps draw a few general conclusions.

1. A type of individualistic thought with strikingly modern features did arise, in conjunction with larger social and cultural forces, out of a liberal and humanitarian movement within the Wang Yang-ming school in the sixteenth century. Thus Confucianism, though the dominant tradition and, to some modern eyes, an authoritarian system, proved capable of fulfilling somewhat the same function as that credited by Professor Butterfield to medieval Christianity in the rise of Western individualism. "If religion produced the authoritarian system, it also produced the rebellion against the system, as though the internal aspect of the faith were at war with the external. The total result over the long medieval period may have been a deepening of personality, a training of conscience, and a heightening of the sense of individual responsibility, particularly in the matter of religion itself."[195]

2. Within this general movement one form of "positive" individualism was represented by Ho Hsin-yin, who attempted to establish it first in the clan community as an egalitarian concept and then in the context of the larger scholarly community. This attempt failed, in the absence of a strong middle-class base, for want of support from the scholar-official class and because of the inability of the schools, academies, and scholarly associations to maintain their independence of the ruling power. To a degree then, the premonition of Lord Acton that the great danger to individual liberty in the twentieth century would come from the monolithic state was borne out in China even before Acton's time.[196]

3. Another radical form of individualism represented by Li Chih, though distinguishable in the originality of its thought

from the traditional forms of dissent, Buddhism and Taoism, tended in the end toward an individualism of disassociation — affirmative with respect to humankind in general and discrete persons in particular, but incapable of establishing itself in any public philosophy or infrastructure of laws and institutions. Though Li too felt the repressive power of the state, if this analysis is correct, the rejection of Li's ideas by leading scholars and prelates was a more fundamental factor in the failure of his type of individualism to sustain itself as a historical movement.

We have been concerned here with that strain of radical thought most nearly resembling individualistic thought in the modern West, and yet in the larger perspective of world history we would have difficulty in holding to the latter as a norm for China. Subsequent history, indeed, has not brought China any closer to such a norm despite even the revolutionary changes of the twentieth century. The possibility must be allowed for that any type of individualism which develops in the future may tend more to keep within the allowable limits of Chinese tradition than to expand to the outer limits of Western forms of individualism.

10. Lü Liu-liang's Radical Orthodoxy

Orthodoxy and radicalism rarely go together, but fundamentalism can lead either way, and, in the Neo-Confucian school, sometimes to both at once. That this could be so is suggested by the case of at least one strong individualist, Lü Liu-liang (1629–83), avowedly both a Confucian fundamentalist and orthodox Neo-Confucian, who proved to be not only a political radical but, in the eyes of the state, a dangerous revolutionary.

Though not considered, like Huang Tsung-hsi, one of the Three Great Scholars of the early Ch'ing period, Lü is without question a figure to be reckoned with. An active partisan in the unsuccessful resistance to the Manchus, who subsequently refused all invitations to serve them, he has gone down in history as a symbol of unremitting hostility to China's foreign conquerors. He is known also, however, as the most articulate spokesman of the orthodox Neo-Confucian revival, which came to be identified ideologically with the very dynasty he struggled against. If this seems too contradictory, anyone who still believed that orthodoxies and establishments always go together, might perhaps explain it in terms of Lü's diehard loyalism, the essential conservatism of which would inevitably prove congenial to the new dynasty, regardless of Lü's personal animus against it. Yet even that characterization of him as an intransigent Tory does not match up well with his radical political views, nor does it hold up in the light of the quixotic turns his life took time and again, later on.

Historians have been intrigued by several facets of that life: by his early friendship with Huang Tsung-hsi—bearing such promise of collaboration between two outstanding scholars—which, however, soon turned into a bitter feud; by the seeming inconsistency of his scorn for those who took part in the civil service examinations and his own great success as an editor of examination essays that they bought in great numbers; by what seems to have been an obsessive hatred and fear of Buddhism, giving way in the end to Lü's enigmatic gesture of taking the tonsure; and by the dramatic way in which he was posthumously charged with inciting a rebellion years after his own demise. With such puzzles and paradoxes to attract them, scholars have worked away at Lü's life and, insofar as the record, heavily censored by the Manchus, would allow them to do so, have established its main outlines with some care.[1] Here a brief summation may suffice.

Lü was born in 1629; his home, like Huang Tsung-hsi's, was in Eastern Chekiang province, an area rich in history and culture, and especially in historians and philosophers. His family were well-established members of the educated elite who had been scholar-officials for generations and local leaders known for their philanthropy and sense of community responsibility. There is nothing unusual about his educational experience except that, from an early age, instead of looking upon his study of the Neo-Confucian curriculum as routine, he described himself as deeply impressed and inspired by the works of Chu Hsi. Several scholars have noted the religious intensity with which he took to Chu Hsi as his guide in life.[2] Along with this went a deep sense of loyalty to the Ming, despite increasing signs of the dynasty's weakness and eventual collapse. With other members of his family and community, he took part, even at a young age, in the resistance movement carried on in his region against the Manchus, but when that proved futile, in 1647 he gave it up and returned home to a more normal pattern of life.

This pattern included passing the first level of civil service examinations, which he did in 1653, thus maintaining his family's membership in the ranks of the official literati, with the status of *sheng-yüan*, i.e., a stipendiary or licentiate, officially registered as a candidate for the higher examinations and some form of public service. He remained in this privileged status for thirteen years, during which he quickly made a name for himself as a scholar and in his sideline occupation as an editor of examination essays. The latter sold well, given the reading public's special orientation toward literature useful for official careers, and given too his own talents for philosophical analysis, lucid exposition, and literary style.

As a conscientious Neo-Confucian, however, Lü could not be insensitive to the ambiguities of his situation. No devoted reader of Chu Hsi could fail to observe what the latter had said about "learning for one's own sake, rather than for the sake of others" (the latter most often understood as studying for the examinations); nor could he have been unaware of the revulsion generations of Neo-Confucians had expressed over the eight-legged essay as a travesty of true classical learning. As we shall see later, Lü had a well-reasoned defense for his work on the essays, but his privileged status as a stipendiary *(sheng-yüan)* was more difficult to justify in one whose Ming loyalist, anti-Manchu sentiments, strictly held to, would seem to preclude any semblance of accepting favors from the new dynasty. Thus by 1666 he had decided to take the drastic step of renouncing *sheng-yüan* status—no easy thing to do in a society providing few alternative careers for the educated outside of officialdom. That Lü could succeed at all in this testifies to his native scholarly talent and resourcefulness at commercial enterprise, but also to his continued willingness to compromise on the eight-legged essay business, which he did more or less actively for some years thereafter.[3]

Meanwhile Lü maintained close personal relations with some of the leading scholars of his day. True, he was a strong-minded, irascible—and some said arrogant—type, whose break with Huang Tsung-hsi, ostensibly over a book-buying deal, was not the only evidence of Lü's being a difficult person to get along with. Nevertheless, he was respected by other prominent figures in the revival of Neo-Confucian orthodoxy, whose thinking he deeply influenced, and it was not for lack of opportunities to enjoy state patronage that he withdrew increasingly from most social involvements, and eventually, as a tactic in resisting pressure upon him to accept distinguished-scholar status at the Manchu court, took the Buddhist tonsure. There is no indication that this represented a religious conversion or a total withdrawal from conventional society. Up until his death in 1683 Lü continued to work on scholarly projects, republishing Chu Hsi's works, editing examination essays, and meeting with his students. He had often pleaded poverty as a condition extenuating his mercenary activities in book-dealing and publishing, but while he no doubt lived in somewhat reduced circumstances during his later years, there is no reason to think that his martyrdom to the cause involved suffering utter destitution, isolation, or abandonment.

Lü's later degradation at the hands of the Yung-cheng Emperor, during the years 1728–33, was the outcome of the failed rebellion of one Tseng Ching (1679–1736), a scholar whose passionate anti-dynastic sentiments were said to have been inspired by the reading of Lü's writings.[4] In consequence of this Lü's remains were desecrated and an ideological campaign was mounted against him, including the publication under Imperial sponsorship of a *Refutation of Lü Liu-liang's Discourses on the Four Books (Po Lü Liu-liang Ssu-shu chiang-i)*, and the subsequent banning and burning of his works in the so-called Inquisition of Ch'ien-lung.[5] Though in a sense an accident of history, this posthumous notoriety was not inconsistent with the role Lü played in life, and one wonders if Lü himself would not have derived satisfaction from learning of this belated tribute to his influence. Indeed, to be so fulminated against by the Manchus might well have seemed an honor.

LÜ AS NEO-CONFUCIAN HERO AND COUNTER-HERO

It was not for his nationalism, however, that Lü was admired by his immediate followers. They saw in him a hero to end all Neo-Confucian heroes—or perhaps it would be more correct to call him a prophet to end all heroes. Lü's disciple, Ch'en Tsung, in a prefatory note of 1686 to Lü's *Discourses on the Four Books (Ssu-shu chiang-i)*, described Lü's heroic role as a champion of orthodoxy in terms evoking both Mencius' classic defense of Confucianism against Mo Tzu and Yang Chu, and Chu Hsi's later rejection of (as Ch'en puts it) the "outward Confucianism and covert Buddhism" of Lu Hsiang-shan. He continues:

Several hundred years after this there appeared Wang [Yang-ming] who, seizing the moment when there was no one standing up for the Way, stole in with the wildcat Ch'an of Lu Chin-hsi [Hsiang-shan], bringing confusion to the eyes and ears of the world. . . . Thus Lu Hsiang-shan's teachings had spread over the earth and the teachings of Chu Hsi had long been obscured when the Master [Lü Liu-liang], following this blocking up of the Way, rose resolutely to take up the Way as his own responsibility, and through a thorough analysis of what was correct and incorrect in the recorded sayings of the Confucians and in the teachings of the Buddhists and Taoists, with a sincere faith in the writings of Chu Hsi and a deep love of them, diagnosed the susceptibility of that age to aberrant doctrines and its inability to reply to them. Consequently he taught men the great essential truths of the investigation of things and the fathoming of principle, insisting on the need to distinguish right from wrong as the first thing to be done.[6]

Lu Lung-chi (1630–93), generally considered to be the prime figure in the establishment of the official Ch'eng-Chu orthodoxy and the only Ching scholar to be honored by installation in the Confucian temple, acknowledged that Lü Liu-liang had had a decisive influence in his own life.[7] He spoke of Lü in similarly heroic terms as one who had risen to challenge deviant doctrines after they had long corrupted men's minds: "In recent years it was our own Master Lü from Chekiang, who alone raised a great outcry, and took upon himself the responsibility for outspokenly criticizing Wang Yang-ming." These were words, incidentally, which, with the later proscription of Lü Liu-liang, became expunged from Lu Lung-chi's writings.[8]

At the end of the Ch'ing, when an effort was made to salvage something of Lü's previously proscribed works, Ch'ien Chen-huang, in a preface to an edition of Lü's *Collected Writings (Wen-chi)*, eulogized Lü for having, "after men's minds and mores were corrupted [by Wang Yang-ming] at the end of the Ming, resolutely taken upon himself the responsibility for setting forth the principles of Ch'eng and Chu, straightforwardly and sternly warning and admonishing the scholars of the day."[9] Late in the day though it was, Ch'ien further claimed that Lü, "having been truly committed to saving the times" should now "be acknowledged as having played an incomparable role in preserving the purity of Ch'eng-Chu doctrine" and for "having been the chief figure in the success of the Learning of the Way during the Ch'ing period."[10]

By now these encomiums will sound like wholly conventional praise, and indeed, we recognize in them the familiar rhetoric of Neo-Confucian hagiography—from the late Sung into the Yüan and Ming, and even into Yi dynasty Korea. Nevertheless it would be a mistake to take it as a mere convention. It is also in a sense Lü's own self-characterization, a script he prepared for himself in many of his own writings, a scenario he was ready to live out. For he conceived of himself truly as a martyr to the same cause as Mencius and Chu Hsi, at a time no less perilous for mankind than theirs had been. Further, he saw this "time" as more than just a crisis created by Wang Yang-ming: it was a long-standing condition which had lasted almost from the passing of Chu Hsi, and had been a threat even before that.

"It is now almost five hundred years since the Way became obscured,"[11] says Lü, referring to Chu Hsi's passing. In his own time, Lü goes on, Chu Hsi had successfully exposed the insidious doctrines of Lu Hsiang-shan, but it was not long afterward that Hsü Heng and Wu Ch'eng betrayed the cause—Hsü by serving the Mongols and Wu by making concessions to Lu Hsiang-shan, patching up a kind of reconciliation between the views of Chu and Lu when a clear break was called for.

> Ostensible followers of Chu Hsi, like Chung-p'ing [Hsü Heng] and Yu-ch'ing [Wu Ch'eng], compromised and brought disgrace upon themselves, all the while professing to "take personal responsibility for the Way," which the whole world took at face value. With the Way thus obscured, it caused many scholars from the Te-yu period [at the end of the Sung] (1275) into the Hung-wu period [of the Ming] (1368–1399) to lose their footing. . . . Thus, the teachings of Tzu-yang [Chu Hsi] have been lost since the time of [Hsü] Chung-p'ing and [Wu] Yu-ch'ing, and what was transmitted as the Way thereafter could not serve as a model or norm.[12]

Elsewhere Lü goes so far as to trace the attenuation and loss of the Way back to the late Sung itself, before any question had arisen of yielding to or compromising with the Mongols. He indicates that only two of Chu Hsi's immediate disciples, Huang Kan (1152–1221) and Fu Kuang, managed to keep to Chu's teaching with some fidelity, but in the next generation Ho Chi (1188–1268), Wang Po (1197–1274), and Chin Lü-hsiang (1232–1303) lost much of Master Chu's teaching.[13] This is a significant admission—that the transmission of Chu's doctrine had begun to lapse so soon after Chu's time, like the breaking off of the original Confucian Way after Mencius. Hence it could not be accounted for simply by foreign intrusion into the process, but would seem to be through some mysterious sapping from within.

Lü is willing to acknowledge, but only grudgingly, that during the Ming some scholars had stood up for the Ch'eng-Chu teaching, though to no real effect:

> Later Yüeh-ch'uan [Tsao Tuan], K'ang-chai [Wu Yü-pi], Ching-chai [Hu Chü-jen], and others wished to rescue something of the Way, but they were only able to pick up a few threads and could not transmit the finer points. At this juncture Pai-sha [Ch'en Hsien-chang] and Yang-ming seized our Way when it had no one [to defend it], and following the hints left behind by [the Chan Master] Ta-hui, they "turned the head and changed the face" of the Way, so that it became "outwardly Confucian and covertly Buddhist."[14]

About others with some claim to having defended Ch'eng-Chu teaching, Lü was similarly reserved in his praise:

> Lo Ch'eng-an [Ch'in-shun], with his work the *Kun-chih chi* (Learning Painfully Acquired), and Ch'ing-lan [Ch'en Chien] (1497–1567), with his *Hsüeh-pu t'ung-pien* (General Critique of the Obscurations to Learning), made a great effort to attack the errors and defects [of those who perverted the Way], but their perception of things was not too sharp. Thereafter Confucians who discoursed on learning *(chiang-hsüeh che)* never failed to pay homage to Confucius, but in their discussions on all the finer points they revealed themselves to have been inwardly poisoned by Chin-hsi [Lu Hsiang-shan].[15]

"Those who discoursed on learning" here represent the followers of Wang Yang-ming, especially in the T'ai-chou school, who had made a special effort to carry the Way of sagehood to a larger, non-elite audience. If Lü's animus against them is on social grounds, it is not evident in his writings. Since he had, in any case, himself renounced membership in the official elite on principled grounds, and his own political views were, for his times, quite radical, we have no a priori basis for suspecting that his grounds for opposing Wang's followers were other than the moral and philosophical ones stated in Lü's own writings. Principal among these is his criticism of the T'ai-chou school's evangelical doctrine proclaiming every man a sage, the kind of born-again religion that stressed finding sagehood directly within, a "getting it oneself" without the need to learn or study—in short by a self-awakening.

Here we encounter two contrasting tendencies in Lü Liu-liang as compared to Li Chih, who likewise reflected disillusionment with some of the modern claims to sagehood.[16] In Li Chih's case those who simply discoursed on learning, and were not prepared to take up the heroic life, had no real claim to sagehood. In Lü's case those who claimed to be heroes, but whose teachings did not show a scrupulous and precise concern for moral principle in every aspect of their daily lives, thereby showed a disrespect for true learning and had no real claim to being either heroes or potential sages.

In his eyes the knights-errant were simply:

> A gang who banded together as daredevils, ready to do anything wild. They took upon themselves the role of hero, saying "Those who aspire to do great deeds need not worry about minor indiscretions." So abroad they would stop at nothing, and in their own persons they could not care less for self-reflection and self-control.[17]

In fact, as can be seen from Lü's account of what had transpired over the centuries since Chu Hsi, there were neither true heroes nor sages to be seen. Even Wu Ch'eng, who had spoken to the same point as Lü just one hundred years after Chu Hsi (see ch. 5, pp. 105–7) had turned out, in Lü's eyes, to be no hero and no sage but a traitor to the cause.

From this emerges the picture of Lü as less an upholder of tradition—for in his eyes it had lapsed long ago—than a fundamentalist trying to restore it. He does not adopt the role of the scholastic, faithfully transmitting a tradition that has come down to him as an honored heritage from the past, nor does he see himself as another in a long line of Confucians passing on the torch from one generation to another. In fact he does not even describe Confucianism in terms of an orthodox transmission: *tao-t'ung* for him, as a patriarchal transmission, is a Buddhist creation which has no place in Confucianism.[18] Instead he dwells on the prophetic role in the *tao-t'ung*. Chu Hsi had clearly thought of himself as more like one of the Ch'eng brothers, a seer proclaiming a long lost Way and declaiming against all those who have bungled or betrayed it. Seen this way, with history a wasteland and the past a nightmare, the function of the prophet is to rouse men from their trance-like state and expose to the light of day the covert forces of evil. As revealed by Lü, these are traceable to one main source: Buddhism, essentially a foreign religion, inimical to all the basic values of the Chinese but, masquerading as the Highest Truth, made cosmetically attractive by Lu Hsiang-shan and Wang Yang-ming. Compared to such subversives and Pied Pipers as these, even foreign conquerors are less cause for indignation and alarm.

LÜ LIU-LIANG AS FUNDAMENTALIST

Fundamentalism, as a professed claim on the pristine values of a teaching, is rarely a simple return to the past and more often proves just simplistic in new ways. Here a question arises as to how much of accumulated tradition is to be dispensed with in order to preserve its essential purity. How much of past learning is to be sacrificed on the altar of orthodoxy? Thought of as a return to the past, fundamentalism may be reactionary, but in its concentration on root values or in the intensity of its commitment, it may prove to be radical. Lü Liu-liang shows us something of both.

From the preceding account we may reasonably conclude that Lü's fundamentalism is Neo-Confucian and not simply Confucian. True, Lü does consider Chu Hsi faithful to the teachings of Confucius and Mencius, but he is not ready to strip down simply to the original deposit of faith in the Confucian classics, or "essential" Confucius of the *Analects*, as others did in the seventeenth century when the lines of Neo-Confucian defense seemed to be collapsing on all sides and a retreat to the original stronghold seemed to be in order. Lü is ready to stand and fight with Ch'eng I and Chu Hsi, who disavowed almost all of Confucian thought after Mencius, even while conceding the loss of the true teaching after them. This is an important difference, as we shall see later in comparing Lü to a Confucian fundamentalist like his contemporary Yen Yüan.

Lü's fundamentalism has two basic requisites: the need to concentrate one's mind and effort in a given direction; the other to make decisive value judgments in rigorously excluding incompatible tendencies. Lü may be faulted for his sharp criticisms of others, so much in contrast to the nuanced judgments of Chu Hsi, but he cannot be charged with trying to be all things to all men.

As to the need for a clear focus in one's studies, Lü is quite ready to say where the concentration should lie: on the Four Books with Chu Hsi's commentary, as represented by the *Sentences and Phrases in the Four Books (Ssu-shu chang-chü)* and Chu's *Questions on the Four Books (Huo-wen)*. He can do without the other "orthodox" writings in the Neo-Confucian canon promulgated in the early Ming, the *Great Compendium on Human Nature and Principle (Hsing-li ta-ch'üan)*. Dispensable too are the writings of most scholars of the Yüan and Ming who do not, in his eyes, make reliable guides because they fail to match the penetration of Chu Hsi, who had distilled the essence of all previous commentaries in a most thoroughgoing way.[19] As a first priority in learning, this choice corresponds exactly to Chu's stated intention that students should first study the Four Books. Moreover it was on these that Chu centered his own scholarship and teaching. Yet when Chu thought beyond the initial stage of education, he had a far broader program of study in mind than Lü.[20]

Two things in particular Lü would exclude from study as beyond the pale of legitimacy. One consists of works other than his own which are meant to prepare examination candidates for the writing of eight-legged essays—a large genre, popular among aspirants to office, with which he identifies the learning of the licentiates *(hsiu-tsai)*. Lü refers to this type of learning as "discursive learning" *(chiang-hsüeh)* mentioned above. As corrupted by the heterodox thinking found in Wang's version of the latter, these essays represent a kind of bastard official orthodoxy or "vulgar learning" *(su-hsüeh)* pervading the examination culture of the day. Worse still, they had even been given a spurious legitimacy in the above-mentioned compendia of the Ming Yung-lo reign.[21] Repeatedly his own *Discourses on the Four Books* belittle this learning, and in the authorized account of his life *(hsing-lüeh)* his view of the matter is expressed in these terms:

> It is now a long time since the Way fell to obscurity. If one wishes to make this Way clearly manifest again, one must have nothing to do with the half-literate *hsiu-tsai,* whose smattering of knowledge they cannot really articulate, or with the kind of learning that lies outside the Four Books and beyond rational discourse.[22]

By the latter type of learning, also to be shunned as incompatible with the true Way, Lü refers to Buddhism, and especially Ch'an (Zen):

> The Ch'an sect has its own [teaching on the] substance of the mind and its own method of practice *(kung-fu),* but it is not what we Confucians consider the substance and method. The principle of the Surangama Sūtra is inconceivably subtle; it could only be carried on through a separate transmission [outside the scriptures] and could not be made to fit into the Four Books. Thus when Wang Yang-ming discoursed on learning [under the influence of Buddhism] he never lectured on the Four Books.[23]

True learning for Lü must be something communicable in words, with actual relevance to one's conduct of the moral life in this world —as is the case with the teachings of the Four Books. A transmission outside the scriptures is not subject to any discussion or verification. As to whether this really applies to Wang Yang-ming is another question. Although Wang did not, it is true, fix his attention so pointedly as did Lü on the Four Books, his important essay entitled "Inquiry into the Great Learning" *(Ta-hsüeh wen)* and his repeated discussions of the "eight items" (especially the first item, the "investigation or rectification of things") which had been given such prominence by Chu, show that Wang did pay much attention to the *Great Learning* as the first and most prominent of the Four Books. On the other hand, it is fair to say that the import of Wang's main teaching, the extension of innate knowing, would be to render the study of the Four Books, or any other supposedly canonical writings, much less essential for him than it was for either Chu or Lü, and Wang did not propose or provide any alternative texts.

Significantly among the forms of learning not to be excluded by Lü from the domain of relevant knowledge is Western astronomy. Lü wrote a preface to the *Treatise on the Western Calendar (Hsi-yang-li chih hsü)* in which he stated that such studies are an important adjunct to Chinese moral philosophy.[24] This, though a theme rarely touched on elsewhere in Lü's writings, shows that he was not necessarily antagonistic to all new learning, but only to those forms of "Outward Confucianism/Covert Buddhism" and of the corrupt examination culture, which he saw as essentially anti-intellectual or amoral.

Just as Lü was clear-cut in deciding his learning priorities, he sought to be decisive and unambiguous in drawing conclusions. Understandably others often found his judgments too sweeping and sharp. In one case Lü was chided for being ungenerous and intemperate in his attacks on Wang Yang-ming. Lü replied:

> In such matters one cannot be mealy-mouthed: there is just the choice of right or wrong. Yang-ming likened Chu Hsi to a "destructive flood" or "wild beast,"[25] thus taking upon himself the role of Mencius [in attacking Yang Chu and Mo Tzu in such terms]. But if Mencius is right, Yang Chu and Mo Tzu are

wrong. There is no middle ground between them for one to stand on.

If you say that Yang-ming was trying to bring others around, to reform and redeem them, then there is nothing Mencius said that could not be considered "reforming" and "redeeming," as if he were trying to get Yang Chu and Mo Tzu to travel the same road in the company of the sages and worthies! When one is discussing the Way it is not like discussing persons. Discussing persons one can make allowances, as with Yang-ming not being without some admirable points, but when one is discussing the Way, one should be straightforward and to the point. There is no room for compromise and accommodation.[26]

From this we can see both the sharpness and narrowness of Lü's fundamentalism.

PRINCIPLE IN THE MIND-AND-HEART

The greater part of Lü's extant writings are devoted to the Four Books: namely, his *Recorded Conversations on the Four Books (Ssu-shu yü-lu)*, his *Discourses on the Four Books (Ssu-shu chiang-i)*,[27] and the very rare *Critical Comments of Master Lü Wan-ts'un (Wan-ts'un Lü Tzu p'ing-yü cheng pien)*. Their content is much the same, but with enough variation so that the more selective and definitive *Discourses* can be confirmed or supplemented by the *Conversations*.[28] This way the main points come through with great clarity and emphasis. Here I present those most germane to the concepts of the individual we have been considering.

Taking up the Four Books in the established order, with the *Great Learning* first, Lü's presentation follows the agenda set by Chu Hsi, i.e., the order of topics—the Three Guiding Principles or Mainstays *(san kang-ling)* and Eight Items or Specifications *(pa tiao-mu)*—which generations of Neo-Confucians discussed or debated thereafter. Some, Lü acknowledges, question the scriptural status of the *Great Learning* and the authoritative character of its teaching on the "investigation of things," but Lü affirms his full faith in the virtually sacred character of Chu Hsi's basic text and dismisses doubters as simply "Outward Confucians/Covert Buddhists." The reference is almost certainly to Wang Yang-ming, so the context of the discussion and its polemical character may be seen from the start.[29]

In the question and answer format characteristic of the Neo-Confucian teaching situation, and recorded in the *Conversations*, the first question deals with the opening lines of the *Great Learning*, characterizing it as education for the adult or for the Great Man who would achieve the full development of his human capacities. It is clearly a leading question:

It has been said "The learning of the Great Man consists simply in employing the mind-and-heart to its fullest." To clarify and manifest lucent virtue is to preserve this mind; to renew the people is to extend this mind to others; and to rest in the highest good is fully to employ this mind so that nothing is left unfulfilled.[30]

The question is a leading one because the Three Guiding Principles are given an interpretation in terms of the Learning of the Mind-and-Heart, which prompts Lü to dispel any possible ambiguity on this score:

The Master said: In the Great Learning if one does not emphasize that the moral principle in the mind is rooted in Heaven, that the employment of the mind is fulfilled only in knowing what is right, and that the preserving of the mind is only possible through its constant rectification, then it cannot be accepted as "clarifying" or "renewing." With regard to the mind, if it is not of the moral nature and the mind replete with lucent virtue, but simply of the mind that one speaks, then it is the learning of the original mind [of Lu Hsiang-shan and the Buddhists] and not the sage learning of which one speaks.[31]

Others in Lü's time who professed fidelity to Ch'eng-Chu teaching might well have taken the initial statement at face value and not made an issue of it.[32] For Lü, since the issue had already been raised by Wang Yang-ming's interpretation of the mind as identical with principle, it is imperative that one specify the exact relationship of the mind to principle. Otherwise it leaves open the dangerous possibility that the mind could be understood as simple, undifferentiated consciousness, naturally good, without the need for moral effort and constant self-rectification to achieve its fulfillment.

A few lines later on in the text of the *Great Learning*, the same question comes up. Someone proposes that the "stability, composure, repose, and deliberation" spoken of in the *Great Learning* text represent the wondrous interaction [of principle and ether] in the Learning of the Mind-and-Heart. The Master says:

> One can speak of the Learning of Heaven, of the [moral] nature, of principle and of the Way, but not of the learning of the mind. The mind is that which learns and cannot be what one learns. It is only to the Original Mind of the Buddhists, which takes the mind as the ultimate reality, and in relation to which Heaven, the moral nature, principle, and the Way are all seen as derivative and subordinate, that one refers when one speaks of the Learning of the Mind *(hsin-hsüeh)*. Indeed whenever one speaks of the Learning of the Mind, it is the Buddhist view they refer to.[33]

Here Lü's comments are directed toward Wang Yang-ming's view of the Learning of the Mind *(hsin-hsüeh)*, which had gained such popularity by Lü's time as to almost completely overshadow or displace the earlier Neo-Confucian Learning of the Mind, previously accepted by the Ch'eng-Chu school as an orthodox alternative to the Buddhist view of the mind.[34] One may take it that Lü is straining to make a point, to differentiate Wang Yang-ming's teaching on the mind from the Learning of the Confucian Sages, and to identify Wang's as originally and essentially Buddhist. I shall defer until later a more thorough evaluation of this contention by Lü, and proceed with the laying out of Lü's argument.

A relevant passage for this purpose is Lü's comment on Confucius' famous statement in the *Analects* (2:4) that "at fifteen he had resolved to pursue learning." Lü seizes this opportunity to demonstrate that "learning" did not mean for Confucius something naturally and spontaneously known but rather something achieved through a lifetime of effort.

> The Learning of the Sage is the learning of the [moral] nature, the learning of Heaven. In ancient times there was no talk of studying the mind. Whenever there was the mind of the Way there was the human mind [to be directed], so the mind [in and by itself] could not be the object of study or learning. Learning is that by which one corrects one's mind. "Directly pointing to the mind of man, seeing into one's own nature and achieving Buddhahood" is learning what itself should do the learning, not learning to be a sage. So all talk in terms of just the "learning of the mind" betrays the confusions of heterodox teachings and leads to [Wang Yang-ming's] "beyond good and evil."
>
> When the Sage [Confucius] spoke about "following his heart's desire without transgressing the norm," he emphasized the three words "without transgressing the norm." What then is the norm? It is the [moral] nature, it is Heaven, the highest good. When the mind-and-heart are one with the nature and Heaven, that is the highest good, that is the Learning of the Sage, something superior to the mind [as mere consciousness]. So if one speaks of the Learning of the Sage as applying one's effort to the mind-and-heart, that is acceptable, but if one speaks of the Learning of the Sage as the Learning of the Mind, it is not acceptable.[35]
>
> From what Confucius said about "not transgressing the norm" one can know that in the Sage's mind there was always this Heavenly Principle present. It is not that the mind itself is the Way. This is the difference between the "original mind" and one rooted in Heaven's principle, which is the basis of the Ch'eng-

Chu teaching that one should give primacy to reverent seriousness.[36]

Here Lü insists that one cannot take the mind-and-heart simply as undifferentiated consciousness ["original mind"]. But because the mind is always the human mind—a compound of Heaven's principles and psychophysical drives—it is imperative (in the sense of the innate Heavenly Imperative, *t'ien-ming*) that the mind as moral agency sees to it that man's emotional and appetitive drives are properly directed—that through the constant exercise of reverent seriousness, principle, as Heaven's imperative, will prevail. In a comment on learning as discussed in *Analects* I, Lü says:

What Confucians are conscious of is principle; what heterodox teachings are conscious of is mind. One can only become conscious of principle through the investigation of things and the extension of knowledge; then with the understanding of human nature and of Heaven comes the fullest employment of the mind. If however one sets aside the principles of things and tries to look directly into the mind, it makes the investigation of things and extension of knowledge seem superfluous and diversionary. If one thinks of oneself as directly perceiving the substance of the mind, the principles of things amount in the final analysis to no more than useless appendages.

Just so, in the theory of the outward Confucians/covert Buddhists the order of learning is reversed so as to seek first the substance of the mind and leave to later the fathoming of the principles of things. Thinking that they hold the secret within themselves, they do not realize that when one first restricts oneself [through the discipline of ritual] and later broadens oneself with culture, or first seeks unity and later engages in learning, the latter turns out to be superfluous and diversionary. This is not the teaching of those who follow the sages.[37]

Lü emphasizes here that the only way to understand principle is through investigation which develops principle in the mind as it explores principles in things and affairs, and thus enables one to fulfill the moral nature or Heavenly endowment. If one assumes that the nature is already perfect and complete, and only needs to be realized by direct self-awareness and self-expression, then even though one speaks of extending such "knowing" outward to others and to things, there is really no need to do so, assuming that the substance is already fully attained. The kind of continuing effort to learn which Confucius speaks of in the opening lines of the *Analects* would be redundant.

Lü makes a similar point in his discussion of the opening lines of the *Mean*, a prime Neo-Confucian source for the doctrine of human nature and principle: "Heaven's Imperative [in the mind of man] is called the [moral] nature; to follow the nature is called the Way, to cultivate the Way is called education." Education and learning should be based on the moral nature, which is Heaven's Imperative in the mind. To seek to know or study the mind in disregard of the moral imperative (Heaven, the nature) contravenes this basic doctrine. Yet, according to Lü, this is exactly what outward Confucians/covert Buddhists do when they try to grasp the mystery of life in a consciousness devoid of moral principles, a mind from which conscience has been ostracized, a mind denatured, in the Confucian sense, by its alienation from the innate moral imperative. They want a Way without any constant norms or fixed imperative, hence they disregard the first of the three statements in the *Mean*. But, says Lü:

In men at birth the [moral] nature is inherent in their consciousness and in the myriad transformations of their psychophysical constituents. The sage says however that this actual form does not represent the highest expression of the common [moral] nature and it is only from such a high point that one can view the ultimate goodness of the created order and the common basis of Heaven's Imperative. Therefore the *Mean* says "Heaven's Imperative [in man] is called the nature." With Confucius' saying "That which continues it is goodness" and "that which completes it is the nature,"[38] and what Mencius said about the goodness of human nature—all these are principles of an unbroken common thread and it cannot be said that one part is more important than another.[39]

Lü tries here to make three related points: first, that human unity is predicated on the common moral nature received from Heaven; that this basic principle is testified to by Confucius, Mencius, and Tzu-ssu, as well as by the Cheng-Chu school (i.e., it is not just a latter-day construct, superimposed by the Neo-Confucians); and that to take the second or third of the three statements in the *Mean* out of context, or to emphasize, say, the second (the Way) at the expense of, or to the exclusion of, the first (the moral imperative), is to do violence to the whole.

As for the "naturalistic" view of the mind which would see it as simply a psycho-physical function, a raw consciousness, Lü says:

> Matter cannot but be the stuff of the nature, but the former is not the master of the latter. Mencius' chapter on the ability of the mouth to taste [6A:7] and the discussions of the Ch'eng brothers, Chang Tsai, and Chu Hsi set forth explanations of principle and ether with the greatest precision. Yet these are not only the words of Mencius, the Ch'eng's, Chang, and Chu, but the words of Confucius and Tzu Ssu as well. Nowadays, however, these words are not generally believed in as an integral whole. It is only believed that the nature is to be found simply in its functions of seeing, hearing, speaking, and moving. . . .[40]

The term "naturalness" has a correct meaning and also a heterodox one. Speaking of the goodness of the moral nature there is an inherent naturalness which is not instilled from outside; this is the correct meaning. If however one says that any action or inaction whatever, without exception, is "natural," this is a heterodox interpretation.

As for the expression "unceasing" [as applied in the *Changes* to the Way of Heaven-and-earth],[41] it too may have a meaning distinct from this. If, by "unceasing" one indicates the constancy of principle, then it is the correct meaning. But if one speaks emptily about unceasingness, it can lead into heterodox views.[42]

For Lü any view of "naturalness" which does not recognize moral principle as inherently natural, while at the same time requiring "unceasing" study for advancement in the Way (as Chu Hsi had said of "getting it oneself"), is incomplete. "It is the naturalness of the Buddhists and Taoists, not of the sages."[43] Further, when Lü speaks above of a natural goodness that is not instilled from outside, he refers to the innate moral imperative as an inner (but not "inward") directedness that man shares with all things in Heaven-and-earth. Thus the second of the three statements from the *Mean* about "following the nature is the Way" is the "common requirement for man and things." "This Way is something inherent in my own self, and just from what one observes of oneself, one finds Heaven, the sage, man, and all things together there. . . . Heaven and the sage are there in myself. The natural moral imperative and the teaching [education] are the Way in myself."[44]

Since much of Lü's discussion is directed against those who celebrated a natural but supra-moral spontaneity as the essence of sagehood, and also since, as a corrective to this, Lü emphasizes the need to study, learn, and practice in accordance with Heaven's imperative, it is significant that for him this implies no loss of autonomy on the part of the individual, only a recognition that conscientious action is integral to the exercise of one's autonomy, as well as to the spontaneous creativity that characterizes the whole natural order. Thus he says:

Once there is Heaven [creating], human beings are necessarily born, and once there are human beings there is sure to be the [moral] nature, and once the nature, there is sure to be this Way of what-ought-to-be. Whether there is one or a hundred, it does not depend on any human arrangement, so it is not only the moral imperative that is natural but the following of it. Thus both the imperative and the following of it partake of Heaven's "unceasingness." If there is something subtle and wondrous about this, it is that the teaching [education] of the sage seems to be man-made and yet it is naturally and necessarily so. Since it derives from Heaven's imperative, if, in the unceasingness of the sage there is something natural and inescapable about it, this is the naturalness and inescapability of Heaven's imperative.[45]

In this way Lü rejects any notion that morality is extrinsic to the self, or that principle stands as an impediment to the natural vitality of the mind. In his explanation of Mencius' final chapters on the full employment of the mind, he cites Chang Tsai's doctrine of the mind as coordinating or combining the nature and the emotions, and refers to Chu Hsi's explanation of this as found in his commentary on "lucent virtue" in the opening lines of the *Great Learning*:

> Chang Heng-ch'ü's dictum, "The mind coordinates the nature and emotions" in one phrase says it all. What Chu Hsi calls "empty, spiritual, and transparent" indicates the substance of the mind; "furnished with a multitude of principles" refers to the coordinating of the moral nature; "responding to all things" refers to the coordinating of the emotions.[46] The mind is an active, living thing. Being empty and spiritual, it can be furnished [filled with] the nature and emotions; being furnished with the virtuous powers of the nature and emotions, its empty spirituality can directly embody Heaven's substance.[47]

The trouble with those who speak about the "Learning of the Mind" under the influence of Buddhism—the so-called "Outward Confucians/Covert Buddhists"—is that they deny the constancy of principle in the structure and direction of the mind and take the mind simply as a stream of consciousness. In other words, using the language of Chu Hsi, they see it as "empty, spiritual, and transparent," but not as structured or directed by principle and not as needing any coordination of the emotions. In fact they see any holding to fixed principle as an obstacle to the transcendent freedom of the mind and an obscuration of its empty transparency and receptivity. This leaves them without any control over the emotions, so that in practice the mind is not only driven by the emotions but dominated by them—human desire prevails over Heaven's principles. Taking the mind's empty spirituality alone as the substance, they speak of it as marvelously subtle, pure, empty, and still—in the same terms as Bodhidharma's description of the Buddha-nature.[48] So, says Lü:

> Lo Ch'eng-an [Ch'in-shun] said "the Buddhists have insight into the mind but not into the nature." In reality, however, they are wrong on both counts. Seeing only the activity of the mind and not its directional norm *(chi)*, on the higher level they cannot match the Heavenly substance, and on the lower level the mind cannot be of any practical use. Hence it is necessary to understand the nature and Heaven, so as to see the ultimate directional norm. Then one can achieve full employment of the mind.[49]

According to his view the key to the mind is understanding or knowing principle and its Heavenly source, and seeing to it that principle or the nature prevails in the direction of the powerful instinctual drives identified with the emotions. The latter derive, like the nature, from Heaven, as Lü indicates when he speaks of them together as "virtuous powers" *(te)*; but it is characteristic of, and natural for, the appetites and emotional desires to seek their own satisfaction, while it is characteristic of principle to provide rational, moral guidance to the emotions so that selfish intent will not predominate over the common interest, which is potentially as broad and far-reaching as Heaven itself. With this proper guidance the emotions can be a creative power like Heaven, and the Mind, "fully employed" in accordance with its inborn nature, can embody Heaven. But without the guidance of principle the mind is lost in emptiness and cannot make creative use of man's physical powers.

GETTING THE WAY ONESELF

What then does this mean for the individual? That one's fulfillment can come only from subordination to principle, in a complete sacrificing of oneself to the common good? Some such conclusion might be drawn from the constant counterposing of Heaven's principle to human desires in Lü's thought, suggesting possibly that principle can only prevail at the expense of human desire. Further there is an ambiguity which attaches to some of Lü's statements about the mind and the desires which precludes a simple answer to the question.

At one point Lü says, "Minds are not the same; moral principle is. This is the difference between Confucianism and Buddhism" [which does not recognize the common moral nature and its constancy in the mind].[50] In the original context this may be taken to mean that one must look to principle because it represents common humanity, the unity and solidarity of humankind. But whether this is necessarily in contrast to a self-interestedness inherent in the individual—and whether that is always to be seen as evil—is questionable. Elsewhere Lü upholds the Neo-Confucian doctrine of the unity of principle and the diversity of its particularizations, a doctrine that reaffirms the equal reality and validity of the one and the many, the commonality and the individual. There is no reason to doubt its relevance and applicability here, for it is in this vein that Lü speaks of human desires and appetites themselves as aspects of common humanity:

> All human minds and hearts are the same in having human desires and Heaven's [corresponding indwelling] principles. For instance, they are the same in their love of material goods and of sensual pleasure. However they should only expect to get what it is proper for them to love. If one speaks only of their being the same in having the love of material goods and sensual pleasure [and not in possessing also the principles to guide and restrain each of them], then human desires in men's minds and hearts become the way to great disorder in the world.[51]

Here Lü stresses the inseparability of desires and principles, affirming them together as aspects of a common humanity as well as of the individual nature. A similar balancing of the two is found in Lü's discussion of "learning for one's self." The question is asked in relation to the Three Guiding Principles of the *Great Learning*, how "learning for one's self" is to be understood in relation to the renewing of one's own nature and the nature of others:

> Some equate the "clarifying of lucent virtue" with "learning for one's self," and "renewing the people" with "for the sake of others." The Master replied: "To speak of it as 'completing oneself and completing others' will do well enough, but to think of it as 'for the sake of others' [approval]' is not the Learning of the Sage. Mixing the two [ideas] will not do."[52]

Lü draws here on the *Mean*[53] where sincerity or integrity *(ch'eng)* is explained as a self-realization that is bound up with the fulfillment of all other things. Yet this truth of the interdependence of self and others should not be confused with the distinction Confucius made with regard to one's motives in learning. Thus Lü says:

> "For the sake of others" means wishing to gain recognition from others. It refers to fishing for fame and trying to make a name for oneself in the world, not to doing something that contributes to the ordering of the world. Doing something of benefit to the world order is also within the scope of "for one's self."[54]

For Lü public service is also "for one's self" because on this level self-fulfillment and the fulfillment of others are as inseparable in Chu Hsi's mind as self-renewal and the renewal of others. So the question "for whose sake it is" is a matter of one's intentions, one's motivations, and not a differentiation among the beneficiaries of one's efforts. "Whether it is for one's self or others is all to be judged according to how one employs one's mind; it does not depend on the object."[55] The decision is to be made in terms of what is right for both one's self and others, rather than of what yields some utilitarian advantage for either.[56]

How then does one know what is right, if this cannot be decided on the basis of self-interest or the interest of others? Lü speaks to this in discussing the problem of "getting or finding it oneself in all life situations [as it comes up in the *Mean* 14:2, where the noble man is defined as one who is at ease or at home with himself in all situations]. Lü says that "there being no place where one is not at home" cannot mean turning oneself around to follow every trend of the times, or "taking off one's clothes and going among naked islanders."[57] He cites Chu Hsi's *Questions on the Mean (Chung-yung huo-wen)* to the effect that "Being all-sufficient within one's own mind-and-heart" is the true explanation of 'getting or finding it (oneself).'[58] Otherwise, in [Chu Hsi's] commentary, where he speaks of 'silent recognition,' what is there to recognize? In 'there being no place where one does not find it oneself,' what is the finding about?" The answer Lü implies to this rhetorical question is that one finds the Way in oneself, as "the multitude of principles in the nature," responding to all life situations. "Wherever one is dealing with affairs and is relating to others, and one deals with them appropriately according to principle, then that is naturally an instance of 'finding it oneself.' "[59]

On this same passage Lü comments further:

> With regard to one's station [in life], if one has [in mind] an ultimate directional norm, there is fixity and stability. Without such a norm, there is no fixity and stability. The noble man's way of according with his station is to take his stand on his own station, wherefore he can rest in it. No matter where he is, that is his station, and the principles of all stations are replete within him, so he can conduct himself in accordance with that station. Thus the following portion of the text speaks of there being no place where he does not find it in himself. In the morning he may be a peasant plowing his fields; in the evening he might be the Son of Heaven. His "according with it" will be all the same.[60]

What it is one finds can be understood as either the Way or principles, depending on whether one has in mind the unity of principle (the Way) or its diverse particularizations (the principles in things and affairs). One's ability to respond appropriately to each situation one encounters in the midst of the constant flux of the universe depends on one's having achieved the "Way of according with one's station," which is the culmination of the learning process, identified by Lü in Chu Hsi's terms, as attaining the "whole substance and great functioning" of one's nature through the complete integration of that nature with the mind.[61]

While affirming that truly "getting it oneself" is a matter of total self-realization, Lü most often emphasizes the starting point in the process, and the specific method of achievement. For him the Way is primarily a method of sustained cultivation, while principles relate to the conduct of the moral life.

Commenting on "getting it oneself" in *Mencius*, Lü first identifies *tzu-te* as the essence of the passage, and then explains that the Way is a method involving specific steps. It is not to be understood as the way of "doing nothing" *(wu-wei)* in the Taoist sense, nor does "being at ease" imply the kind of effortlessness associated with Taoist *wu-wei*. Even in action, when he is not at rest, the noble man can always rest at ease because he has first examined and rectified himself. And this is because he has taken responsibility for the Way himself and accepts the blame for whatever is not right.[62]

We recall that in discussing Mencius' "finding the Way in oneself" *(tzu-te)*, Chu Hsi had talked about the Way in a more concrete and somewhat less mystical sense than earlier commentators (see chapter 3). Lü shares that approach, stressing it, if anything, even more than Chu Hsi:

> To cultivate the Way deeply (or "steep oneself in the Way," *shen ts'ao i tao)* has the meaning to penetrate, to accumulate, and never to let up. . . . [It] has two meanings. "In or with the Way" is the step-by-step, specific method of study. "Deeply cultivate (steep)" means to advance and never let up. . . . It is only by virtue of this Way that one has something to adhere to in order to get it oneself. Otherwise what is there to cultivate deeply? Many people leave out the part about the Way and just talk about steeping or cultivating deeply; some even slur over

[Chu Hsi's commentary about] "advancing gradually" or pay no attention to what he said about Way or method. So they talk about the noble man steeping himself [with no mention of advancing], not recognizing that in what Chu said about "the method of advancing in the Way," the "method" was definitely meant as the real business at hand. To treat this in a vague way and talk about it as a dark mystery or subtle beyond words, is not at all to the point.[63]

In the foregoing Lü (like Chu Hsi) understands *shen-ts'ao* more in the sense of "cultivate deeply" than of "steep" (D. C. Lau's appropriate translation in the Mencian context). I have used either rendering in accordance with whichever sense is primarily intended in the passage at hand, trying to preserve something of the original ambiguity which allows of different interpretations. Lü, however, makes his own preference clear:

In this passage Master Chu particularly emphasized the words "according to the Way." Later scholars have only understood it in terms of steeping oneself in the Way and unfortunately they did not pay attention to the essential principle.[64]

Often misunderstood in this passage is the matter of depth. It should be seen as making unceasing advancement. When it speaks of "in or with the Way," there is a definite method of moral practice.[65]

The reason Lü stresses a definite method of moral practice is not difficult to fathom, given his repeated admonitions against any short-cut or easy way to self-realization:

To cultivate the Way deeply is the heart of "getting it oneself." Mencius strictly enjoins upon men the method of cultivating the Way deeply and does not simply tell them to look for some kind of sudden discovery of the Way in oneself or self-realization *(tzu-te)*. To talk about *tzu-te*, leaving out the deep cultivation, is wrong; to talk about "deep cultivation" while leaving out the method of practice, is wrong.[66]

It will be recalled that earlier Chu Hsi had spoken of "getting it oneself" in relation to Confucius' famous statement in *Analects* 2:11 that "he who can cherish the old while learning the new can be a teacher of men." In commenting on this passage Chu had in mind that by his own time study of the old had become for many a deadly routine, either because as scholars they had become mere antiquarians or philologues who failed to relate what they learned to their own conduct of life, or because as candidates for office they sought only the kind of rote learning and memorization that would bring success in the examinations. Therefore Chu explains:

Wen [translated by Legge as "cherish"] means "inquire into." *Ku* [the old] is what one formerly heard about. *Hsin* ["new"] is what one now acquires. It means that if one can review one's old learning and each time get something new out of it, then what one has learned is within one and can be endlessly responsive [to any situation]. Thus one can be a teacher of men. If it is learning just memorized by rote, it is not something gotten in one's own mind-and-heart, and thus is limited [in its applicability].[67]

Chu Hsi's discussion of the same passage in his *Classified Conversations* emphasizes grasping principle within one as "getting it oneself."[68] This then gives rise to the question put to Lü in his *Discourses*, which is based on a plausible reading of Chu's comments:

Some say that in the pursuit of learning one hobbles himself by too much reading and listening [i.e., external knowledge received through the senses]. The noble man's learning is to be "gotten oneself" in one's own mind-and-heart.

The Master replied, " 'Old' here refers to what is already known [from the past]. 'New' refers to what is not yet known. Both refer to reading and listening." It is asserted here that one should follow up what one has already learned by further adding to and refining one's knowledge, daily learning what was not known or understood before. It does not mean that "what is old" comes from reading and listening [external knowledge] while what is new comes from enlightenment within the mind.

It is like reading books. At first one's reading is superficial but if one can reflect on it unceasingly *(pu-i)* and analyze what one has learned, one may become aware of how crude were the interpretations accepted before; or discover how false were those of others; or learn about points not previously understood, or penetrate to alternative readings—this is all new knowledge. If so, one can then be a teacher of men, explaining texts and solving problems. What Chu's commentary refers to as rote learning *[chi-wen chih hsüeh]* is something not truly gotten in or by one's own mind-and-heart.[69]

In this passage we note, in passing, another use to which Lü puts the expression "unceasing" *(pu-i)*. Earlier, in discussing the inescapable inherence of principle in the mind, he had argued against interpreting this expression from the *Changes (I-ching)* as simply an irrepressible vitality of the Way in the form of psycho-physical consciousness, and had insisted on it also as a moral constant in the mind. Here he speaks of the "unceasing" active effort which this moral imperative commands. It may take the form, as here, of intellectual activities such as reading, reflecting, analyzing, weighing, etc., but these only demonstrate the inseparability of intellectual and moral effort.

The phrase *pu-i*, as we have seen, comes from Chu Hsi's comment on *tzu-te* in relation to *Mencius* 4B:4; not only does Lü accurately express Chu Hsi's own view of the intellectual/moral effort required, but since Lü repeatedly emphasizes this unceasingness in refutation of the Wang Yang-ming school's philosophy of mind, it demonstrates how crucial to the issue was this interpretation of "getting it oneself" to the combination of unceasing moral effort with the *I-ching*'s more metaphysical use of *pu-i*.

Lü's interpretation of this passage, which undoubtedly expresses in significant measure what Chu Hsi had intended, further sharpens the point in order to counter the anti-intellectualism which, in his view, dominates the contemporary scene, owing not only to Wang Yang-ming's popular teachings but to other evil tendencies as well. That his own situation was unique in this respect, Lü would be unlikely to claim, for these evils had already been addressed by Chu Hsi, but the corruption is now widespread and takes many forms. The officially certified scholars *(hsiu-tsai)* are, as we have seen, one target of attack. They read trashy counterfeits of the classics as if these were the equal of the originals and of Chu's commentaries. Thinking that they have thus mastered "the old," they see no need to study anything new. There are, too, those who congratulate themselves on being broadly learned because they have read through the *Great Compendium* of the early Ming; they too think they have nothing more to learn, even though, since the *Compendia* reflect an "orthodoxy" that was already distorted and misleading, according to Lü they remain ignorant of the true meaning of the classics. Others, like the popular thinker and writer of "morality books," Yüan Huang[70] (1533–1606) take it upon themselves to revise and update Chu's commentaries, professing to offer a learning that is new, though it is not at all what the Sage meant by the new (i.e., knowledge tested in the present and found to be applicable). The new is not something to be found outside the Four Books and Chu's commentaries which allows one to discard the latter and look for something original in the mind. The sage clearly meant by "cherishing the old and learning the new" that the new is to be found within the old and the "getting" within the "cherishing." Lü brings this out by interpreting *wen* (Legge's "cherishing") as Chu's commentary does, to mean inquiry and investigation. This could be potentially of a creative kind, producing both new discoveries and richer life experiences, but in the context of the old. "Confucius never meant that one should set aside the old in order to learn the new."[71]

In a related comment the *Discourses* record Lü's awareness of the cumulative character of learning:

[Question:] Some say the "old" refers to physical objects and the "new" to the metaphysical way. The Master said: "Inquiring *(wen)* into the old and learning the new" means each day learning what one has not known before, not that the old lies in the physical domain [apprehended through sense knowledge] and the new in the metaphysical [apprehended in the inner mind]. What is new today becomes the old tomorrow.[72]

Here Lü not only transcends the dichotomy of new and old, but also the dichotomy of physical and metaphysical which might be read into Chu Hsi's commentary if one dwelt on the contrast between knowledge deriving from sense data and some a priori truth supplied wholly from within the mind. He wishes to sanction neither the view that there are two kinds of learning, inner and outer, nor that either of these can be pursued to the exclusion of the other. Discussing the phrase "meeting its source right and left" as the fruit of "getting it oneself," he says that it should involve no consciousness of inner versus outer, no sense of anything being alien to oneself.[73] Nor, on the other hand, can it mean doing away with such a distinction by the one overcoming the other, or the one imposing itself on the other.

"Getting it" remains, in that respect, a thoroughly individual process which cannot be reduced to a stated formula. If numinous principle is to be found in one's engagement in ordinary affairs and day-to-day learning, not in some transcendent state removed from ordinary intellection, still the recognizing of principle, within and without, is a potentially limitless process. It partakes of both the unity and diversity of principle, of the particular as well as the non-finite Supreme Ultimate in each individual. In this sense Lü would not, I think, object to the word "steeping" as a description of the natural, autonomous character of the learning experience. "Getting it oneself" and "meeting its source right and left" was something which should not, he says, be forced, strained for, or manipulated willfully. One could, with respect to the study of the classics and commentaries, only immerse oneself in the spirit conveyed by the words, let the mind-and-heart silently recognize principle, and naturally get the deeper meaning from the outward signs.[74] This will always remain an experience that is both common and unique, and if there is any recipe for it, it will have to allow for variation according to the differences in each person's psycho-physical makeup and disposition.[75]

FUNDAMENTALISM AS REVISIONISM

Fundamentalism, as an effort to return to the root values of a tradition, necessarily implies some redefinition of them, either by selecting and emphasizing certain values at the expense of others or by a process of reassembling or refocusing them. Either explicitly or implicitly this also involves some revision of the tradition as it has emerged from the original source—in this case Chu Hsi. Thus Lü is most obviously revisionist in regard to such Ming thinkers as Ch'en Hsien-chang and Wang Yang-ming, who had themselves come out of the Chu Hsi school but took certain of its teachings in a new direction. Insofar as Lü's negative judgments were later confirmed as orthodox, Ch'en and Wang would be seen as heterodox.[76]

In addition, however, Lü criticized others (though no doubt to a lesser degree) who had been, and continued to be, seen as still within the bounds of orthodoxy. Among the most obvious cases cited by Lü are Hsü Heng, Ts'ao Tuan, Lo Ch'in-shun, Ch'en Chien, and Ku Hsien-ch'eng, most of whom survived Lü's critique to become included in Chang Po-hsing's celebrated collectanea of orthodox scholars, the *Cheng-i t'ang ch'üan-shu*.

From this it is plain that there continued to be more than one type or strand of orthodox Neo-Confucianism in Ch'ing China, and this was true also in Korea and Japan. What I propose to discuss as "revisionism" here is mostly those ways in which Lü significantly took issue with "orthodoxy" as he found it or influenced its later direction. These largely concern the nature and uses of the mind-and-heart.

As we have seen, for Lü a key formulation in the Ch'eng-Chu teaching, at issue in the debate with Ch'en and Wang (that is, in the theoretical discourse continuing over time) had been that of "the mind coordinating the nature and the emotions." As this formulation came from Chang Tsai and Chu Hsi, the mind was seen as the central, coordinating conception, but in terms of Neo-Confucianism's contest with Buddhism for the minds of men, the significant new elements were the Neo-Confucian reaffirmation of the basic reality of moral principle, as expressed in "the nature," and of the emotions, as expressed in the psycho-physical constitution. By "basic reality" is meant here a conception of reality not ultimately qualified by the Buddhist principle of "emptiness" or indeterminacy, against which Lü asserted the constancy and immutability of principle in the moral nature.

In the original Ch'eng-Chu formulation the idea of the "mind coordinating the nature and emotions" reflected the new sense of reality accorded to the psycho-physical element by Chang Tsai and to principle by Ch'eng I, as the two were synthesized ("coordinated") and refined in Chu Hsi's conception of the mind of the sage, which served as the ideal for self-cultivation.

As Lü looks back on the Ming development of Neo-Confucianism, he becomes preoccupied with three main problems: 1) something has gone seriously wrong with the teaching, and accounting for this failure he finds that, 2) there has been an undue emphasis on the psycho-physical consciousness, which has resulted in the overshadowing of the moral nature (whereas properly speaking, in the complementary relationship between the two, the latter should function as yang and the former as yin); and 3) in this unbalanced condition, the relative weakness of principle has reopened the door to infiltration by the Buddhist view of adaptability or expediency in all worldly affairs.

In this situation Lü feels compelled to reassert the primacy of principle. The emotions are not to be denied, for their appetitive drive energizes the Way, but this energy must once again be harnessed to the rational and moral imperative rather than be dissipated in the uncontrolled hedonism which Buddhism tolerates. At this point the mind, while still the area of crucial conflict, recedes in importance for Lü. Unless it can be decisively controlled by principle, and can serve as an instrument of rationality and morality, it can be a dangerous, destructive power, lending itself to alien, fundamentally inhumane, and uncivilized forces. This, I believe, is the proximate, if perhaps not the underlying, source of Lü's repudiation of the term "Learning of the Mind-and-Heart," which so redoubtable a defender of orthodoxy, against Wang Yang-ming, as Ch'en Chien had insisted was at the heart of Neo-Confucian orthodoxy.[77]

Among the first signs of this change is Lü's denial above of the Mind-and-Heart as an object or subject of study, rather than as an instrument for the learning of principle. Here a clear antithesis is set up by Lü between mind and principle. Traditionally it had been assumed that the two always went together (which is not necessarily the same as asserting their identity, as Wang Yang-ming did, thus precipitating the issue). For Lü to say that the mind was an instrument of learning and not the object of learning, meant also that for him there was no such thing as the mind-in-itself as an object of inward contemplation. The substance of the mind could only be principle or the Heaven-instilled, inborn nature; and since principle in its essence allowed of no distinction between inner and outer (self and things), one could not, Lü said, apprehend principle by any method or practice that involved a purely inward contemplation.

Ch'ien Mu has pointed out a significant difference between Huang Tsung-hsi and Lü Liu-liang on this issue of the substance of the mind. He says that Huang believed the basic stuff of the universe to be a dynamic psycho-physical consciousness *(hsin)*, and that the mind-and-heart had no substance-in-itself apart from what was arrived at through its operation or application *(kung-fu)*. Lü, on the other hand, did believe the mind had a substance.[78] Since, however, in Lü's terms that substance was understood as principle and not the mind-in-itself, and in order to understand the substance one had to learn and come to understand principle both within and without, the practical outcome was not so different as to method. For both Huang and Lü it still required intellectual and moral effort as the prime means of self-cultivation.

One indication of Lü's revisionism in respect to the Learning of the Mind-and-Heart is his rejection of quiet-sitting as an orthodox method of moral and spiritual praxis. Quiet-sitting had been a common practice in the early Ch'eng-Chu school and even in the late Ming return to orthodoxy in the Tung-lin movement it had been strongly recommended as a discipline of mind-control by Kao P'an-lung.[79] In the Neo-Confucian orthodoxy carried to Korea in the Yüan and early Ming periods, quiet-sitting had been a standard practice particularly favored by Yi T'oegye, and the same was to be true in Japan of the most influential form of orthodox Neo-Confucianism in the school of Yamazaki Ansai.[80] Yet here in the later seventeenth century Lü downgrades it as a practice susceptible of misunderstanding and abuse, easily leading into Buddhism.

The proper Confucian discipline was to be found in being watchful over one's solitary self, or watchful over oneself when alone and unobserved by others *(shen-tu)*. Here the practice of caution in and vigilance over one's own conduct *(chieh-shen)* was described by Lü as the true method of the mind-and-heart *(hsin-fa)*; this confirmed the content of Chu Hsi's doctrine of the mind-and-heart, with its distinction between the mind of the Way and the mind of man, even while Lü was disavowing the name, Learning of the Mind, which had become such an embarrassment to him.[81] On solid Neo-Confucian textual grounds Lü argues that this recognition of the need for the human mind to be brought under the control and direction of the mind of the Way is the fundamental principle of Chu Hsi's doctrine of the mind, by which the noble man exercises self-control and preserves the mind. There is no situation in life to which it is not applicable and no time in which it is not practicable.[82]

Unfortunately, says Lü, there were many later Confucians who misinterpreted the doctrine of self-watchfulness. "Being by oneself" or "solitariness" *(tu)* they understood to be "solitary sitting," which they equated with Chou Tun-i's practice of quiescence.[83] The *Mean's* reference to "what is not seen or heard" they took as describing a state of mind beyond tangible grasp or conceptual formulation,[84] either because of its transcendence of ordinary experience or its miraculous dynamism and creativity. But, says Lü:

> The learning of the sages applies its method [of vigilance and restraint] to both action and quiescence, so that the mind would be reverent and conscientious at all times; the principle was not to avoid action and seek quiescence. Someone asked if that was not the case with Chou Tun-i's giving primacy to quiescence and with Ch'eng I's expression of delight when he saw men practicing quiet-sitting. The Master replied, "It was not that kind of quiescence. As for action and quiescence, one may speak of it with respect to its application to principle, or its application to the psycho-physical consciousness, or its application to times and circumstances. Chou Tun-i's giving "primacy to quiescence" spoke of its application to principle, but fearing lest men misconstrue this, he specifically noted that quiescence was aimed at desirelessness [thus precluding any uncontrolled expression of the psycho-physical consciousness]. When Master Ch'eng saw men practicing quiet-sitting,[85] he was delighted to have them seek the Way within rather than chase after externals, but still he did not base his teaching on the practice of quiescence [rather he emphasized reverent seriousness *(ching)* in place of Chou's quiescence *(ching)*].[86]

Thus Chou's method, according to Lü, was safeguarded against quietism, being applicable to both action and quiescence, while Cheng I's method of maintaining reverent seriousness at all times obviated any tendency to separate out quiescence and emphasize it over action; in this way he preserved the constant unity of the mind with principle. In the Ming, however, followers of Wang Yang-ming like Wang Chi applied the method of self-watchfulness to the psycho-physical consciousness, emphasizing its irrepressible spontaneity and rejecting, as obstructive of that spontaneity, any idea of the nature as a constant or fixed principle (see chapter 7). Lacking any such principle of unity, says Lü, Wang Chi in the end had to seek the unity of mind in an undifferentiated quiescent state. From this then he was led to favor quiescence over action and the state of non-differentiation over differentiation—in other words a state very close to Zen.[87]

This outcome Lü contrasts to the true self-watchfulness of the *Mean* which is applied to one's active involvements with the world, according to the specific circumstances of time and place, and not to some separate entity or state within the mind.[88] (See chapter 4, pp. 88–90, for Chu Hsi's caution on this point.) Quiet-sitting is also incompatible with the original message and method of the mind-and-heart coming down from the sage kings:

> Yao and Shun transmitted the teaching that the human mind is precarious and insecure, while the mind of the Way is subtle and barely perceptible. From this one can see that [Wang Chi's interpretation of the substance of the mind as] beyond good and evil won't do. Even the sage-kings had to practice caution, vigilance, and apprehension, and to strive to make refinement, singleness, and holding to the Mean the master of the mind. In the Sage Learning there can be no difference of ease and effort [as is implied by distinctions, allegedly made by Wang Yang-ming according to Wang Chi, between the naturally gifted and perceptive and those slower of wit], or between sudden and gradual enlightenment. "Sudden or gradual" is the way heterodox teachers speak about enlightenment; it is a distinction made by the Ch'an Buddhists in their teaching and training.[89]

On this Lü says:

> The Five Constant Virtues are the moral nature which inheres within one. Before action takes place, they are spoken of as in a state of centrality (or equilibrium). This is like the Supreme Ultimate's being non-finite *(wu-chi)*; it is not as if there were a

separate centrality added to the nature, any more than there is an Infinity added to the Supreme Ultimate.

Heterodox teachings, when they "point to the mind as the nature," say one must forget principles and attend to the psycho-physical [consciousness], believing that humaneness and right-ness are only superficial realities, above and beyond which they point to something separate, empty, and indescribable. They do not realize that it is actually subordinate to principle.[90]

Among the issues involved here for Lü is the question of what is meant by a "natural mind," what kind of learning is truly natural, and whether making a conscious effort is to be considered unnatu-ral. Lü proceeds to discuss this issue in relation to the process of learning and knowing as taught by Chu Hsi:

What the sage spoke of in relation to the investigation of things and the extension of knowledge was the point of thorough pene-tration where there is integral comprehension, as the principles in things and affairs meet, through inquiry and discussion, with principles in the substance of the mind. In this there is no distinction of inner and outer. If one talks of freeing oneself from externals in order to seek knowledge within the mind, then there is a distinction between inner and outer. The sages only sought to understand principles in order to practice the Way.[91]

At this point in Lü's discussion of the *Great Learning's* investi-gation of things and extension of learning, he does not make any direct comment on Chu Hsi's special note on the subject (discussed above in chapter 3 on "Getting It Oneself" and chapter 4 on "Neo-Confucian Individualism and Holism"). This had been a striking intervention on Chu Hsi's part into the text of the *Great Learning* and in his *Questions on the Great Learning (Ta-hsüeh huo-wen)*. It was also often commented on by later Neo-Confucians since it pointed to the culmination of the learning process in a kind of breakthrough to integral comprehension. Whether this should be understood as a *sudden* breakthrough is debatable, but it was inter-

preted by many as an experience of self-transcendence and wholeness, analogous in some ways to Ch'an enlightenment, yet dis-
tinctly Neo-Confucian in other ways. Ch'ien Mu, for instance,
says: "If one wishes to discuss Chu Hsi's thought concerning the
investigation of things, it is imperative to take his supplementary
comment on *ko-wu chih-chih* in the *Great Learning* as the most
important source."[92] For Lü not to address it directly raises a
question as to whether he might not have wished to deemphasize
the point; to avoid drawing unnecessary attention to this "breakthrough" could have been part of his strategy for discounting or
minimizing any attempt to equate Chu Hsi's experience of integral
comprehension with Wang Yang-ming's innate knowing.

If a modern account of it could describe Neo-Confucian "self-
cultivation" as leading to "a type of enlightenment that is, as
described by Chu Hsi, strongly reminiscent of Zen ideas,"[93] one
can believe that it is this passage which is referred to. Even though
Chu Hsi himself would have rejected such an interpretation, Lü
might have sensed the danger lurking there.

In any case, there can be no doubt whatever that Lü spoke to the
essential issue again and again elsewhere in his *Discourses* and
Recorded Conversations on the Four Books. This is especially evident in his discussion of the chapter in the *Great Learning* immediately preceding Chu Hsi's supplementary note. Here Lü goes out
of his way to specify the different senses in which Chu Hsi discusses "knowing," to make clear that Chu is referring to a gradual
step-by-step process, and to preclude any possible interpretation of
this in terms of Wang Yang-ming's innate knowing:

> This chapter just stresses the root and does not stress "knowing."
> As used here "knowing" *(chih)* corresponds to the *chih* in the
> text of the classic *[Great Learning]* which speaks of knowing the
> order of stem and branch *(chih pen-mo)*, and has nothing to do
> with the *chih* of "extending knowledge" *(chih chih)*. Many peo-
> ple confuse the two and from this get it involved with the inves-
> tigation of things, thus equating the things of "the investigation

of things" with the "thing" of "things having their stem and branch." The misleading assertions of one school about this have their source in Hsin-chien's[94] [Wang Yang-ming's] attack on Chu Hsi's supplementary comment on the investigation of things and extension of knowing,[95] by which this school seeks to extend the meaning of the text so as to justify their linking of the terms. In the Classic and its commentaries, when the same character has different meanings, they should each be analyzed one by one. . . .

[If a loose usage is allowed,] it can lead to such things as later scholars taking the practice of quiet-sitting *(hsi-ching)* to mean giving primacy to quiescence *(chu-ching)*, or to taking "innate knowing" and making it "the extension of knowing," all of which fails to analyze the meaning of the words and only gives license to their own theories.[96] This is exactly what Confucius called "acting in ignorance." . . .[97]

The knowing of "knowing the stem" and "knowing the order of priority" is not the same as the knowing of the "extension of knowing" or "knowing when to rest." The "things" of "things and affairs having their stem and branch" is not the same as the things of the "investigation of things," but the lecturers of the Cheng-te and Chia-ching periods (1506–1566) likened and identified them so that they could take the chapter about things and affairs having their stem and branch and use it to emend the commentary on the method of investigating and extending. With this inadequate understanding of the terms, they proceeded to propound their own theories. Thus, starting with such exegetical amendments to Ch'eng and Chu, they ended up entirely propagating aberrant doctrines.[98]

A similar concern is evident in Lü's discussion of the oneness or singleness referred to in the sages' "method of the mind-and-heart." In the latter case, the oneness, unity or singleness of mind is a means to preserve the centrality or equilibrium of the mind, and not the pursuit of a separate essence or object of contemplation. Here "equilibrium," "centrality," or the Mean *(chung)* is seen by

Lü as "the essence of the method of the mind" but, as indicated above, it is only a condition to be attained through the practice of refinement and singleness.[99] In this respect refinement and singleness are akin to the "caution," "apprehension," and "vigilance" spoken of in the *Mean*. "Caution and vigilance sum up the whole method of the mind-and-heart *(hsin-fa)*, by which the noble man exercises self-control and preserves the mind."[100]

Here Lü may have in mind not only sixteenth-century "lecturers" of the Wang school, but his contemporary Li Yung (1627–1705)[101] who expressed views similar to those attacked here when he lectured at the Tung-lin Academy and elsewhere in the Kiangnan area during the early 1670s.[102]

Further, explaining Mencius' teaching concerning the "lost mind," Lü says, again on the basis of Chu Hsi's view of "the mind as coordinating the nature and emotions":

> The mind coordinates the nature and emotions. The movements of the mind, their coming and going, their loss or preservation, all have to do with the spirituality of the psycho-physical [consciousness], and the subtlety of its control consists in preserving the mind of humaneness and rightness. "Losing the mind" is the loss of control by humaneness and rightness, and "seeking the lost mind" means seeking what should control the mind. If this mind is preserved, then what gives this control is preserved, and principle and the psycho-physical [consciousness] are unified. . . . If this mind is lost, then the psycho-physical consciousness runs off by itself. Wherefore it becomes imperative to employ the method of inquiry and learning to recover and nourish it through the correcting power of principle, so as to restore unity. . . .[103]
>
> Heterodox teachings also seek the mind, but having rejected the search for the principles of things-and-affairs, what they pursue is no more than the spiritual activity of the psycho-physical consciousness, and so they cannot employ the multitude of principles in the mind to deal with things-and-affairs.[104]

Here Lü asserts the importance of method or process, combining moral effort and intellectual inquiry, as the requisite means for achieving and preserving the unity of the mind. Deviant teachings, such as those of the Ch'an masters Lin-chi and Ts'ao-tung, Lu Hsiang-shan, Ch'en Hsien-chang, and Wang Yang-ming, discard this method in order to pursue the substance of the mind-in-itself, apart from things-and-affairs, thereby seeking a unity devoid of principle. This then leads also to dispensing with specific steps taught in the *Great Learning* (the Eight Items or Specifications) and the *Mean* (the five procedures of broad learning, accurate inquiry, etc.).[105] Lü's line of analysis is clearly meant to underscore the difference between Lu Hsiang-shan's primary emphasis on first establishing the moral nature and Chu Hsi's on the method of inquiry and learning—a difference which some earlier proponents of the Learning of the Mind-and-Heart had tried to minimize and reconcile. At the same time Lü is differentiating Chu Hsi's method of the mind-and-heart *(hsin-fa)* from the looser and more general concept of the Learning of the Mind-and-Heart *(hsin-hsüeh)* as taught by Wang Yang-ming.

Against this background one can appreciate the significance of Lü's explanation of Confucius' "One Thread Running Through It All": "The expression one thread running through it all points to an overall coordination and integration on the basis of what one has studied and learned. The point of comprehension is not something special to be perceived before one begins studying and learning."[106]

From this Lü argues that if there was nothing learned there was nothing to be threaded, and if there was no threading there could be no integration to speak of. Chu Hsi, he believes, correctly understood and expressed what Confucius meant about the One Thread, i.e., first learning much and through this coming to a sense of the coherence of all principles, as well as a sense of the unity of the self with all things.[107] "All talk about first having an experience of unity or wholeness, and then proceeding to study and learn is lapsing into Ch'an. It is the counterfeit of the way to virtue."[108]

In the *Analects* it is loyalty (being true to oneself, *chung*) and reciprocity toward others *(shu)* that are said by Confucius to have a single thread running through them. One cannot, says Lü, take this kind of "one thread," treat it as a special transmission outside the scriptures, and assimilate it to the One Mind of the Buddhists as if it were a kind of Confucian Hinayana, to be sublimated in an all-encompassing Mahayana vision. In the one original mind of the Buddhists, there would have been no distinction of loyalty and reciprocity to start with and no need for "one thread."[109]

If, says Lü, book-learning and the fathoming of principles are to be regarded as diversionary and divisive, alienating the self from itself, and are not, instead, precisely what Confucius thought was to be threaded, what could there have been [for Confucius] either to thread or integrate? Therefore Lü says "The 'one thread' [integration] lies right in the cognitive learning itself."[110]

In the context of the Chu-Lü debate over the priority of "honoring the moral nature" versus "the path of inquiry and learning" it was to be expected that Lü would favor the latter. What is noteworthy in his discussion, however, is the specific emphasis Lü puts on knowing or learning *(chih)* as cognitive learning or intellection *(chih-shih)*. This is not put forward at the expense of moral cultivation, but as a way of asserting the inseparability of rationality and morality, intellection and experience or practice. One can only achieve moral integration through the making of cognitive distinctions. The different virtues and their corresponding obligations must be respected for their distinctiveness before one can talk meaningfully about any underlying unity or coherence.

It is true that Chu Hsi spoke about principle as an "undifferentiated unity," but he was careful to explain how this was to be achieved, so as to avoid any confusion with the One Mind of the Buddhists into which all distinctions were ultimately dissolved.[111] Lü offers two analogies to illustrate the Neo-Confucian alternative to the Buddhist view of the mind, seen as one moon with many essentially unreal reflections:

All principle in the world originates from one source but flows out through many streams; it starts from one stem and reaches out to many branches. But the learner, in making his own effort, must go from the branch or stream and work back to the source. As to when, where, and how one applies this effort, Tseng Tzu every day continuously and consistently applied himself to one task after another; this too is going from the branch or stream back to the source. . . .[112]

The principle of the Way is just one. In the person of each individual it becomes many principles, but it is still just one principle. So the "one thread" truly arises out of individual differences. It is like people's having a fever. It may be just the same fever, but those who suffer from it differ in how strong of body or how weak of disposition they may be, and so there are differences in the diagnosis of each case and in the prescription for how to deal with it. The basic principle is the same for all fevers—how to dispel the infection and restore the body to its natural strength and vitality—but if one uses the same exact remedy in all cases, there are bound to be failures.[113]

As he does so often in the *Conversations* and *Discourses*, Lü bases himself here on the Neo-Confucian principle of the unity of principle and the diversity of its particularizations *(li-i fen shu)*. The applications he gives it, however, are significant. One is the need to deal with specific circumstances by analyzing them correctly. One cannot fulfill the principle by being vaguely sentimental or mystical about the unity of all things, but only by coming to terms with concrete realities. In this sense the individual must adjust or adapt himself to the facts; he cannot be subjective or self-assertive.

Every thing and affair has its own proper principle of what is fitting. If I can understand the proper way to deal with something, then that is its principle. If I do not understand it, I will make a mistake. Inherent in every thing and affair is its principle. The noble man, in regard to each thing and affair, seeks to make his handling of it accord with the principle of what is fitting in each case, so that they are one [integrated].[114]

Lest one conclude from this that Lü's point is simply to insist on the individual's following a specific moral requirement in each situation—perhaps even conforming to detailed moral prescriptions—one should note further, in the same discussion, how the principle of particularization also applies to the individual himself:

In the final analysis loyalty and reciprocity are just one thread, one substance, and one item, yet where and how the sages apply their effort is not the same. Each has his own way of working at it.[115]

The sage has his own particular application to make. The worthy has his own particular application to make. The ordinary man has his own particular application to make. The particularization differs but the principle is one.[116]

One can see from this how consistent Lü's discussion of these matters is with his interpretation of "getting it oneself" as "finding the Way oneself," "meeting its source wherever one turns," and "according with it in whatever situation one finds oneself."

In this basic formulation, "particularization" is often understood as one's lot, function, or duty—an interpretation which lends itself to the idea that prescribed moral duties or ritual requirements are to be accepted by, and internalized by, the individual. But, as in the medical analogy cited above, Lü most often has in mind a process that is far more general in its application to a variety of human activities, with the emphasis being put on the need for cognitive learning and the recognition of facts as the primary task. Again and again he presents Confucius as the example of one who worked at such learning throughout his lifetime, accumulating both knowledge and experience. Similarly with the insistence, cited earlier, on broad learning as taking precedence over "restraining oneself with ritual," and on the basic intellectual operations of studying widely, inquiring accurately, sifting, judging, etc., which Chu Hsi had highlighted in his "Articles of the White Deer Grotto Academy." Hence, although Lü will never sanction the divorcing of cognitive learning from moral practice, he is willing to pair them, with the former ahead of the latter:

> Someone asked about Master Chu's distinction between knowing and doing [learning and practice]. The Master replied, "When Master Chu said that Confucius' 'resolving to study' had learning as one aspect and energetic practice as another, he put the emphasis on [cognitive] learning." If one establishes learning as the base, while giving importance to practice, then from the start they are completely inseparable.[117]

In this case Lü opposes any divorce of knowing from doing, or learning from practice, lest it encourage the thought that the substance of the mind can be isolated and known in itself, apart from its engagement with things and affairs. While affirming that there is indeed a substance of the mind, i.e., the moral nature (in contrast to Huang Tsung-hsi's denial of such a substance), practically speaking Lü believes that one can only know it through its active employment or functioning, and that this begins with cognitive learning. Thus, in effect Lü's position is not so very different from Huang's—that the substance of the mind is what works out in practice; and in respect to "broad learning," no reader of Lü's *Discourses* and *Conversations* with their constant reiteration of this theme, could conclude that Lü was any less committed to scholarly study than Huang.

Ch'ien Mu is no doubt right when he singles out Huang as the outstanding scholar of the day for the breadth of his learning and the comprehensive scope of his thought.[118] Lü, if we can judge from what survives of his writing, does not compare with Huang in this respect. Nor would he, I think, wish to be so compared, for with all the value Lü set on breadth of scholarly learning, he assigned an almost equal status to selectivity: to the setting of scholarly priorities and to concentrating on first things first.

In this respect Lü again follows Chu Hsi. Thus, on the one hand, he subscribes fully to the extraordinary variety of ways in which Chu says "the investigation of things" should be pursued in what we would call the natural world, social relations, and the humanities [history, literature, philosophy, religion, etc.].[119] On the other hand, in his teaching Lü focuses narrowly on the Four Books—indeed, to an even greater extent than Chu Hsi had. It is no accident then that his extant writings, even taking into account the effects of their later proscription, are mainly concerned with the Four Books, or that, among the topics so selectively emphasized is broad learning!

Broad learning and fine distinctions might well be the mottoes of the scholarship Lü advocates as a remedy for the nondiscrimination and nondifferentiation of the Buddhists, who have emptied fullness of any clear meaning or value.

> When the sages and worthies discussed principle they insisted on making clear analyses and fine distinctions. The more precise the distinctions, the more solid and genuine would be the area of agreement. Thus the sages spoke of both refinement and unity. Aberrant teachings greatly feared such distinctions and discriminations, and wanted to sweep them all away so that they could see the substance of the mind directly. They did not realize that what they called the substance was a delusion, not the real thing. This represents the essential difference between Confucianism and Buddhism, orthodoxy and heterodoxy. Later those who became "outward Confucians and covert Buddhists" also wanted to give priority to seeing the substance of the mind directly, after which one was to undertake investigation and seek out principles through precise analysis. Though at first sight this theory seems very comprehensive and appealing, nevertheless, first to restrain the mind and only later to broaden it, first seeking unity and only later refinement of detail, is most contrary to the method men were taught by the sages. It is the greatest of delusions, a heresy beyond even the bounds of heresy![120]

Lü extends and develops this line of rational analysis into a full-scale attack on the idea that "getting" the Way is just an inner, private experience. Rather the Way is something both social and public. In ancient times, he says, scholars loved to gather together with friends to share their experiences and discuss them in writing. In this way the intimate relation between principle and the conduct of human relations, and between both of these and literature, was made manifest.

Lü is especially eloquent in advancing the argument that speech and writing, rather than being inadequate and undependable for conveying truth, as Ch'an Buddhism would have it, constitutes the very means by which essential virtue is produced, by which humaneness is achieved. It is through communicating with others that one engages in mutual encouragement for the fulfillment of each other's humanity *(fu-jen)* as Confucius had described it in the *Analects:* "The noble man, through letters, meets with friends, and through friends, strengthens his virtue (12:23)." It is through writing and literature that one comes together with others—sharing thoughts, discussing, debating, clarifying, and refining ideas.[121] "Spoken words are the voice of the heart, written words the brush-strokes of the heart.[122] If in the mind-and-heart there are hidden weaknesses or secret longings, they must be given expression in words, spoken and written. For spoken and written words all represent the mind-and-heart."[123]

Here Lü gives new voice to one of the earliest impulses of Neo-Confucianism, as articulated by northern Sung scholars in their threefold formulation of the Way as substance, function, and literary expression. That Lü's is a "new" voice may be seen against the background of two important developments in the Sung and Ming. Following Hu Yüan's early reaffirmation of the Way as substance, function, and literary expression in rejoinder to Ch'an Buddhism's teaching of "non-dependence on words,"[124] came the Ch'eng-Chu conception of the repossession of the Way, or Succession to the Way *(tao-t'ung)*, accompanied by the Method of the Mind-and-

Heart. At this point a literal reading of texts, as Han and T'ang scholars had commented on them, was superseded by the inspired reinterpretations and reconstructions of Ch'eng and Chu, especially of the *Great Learning* and the *Mean,* in some disregard of received traditions of textual exegesis.[125] Then, among Chu's disciples, Ch'en Ch'un and, in the next generation, Chen Te-hsiu, a prime exponent of the Ch'eng-Chu Learning of the Mind-and-Heart, had confirmed this shift by speaking of the substance, function, and transmission (rather than literary expression) of the Way, as if to allow for the heightened role of the mind in the revival and reconstitution of the Way.[126] Neither Ch'en, Chen, nor Chu Hsi himself had meant, of course, to jettison literature or textual tradition, but in the ongoing struggle with Buddhism, Confucianism's possession of its own philosophy and discipline of the mind had assumed a new importance.

Now Lü, in turn, having called into question this same learning as a subtle intrusion by Buddhism, assumes the revisionist role of challenging the credentials as bona fide Confucians of late Sung and Yüan scholars like Chen Te-hsiu, Hsü Heng, and Wu Ch'eng. It is of some significance then that Lü should at the same time reaffirm the fundamental value of expository literature, the basic Neo-Confucian texts, and the authoritative commentaries of Chu Hsi. Here we have a revisionist tactic in the service of a new fundamentalism, by which the latest of the Neo-Confucian prophets attempts to restore, of all things, the genuine scholastic tradition. Lü's "spoken and written words are all the mind-and-heart" signifies that classic texts and scholarly discourse are being brought back to the forefront of attention in place of the new Learning of the Mind-and-Heart as taught by Wang Yang-ming.

Good grounds for this were ready at hand for Lü Liu-liang. The second stage in the evolution of the Learning of the Mind-and-Heart had been identified by Lü with Ch'en Hsien-chang and Wang Yang-ming, both known for their independent interpretation of the Way, as they had "gotten it themselves."[127] In this situation Lü cannot rule out such independent "getting" of the Way, for it has a scriptural basis in classical and Neo-Confucian texts; but perhaps even more to the point is his own exercise of the same birthright when he overrules a great deal of intervening tradition.

Literarily, however, this second development had culminated in the romantic, self-expressionist movement led by Li Chih and the Yüan brothers, who celebrated in literature the unfettered expression of the emotions—the natural, spontaneous outpouring of the innocent, childlike heart.[128] Now when Lü seems to adopt a similar expressionist view of the function of literature, it might make one wonder. The fact is, however, that they do share a common Neo-Confucian conviction concerning the reality of the appetitive and instinctual life of man. The sticking point for Lü comes, not with the acceptance of the emotions, but with the tendency of others to think of these as unconditional and incontestable expressions of personal experience, rather than as having a social and public dimension as well. For it was in the open arena of public discourse, in the give-and-take of literary exchanges and rational debate—that an appropriate place and natural limit could be found for one's own self-expression or self-satisfaction in relation to others'. It was through this kind of exchange that the corrective power of principle, according to Lü, naturally emerged. One did not engage in literary communication and exchange with others as a means to attract attention to oneself and display one's own talents, but out of the natural enjoyment one derives from sharing one's feelings with friends and teachers who can help one clarify and refine them through literate discourse.[129]

If in this respect Lü may be thought of as returning to a scholastic tradition, it is not to a school of which he claims to be the direct heir and spokesman. At best one could only say that he is carrying on the kind of discourse that once had flourished in the academies of the Sung and Ming. As prophet and revisionist, he rebukes those identified with "lecturing or discoursing" on philosophy in the late Ming, not because they engaged in public lecturing and discussion, but precisely because they had betrayed it, turning in a direction that exalted private experience and led off into the trackless mysteries of Ch'an where no principles applied, no standards could be upheld and no rational conclusions could be reached.

The essential elements, then, in Lü's return to a kind of academic or scholastic tradition are his refocusing of that discourse on the Four Books and Chu Hsi's Commentaries, along with his promotion of the examination essay as a means of scholarly communication. The first followed from the inherent superiority, in Lü's eyes, of Chu Hsi's orderly and systematic approach to the study of the classics and from the lucidity of his expositions. It was a method combining definite commitment to the life of learning, specific steps by which to achieve the goal, and a recognition of the need to support one's claims with evidence and verify one's conclusions. The subjective conviction that one had "gotten it" in a silent unspoken way was not enough.[130]

Lü's second choice was far less obvious. Given the low esteem in which the so-called eight-legged essay was held by most Neo-Confucians, Lü's first task was to rescue this expository form from the hands of those popular, but vulgar and corrupt writers who had degraded themselves in the eyes of many Confucians, and who in Lü's own eyes had perverted the contents of the essays by turning away from Chu Hsi's authoritative interpretations.

We have noted before that Lü had qualms about making a living as a critic, editor, and publisher of examination essays. If we are to rely on the evidence presented in Tom Fisher's very thorough and judicious consideration of this question in his biographical studies of Lü, the primary issue for Lü was a conflict of conscience, not so much over the inherent unworthiness of essay composition as an intellectual pursuit, as over the seeming inconsistency of his refusal to take office or accept any favor from the Manchus, while at the same time he was deeply involved in an unseemly commercial enterprise directly related to the official recruitment process. Lü's great talent for this kind of work—his literary gifts and skill in philosophical exposition—had shown themselves quite early, and it was natural enough for him to exploit this talent, given the limited number of careers in which an educated man might make a living outside of officialdom. But for Lü it was surely more than a matter of expediency. Ch'ien Mu has observed that in the last years of the Ming, Chang Pu (1602–41) as leader of the Restoration Society *(Fu she)* had already made the case for the writing of examination essays as a legitimate form in which to convey one's Confucian concerns for the application of classical principles to contemporary problems.[131] Lü seems genuinely to have shared that conviction. To him it meant that there was a medium for enlarging the arena of discourse and debate over right principles, and further, through the printing press, for engaging far larger numbers of educated men in the process—creating, so to speak, an academy without walls. Indeed, had it not been for the success Lü achieved in this form of scholastic dialogue, he might well have been just another prophet without a people.

As Fisher concludes his discussion of the matter:

> Lü believed that departure from the philosophy and ethics of the Sung master [Chu Hsi] had produced the moral decay of his own times and was ultimately responsible for the downfall of his beloved Ming dynasty. He saw no more effective way of spreading his point of view to the educated segment of society than by using as a vehicle the type of literature every aspiring official had to master. Furthermore, unlike giving public lectures or teaching in the houses of the rich and influential, this method kept him out of the public eye and relatively free from potential government interference, for after all he was utilizing the very foundation of state orthodoxy as his means for criticizing contemporary society.[132]

This being the case, it must be recognized how much we rely on a source for Lü's ideas which has a specific orientation to the educated class of would-be scholar-officials. So far as one can tell, these sources—the *Discourses, Conversations,* and *Critical Comments*—constitute the great bulk of the written record of Lü's thought, and in this sense they are representative of his views on matters that preoccupied the literati in his time. But if one looks instead at his *Family Instructions*, a short piece that does not figure prominently in Lü's Collected Writings, one gets a different perspective on his thought. Here in a few brief admonitions on respect for those in the family hierarchy, on unselfishness, on diligence and thrift, on the avoidance of religious superstitions, one can observe some of the social assumptions that underlie Lü's views on the individual and society. Among these, for instance, is the belief that women have a limited outlook on life, tend to be narrow and selfish if not properly trained or restrained, and are (especially sisters-in-law) the greatest single source of discord in the family.[133] To say this is not necessarily to detract from what Lü has to say about the more high-minded concerns of the literati, but it reminds us that the same critical intelligence was not often focused (as in the case of Li Chih) on the problems of the lower orders of society. Progress on this level lagged behind what great scholars of the day were able to contribute to the understanding of other matters.

FUNDAMENTALISM AS RADICALISM

For those who have not heard of Savonarola, the Ayatollah Khomeini probably typifies today the fundamentalist who was also a radical. To be not only a fundamentalist and radical but at the same time orthodox, is a more difficult thing to achieve, but arguably Lü Liu-liang did it.

Radical, as applied to Lü, can only refer to the ends he sought and not to the means he would use, for the possibility of resorting to provocative advocacy or violent activism was virtually precluded by the failure of the Ming resistance and Lü's resignation to more passive means of struggle against the Manchus. As to ends, "radical" here refers to the totalistic nature of the political and social changes he called for, to the sweeping nature of the critique he made of existing institutions, and to the thoroughness with which he rooted this in his thought as a whole. One may find evidences of

Lü's loyalism or nationalism here and there in his surviving works, but on the whole, even allowing for the effects of censorship, Lü made less of a direct issue of this in his writings than he did in his conduct of life. By contrast his radical views on political and social questions permeate all of his discourses and recorded conversations. The practical and theoretical aspects of his thought are thoroughly interwoven. It is on this basis that we consider them here: not with a view to making a full assessment of his political philosophy and program as such, but only so as to grasp their implications for his view of the individual.

In his pioneering study of Lü, Jung Chao-tsu expressed admiration for Lü as a nationalist and rationalist but regretted his conservatism.[134] Ch'ien Mu, at about the same time, saw Lü as reviving the reformist spirit of the Northern Sung,[135] which seems to me more apt. But this spirit, which I have called "restorationist,"[136] tended to reject all existing institutions as flawed and corrupt in comparison to those of higher antiquity; hence not only was it far from conservative of the status quo, it was no less than radical in its attack on the established order. Sung reformers, and even Chu Hsi in his more seasoned judgments, found it necessary to moderate that critique and make concessions to the fact of historical change, so as to come to terms with existing realities. When, then, Lü in the late seventeenth century, returns to and reaffirms the earlier Sung view, it involves much more: the shelving of another five centuries of dynastic history, which in turn implies a far more intransigent defense of the original Neo-Confucian position.

This position rests for Lü, as it did not for early Sung reformers, on the more fully developed Neo-Confucian doctrine of human nature. Here Heaven's Imperative (*t'ien-ming*, politically the Mandate of Heaven) is conceived primarily in terms of man's moral nature. It is the moral imperative inherent in every human mind-and-heart that must be answered to for the validation of any regime's claimed legitimacy. There can be no mandate from Heaven for any ruler or regime that violates the basic life-giving principles constitutive of human nature. Indeed government exists only to advance and enhance those human values, and not to serve the interests of the ruler or ruling house:

> During the Three Dynasties every measure the sage-kings took to provide for the people's livelihood and maintain the social order, including the enfeoffment, military and penal systems, no matter how minute in detail or long-range their consequences, were only instituted for the sake of all-under-Heaven and their posterity. . . . Not a thing was done nor a law enacted simply for the ruler's own enrichment or aggrandizement, nor was their aim in the slightest to secure for their descendants an estate to be held onto forever, for fear of others trying to seize it. Thus in the *Mean (Chung yung)* was the sages' humaneness acclaimed for the warmth of its earnest solicitude [for the people].
>
> After the Ch'in and Han [however], even though among the many systems and institutions adopted from time to time there may have been some good ones ostensibly of benefit to the people or enriching the world, the underlying motive in government has been purely selfish and expedient, the fear being that otherwise one might suffer the loss of what belonged to one's family. . . . This is why Master Chu said that for over two thousand years the Way had not been practiced for even a single day.[137]

Elsewhere Lü identifies rulership with Heaven in order to emphasize both the overarching responsibility of the ruler to the people and the universality of the principles that should govern the ruler's conduct: "The Son of Heaven occupies Heaven's Position *(t'ien-wei)* in order to bring together the common human family within the Four Seas, not just to serve the self-interest of one family."[138] Lü explains that during the Three Dynasties the throne was passed on to others with the idea of sharing responsibility, of doing what was best for the people. "Heaven's Imperative and the minds-and-hearts of the people weighed heavily on them, and the world lightly. [Such being the case, as Mencius said] the sages would not commit even one unrighteous deed or kill even one person, though to do so might gain them the whole world."[139]

Yet after the Three Dynasties this attitude of shared concern disappeared:

> Since the three dynasties men's mores have changed, so that it has become a utilitarian world. Both our own [the ruler's own] and the people's hearts have lost their correctness. All rites and music, civil and penal administration, institutions and letters [supposedly incorporated in the Rites], as well as the management of resources and men, are governed purely by selfishness.[140]

Although some people talk about the ruler's loving and caring for the people, at best under dynastic rule one could hope for no more than was accomplished by Han Kao-tsu and T'ang T'ai-tsung, founding fathers of their respective dynasties, and this, says Lü, fell far short of the peace and order which prevailed under the Three Dynasties.[141]

This line of argument is, of course, quite similar to that of Northern Sung scholars who rejected the Han and T'ang as models for their own rulers. Familiar too is the example of the Ch'eng brothers and Chu Hsi, cited by Lü for their trenchant criticism of the rulers of their time, insisting that the latter "rectify their minds-and-hearts and make their intentions sincere."[142] Yet, for all these Sung precedents, there are significant differences of emphasis in Lü's reformulation of them. His situation differs from theirs not only in virtue of the passage of time, during which generations of Neo-Confucian mentors to the throne have failed to accomplish the needed change in attitude, but also in that Lü has no prospect himself of fulfilling that role—lecturing to the Emperor or writing admonitory memorials as Chu Hsi and Chen Te-hsiu had done. In consequence of this, we find him addressing, not the reigning emperor as they had done, but all those in the official ranks who should be sharing in the responsibility of rulership. Remembering, in fact, that Lü's audience consisted largely of candidates for office, it is of some importance that he magnifies the role of the minister, while also including officialdom as a whole in his scathing condemnation of those who have failed to fulfill the responsibility of upholding the True Way.

This reformulation of the problem emerges clearly in Lü's analysis of dynastic rule, for the latter is in his eyes the perversion of a ruler-minister relationship posited as the most serious of all moral relations. Some scholars had justified the dynastic system as a natural extension of the parent-child relationship, and had tried to promote the idea that the ruler was the loving parent of all the people. Lü dismissed this paternalism as a fraudulent claim and instead equated rulership with ministership. The original basis of rulership was no different from that of ministership; the only criterion for holding the office should be individual human merit:

> Lineal succession is founded on the parent-child relationship; the passing on of rulership is founded on the ruler-minister relation. The former derives from [the principle of] humaneness; the latter from that of rightness. On this basis these two great principles coexisted and were never confused. Thus Heaven's position [rulership] was originally conferred on the basis of individual worth.[143]

Elsewhere Lü emphasizes that this basic moral relation is rooted in the nature received from Heaven:

> People understand that the relation between parent and child is inherent in the moral nature received from Heaven; they do not realize that the same is true of ruler and minister; that it is a natural and not an artificial joining of the two. Heaven gives birth to the people and establishes rulers and ministers for them. Rulers and ministers are for sustaining the life of the people. The minister seeks out a ruler to head the government, and the ruler seeks out the minister to share in the governing. Together they represent Heaven's presence in the world. Thus the ruler's position is called "Heaven's position; official emoluments are called

Heaven's emoluments." Heaven's order and Heaven's justice are not something the ruler and minister can take and make their own. Though there is a definite difference in the honor done to ruler and minister, it is still only a difference of one degree in the relative distance between them.[144]

Here Lü emphasizes the organic nature of the social order and of the moral imperatives governing human relations. Among these, he says elsewhere, the moral relation between ruler and minister is the most important of all:

The rightness (i) of the ruler-minister relation is of the first importance in the world (yü chung ti-i shih). It is the greatest of the human moral relations. If one does not keep to this principle, then no matter what one's accomplishments or meritorious deeds, they will count for nothing against the guilt so incurred.[145]

While the moral responsibility which attaches to this relation is heavy and inescapable—as fixed and unalterable as the imperatives of Heaven's mandate—this does not mean that the personal relationship between ruler and minister is similarly fixed and unalterable:

Ruler and minister come together in agreement on what is right (i). If they can agree on what is right, they can form the relation of ruler-minister; if not, they should part, as is the case in the relation between friends. It is not like father and son, or older and younger brother [i.e., a blood relation which cannot be changed]. If they do not agree, there is no need for personal resentment or recrimination. If their commitment is not the same, their Way cannot be carried out, and it is best to part.

Parting is in accordance with the rite of ruler and minister, not a departure from that relation. It was only in later times, with the abandonment of the enfeoffment system and adoption of centralized prefectures and counties, that the world came under the control of one ruler and consequently there was "advancement and retirement" [from office] but no parting. When the Ch'in abandoned the Way, they established the "rite" of honoring the ruler and abasing the minister, and created an unbridgeable gap between the one on high and the other below, giving the ruler complete control over the minister's advancement and retirement, while leaving him nowhere to go. That was when the relation of rightness between ruler and minister underwent a complete change.[146]

In consequence of this change the conception of ministership, as well as rulership, was corrupted when Heaven's authority was no longer recognized:

After the Three Dynasties' rulers and ministers forgot about Heaven. Rulership came to be thought of as for one's own self-gratification. Ministers thought that life and death, reward and punishment, were all at the ruler's disposal and it could not be otherwise. Thereupon the ruler became honored and the minister abased, with the two completely separated. Government, insofar as it now involved a sharing of power and prestige, could not possibly be shared. Thereupon usurpations and assassinations followed; a world of selfishness and expediency was produced. Cut off from Heaven, rulers did not understand that rites come from Heaven, ministers did not realize that loyalty [being true] is rooted in the moral nature, that the nature is Heaven, that Heaven is the moral imperative [and political mandate], that it is principle, and the nature is principle.[147]

By now the reader should be able to complete the argument for himself: it was the great contribution of Chu Hsi, says Lü to have articulated the idea that everything depended on the recognition of principle, and it was the disastrous error of Wang Yang-ming's "innate knowing" in subverting principle, by assimilating it into the mind, which frustrated the effort to establish principle in the halls of power.

Still Wang's fault was only to thwart the needed reformation;

others were to blame for the original corruption. If one compares what Lü has to say about this sorry state of things with what Chen Te-hsiu had said about it earlier in his *Extended Meaning of the Great Learning (Ta-hsüeh yen-i)*, one notices that Lü has reduced the problem to much simpler terms: he has given up on the hope of reforming dynastic rulers, and concentrates far more of his attention on evils prevailing among scholar-officials, who by now have been thoroughly infected by the selfishness, acquisitiveness, and expedience characteristic of dynastic rule.

Properly the role of minister or scholar-official was to speak out against existing evils and abuses. Although the *Mean* (27) speaks of the noble man as, by his very silence, commanding respect through the force of his own character, Lü is concerned lest this be misunderstood as sanctioning the toleration of evil. At court, he says, it is a shame and a disgrace for the noble man if the Way is not carried out. "When he stands at court, there is no way he can keep silence. If something is done contrary to the Way, he can only withdraw from participation in it. To keep silence is what base officials and unworthy scholars do." [148]

Since the Ch'in and Han, however, scholar-officials have not only kept silence in the face of evil; they have actively cooperated with it, seeking only to gratify the wishes of the ruler. Even when they have paid lip service to what was right, in the form of rites, they have been motivated by one concern only—to cater to the ruler and advance their own ambitions. This, says Lü, is why they are unwilling to advocate fundamental changes and, indeed, go so far as to argue against restoring the institutions of the sage-kings as impractical. [149]

In his own time, says Lü, this situation does not arise from any lack of natural sympathy on the part of scholars for the people and their needs, but from the fact that the examination and civil service system mass-produce scholars on the wrong model. "Scholars' mind-and-hearts become like block-prints, and just as errors in the text of the block are reproduced in what is printed, they all repeat the same errors." [150]

Initially . . . when they are poor and have not yet become licentiates, they identify with the people and sympathize with their feelings on what is good and evil. But once [as licentiates] they have put on the robes of office and taken up their administrative duties, in their ruthless greed and harsh rapacity, they come to see things, good and ill, differently from the people. The reason is that when they are licentiates their feelings about good and evil begin to change from what is correct, and everything becomes dominated by selfish desires. How then, on becoming officials, could they be expected all of a sudden to start adhering to principle?[151]

RITES AND RIGHTS

If principle is the main focus of Lü's Neo-Confucian fundamentalism, rites are the main substance of his radicalism (as, we recall, was the case with Li Chih). His preoccupation with the former, however, tends to direct and define his treatment of the latter. This is shown in his choice of the Four Books as his primary texts. For in this context rites are discussed essentially in terms of principles, in a theoretical way. They are no less important to him for all that, as we shall presently see, but his approach to the subject is less practical and detailed than was the case with Chu Hsi, Chen Te-hsiu, Ch'iu Chün, and other scholars of the Ch'eng-Chu school who devoted particular attention to rites. Largely ignored in his discourses are the *Family Ritual of Master Chu (Chu Tzu chia-li* or *Wen-kung chia-li);* the *Elementary Learning (Hsiao-hsüeh)*, the manual of basic personal, household, and community ritual; Chu's commentary on the classic of *Ceremonial Rites (I-li);* his revision of the *Lü Family Community Compact (Lu-shih hsiang-yüeh)* and many other writings within the scope of ritual as Neo-Confucians had broadly conceived of it. The practical reason for this is obvious enough—Lü's concentration on a particular audience and on their preoccupation with the Four Books—but it is nonetheless indicative of his particular revisionist brand of Neo-Confucian fundamentalism that he excludes large areas of traditional scholarly and practical endeavor, and not just the Learning of the Mind-and-Heart. This then, in turn, shapes his radicalism and what it has to say about the individual.

Many of the points made by Lü concerning the illegitimacy of dynastic rule are similar to those found in Huang Tsung-hsi's *Plan for the Prince (Ming-i tai-fang lu)*, where Huang challenges the legitimacy of dynastic law and speaks of it as "unlawful law."[152] Lü resists the idea that fundamental institutions should be thought of in terms of law, preferring to stay with the traditional Confucian view of them as rites, and of law as only a last, coercive recourse when the possibility of voluntary cooperation through rites no longer exists. But he makes a like distinction to Huang's when he speaks of existing institutions in Mencian terms as "rites that are not rite" *(fei-li chih li)* and "rightness that is not right" *(fei-i chih i)*. Commenting on this passage in *Mencius* 4B:6, Lü asserts an intrinsic link between rites, rightness, and principles:

Rites represent the principles of things and affairs. Rightness represents what is thought appropriate to the time. As to their source, although they are there in our minds-and-hearts, rites and rightness have no pertinence apart from given matters or specific instances in time. Once there is a matter at hand and the time comes, then rites and rightness are there. If one does not analyze this correctly, saying for example that the rite follows upon the matter-at-hand or rightness upon the time, one has already bifurcated them beforehand.

Having the manifestation (*chi*, lit. traces) one has this mind. Rites that are not rite, rightness that is not right, come about by one's own conscious action when one's mind takes something as rite or right erroneously. Therefore I say that if one is not precise in one's judgment of principles, it will not fit the manifest facts and will not be rite or right.

The school of innate knowing sees everything in the world as a residual manifestation of conscious activity—as outward ephemera—and says it is only the consciousness of our mind that constitutes innate knowing, is Heaven's principle, or is in effect rite or right. They do not judge that the rites and rightness of the sages and worthies are to be found precisely in the matter at hand and in the time. If one gets the principle of the matter and hits what is appropriate to the time, then the rite and rightness of our mind is complete. But if one's judgment with regard to the matter at hand or the time is imprecise, one will be misled by vain imaginings and rash judgments.[153]

Here one sees that Lü uses "rite" to mean a formulation of principle directly in relation to facts and circumstances. It combines the constancy and universality of principle with its differentiated application to all human affairs, while "right" or "rightness" represent a human response as to the appropriateness of an action in time. Both are indispensable to the employment and fulfillment of principle in the mind. Hence Lü speaks of rites as the substance or embodiment *(t'i)* of the Way. They are not mere residual excrescences of some hidden virtue, as Lao Tzu and Chuang Tzu would have it, or momentary and ephemeral traces of an inconceivable Truth, as the Buddhists would see them, but are indeed the very reality of the Way.[154]

A secondary implication is that "rite," as the formal definition and concrete embodiment of principle, covers some of the same ground as our rational and moral conception of "rights," expressing the principles of propriety and respect toward others in the broadest sense, i.e., not only in the respect to be shown other human beings, but also in things and affairs in the world at large, including the entire natural order. This is, however, not wholly original with Lü. Ch'iu Chün had said something similar in the fifteenth century in his discussion of rites in his *Supplement to the "Extended Meaning of the Great Learning,"* again based squarely on Chu Hsi's view of both principles and rites.[155]

Of special significance is the way Lü relates this conception to the human emotions. As we have seen earlier, Lü believed the emotional and instinctual drives in man always were accompanied by their corresponding innate principles in the mind-and-heart, with the former providing the energy and the latter the direction for human activities. As Lü puts it:

Rites derive from Heaven [i.e., principle], emotions from the mind-and-heart. Rites are always joined to human emotions, but this must mean to be in accord with the norms of the highest excellence in human emotions, i.e., with Heaven. To weigh the emotions, evaluate them, adjust and modulate, correct and check them, is all according to Heaven. Whether to set rites forth clearly, so that emotions attain their proper fulfillment, or [contrarily] for the emotion alone to be relied upon, allowing Heaven's principles to be overruled—this is the essential difference between orthodoxy and heterodoxy.[156]

Earlier we have seen how Lü spoke of the emotions as natural powers or virtues *(te)*. Here rites are spoken of as giving formal embodiment to the principles which should guide the appetites. Lü does not refer to Li Chih in this connection, but what he says in the following could well be taken as a comment on Li's views as presented in chapter 9. Lü says:

All human hearts are the same in having desires and [their corresponding indwelling] principles. For instance, they are the same in their love of goods and sex. However they should only get what is right for them to love. If one speaks only of their being the same in the love of goods and sex [and not in having principles], then human desires can become a source of great disorder in the world. Therefore when Mencius spoke of what makes human hearts the same, he referred to principle, to what is right and proper. Filiality, brotherliness, and commiseration are common principles of what is right and proper; therefore the text [of the *Great Learning*] speaks of them as norms or standards. Rites, music, penal and administrative systems are also the common principles of what is right and proper; therefore they are called the Way. Extrapolating from these norms one projects the Way, which is the common basis for putting these principles into practice. Therefore what is spoken of as the Way of the measuring square, refers to taking those common principles for measuring human hearts and making them the means of governance which brings peace to the world. Simply to pursue the satisfaction of the physical appetites and let everyone gratify his own desires is the naturalness and laissez-faire of the Taoists or the expedient adaptability of the Buddhists. It is not the Sages' way of the measuring square.[157]

Critics of Neo-Confucianism in Lü's time and after often criticized its concept of principles and its practice of rites as a deadly attack on the human emotions, reflecting the influence on Neo-Confucianism of Buddhism and Taoism with their negative view of human desires. In Lü's case, however, as in Chu Hsi's,[158] the emotions are not seen as intrinsically evil but as natural. Thus the issue for Lü is whether the norms for directing these desires are not also natural, so that one need not regard the desires as inherently selfish and anarchic.

Here two points should be observed. The first, which we simply note for further discussion later, is that Lü treats the matter less as a great struggle for the moral will in overcoming the physical appetites than as a question of recognizing the reality of principle in the universe and in the mind of man—that is, of dealing with the philosophical errors of Buddhism and Taoism. The second point is that when Lü does attack selfishness in man it is almost always in the form of the greed and acquisitiveness of those who hold power and influence over others through the dynastic system. As far as the common man is concerned, Lü is all sympathy for the satisfaction of their basic physical needs. In this, of course, he is following Mencius, who diagnosed the essential problem as the failure of the ruler and his henchmen to identify with the needs and feelings of the common man.

The extent to which Lü also reflects the growing trend in the late

Ming and early Ch'ing to enlarge the scope of human desires *(jen yü)* accepted as natural is difficult to judge, though his view of the matter certainly allows for this. What seems clear, in any case, is the difference in emphasis between him and Chen Te-hsiu earlier. Chen was preoccupied with the personal weaknesses and self-indulgence of Sung emperors, of which he had close experience himself. Therefore he greatly stressed the need for the individual to gain self-control. This was not the case so much with Lü, who sees the matter more as one of institutionalized selfishness in the dynasty and in those who serve it who have become corrupted by this systemic evil.

This would accord with an increasing consciousness among late Ming-early Ch'ing thinkers on the institutional factors, in contrast to the individual's personal role, in politics. But none of this requires that Lü amend Chu Hsi's basic view with respect to the legitimacy of natural desires, shared with others, and the ruler's obligation to provide for the satisfaction of these desires and needs on the part of the people.

Indeed, if Lü can be accused of being too moralistic in such matters, it would have to be for reducing the whole problem of dynastic rule simply to a question of selfishness on the part of power-holders. This simplistic tendency shows itself in a disinclination to deal in a more realistic way with the historical factors that underlie the development of the dynastic system—as for instance Huang Tsung-hsi, Ku Yen-wu, and Wang Fu-chih (1619–92) did.[159] More often than not Lü is content to dismiss these as simply considerations of expediency and utilitarianism, and then to turn the analysis in the direction of those philosophical errors—typified by Wang Yang-ming and other ostensible Confucians but covert Buddhists—that allow principle to be taken as whatever circumstances dictate.

If this is not uniformly the case with Lü, it is because he often detects some other moral issue at stake in the discussion of particular institutions, such as the well-field system or the school system. Often enough he simply refers to the ancient rites or institutions in a formulaic way as "the enfeoffment system, the well fields, the schools, the penal and administrative systems. . . ." What is more, for one seemingly so devoted to Chu Hsi, it is striking that nowhere in his extant writings do we find any recognition by Lü of Chu Hsi's own quite specific contributions to the creation of an adequate infrastructure for the "renewal of the people," as for instance in the community compacts and other intermediate forms of social and economic organization. Occasionally, however, he can be quite acute in singling out fundamental principles at issue in the neglect or abandonment of such institutions. Thus, for him, a prime principle underlying the well-field system was its provision of the basic means of subsistence for all. Lü stubbornly held to this egalitarian economic model against those who believed it to be impossible of realization in existing circumstances. Concerning one such argument, Lü had this to say:

> Some say that schools are not difficult to set up but the well-field system is far from easy to carry out, in witness whereof is the fact that today there are schools but no well-fields. To this the Master said: "They do not realize that the schools of today are not the same as the schools of antiquity. The latter were set up only after the well-fields had been instituted [to provide the material support prerequisite to education]. For the whole purpose and organization of schools was linked to the well-field system, which is not at all the case with the schools of today. So if it is easy for one [to be established], it is easy for both, and if it is difficult for one, it is equally difficult for both. There is no difference between them in this."[160]

Such an argument does not, of course, dispose of the practical difficulties, but it does show an awareness on Lü's part that the existing school system is inadequate (something his questioner had not apparently thought of) and that the educational problem could not be solved except on the basis of an improvement in the economic condition of the ordinary man. Since other Neo-Confucians, as we have seen, were not unconscious of the failure to establish a universal school system of the kind Chu Hsi had advocated, it is significant that Lü has not forgotten the point either.

Lü was by no means a complete leveler. He believes like Mencius in a hierarchy of merit—the "nobility of Heaven" as Mencius had put it. But he thought of himself as a poor man and identified with the poor in their suffering at the hands of grasping officials. Thus he took the welfare of the common man, and provision for it, as the basic measure of what may be considered an adequate income for those of higher status. The well-field system had provided the ordinary man with 100 *mou* of land to cultivate, which was enough to insure a decent livelihood. The emoluments of officials, though meant to be somewhat more ample, should, as Mencius (5B:2) said, be thought of as in lieu of their own cultivation of the land and the income thereby produced.

> [In ancient times] the whole system of emoluments was based on the usufruct of the land, and likewise the whole system of official ranks was based on it. In Heaven's creating of the people and providing for rulers and teachers, the basic principle was thus all-embracing. . . . Looked at from the top it might seem to some as if ranks and emoluments were projected downward to the common people; they do not realize that looked at in terms of Heaven's bestowing of life on the people, the principle originates with the people and reaches up to the ruler.[161]

In this emphasis on the fundamental importance of the common man we see not only a reflection of Mencius' emphasis on the people, but a further application of Lü's basic doctrine that all life comes from Heaven, that all human beings are endowed with the moral nature, and that in each individual lies the imperative to act in accordance with the principles inhering in that nature. It is not a "mandate" solely for the ruler.

This is a point of great potential significance. Confucius and Mencius had stressed the responsibility of noble men *(chün tzu)* to provide for the needs of the common man *(min)*, but not the responsibility of the *min* themselves. Here the heightened emphasis on the indwelling of principle, as the Heavenly endowed moral nature, suggests that all individuals share to some degree in this responsibility, even though Lü does not elaborate any new political mechanisms by which this responsibility might be actively discharged.[162]

All of this is consistent with what Chu Hsi sets forth in his commentary on the opening chapter of the *Great Learning,* but the particular emphasis on Heaven's Imperative comes from the *Mean.* We have seen earlier that this has special meaning for Lü as the basis for his refutation of Wang Yang-ming's view of the mind-and-heart, but this is not all. Considering that the *Mean* is the most metaphysical of the Four Books it is significant how much of Lü's commentary on it is devoted to political and social matters, as if especially to ground the social order in the underlying structure of the universe, and at the same time show how principle, in the form of human nature, must find embodiment in the social order. Thus, discussing the opening lines of the *Mean,* he says "whenever one speaks of rites, music, law, and government one is speaking about the moral nature which derives from Heaven's Imperative."[163]

If the universal moral nature is the most fundamental principle of the social order, and rites are the embodiment or substance of the Way governing human affairs, it establishes a certain basic human equality as the touchstone of government. Speaking to the Ch'eng-Chu doctrine of "renewing the people," Lü says:

> Both the common man and the Son of Heaven are rooted in the same principle. Speaking of it in terms of rank from the top down, the *Great Learning* says "from the Son of Heaven down to the common man," but in terms of principle, in reality, it goes from the common man up to the Son of Heaven. The Son of Heaven's renewing of the people should proceed on the same principle, and conform to the common man's regulation of his own family.[164]

The *Recorded Conversations* adds the further note:

This is not only a responsibility that weighs on the ruler. Everyone has his own self [to govern] and therefore there is no one on whom the responsibility does not lie. Just as there are the myriad things and one Supreme Ultimate, so each thing has its own Supreme Norm to follow.[165]

Although the matter is discussed in terms of responsibilities rather than entitlements, it is clear that each thing's having its own norm to follow confers on it a certain irreducible autonomy, which governance must take into account and respect. Thus Lü also says:

There are many gradations from the Son of Heaven down to the common man, and each in performing his own proper function is different, but the differentiation lies in one's lot or function and not in the principle. Therefore it is said "Principle is one and its particularizations diverse. . . ." No matter how low the commoner is, it is the same underlying principle and not a different case. The commoner may not have the official function of ordering the state and bringing peace to the world, but inherent in the fulfilling of his self-cultivation is the principle of ordering the state and bringing peace to the world.[166]

From this one can see that the structure of authority, which in Lü's mind derives from the imperative of Heaven, is based on the moral nature as expressed through the minds and hearts of the common people, and that it works upward from them, not downward from the Son of Heaven, in a manner parallel to the workings of the economic principle referred to earlier. This is all of one piece with the interdependent structure of economic welfare and educational opportunity discussed in relation to the school system.

Since the rites represent a voluntaristic ordering of human life and activity, for Lü they rest on a foundation of self-cultivation by the people at large. It is typical of Lü's approach, as it was of Chu Hsi's, that the macrocosmic view of world-ordering should rest on the microcosmic view of self-cultivation, and that the discussion—whether it be of the *Great Learning* or the *Mean*—would always be brought back to his conception of the self. This much, one could say recalling Li Chih's views on rites, was common to them both. But, having presented the theoretical basis in relation to the opening lines of the *Mean*, Lü concludes by reiterating Confucius' dictum that the process of self-cultivation must begin with a commitment to learning, a commitment of the mind-and-heart to "learning for one's self."[167] The essential method to be followed is that of vigilant self-watchfulness, in a reverential and respectful spirit, to be exercised in relation to every matter, every action, every thought one becomes engaged in. It is here then, recalling Li Chih's view on reverence, that an essential difference lies between the two.

Lü is careful to distinguish this self-watchfulness from any conception of a self to be contemplated in itself, apart from one's engagement with the world. And he reiterates his opposition to any method which would set aside either rational thought or value judgments in arriving at a direct intuition, sudden enlightenment, or transcendent self-awakening. It must work through careful observation of things and the making of fine distinctions in regard to the matters at hand, with the greatest acuteness and precision of thought, since there is no holistic understanding that does not work through subtle analysis.[168] In this respect it is probably significant that Lü does refer to Chu Hsi's concluding remarks at the end of the *Mean*, which include the preceding points, whereas he has drawn no attention to Chu's special note on the extension of learning that culminates in a "breakthrough to integral comprehension" *(huo-jan kuan-t'ung)*.

Nevertheless, principle in the mind has its transcendent, numinous aspect, just as does the Supreme Ultimate. It has its unity as well as its diverse particularity. This applies even to so sensitive an issue as innate knowing, which Lü accepts as a valid concept in the Mencian sense even if not Wang Yang-ming's: "Innate knowing and innate ability are Heaven's [natural] principles, the same in every man. . . . What one has learned and can do, are necessary principles *(pi-jan chih li)*. In this every man is different, and yet there is no man that does not possess his own learning and abilities."[169]

Hence there is also, even in a "learning for one's self" that insists on the validity of rational concepts and moral distinctions, an irreducible element of individual "getting it" that goes beyond such concepts: "In the way of the sage there is always something that cannot be exhausted by words. No matter how far one may go with the discursive method, at the point of getting it oneself, its meaning is subtle and mysterious, and varies with the individual."[170]

There is significance in Lü's equal insistence here on the transcendence and immanence, the unity and particularity, of principle. The former provides the ground for his radical challenge to existing institutions and his revisionist critique of Neo-Confucian tradition, the latter the basis for his adaptation of tradition in the form of a new fundamentalism appropriate to his own age and circumstances.

To one way of thinking Lü's belief in the enduring character of principle and of the Way represents the quintessence of his "orthodoxy." Without doubt it is the main theme of his attacks on all forms of heterodoxy, and it underlies his stubborn adherence to political ideals at odds with later traditions, as well as his upholding of ancient models in contrast to existing institutions. Here then lies a seeming paradox: that Lü's radical program and wholesale rejection of the established order rest squarely on his uncompromising insistence on principles at the heart of Ch'eng-Chu orthodoxy.[171]

Lü's identification with the basic outlook and style of Sung learning has already been noted by Ch'ien Mu, who quotes Lü to the effect that "the Sung Learning passed over the Han and T'ang and went directly back to the Three Dynasties."[172] That Lü thought of himself as doing the same kind of "passing over" is plain from the context of his quotation, since he goes on to associate with it his own approach to learning: "Likewise I prefer to discuss the Four Books and their commentaries [by Chu Hsi] and on this basis to criticize the examination essays in terms of whether they are correct or incorrect, conform or depart from [this standard]." Thus Lü dismisses in one stroke all scholarly discussion and interpretation subsequent to Chu Hsi, who stands as both the prime and ultimate authority for him, just as, for the Sung masters, the Three Dynasties symbolized an absolute standard of value.

Similarly with Lü's view of the social order. Compared to the Three Dynasties, everything subsequent to it has become flawed and corrupt, and even reform efforts have proven to be ephemeral.[173] Yet, though it has not been possible to restore the institutions of the sage-kings, "it is absolutely essential that scholars preserve these principles in order to keep alive the hope of restoration."[174] Whether they succeed or not, however, the Way remains. "Although the Way of the Sages has not been practiced for at least two thousand five hundred years, it is still there. This is what is meant by the Way not being lost [in *Analects* 29:22].[175]

Principles endure, and not only as abstractions. In the specific form of rites as recorded in the Classics, they are given expression, can become known, and even when not put into practice, can serve to remind men of what is rite and can be made right. How this works is illustrated by the example of the schools given earlier. There Lü's questioner assumes uncritically the existence of an adequate school system, which suffices in his mind to demonstrate the practicability of schools, while the nonexistence of well-fields implies their impracticability. Yet Lü, having in mind an ancient model of schools based on a well-field system, can question the adequacy of the present schools and suggest how, with the linking of economics and education, a better organization of the land could make education more widely affordable. From the perspective of his ideal model then, Lü is able to diagnose an actual weakness in the limited availability of education in his own time. The principle embodied in the "rite" becomes the basis for setting things "right."

Jung Chao-tsu is not wrong when he sees Lü's belief in the rites as something pure and sacred, a kind of blind religious faith.[176] This is true not only of his high ideals politically, but also of those unquestioned social assumptions noted earlier in connection with

Lü's *Family Instructions*. Yet for Jung to speak of Lü simply as a conservative, across-the-board, misses the point. In Lü's thought as a whole there is no clinging to the familiar, comfortable way of life; nor is he uncritical of conventional thinking on many social questions (remember his distinction between true and false rites: "rites that are not rite," and his readiness to debate the difference on rational grounds). Indeed there is no blind attachment to things as they are,[177] for Lü challenges his reader with radical alternatives. He calls for a great exodus from the present state, refusing to accept things as they are and offering instead the prophetic prospect of a paradisal state, even if not a promised land. In a sense indeed Lü's vision is revolutionary, yet given his acceptance of Mencius' stricture against sacrificing even a single human life to achieve one's ambition, it stands (with some apologies to Herbert Fingarette)[178] as a human rite that also respects human rights.

In the Sung there was the idea, expressed by Fan Tsu-yü (1041–98) and others, that even when the Way was not practiced by rulers, scholars like Confucius preserved it as a way of learning.[179] Lü has something of the same notion, but for him it is more of an unrealized hope than a fact of history. Nowhere between Mencius and the Ch'eng brothers, between Chu Hsi and himself, does he find scholars who have measured up to the high calling of those who truly perpetuate the Way. Thus for him there has been no transmission of the orthodox way in the scholastic sense,[180] no succession *(tao-t'ung)* as more conventional Ch'eng-Chu scholars think of it being passed from one generation of scholars to another. In fact, he sees it as a misconception based on an improper analogy to the patriarchal succession in Ch'an Buddhism—another sign of the latter's penetration of the Confucian ranks.[181]

In his important study of the *Hsing-li ching-i* (Essential Ideas of Nature and Principle), an official Ch'ing anthology of essential Neo-Confucian doctrines compiled in 1715, Wing-tsit Chan notes what he calls a contradiction in its handling of the *tao-t'ung* concept. On the one hand its presentation of material follows "strictly the order of the *tao-t'ung* as found in the *Hsing-li ta-ch'üan*";[182]

on the other hand, in the explanatory note at the beginning of the work, it said that the section on the *tao-tung* which would have dealt with this subject as in its Ming prototype, has been omitted as "too controversial." [183] Professor Chan finds this puzzling, but attributes it to a distaste for controversy at this time, following the bitter polemics of the preceding period. I believe the controversial views referred to may well have been those of Lü Liu-liang (or his admirer Lu Lung-chi). As perhaps the best-known, most articulate, and controversial exponent of Ch'eng-Chu orthodoxy in the previous generation, Lü and his views on the *tao-t'ung*, as well as his negative comments on many of the scholars frequently included in the orthodox succession as a scholastic lineage, such as Hsü Heng and Hsüeh Hsüan, must have been known to the compilers of the *Hsing-li ching-i*.

It also seems likely that Lü's views lie behind another anomaly in the order of succession as presented by the compilers of the *Hsing-li ching-i*. Professor Chan says: "Curiously enough, outside of the list of Neo-Confucianists in the *Hsing-li ta-ch'üan*, only Ouyang Hsiu [i.e., an earlier Sung scholar] is new. And none of the prominent Ming Neo-Confucianists. Wu Yü-pi (1392–1469), Hu Chü-jen (1434–84), Ts'ao Tuan, or Hsüeh Hsüan is included. One is inclined to say that not only was the *tao-t'ung* reaffirmed, but it was reaffirmed without even such modification as would bring it up to date." [184] Here again it seems to me the compilers are influenced by Lü's disqualification of all Yüan and Ming Confucians as upholders of the Way; their dodging of the issue lets stand Lü's decisive rejection of the scholastic transmission and his reaffirmation of Chu Hsi as, so to speak, "the last of the prophets." In fact the principal compiler of the *Hsing-li ching-li*, Li Kuang-ti (1642–1718), says in a memorial to the K'ang-hsi emperor that there was no one to carry on the Way for five hundred years after Chu Hsi, until his and K'ang-hsi's time. [185]

This point, it seems to me, bears upon another major feature of the Ch'eng-Chu school in the early Ch'ing emphasized by Professor Chan: "the increased reverence for Chu Hsi . . . as the central figure of the whole Neo-Confucian tradition," reflecting, "the long tendency to assert Chu Hsi's supremacy among the Neo-Confucians."[186] In one sense this is a quite understandable development. We can appreciate the increasing respect shown to Chu Hsi for his impressive philosophical synthesis, which commands even more admiration today as its depths are penetrated and its heights stand out in the long perspective of history. Yet in another sense, as a tradition, Neo-Confucianism seems less viable if its own adherents are diminished in stature and its own self-criticism is dismissed as making no constructive contribution to the "advancement of the Way" (as Lü put it).[187] To the extent that the succession has failed to produce worthy heirs, and one master (Chu Hsi) or perhaps two or three (Ch'eng-Chu) stand alone as preeminent for their profound pronouncements on the Way, the tradition has been placed in some jeopardy. In its latter-day, weakened condition it is dangerously exposed to infection, if not to direct attack. For if its own paradigm calls for a prophet or sage to make his appearance when the Way has long been in decline, some "hero" will no doubt come forth to assume that role. It may not, however, be simply a revisionist like Lü, but another kind of fundamentalist who, instead of just passing over the Yüan and Ming, goes one step further to pass over Ch'eng and Chu, and even as they did, reach back to Confucius and Mencius. Such indeed was Yen Yüan (1635–1704).

Yen Yüan is well known today, even more than in his own time, for his early and radical challenge to the Ch'eng-Chu school, especially its doctrine of human nature and its alleged impracticality.[188] Instead he offered a real or practical learning *(shih-hsüeh)* which would have more actual effect on the transformation of society than generations of Neo-Confucians had had.[189] From this some modern writers have acclaimed him for his utilitarianism and pragmatism. In an important recent interpretive essay, however, Tu Wei-ming has shown how the basic spiritual values of the Confucian tradition remain the primary context in which Yen should be seen.[190] In this light Yen bears significant comparison and contrast to Lü Liu-liang.

Yen's life has many resemblances to Lü's—in his early intense commitment to Neo-Confucian self-cultivation, in his taking the first step on the examination route and then renouncing it, in the problems he faced trying to survive outside the official support system by a combination of teaching, farming, and medical practice; in the years of relative isolation from the political and social world of the time—a fact so sharply in contrast to the professed commitment each held to doing something of practical benefit for human society.

Perhaps the most significant difference between them lies in how each tried to fulfill this commitment: in Lü's case by making a tactical compromise with the examination system through his involvement with the examination essays as a business—necessarily an intellectual and literary enterprise, as well as a commercial one —and in Yen's case by his denunciation of book-learning, belles-lettres, and scholasticism, a view with which he had to make the inevitable compromise of writing books himself, lest his message not be communicated and he became totally cut off from those he so wanted to reach. In this respect Lü appears to have made the more realistic compromise and gained the most immediate returns in reaching a large audience, but the move was not without its own costs, as we shall see.

It is often observed of Confucian scholars in the early Ch'ing that they were deeply marked by the fall of the Ming and the fate of so many scholars who sacrificed their lives on behalf of a doomed dynasty—uselessly as Yen judged it to be. Tu Wei-ming says of Yen, "He was so impressed with the heroic sacrifices of those Confucian loyalists, yet so disheartened by their powerlessness that he felt it necessary to conclude that, judging by the criterion of practicality, they all died a meaningless death."[191] That this was a most serious problem for Huang Tsung-hsi, who also survived from the Ming into the Ch'ing is undoubted,[192] and it was no less so for Lü Liu-liang, who lost relatives and friends in the resistance movement and whose intense, life-long loyalism, gave him much reason to confront this problem in his own mind. His essential resolution of it may well be seen in his citing with obvious approval Confucius' exoneration of Kuan Chung for not sacrificing his life in the losing cause of his brother.[193] For Confucius, it was not reasonable to sacrifice one's life uselessly if one could live to make a greater contribution to human civilization. In this case, it was not a question of expediency or opportunism since Kuan Chung acted out of devotion to principle rather than with a view to achieving personal success.[194] No doubt this practical concern was an important motive for Lü's own holding on to life and trying to perpetuate what he considered the heart of human civilization, even by means he recognized as in some ways open to question. Yet if this motivation is common to Lü and Yen, it does not in itself explain the difference in their views of what "practicality" consisted in.

Theoretically the main difference between Yen and Lü lies in their views on human nature, with Yen attacking Chu Hsi's distinction between the moral nature (identified with Heaven's principle) and the psycho-physical nature, and with Lü defending it. In Yen's eyes Chu Hsi had taken too negative a position on human desires and man's physical nature, seeing them only as destructive forces rather than as the dynamic and creative powers they should be. One damaging result was the practice of quiet-sitting, a stultifying exercise in self-subjugation. Both in theory and practice, according to Yen, this reflected the influence upon Neo-Confucianism of Buddhist nihilism.

Lü, who wrote and published some years before Yen, had already declared his full support of Chu Hsi's position, and if anything put even more stress on the moral nature and Heaven's principle, believing that there could be no true practicality that did not rest on the base of moral principle immanent in the mind-and-heart. Yet in other respects, as we have seen earlier, Lü has already aligned himself against many of the same alleged Buddhist errors, and, in his revisionist purge of such influences in Yüan and Ming Neo-Confucianism, including quiet-sitting, anticipated many of Yen's criticisms.

Tu speaks of Yen as differentiating "authentic Confucian cultivation from other non-Confucian methods of spiritual self-discipline," such as quiet-sitting. Further he says that for Yen "The mysterious experiences of the Ch'an masters were merely flowers in the mirror or the moon in the water," and that "Yen Yüan realized that for generations many of the great personalities in the Confucian tradition had devoted themselves to the cultivation of a kind of inner experience . . . and had no useful role to play in the socio-political realm."[195] On these points one can find many passages in Lü's *Discourses* and *Conversations* with a familiar ring, except that, in Lü's revisionist version of Neo-Confucianism, instead of these defects being attributed to the "great personalities of the Confucian tradition," they would be ascribed to "outward Confucians and covert Buddhists," who in Yen's terms were "using the empty form of Confucian terms to do the real work of Buddhism."[196]

Essential agreement on these points does not keep Yen and Lü from differing greatly on others. Symptomatic of such disagreement would be their respective handling of the injunction in the *Analects:* "Conquer self and restore riteness." For Yen this is still a canonical injunction and, purged of any depreciation of human desires, remains a basic formulation of what Tu characterizes in Yen as a life of ritualized action.[197] For Lü, in some contrast to Yen, it is important that "selfish desires" not be allowed to dominate the mind-and-heart. Yet, like Yen, he is greatly concerned that this discipline not be directed at some interior self, isolated from the affairs of life. Repeatedly he emphasizes that "conquering" and "restoring," though distinct, are as inseparable as substance and function, principle and practice. And if the two together define what it means to be humane or to lead the virtuous life, it is only on the condition that they can be constantly exercised in relation to the concrete affairs of daily life *(shih-shih),* in every thought, word, and action.[198]

Lü saw this simple, straightforward practice as endangered by more than one misconception. Some people viewed the essential self as something removed from sensible contact with the world, and humaneness as a separate state of mind to be cultivated prior to one's engagement with the world. Lü thought this led to the neglect of practice *(kung-fu)* in the conduct of affairs through specific actions that are, as he had said, both rite and right. According to him:

> Ch'eng I had said "to conquer self is itself to restore riteness" but master Chu feared lest scholars take this as too direct and quick an approach, leading to such errors as seeing the mind itself as Buddhahood; therefore he explained it as overcoming selfish desires and restoring riteness. By emphasizing that self-conquest also required [the practical effort of] restoring riteness, he gave greater precision to it.[199]

Another misconception was found in starting from a view of the self as in isolation or opposition to the world, i.e., self versus society, and then trying to overcome this conflict by resolving to "take the whole world as one's own responsibility" *(i t'ien-hsia wei chi-jen)*, thus bringing both self and world back to humaneness. This, Lü feels, is to reach too directly for an all-encompassing solution that could lead, like the undifferentiated compassion of Buddhism, to the neglect of specific moral tasks, whereas Confucian humaneness must start at the center, with the concrete moral responsibility nearest at hand, and work out from there.[200]

On this point, as we have seen, Yen and Lü would be unlikely to disagree. Where some difference might arise is in Lü's greater emphasis on the need for the moral task to be guided by cognitive learning, aided by the study of books, in contrast to Yen's impatience with book-learning as enervating to the moral will. We must not exaggerate the difference, because Yen obviously did not forswear all study of books, while Lü, for his part, was careful to limit his own learning priorities to what was manageable; concentrating first on the Four Books and only then going to a wider range of scholarly investigation. Yet, while each no doubt thought of himself as speaking for and to every man, Lü's words were more directed toward that relatively elite group who "read books" *(tu-shu jen)* and were potential candidates for official service, while Yen spoke for, and hopefully to, a larger class of potential learners—closer to the soil and to the hard facts of physical labor—whose needs were more practical and who by that very fact were less able to appreciate the philosophical and scholarly niceties Lü considered so fundamental to the intellectual life. Lü's orientation was to the leisured, educated class, whom he sought to deliver from a confused mixture of Buddhist mysticism and a corrupt scholarly tradition. Yen's concern was with the ordinary man in need of education, who could, however, dispense with spiritual and philosophical refinements—the higher life of the mind—as of no immediate, practical relevance. This has been an enduring tension in Chinese life between the educated elite and less educated masses, and even today it has not been completely resolved.

At first glance one might think that Lü achieved more practical success with his approach, since his works had a direct relevance to the concerns of examination candidates and his talents served their purposes well, whereas Yen was largely ignored until the twentieth century. Yet, we remember Lü's own concern for universal schooling—a very orthodox concern of Chu Hsi—and we cannot be unmindful of the criticism made by generations of Neo-Confucians that it was preoccupation with the examinations and official recruitment process that seriously distorted Chinese educational efforts, leaving masses of people without the benefit of any schooling adapted to their own needs. On these terms it could be argued that Lü's compromise with the system, and such success as he achieved, while perhaps representing a tactical gain, also entailed a strategic loss to the advancement of his own principles. To this it could be said in reply that there was no other option for Lü at the time, and that in any case his writings made no concessions to any class interest—they spoke as much to the troubled consciences of the educated as to their immediate personal ambitions.

In Lü's discussion of "conquering self and restoring riteness" he mainly emphasizes the reality of moral principle, common to what is within the mind and what is without, as well as the application of principle to everyday affairs through methodical effort *(kung-fu).*

For the rest he dwells on those erroneous conceptions of crypto-Buddhists who lead people astray. Nothing is said about the psycho-physical nature of man as evil. Human desires are a threat only when ungoverned by principle, as they would not be except for these misconceptions. Moreover, in Lü's writings as a whole, the main targets of attack on grounds of selfishness are not the common man's basic instincts for sex, material goods, etc., but the drive for power and the greed for wealth so conspicuous in the ruling class. As seen and employed by Lü, principle is not an instrument for the repression of vital instincts among the people but only for protecting them against oppressors both selfish and powerful.

If we compare this insistent critique of selfishness in high places with the earlier Neo-Confucian view of Chen Te-hsiu in the thirteenth century, two things emerge. First, the concern over selfishness among those in power is common to both Chen and Lü. Second, in Chen Te-hsiu there is also a powerful sense of almost Manichaean struggle between principle and selfish desires, which is the central theme of the early Learning of the Mind-and-Heart as a moral discipline for the leadership elite,[201] but in Lü this rigorist, if not puritanical, leaning is replaced by a greater emphasis on intellectual clarity and finesse in moral judgments generally. The mind is less a battle ground of warring wills and more a field of scholarly inquiry, intellectual debate, and analytical precision. As Lü said, "If one establishes oneself in cognitive learning and also emphasizes practice, then from the start the two are inseparable."[202] This is in line with the general shift in early Ch'ing thought, away from the sageliness of deep interior virtue—achieved through intense inner struggle and culminating in an experience of sage-like "integral comprehension" or self-realization—toward a scholarship of greater intellectual complexity and sophistication. Yet it is not surprising that such a tendency should have been accompanied by the kind of reaction evoked from Yen Yüan, who rejected either alternative as too far removed from ordinary life.

Professor Chan has shown that this growing scholarly extroversion was no less a trend in the Ch'eng-Chu school of the seventeenth century than in Ch'ing thought generally,[203] and Lü may well have exerted an early influence in this direction. Though so tidal a change cannot be explained as any one man's doing, it is not insignificant that several leaders of the so-called Sung school paid tribute to Lü's vanguard role,[204] made use of his arguments, and followed him in some of his revisionist directions. We have already seen signs of the latter in the *Hsing-li ching-i's* avoidance of the subject of the "orthodox succession" *(tao-t'ung)* as too controversial—a noteworthy distancing of the official orthodoxy from what had been a central concept after Chu Hsi. Moreover in that same official compilation leading Neo-Confucians after Hsü Heng in the thirteenth century drop from sight—leaving a gap in continuity incongruous for any school that would claim legitimacy on the basis of scholarly filiation or lineal inheritance. Still another indication of this influence is Lu Lung-chi's diffidence in regard to quiet-sitting, which had been a practice in the Ch'eng-Chu school of the Ming and in the Tung-lin neoorthodoxy of the early seventeenth century, but had been disapproved by Lü Liu-liang. Here Lu Lung-chi seems to line up with Lü when he excludes from the ranks of the orthodox those who favor quiet-sitting.[205] Also symptomatic would be Li Kuang-ti's dropping from the text of the *Great Learning* Chu Hsi's special note on the investigation of things, culminating in a "breakthrough to integral comprehension";[206] this too had been a key text for the earlier Learning of the Mind-and-Heart (and remained so for its Korean and Japanese adherents),[207] but Lü Liu-liang had conspicuously avoided it.

There are, of course, contrary opinions and counter-indications as well. One of the most prominent reactions against Lü is the official "Refutation of Lü Liu-liang's *Discourses on the Four Books*,"[208] which took special exception to Lü's views on the Learning of the Mind-and-Heart. Another is the persistence of certain features of the earlier Learning of the Mind-and-Heart, such as quiet-sitting and the keeping of accounts of merit-and-demerit in one's practice of self-scrutiny. As conservative features of the so-called Sung school in the Ch'ing, these practices of syncretic origin must be kept in mind along with the more positivistic trends reported above. But such vestiges of Sung and Ming spiritual cultivation seem increasingly isolated from the main intellectual currents of the eighteenth century, and may have had less influence over scholars generally than the kind of broad learning and objective inquiry Lü Liu-liang spoke for.[209]

This is not the place for a further evaluation of such differences within Neo-Confucian orthodoxy in the Ch'ing, a matter I have taken up in *The Message of the Mind in Neo-Confucianism*.[210] For present purposes it may suffice to note some significant continuities and discontinuities in the Neo-Confucian view of the self and individual.

1. Although the new Ch'ing learning was ramified in many directions, self-cultivation retained a central importance in Neo-Confucian thought and education. Huang Tsung-hsi, and more recently T'ang Chün-i, might lament the failure of Ch'ing scholars to carry on as full a discourse on the philosophy of mind and nature as had the Sung and Ming,[211] but "learning for one's self" remained, implicitly or explicitly, a basic value. That this is so of the most "orthodox" of Neo Confucians may be seen later in the works of so prominent a scholar-official and educator as Chang Po-hsing, no less than in many other Ch'ing scholars of different persuasions.[212] Whatever the relative weight given by individual thinkers to intuition or intellection, contemplative practice or cognitive learning, involvement with the social order or disengagement from it, among Ch'ing scholars there was little inclination to question the fundamental importance of "learning for oneself," or to divest the self/person of its essential functions, as expressed in terms of taking responsibility for oneself *(tzu-jen)* in shaping and directing one's own life, and "getting it oneself" *(tzu-te)*, whether understood as achieving self-fulfillment or perhaps simply gaining one's own insights into the Way. Their interpretations of these Confucian and Men-

cian concepts might vary greatly but not their acceptance of
them as basic values.

The first of these concepts, often expressed in terms reminiscent of Confucius' resolving early in life to pursue a life of
learning, or to take responsibility for the Way, was shared in
common by Confucians as different as Lü Liu-liang and Yen
Yüan. The manner of its pursuit and the outcome in each case
varied with their own experience of life, conditioned by the
diverse social and cultural circumstances in which Confucians
"found" themselves. New achievements in textual and historical scholarship could not be as much appreciated by Yen Yüan
as, say, by Huang Tsung-hsi, but from his own vantage point
Yen helped to keep these in perspective—as they would be
seen by many unable to enjoy the refinements of the higher
learning, yet whose lives could not be unaffected by the
conduct or decisions of those whose education gave them
power over others. In his own way Yen sought to fulfill the
Neo-Confucian aim of education for Everyman, but found
that he could not do so working with an ideal of sagehood too
closely tied to Sung scholarly ambitions or spiritual aspirations, too greatly affected by the encounter with Buddhism,
and too far removed from the ordinary man's daily life.

2. Lü Liu-liang opposed any tendency to isolate an originally
pure mind, "mind-in-itself," or transcendental consciousness,
not because he was ready to abandon the quest for the purity
of principle or deny a dimension of transcendence in human
nature, but because he saw this nature as inseparable from
the interdependent structure of principle—the unity of principle and its diverse particularizations—symbolized by Heaven
and made manifest through the moral imperative immanent
in each individual and the bonds of human relationship. Isolate man from that creative principle and his self would become insubstantial and unreal, enjoying only an illusory freedom—insubstantial because without recognition of the moral

imperative in the mind there is no firm ground on which to construct a life or stand in defense of humane values; illusory because one's growth and maturation could only be stultified by the suspension of conscience or abandonment of active concern for others. Put another way, no view of the mind or self would suffice which could not also serve as the ground of a public philosophy. Nor would any political doctrine succeed if it failed to respect the exercise of individual conscience in human affairs or recognize self-discipline as the keystone of human governance *(hsiu-chi chih-jen)*. Thus the interdependence of Heaven and man, self and society, are constant themes in Lü's discourses, as are the indispensability of the rational and moral faculties to the full realization of these values. In this way Lü upheld Chu Hsi's intellectual standards and moral ideals for the educated man as scholar and leader, even if he backed off from the earlier vision of sagehood as something anyone could hope to experience in one's own life.

On this basis Lü claimed an authority from Heaven and its principles for challenging dynastic rule and what he saw as its inherent selfishness—the worst of selfish "human desires." That this claim should stand, in writings which circulated as widely and for as long as did Lü's, without this challenge to imperial authority being taken up, is in a way remarkable. It reminds us that, even if the imperial ideology claimed ultimate and total authority for the ruler, Chu Hsi's teachings qualified that claim and restrained its application. Thus, the K'ang-hsi emperor, as a deep student of Chu Hsi, was more liberal in the exercise of this authority than his successor proved to be. When finally the issue was precipitated in the Tseng Ching case, the rival claims of the Manchu's Imperial Mandate and Lü's Heavenly Imperative were unmistakably in conflict: absolutist rule confronted by the claims of fixed, unyielding principle.[213] As it happened in this case, there was a particular irony in that the Yung-cheng emperor, in condemning Lü, exercised his autocratic authority on behalf of a view of the mind quite questionably Neo-Confucian and far more congenial to his own predilection for Ch'an Buddhism.[214] It is as if Lü's prophetic warnings about Ch'an had been confirmed at his own expense.

In nineteenth-century Japan when Nakae Chōmin, probably the first advocate in East Asia of human rights in the Western sense, tried to express these in terms that would be familiar to Japanese readers, he reached for the same Neo-Confucian concepts as Lü Liu-liang had employed in his analysis of human nature and critique of dynastic rule—Heaven *(t'ien/ ten)*, Heaven's principles *(t'ien-li/tenri)*, the Heavenly Imperative *(t'ien ming/tenmei)*, Heaven's endowment *(t'ien-fu/ tempu)*, and the moral nature of man *(t'ien hsing/tensei)*— all terms as useful to the Chinese and Koreans as to the Japanese.[215] The significance of this conjunction of Confucian and Western ideas for the larger Neo-Confucian world of East Asia should not be overlooked.

3. The new objectivity and emphasis on empirical learning in the early Ch'ing, to which Lü contributed, was largely directed toward humanistic learning in the Confucian tradition (what Shimada Kenji has called "solid learning in the study of texts"—*bunken jitsugaku*), and to the developing technologies relevant to the practical concerns of officials. It was not oriented toward the kind of "scientific empiricism" then developing in the West,[216] but some of the new scholarly attitudes represented by Lü Liu-liang were open to this possibility and in some cases actually lent themselves to the study of Western science.[217]

4. Confucians are usually thought to have a strong sense of history and tradition, but Yen Yüan and Lü Liu-liang show little of either. This may not be surprising in the case of Yen Yüan, since his being "discovered" in the twentieth century was from the start an attempt to validate new ideas and direct experience, rather than to draw upon or mediate with the

past.[218] It is true of Yen, as Ch'ien Mu says,[219] that he had a worshipful view of antiquity, and so indeed did Lü, but this kind of archaism has a different meaning from traditionalism: whether taken literally or figuratively, symbols appropriated from the remote past are meant to stand in vivid contrast to the established order as it claims the sanction of received tradition. This, radical juxtaposition, rather than any dogged conservatism, is the significance of Lü's passing over most of history in order to reach the higher ground in antiquity from which he could attack the present.

In the Neo-Confucian discourse we have been following here there is ample precedent for Lü's visionary invocation of the past, and for the Neo-Confucian taking upon himself a prophetic role in relation to it. That vision of the past does not offer a promised land, a millennial future in the Old Testament sense. The myth of the exodus had more of an attraction to the nomadic and migratory peoples of the desert and steppe than for a people whose sedentary, agricultural ways and deep attachment to the soil would render them immune to such an appeal. Instead the dominant motif is one of reclaiming and repossessing ancient soil, to make it productive and thrive again. Restoration and renewal is the theme of those who speak with a prophetic voice in China, as warners against prevailing corruption and decline.

In the latter vision, the dominant models for Neo-Confucians are the noble man and sage. Self-cultivation, scholarship, and learning have a large place in this conception of the educated elite, but along with these, there is a strong sense of responsibility for leadership in society, typified by the heroic figure of the noble man. "Taking responsibility for the Way" signified one's acceptance of that leadership responsibility. "Getting it oneself" or "finding the Way in oneself" could mean either being fully at home and at ease with that understanding and responsibility, or in more modest terms, making one's own contribution to learning. In Neo-Confucian discourse it mostly has to do with learning, but together, leading and learning constitute the two main functions of the self-elected—because self-committed—moral and intellectual elite.

In the period covered here significant changes took place in the relative importance of these concepts and roles as models for the individual or ideals for the self. During the Confucian revival of the Northern Sung, with hopes for reform and restoration running high, Fan Chung-yen's ideal of the Noble Man taking personal responsibility for the Way in the world, expressed as "first in worrying about the world's worries and last in enjoying its pleasures," was advanced as a Confucian alternative to the self-sacrificing ideal of the Bodhisattva. Then, with the fracturing of the reform movement and later its eclipse, the ideal of the sage, personifying the lofty spirituality of the learning of the Way *(tao-hsüeh)*, as a religious alternative to the contemplative ideal of Buddhahood, became embodied in the cult to Yen Hui, with his total dedication to learning as an aspirant to sagehood, and later in the figure of Chu Hsi as the supreme master of all sagely learning. Here "getting it" meant self-realization in a Way that endured regardless of the failure of rulers and dynasties to achieve it.

Both the Noble Man and the Sage remained operative ideals of the Neo-Confucian movement as it struggled to gain its educational and political footing in the difficult days of the late Sung, Yüan, and early Ming. Chen Te-hsiu in the late Sung, Hsü Heng in the Yüan, and Fang Hsiao-ju in the early Ming, assume the heroic role of the Noble Man, endeavoring as scholar-officials to advance the Confucian Way and convert China's rulers (domestic or foreign) to the Way of the Sage-Kings, but suffering the unforeseen consequences of rule by Imperial Sages who turn out not to be Sage-Kings. In the Yüan, Liu Yin, and in the early Ming, Wu Yu-pi, may be taken as examples of the contrasting, more uncompromising ideal of the aspirant to sagely integrity whose ideals would allow of no concession to serving the established order.

Meanwhile, in the youthful Wu Ch'eng of the Yüan period we can see the tension rising between the noble man and sage, the activist and the contemplative, the official and scholarly roles, when

Wu, as a young man trying to identify his goals in life, sought to reconcile the heroic and sagely ideals in his time.

The tension between the ideal and the reality was only heightened by the educational and scholarly successes of Ming Neo-Confucians, a strain showing itself especially in Wang Yang-ming, the Noble Man par excellence, worried like Fan Chung-yen about "the world's worries," but committed also to the sagely ideal of Chu Hsi, and burdened not only by the increasing demands of scholarship—broad learning and searching inquiry—but by the seeming artificialities of a more and more complex culture, resistant alike to Chu Hsi's painstaking methodical approach to "integral comprehension," and to the simplicities of dedicated social activism. Wang and his school, in their educational outreach, attempted to fulfill the long-standing Neo-Confucian promise of education for all, based on his redefinition of sageliness. Initially an answer to his own spiritual malaise, his view of "innate knowing (or innate learning)" was far more accessible to the common man, but with the spread of Neo-Confucian education, it came increasingly into contact with commoners, and especially townspeople, for whom the earlier Neo-Confucian rigorism so much demanded of the leadership elite, as well as the learning required of the scholar, had little meaning. In these circumstances the naturalism—or natural morality—which had had both a moral and physical value in the Neo-Confucian encounter with Buddhism, saw an enlargement in the scope given to the expression of human feelings and a diminution in the demand for heroic self-denial and self-sacrifice. In the late Ming the brilliant but quixotic individualism of Li Chih reflects the tension this produces between the self-sacrificing ideal of the activist hero, supposedly infused with the lofty spirituality of the sage, and the earthy realities of life among the common people, whose basic desires and needs are given expression by the new, ready-made sages of the T'ai-chou school.

With the fall of the Ming, there is a noticeable retrenchment, a pulling back from and a reexamination of the moral idealism that had characterized the Neo-Confucian movement up to this time but had come into increasing question in the Ming itself. Even Lü Liu-liang, who reaffirms the orthodox position that moral principle must guide and control the desires, does not couch this in terms of a desperate struggle with evil "human desires," as had Chen Te-hsiu earlier, but rather as a struggle to be waged against the systemic greed for power and wealth represented by the dynasty—a view shared with Huang Tsung-hsi and other scholars of the day.

From this point on the pursuit of sagehood as something to be experienced all at once recedes as an operative spiritual ideal among even those, like Lü, who still revere Confucius and Chu Hsi as sages. Indeed Ch'ing orthodoxy, which enshrined Chu Hsi with ever more towering authority, seemed to concede that he was beyond individual emulation. With learning of all kinds expanding and practice becoming more specialized in virtually every field of human endeavor—including the study of the classics—the thought of one's achieving the breadth and balance of Chu Hsi, while still an honored ideal, was about as far removed from practical realization as the ideal of the Renaissance man became for twentieth-century man in the West.

As we have seen, both Li Chih and Lü Liu-liang, fiercely independent though each is, reflect or anticipate many of these divergent trends, which together emerge, like them, out of Neo-Confucianism as interwoven threads in an evolving historical process. At the core of their thought are certain basic assumptions, expressed in the terms studied here through at least five centuries of Neo-Confucian thought, which despite the philosophical differences between them establish an underlying kinship between these seeming polar opposites. Each had renounced an official career, but managed to live by his wits in the interstices of the established order, fitting exactly into none of the usual classes—official, scholarly, clerical, agricultural, or commercial—but involved to some degree with them all and certainly not marginal in personal influence on them for all of Li's and Lü's independence of them. (With lives so similar it would take tortuous logic indeed to establish any one-to-one relation between their thought—at once so different in certain respects and strikingly alike in others—and any given economic interest or social class.) But each managed somehow to survive into old age and win posthumous fame as martyrs to their own convictions—won through "learning for one's self." Each in his own way had found the Way for himself, and who knows, may even have learned what Confucius meant when he said "Hearing the Way in the morning, one can die content in the evening."

Notes

The following sinological abbreviations are used:

CKTHMCCC Chung-kuo tzu-hsüeh ming-chu chi-ch'eng 中國子學名著集成

DMB Dictionary of Ming Biography

ECCP Eminent Chinese of the Ching Period

KHCPTS Kuo-hsüeh chi-pen ts'ung-shu 國學基本叢書

KSKSSK Kinsei kanseki sōkan 近世漢籍叢刊

MJCCTLSY Ming-jen chuan-chi tzu-liao so yin 明人傳記資料索引

MJHA Ming-ju hsüeh-an 明儒學案

MS Ming shih 明史

SKCS Ssu-k'u ch'üan-shu 四庫全書

SKCSCP Ssu-k'u ch'üan-shu chen-pen 四庫全書珍本

SPPY Ssu-pu pei-yao 四部備要

SPTK Ssu-pu ts'ung-k'an 四部叢刊

SSGTK Shushigaku taikei 朱子學大系

SYHA Sung-Yüan hsüeh-an 宋元學案

TSCC Ts'ung-shu chi-ch'eng 叢書集成

1. LEARNING FOR ONE'S SELF

1. See de Bary, Chan, and Watson, *Sources of Chinese Tradition*, p. 813.

2. *Ibid.*, p. 768. The same view is found in Wing-tsit Chan's "Chinese Theory and Practice," pp. 92–93.

3. *Sources*, pp. 858–861.

4. To name only two of the more prominent examples: Hou Wai-lu, *Chung-kuo ssu-hsiang t'ung-shih*, hereafter referred to as Hou, *T'ung-shih 4*, pp. 875–1290; Shimada Kenji, *Chūgoku ni okeru kindai shii no zasetsu*, hereafter referred to as *Zasetsu*.

5. Such a distinction might well apply to the subject matter discussed by Max Loehr in his "Individualism in Chinese Art" and J. R. Hightower in "Individualism in Chinese Literature." For the most part they are concerned with "individuality" in arts and letters and touch only negatively on the question of "individualism" in the sense that it is discussed by Herbert Butterfield, for instance, in his paper for the same conference, "Reflections on Religion and Modern Individualism."

6. This type of individualism as it flourished in the third century B.C. is discussed by Etienne Balazs in an article translated into English under the title "Nihilistic Revolt or Mystical Escapism" and published in his collected papers under the editorship of Arthur Wright.

7. That this is an important, if not essential, element in modern Western individualism is implied by Butterfield in his description of it as a "heightening of the notion of individual responsibility and the dissemination of this amongst wider sections of the population" (p. 40) and as "the autonomy of men who are determined to decide the main purpose of their lives and feel a similar responsibility for public affairs . . ." (p. 46). "Reflections on Religion and Modern Individualism."

8. See Robert Hartwell, "Patterns of Settlement, the Structure of Government, and the Social Transformation of the Chinese Political Elite, ca. 750–1550," esp. 18–19; and Shiba Yoshinobu, *Commerce and Society in Sung China*, esp. 45–50, 202–213; Saeki Tomi, *Sō-no shin bunka* [The new culture of the Sung], pps. 141–168, 370–385.

9. See Saeki Tomi, *Sō-no shin bunka*, pps. 381–385.

10. Huang Tsung-hsi and Ch'üan Tsu-wang, *Sung Yüan hsüeh-an*, 1:26.

11. See Chu Hsi, "Ta Lü Tzu-yüeh" [Letter to Lü Tsu-ch'ien], in *Chu Tzu ta-ch'üan*, 47.17b–18a; and my *Neo-Confucian Orthodoxy and the Learning of the Mind-and-Heart*, pp. 8, 22–24.

12. See Saeki Tomi, *Sō no shin bunka*, pp. 370ff. On the crisis in education from the lack of a sense of higher purpose, see Thomas H. C. Lee, "Life in the Schools of Sung China."

13. *Mencius*, 6A:16.

14. *Hsün Tzu*, Harvard-Yenching Institute Sinological Index Series, Supplement 22, 2/1/32.

15. Chu Hsi, *Wen-chi*, 74:1b.

16. Mao Hsing-lai, *Chin-ssu-lu chi chu*, 2:13b.

17. *Mencius*, 4B:14; trans. adapted from D. C. Lau, *Mencius*, p. 130.

18. *Chin-ssu-lu chi-chu*, 2:32a; Wing-tsit Chan, tr., *Reflections on Things at Hand*, p. 68. Hereafter abbreviated as *Things at Hand* or, following references to *Chin-ssu-lu*, simply as "Chan."

19. *Lun-yü chi-chu*, 7:17a.

20. *Lun-yu ching-i*, 7b:22a–b.

21. *Chin-ssu lu chi-chu*, 6:1a; see Chan, p. 171.

22. Chu, *Wen-chi*, 79:23b (Chūbun ed., p. 1445), Heng chou Shih-ku shu-yüan chi.

23. *Ibid.*, 74:19b.

24. Abe Takeo, *Gendai no kenkyū*, pp. 45–57.

25. Makino Shūji, "Gendai no jugaku kyōiku," pp. 71–74.

26. Martina Deuchler, "Self-Cultivation for the Governance of Men," p. 16.

27. Chan *Things at Hand*, p. 154; Yeh T'sai, *Chin-ssu-lu chi-chieh*, p. 297.

28. Chu Hsi, *Ssu-shu chi-chu, Lun-yu chi-chu*, 12:1.

29. Chou Tun-i, *T'ung-shu*, 1:65; translated in Wing-tsit Chan, *Sourcebook in Chinese Philosophy*, p. 473.

30. de Bary, *Neo-Confucian Orthodoxy*, p. 82.

31. *Erh Ch'eng wai-shu*, 3:1b; *Chin-ssu-lu chi chu*, 5:14a; translation adapted from Chan, p. 165.

32. Roger T. Ames, "Chinese Conceptions of the Body," pp. 39–59.

33. Roger T. Ames, "Co-extending Arising, *Te*," p. 121.

34. See Ren Jiyu, "Ju-chia yü ju-chiao." See also his "Confucianism as a Religion," pp. 128–152. See also Fung Yu-lan, "Lüeh-lun tao-hsüeh ti t'e-tien, ming-ch'eng ho hsing-chih," pp. 35–43.

2. THE SELF IN NEO-CONFUCIAN DISCOURSE

1. See my *Unfolding*, p. 169; *Lin-ch'uan Wu Wen-ch'eng kung chi*, *Wai-chi*, 2:10b–11a.

2. See Morohashi Tetsuji, *Dai kanwa jiten*, No. 30095-59; Chang Sankyon *Tae han han chachon*, p. 1226; The *Nihon kokugo daijiten*, 9:387d, citing a Sung source, has it used in Japanese to mean both oneself and one's home or family. The term does not appear in the original editions of either the *Tzu-hai* or *Tzu-yüan* dictionaries, but is listed in the more recent *Tzu-yüan* and *Xiandai hanyu cidian*, Morohashi, no. 7169, citing *Hsün Tzu*, gives as one of the meanings of *chia* "one's own *(tzu chia)* in contradistinction to others."

3. *Yü-lei*, 11:5a, Item 38; see also 8:9a, Item 88.

4. *Chu Tzu ch'üan-shu*, 42:9b, trans. adapted from Chan, *Sourcebook*, p. 616.

5. On Chu Hsi's concept of moral agency, see Kirill O. Thompson, "A Comparative Study of Chu Hsi's and Kant's Ethical Theories."

6. *Chu Tzu yü-lei* (Cheng-chung/Chubun ed., p. 213), 8:4a.

7. Chu Hsi, *Wen-chi*, 74:4a Tse wen.

8. *Ibid.*, 4b–5a.

9. Ch'eng Hao, *Ming-tao wen-chi*, 2:1a.

10. *Mencius*, 4A:20.

11. Tung Chung-shu in *Han shu*, Po-na pen 56:6b, and *Tung Tzu wen-chi* (Chi-fu ts'ung-shu ed.), 1:51.

12. Ch'eng Hao, *I-shu*, 15:17a; Mao Hsing-lai, *Chin-ssu-lu chi-chu*, 8:16b–17a; Chan, p. 213.

13. Ch'eng I, *I-ch'uan wen-chi*, 1:3a.

14. Chu, *Wen-chi*, 11:4b.

15. See Robert Hartwell, "Patterns of Settlement, the Structure of Government, and the Social Transformation of the Chinese Political Elite, ca. 750–1550," pp. 9, 18–19.

16. Fan Tsu-yü, *Ti hsüeh*, 3:6b–7a.

17. See Saeki Tomi, *Sō no shin bunka*, p. 372.

18. *Ibid.*, esp. pp. 373 ff. On the expansion of schools, rise in scholarly population, and increased participation in examinations, see John W. Chaffee, *The Thorny Gates of Learning in Sung China*, pp. 119–142.

19. There has been extensive scholarly discussion of this question. Those not already familiar with the literature may wish to consult E. Balazs, *Chinese Civilization and Bureaucracy* (New Haven: Yale University Press, 1974), ch. 4, esp. pp. 53–54; and Hartwell, "Patterns," pp. 32–33.

20. C. Schirokauer, in A. Wright, ed., *Confucian Personalities,* pp. 165–66. The conclusion of Wing-tsit Chan, based on many years' study of Chu's life and work, is that he lived in extremely modest circumstances, and managed to support himself partly from a small printing business on the side. See Wing-tsit Chan, "Chu Tzu ku-ch'iung," in his *Chu-hsüeh lun-chi* (Taipei: Hsüeh-sheng, 1982), pp. 205–32.

21. See, for example, Wei-ming Tu, "Toward an Understanding of Liu Yin's Confucian Eremitism," p. 259; and John Dardess, "Confucianism, Local Reform and Centralization," p. 357.

22. Ch'eng Hao, *I-shu,* 19:9a–b.

23. *Mencius,* 2B:2.

24. Ch'eng I, *I-ch'uan wen-chi,* 4:21b; Mao Hsing-lai, *Chin-ssu-lu chi-chu,* 7:8b; Chan, p. 190. See also Franklin Houn, "Rejection of Blind Obedience as a Traditional Chinese and Maoist Concept," pp. 266–69.

25. *I-shu,* 15:3b–4a; *Chin-ssu-lu chi-chu,* 7:11a; translation adapted from Chan, p. 193.

26. Julia Ching, "The Goose Lake Monastery Debate," p. 175.

27. L. C. Goodrich and C. Y. Fang, *Dictionary of Ming Biography,* pp. 426–33, 474–79.

28. Chu, *Wen-chi,* 69:18b.

29. See Wing-tsit Chan, *Source Book in Chinese Philosophy,* pp. 465ff.

30. *Chin-ssu-lu chi-chu,* 2:1a–b; Chan, *Things at Hand,* p. 37.

31. *I-ch'uan wen-chi,* 4:1a–2a; Chan, *Source Book,* pp. 547ff.

32. Chan, *Source Book,* p. 473.

33. *I-ch'uan wen-chi,* 4:1a; Chan, *Source Book,* p. 548.

34. *I-ch'uan wen-chi,* 4:1b–2a.

35. Uno, *Shōgaku,* 3:139.

36. *Chu Tzu yü-lei* (Kyoto: Chūbun shuppansha, 1979), 93:9a; cf. Chan, *Things at Hand,* pp. 204–5.

37. *Chu Tzu yü-lei,* 94:8a–b.

38. Chan, *Things at Hand,* p. 2.

39. Uno, *Shōgaku,* 3:139.

3. GETTING IT ONESELF

1. Translation adapted from D. C. Lau, *Mencius,* p. 130.

2. E.g., Chuang Tzu: Harvard-Yenching Index ed., 22/8/31, 77/28/7, 78/28/54; Burton Watson, *Complete Works of Chuang Tzu,* pp. 102–103, 310, 317. See also the discussion of James D. Sellman, who translates *tzu-te* in the Taoist context as "self-actualization," in his "Three Models of Self-Integration in Early China."

3. *Huai-nan Tzu,* ch. 1, Yüan tao, passim.

4. *Ibid.,* 1:15a, 20:12b.

5. David Hall and Roger Ames, "Getting It Right: On Saving Confucius from the Confucians," pp. 5–6.

6. Cf. Chu Hsi, *Ssu-shu chi-chu,* commentary on *Mencius,* 4B:14; Mao Hsing-lai, *Chin-ssu-lu chi-chu,* 2:22b, no. 41; and Ch'eng Hao, *I-shu,* 11:4a. My translation follows in part the renderings and annotation of Yamazaki Michio in SSGTK, 9:41, rather than that of Chan, pp. 57–58.

7. D. C. Lau, *Mencius,* p. 130.

8. *Ssu-shu chi-chu,* Comm. on Mencius, 4B:14; pp. 696–697.

9. Chu Hsi, *Meng Tzu huo-wen,* 8:3b–5a.

10. *Ta-hsüeh chang-chü* 1–2.

11. *Meng-Tzu huo-wen,* 8:4a, 4b.

12. Legge, *Chinese Classics, Mencius,* 2:373.

13. *Shih-san ching chu-su,* Meng Tzu, 4B:14.

14. Legge, *Chinese Classics, Mencius,* 2:22.

15. Hu Kuang, *Hsing-li ta-ch'üan,* Ssu-k'u chen-pen ed., 43:9b, citing *Erh Ch'eng i-shu,* 6:6b.

16. *I-shu,* 2A:2a, *Chin-ssu-lu chi-chu,* 4:6b, No. 14; SSGTK (Shushigaku taikei), 9(4):129, 310; cf. Chan, *Things at Hand,* p. 128. Here and in the passage which follows my translation benefits from Prof. Chan's, but differs somewhat in the handling of the key terms at issue in my discussion of the problem.

17. *Analects,* 8:2; 7:37.

18. *I-shu,* 2A:16a; *Chin-ssu-lu chi-chu,* 4:7a–b, No. 16; SSGTK ed., 4:130, 310; Chan, *Things at Hand,* p. 128.

19. For a near analogy of the Buddhist tradition, one might compare this with the *jinen honi (tzu-jan fa-erh)* of the Pure Land "saint" Shinran in Japan or with the problem of moral effort *(kūfu; kung-fu)* in the Zen master Dōgen. See Tsunoda, de Bary, and Keene, *Sources of Japanese Tradition,* pp. 212–18, 249–251.

20. *Mean (Chung-yung),* 14. Trans. adapted from Legge.

21. Chu Hsi, *Chung-yung huo-wen,* 28a, p. 55.

22. Chu Hsi, *Chung-yung chang-chü,* p. 49, Commentary on ch. 1.

23. Ch'en Chang-fang, *Wei-shih chi,* 1a–3b; SYHA 29:9–10. Wing-tsit Chan, "Chu Hsi's Completion of Neo-Confucianism," pp. 76, 78. Richard Lynn, "Chu Hsi as Literary Theorist and Critic," p. 349.

24. Wing-tsit Chan, "Neo-Confucian Philosophical Poems," p. 11.

25. Ch'eng Hao, *Ming-tao wen-chi* 1:6b.

26. Chu Hsi, *Wen-chi* 47:17b, letter to Lu Tsu-ch'ien.

27. *Analects* 1:6. Trans. adapted from Legge.

28. Note that scholarship is not seen here as an unalloyed good but as much of a problem for the Confucians as a plus. The scholarly character of Confucianism is neither cited as a credit to it, nor as a reflection upon other religions, but in view of the absence in Confucianism of any emphasis on the religious functions common to the others. It does not require extended comparative study to recognize that Confucians are identified in the record, not as priests, pastors, monks, nuns, missionaries, pilgrims, and the like, but most commonly as scholars and sometimes as ministers (though ministers to the throne and not to the laity).

29. *Sung shih*, chüan 427–430, pp. 12709–12792.

30. For a negative view of this kind of cultural qualification from a Buddhist standpoint, see the rejoinder of the Chan master Hai-yün (1202–1257) to the proposal that Buddhist monks be required to take examinations, in Hok-lam Chan and W. T. de Bary, *Yüan Thought*, pp. 16–17, 388.

31. *Chung-yung huo-wen*, Kinsei Kanseki sōkan shisō sampen ed. (Kyoto: Chūbun shuppansha, 1976), p. 82, tr. adapted from Chan, *Things at Hand*, p. 69.

32. *I-shu*, 22A:14a; *Chin-ssu lu chi-chu*, 3:10b–11a; Chan, p. 97.

33. *I-shu*, 15:19b; *Chin-ssu-lu chi-chu*, 11:7a; tr. adapted from Chan, p. 264.

34. Ch'eng I, *I-ch'uan wen chi*, supplement, p. 3a, letter to Fang Tao fu; *Chin-ssu-lu chi-chu*, 2:14a, No. 15; tr. adapted from Chan, pp. 47–48.

35. *I-shu*, 19:11a; *Chin-ssu-lu chi-chu*, 3:14a, No. 30; Chan, p. 100.

36. *I-shu*, 19:11a; *Chin-ssu-lu chi-chu*, 3:16b, No. 38; Chan, p. 103.

37. *I-shu*, 2A:21a, 6:6b, 19:11a, 22A:2a, 6b; *Wai-shu* 3:1a, 5:1b, 12:4b, 6a.

38. *Wai-shu*, 11:2b; Chan, p. 94.

39. Chang Tsai as quoted in *Chin-ssu-lu*, 3:10b; Chan, p. 97.

40. *Lu Chiu-yüan chi*, Chung-hua shu-chu edition, pp. 388–389, CP edition, 34:400, Yü-lu shang; Chan, *Sourcebook*, p. 582.

41. *Lu Chiu-yüan chi*, 36:491; Ch'ien Mu, *Hsin hsueh-an* III, 615.

42. Chu *Wen-chi*, 43:7a, p. 2882, Ta Ch'en Ming-chung.

43. Chu, *Chu Tzu yü-lei*, 11:5a, p. 287, Item No. 38.

44. *Ibid.*, 24:8b–9a, p. 929, Item No. 39.

45. Chu, *Chu Tzu ta-chüan*, 43:13b–14a, translation adapted from Kirill Thompson "The Maturation of Chu Hsi's Mind and Moral Self-Cultivation," p. 10.

46. Chu, *Wen-chi*, 80:20b–21a, pp. 5816–5817; Chi Ching-shih-ko.

47. Chu, *Wen-chi*, 80:9b–10a, pp. 5794–5795; Chi-ku-ko chi also quoted

in "The Reading Schedule of the Ch'eng Family School," *Ch'eng shih chia-shu tu-shu fen-hien jih-ch'eng,* p. 9, Kang ling.

48. See W. T. de Bary and J. Chaffee, eds., *Neo-Confucian Education: the Formative Stage,* pp. 186–218.

49. *Chu Tzu yü-lei* 16:4a, Item 22; 1:6b (p. 266), Item 55.

50. *Ibid.,* 10:1b, Item 5; 10:7a, Items 56, 57.

51. *Ibid.,* 10:7a (pp. 267–286m), Items 60, 61.

52. *Ibid.,* 10:7a (p. 267), Item 60.

53. *Ta-hsüeh chang-chü,* 6b (p. 18).

54. I have discussed this more fully in "Chu Hsi's Aims as an Educator," in de Bary and Chaffee, *Neo-Confucian Education, the Formative Stage,* pp. 196–197. See also the analysis of Liu Shu-hsien, "The Functions of Mind in Chu Hsi's Philosophy," p. 204.

55. *Wai-shu* 11:2b; Chan, *Things at Hand,* p. 94.

56. Chang Tsai, *Chang Tzu ch'üan-shu,* 7:5a.

57. Chu, *Wen-chi,* 47:30a–b, letter to Lü Tsu-ch'ien, and *Chin-ssu-lu chi-chu,* 3:10a; Chan, p. 96.

58. See Morohashi Tetsuji, *Jukyō no mokuteki to Sōju no katsudō,* p. 798.

59. de Bary, *Unfolding,* pp. 143–7.

60. de Bary et al., *Sources of Chinese Tradition,* pp. 492–509; James T. C. Liu, *Ou-yang Hsiu,* pp. 90–102; and Hok-lam Chan, " 'Comprehensiveness' and 'Change' in Ma Tuan-lin's Historical Thought," in *Yüan Thought,* pp. 41–45.

61. See Chan, *Things at Hand,* pp. 88–122.

62. *I-shu,* 24:7b; *Wen-chi,* 5:11b.

63. *Chu Tzu yü-lei,* 4:12b, p. 112.

64. *Ibid.,* 67:6b, p. 2628.

65. *Ibid.,* 12:9b, p. 334.

66. *Hsi-shan wen-chi,* 24:410.

67. *Ssu-k'u t'i-yao* (Shanghai: Commercial Press, 1933 ed.), 36:742.

68. See Christian Murck, "Chu Yün-ming (1461–1527) and Cultural Commitment in Su-chou," 2:311–312.

69. *Chang Tzu ch'üan-shu,* 7:5a.

4. NEO-CONFUCIAN INDIVIDUALISM AND HOLISM

1. *Ta-hsüeh chang-chü,* in *Ssu-shu chi-chu* (Collected commentaries on the Four Books) 1a–b, 6a–b (7–8, 17–18); *Ta-hsüeh huo-wen* (Kinsei kanseki sōkan, shisō sampen ed.), 4b (8). (Page numbers in parentheses refer to consecutive pagination in reprint edition cited.)

2. *Chu Tzu yü-lei* (Classified conversations of Master Chu), 20.21a (759). (Note: page references appearing in parentheses after citations of the *Chu Tzu yü-lei* provide the reader with a cross-reference to the Chūbun shuppansha ed., 1979.)

3. Ch'eng I, *I-shu* (Written legacy), in *Erh-Ch'eng ch'üan-shu* (Complete works of the two Ch'engs), 19.3b; Mao Hsing-lai, *Chin-ssu lu chi-chu* (Collected notes on the *Chin-ssu lu*) (KHCPTS ed.), 3.13b; Wing-tsit Chan, *Reflections on Things at Hand*, pp. 99–100.

4. Chu Hsi, *T'ai-chi-t'u chieh*, in *Chou-Chang ch'üan-shu* (Complete works of Chou and Chang), 1:39; Mao Hsing-lai, *Chin-ssu lu chi-chu*, 1a–2a; Chan, *Things at Hand*, p. 5.

5. *Chu Tzu yü-lei*, 94.2b (3758).

6. Chu Hsi, *T'ai-chi-t'u chieh*, 43; Mao Hsing-lai, *Chin-ssu lu chi-chu* 1.1b; *Chu Tzu wen-chi*, 36.9b; *Chu Tzu yü-lei*, 94.1a, 5b (3755, 3764).

7. *Chu Tzu yü-lei*, 94.1a–b, 4a–b, 6a (3755–56, 3762–63, 3765); *Chu Tzu wen-chi*, 36.14a.

8. Masao Maruyama, *Studies in the Intellectual History of Modern Japan*, pp. 20–31; see also de Bary and Bloom, *Principle and Practicality*, pp. 136–138; Ishida Ichirō, "Tokugawa hōken shakai to Shushigakuha no shisō (Tokugawa feudal society and Neo-Confucian thought), partial English translation in *Philosophical Studies of Japan* v. 5, (1964), Japan Society for the Promotion of Science, 5:17–24.

9. This development and discussion is analyzed in detail by Tomoeda Ryūtarō in his *Shushi no shisō keisei*, pp. 142, 154–157, 183–184, 214–218, 227–238.

10. *Chu Tzu wen-chi*, 36.10a–b, 11b–12a.

11. *Chu Tzu yü-lei*, 94.1b, 2a (3756–57).

12. See also Tomoeda Ryūtarō, *Shushi no shisō keisei*, pp. 227–238.

13. *Ibid.*, 238ff.

14. Ch'eng I, *Wai-shu* (Outer works), in *Erh-Ch'eng ch'üan-shu*, 3.1b, quoted in Mao Hsing-lai, *Chin-ssu lu chi-chu*, 5.14a; Chan, *Things at Hand*, p. 165; *Chu Tzu yü-lei*, 20.21a (759).

15. See Chu Hsi, *Ta-hsüeh huo-wen*, 2b–3a (4–5).

16. *Ibid.*, 4b (3).

17. See Tomoeda Ryūtarō, *Shushi no shisō keisei*, p. 15.

18. Chu Hsi, *Ta-hsüeh huo-wen*, 3a–b (5–6).

19. "Ta Ch'en Ch'i-chih" (Reply to Ch'en Ch'i-chih), in *Chu Tzu wen-chi* (Sppy ed.), 58.21a–b.

20. *Ta-hsüeh chang-chü*, 6a–b (17–18).

21. *Ta-hsüeh huo-wen*, 20b–21a (39–41).

22. Chu Hsi, "Wei-cheng" (Governing), in *Lun-yü chi-chu* (Collected

Commentaries on the *Analects*), 2.9a; *Ta-hsüeh huo-wen*, 4b–7a (8–13); *Chu Tzu yü-lei*, 1.1a–b, 23.16b, 117.9a (1, 892, 4491).

23. *Chu Tzu yü-lei*, 94.8a–b (3769–70).

24. *Chu Tzu wen-chi*, 38.34a–b (first letter in response to Chiang Yüan-shih). For the sequence of Chu's learning experiences, see Wing-tsit Chan, "Patterns for Neo-Confucianism: Why Chu Hsi Differed from Ch'eng I," and Tomoeda Ryūtarō, *Shushi no shisō keisei*.

25. Ch'eng I, *I-shu*, 2A.2a.

26. *Ibid.*, 2A.3a; Tomoeda Ryūtarō, *Shushi no shisō keisei*, p. 110.

27. Okada Takehiko, "Shushi no chichi to shi, pt. 2, p. 20."

28. Chu Hsi, *Yen-p'ing ta-wen*, 70, 89–92, 99–103. Iki Hiroyuki, "*Empei tomon wo yomu*" (On reading *Responses of Yen-p'ing*), in *Tōyō no risō to eichi* (The ideals and wisdom of the East), Okada Takehiko, ed. (Fukuoka: Tōyō Shisō Kenkyūkai, 1963), pp. 51–64.

29. Chu Hsi, *Yen-p'ing ta-wen*, 111.

30. On Huang T'ing-chien, see *Sung-shih* (Sung history), 444.1; *Sung-Yüan hsüeh-an*, 19.28.

31. Chu Hsi, *Yen-p'ing ta-wen*, 65, quoting Huang T'ing-chien's preface to the poetry *(shih)* of Chou Tun-i found in *Yü-chang Huang hsien-sheng wen-chi* (Collected writings of Mr. Huang of Yü-chang) (SPTK ed.), 1.14b.

32. Mao Hsing-lai, *Chin-ssu lu chi-chu*, 14.6a; Chan, *Things at Hand*, p. 298.

33. Chu Hsi, *Yen-p'ing ta-wen*, 83–84.

34. *Ibid.*, 67–68.

35. *Ibid.*, 60, 63–64, 62.

36. *Ibid.*, 61–62.

37. *Yen-p'ing ta-wen fu fu-lu* (Supplement to the *Responses of Yen-p'ing*), 135.

38. Mao Hsing-lai, *Chin-ssu lu chi-chu*, 3.11a, no. 25; Chan, *Things at Hand*, p. 7.

39. Ch'eng I, *I-shu*, 18.5b; Mao Hsing-lai, *Chin-ssu lu chi-chu*, 3.5b, no. 9; Chan, *Things at Hand*, p. 92.

40. *Yen-p'ing ta-wen*, 72, 109; Mou Tsung-san, *Hsin-t'i yü hsing-t'i* (Substance of mind and substance of its nature), vol. 3, chs. 2–4; Tomoeda Ryūtarō, Introduction to *Yen-p'ing ta-wen*, 1–11; Okada Takehiko, "Shushi no chichi to shi," 85, 93.

41. Chu Hsi, *Yen-p'ing ta-wen*, 93, 111, 114; Okada Takehiko, "Shushi no chichi to shi," 86.

42. See my "Neo-Confucian Cultivation and Enlightenment," in

The Unfolding of Neo-Confucianism, Wm. Theodore de Bary, ed., pp. 170–172.

43. Chu Hsi, *Yen-p'ing ta-wen*, 42, 63, 114; Okada Takehiko, "Shushi no chichi to shi," 86.

44. Chu Hsi, Yen-p'ing ta-wen, 114.

45. Tomoeda Ryūtarō, Introduction to *Yen-p'ing ta-wen*, 9–10.

46. Chu Hsi, *Yen-p'ing ta-wen*, 92, 102, 107, 109; Tomoeda Ryūtarō, *Shushi no shisō keisei*, 248; Okada Takehiko, "Shushi no chichi to shi," 81–82.

47. Tomoeda, *Shushi no shisō keisei*, 60; Chan, "Patterns for Neo-Confucianism," 112–13.

48. Ch'eng I, *I-shu*, 24.2a.

49. The classic study of the evolution of this doctrine and its relation to modern reformism and radicalism is Shimada Kenji's "Subjective Idealism in Sung and Post-Sung China: The All Things are One Theory of *Jen*," 28:1–80.

50. Adapted from Wing-tsit Chan, *A Source Book in Chinese Philosophy*, pp. 497–98.

51. Shimada Kenji, *Shushigaku to Yōmeigaku* (The learning of Chu Hsi and Wang Yang-ming), pp. 67–70.

52. Ch'eng I, *I-ch'uan wen-chi* (Collected writings of Ch'eng I), 5.11b; Mao Hsing-lai, *Chin-ssu lu chi-chu*, 2.42b–46b; *Chu Tzu yü-lei*, 98.12a–20b (pp. 4003–16); *Yen-p'ing ta-wen*, 26–29; Chan, *Source Book*, pp. 498–499, and *Things at Hand*, pp. 79–81.

53. Ch'eng I, *I-shu*, 18.1a; Mao Hsing-lai, *Chin-ssu lu chi-chu*, 1.31b–32a (translated in Chan, *Things at Hand*, p. 27).

54. "Jen shuo," in *Chu Tzu wen-chi*, 67.21b; translation adapted from Chan, *Source Book*, 596.

55. *Chu Tzu yü-lei*, 126.20b (4858).

56. *Ta-hsüeh chang-chü*, 4a–5a (13–15); *Ta-hsüeh huo-wen*, 4a, 5b, 7b, 8b, 11a, 13a–14a, 18b, 31b (7, 10, 14, 16, 21, 25–27, 36, 62).

57. Chan, "Patterns for Neo-Confucianism," p. 110.

58. Chu Hsi, *Chung-yung chang-chü* (Commentary on the *Mean*), in *Ssu-shu chi-chu*, 49.

59. The notable exception, of course, is the work of Shimada Kenji. See note 49 above.

60. Chu Hsi, *Ta-hsüeh chang-chü*, 1a–6a (7–17). See also my "Individualism and Humanitarianism in Late Ming Thought," pp. 146–48.

61. See Matsumoto Sannosuke, "The Idea of Heaven: A Tokugawa Foundation for Natural Rights Theory."

5. LEARNING FOR ONE'S SELF IN THE YÜAN AND EARLY MING

1. Wei Liao-weng, *Ho-shan hsien-sheng ta-ch'üan chi*, 69:21a–b; *Sung shih*, 437:12964.

2. Ou-yang Hsüan, *Kuei-chai wen-chi*, 9:1a.

3. Hsü Heng, *Lu-chai ch'üan-shu*, 2:32a–33b.

4. Tu Wei-ming, "Toward an Understanding of Liu Yin's Confucian Eremitism," p. 256.

5. *Ibid.*, p. 255.

6. *Ibid.*, p. 256.

7. Hsü Heng, *Lu-chai ch'üan-shu*, 4:14b.

8. Liu Yin, *Ching-hsiu wen-chi*, 1:4ab. Hsü hsüeh.

9. See my *Neo-Confucian Orthodoxy*, p. 150; Wu Ch'eng, *Ts'ao-lu Wu Wen-cheng kung ch'üan-chi*, Wai-chi, 2:14a–15b, "Tao-t'ung."

10. Yü Chi, *Tao-yuan hsüeh-ku lu*, 44:54ab, 52b, *Hsing chuang*.

11. See my *Neo-Confucian Orthodoxy*, pp. 59–60.

12. On this point see Ch'ien Mu, *Chung-kuo hsüeh-shu ssu-hsiang shih lun-tsung*, p. 72.

13. Wu Ch'eng, *Tsao-lu Wu Wen-cheng kung ch'üan-chi*, Wai-chi, 2:14b, Tsa-shih, 14.

14. Wu, *Ch'üan-chi*, 24:8b–9b.

15. *Ch'üan-chi*, Wai-chi, 2 7b–8a, Tsa shih, 5.

16. *Ibid.*, 2:8a, 10b.

17. See my *Unfolding*, pp. 153–160, and *Neo-Confucian Orthodoxy*, pp. 5–10; Yü Chi, *Tao-yuan hsüeh-ku lu*, 44:5a–6a, Hsing chuang.

18. Wu, *Ch'üan-chi*, Wai-chi, 3:1a–2b, Yeh Chao pan-pu shu. An abbreviated version of this letter is quoted in Yü Chi's account of Wu's conduct of life *(hsing-chuang)* cited above. My translation includes all of the latter, but reinstates some of the original, fuller version which is so revealing of the inspirational nature of Wu's conception of the heroes' role in the repossession of the Way *(tao-t'ung)* and his contradistinction of it from the popular conception of the hero.

19. Cf. Yü Chi, *Hsing-chuang*, 44:3a–18b.

20. Ch'ien Mu, *Ts'ung Chung-kuo li-shih lai k'an Chung-kuo min-tsu hsing chi Chung-kuo wen hua*, pp. 47–59.

21. It is an intriguing coincidence that in the sixth volume of his *Chung-kuo hsüeh-shu ssu-hsiang-shih lun-ts'ung*, published the year before his lectures on the Chinese national character, Professor Ch'ien has a discussion of Wu Ch'eng which includes a quotation from the same letter discussing the hero cited above. Ch'ien Mu, *Chung kuo hsüeh-shu ssu-*

hsiang shih lun-ts'ung (Taipei: Tung-ta Publishing, 1948), p. 55. The quotation, however, is drawn from the much abbreviated version given by Yü Chi in his *Hsing-chuang* (pp. 5a–6a) which does not bring out so clearly as the full original text the terms in which Wu takes issue with the popular conception of the hero. In his later work, of course, Professor Ch'ien is discussing the general features of Wu Ch'eng's thought, not the issue of individualism, while in the earlier lectures he is addressing the general character of Chinese tradition, not specific Neo-Confucian developments. Between the two I have judged that there would still be room for him to agree with the interpretation offered here, and in personal conversation he has confirmed this.

22. Wu Yü-pi, *Jih-lu, K'ang-chai chi*, 8:16b; as cited by Theresa Kelleher in "Personal Reflections on the Pursuit of Sagehood: The Life and Journal of Wu Yü-pi (1392–1469)," p. 405.

23. *Mencius*, 4B:11, 12; 7A:33, "Dwelling in benevolence and acting out of righteousness, the business of the great man is complete." Cf. *K'ang-chai chi*, 11:2b.

24. *Mencius*, 3B:2: "He who dwells in the wide house of the world, stands in the correct station of the world, and walks in the great path of the world; he who, when successful, practices virtue along with the people, and when disappointed, still practices it alone; he who is above the power of riches and honors to corrupt, of poverty and mean condition to turn away from principle, of power and force to bend—he may be called a great man."

25. Wu, *Jih-lu, K'ang-chai chi*, 11:38b.

26. Chu Hsi, *Ta-hsüeh chang-chü*, 1:1.

27. Wing-tsit Chan, "Neo-Confucian Philosophical Poems," p. 11.

28. Hsü Heng, *Hsü Wen-cheng kung i-shu*, 4:1a, *Ta-hsüeh chih chieh*. On the importance of this concept later in the Wang Yang-ming school see T'ang Chün-i, *Chung-kuo che-hsüeh yüan-lun, Yüan chiao p'ien*, chs. 14, 16.

29. Lou Liang, "K'ang-chai hsien-sheng hsing-chuang," 10:13a.

30. E.g., *K'ang-chai chi*, 11:2b, 14a, 31b.

31. *Ibid.*, 8:15b, "Letter to Hsü Hsi-jen"; cited by Kelleher, p. 403.

32. *Ibid.*, 8:29a–b; cited by Kelleher, p. 425.

33. Wu, *Jih-lu, K'ang-chai chi*, 3:30a–b, 11:40b; Kelleher, p. 140, identifies a poem of Ch'eng Hao as the inspiration for this.

34. Jen Yu-wen, "Ch'en Hsien-chang's Philosophy of the Natural," in de Bary, ed., *Self and Society in Ming Thought*, pp. 53–82; Paul Jiang, *The Search for Mind: Ch'en Pai-sha, Philosopher Poet*, pp. 49–50, 74–78, 156–59, 181–82.

35. Jiang, p. 35.

36. Ch'en Hsien-chang, *Pai-sha Tzu ch'üan-chi*, 3:80b, letter to Ho Huang-men.

37. *Chu Tzu yü-lei*, 95:35b–36a, p. 3902; tr. adapted from Chan in *Things at Hand*, p. 70.

38. *Erh Ch'eng ch'üan-shu*, "Ts'ui-yen," 1:32a.

39. Ch'en Hsien-chang, *Pai-sha Tzu ch'üan-chi*, 1:41b–42a, "Hsin ch'ien Tien-pai hsien ju-hsüeh chi."

40. de Bary, *Neo-Confucian Orthodoxy*, p. 44–45.

41. This fact was noted by Dr. Hu Shih in his early advocacy of the *paihua* literature movement, and its importance in his eyes was reiterated to me in personal conversations in 1960.

42. Ōta Tatsuo, *Chūgoku rekidai kogobun*, pp. 70–71; de Bary, *Neo-Confucian Orthodoxy*, pp. 46–50, 134–147. I have been unable myself to locate the lectures in the vernacular by Wu Ch'eng, cited by Prof. Ōta, in any available editions of Wu's collected works.

43. W. T. de Bary, "Individualism and Humanitarianism in Late Ming Thought," in *Self and Society in Ming Thought*, pp. 154–157.

44. Ho Ping-ti, *The Ladder of Success in Imperial China*, p. 197; de Bary, *Neo-Confucian Orthodoxy*, p. 50.

45. Legge, *Shoo King*, pp. 41, 66.

46. *Kan-ch'uan wen-chi*, 1580 ed., 7:30b–21a. Letter in reply to Wang Yang-ming *(Ta Yang-ming)*; Shiga Ichirō, *Tan Kansen no kenkyū*, 2:128–129.

47. Legge, *Shoo King*, 396.

48. Chan, *Wen-chi*, 8:23a, *Hsin-ch'üan wen-pien lu*, "T'ien-li"; text as in Shiga, 2:190–191.

49. Chan, *Wen-chi*, 17:10b, Preface to the reprint of the *Collected Poems of Master Pai-sha*, text as in Shiga, 2:289–290. On this point Thomas Metzger in *Escape from Predicament*, p. 55, takes my reference to a "spiritual ideal that eludes precise definition" to imply a denial that "Chinese thinkers were very verbal and often consciously valued words." This does not, I regret to say, represent my view of the matter, as the reader will know from my discussion at the beginning of chapter 4. In my earlier writings on Neo-Confucianism I have tried to make clear the importance Neo-Confucians attached to the spoken and written word, and their fundamental rejection of the Ch'anist position that "one should not depend on words." What Chan Jo-shui says here about "words being the sounds of the mind-and-heart" and the importance of words in leading one to an experience of the Way, comes close to expressing a Neo-Confucian consensus on this point, and anticipates by some 150 years the quotation Metzger

offers from Lü Wan-tsun (1629–1683) that "spoken words are the sounds of the mind and written words are the brush-strokes of the mind."

50. Chan, *Wen-chi*, 7:30b–34a, "Ta Yang-ming Wang tu-hsien lun ko-wu," text as in Shiga, 2:133.

51. *Ibid.*, Shiga, 2:1.134.

52. *Wang Yang-ming ch'üan chi* 1(1):4–5, Pieh Chan Kan-chuan hsü; Okada Takehiko ed., *Ōyōmei zenshū*, 2:334 (187).

53. Chan, *Wen-chi*, "Ta Yang-ming Wang tu-hsien lun ko-wu," Shiga, 2:134–135.

54. See the biography of Chan by Fang Chao-ying, in *DMB*, pp. 36–42.

6. WANG YANG-MING: SAGEHOOD AND THE SELF

1. *Wang Yang-ming ch'üan-chi*, Wen-chi, 6:89–90; tr. adapted from Wing-tsit Chan, *Instructions for Practical Learning*, pp. 272–3.

2. *Wang Yang-ming ch'üan-chi*, Ch'uan-hsi-lu, 2:62, "Ta Nieh Wen-yü"; tr. adapted from Chan, *Instructions*, pp. 168–169.

3. See Chan, *Instructions*, pp. 13, 16, 45–48, 58–60.

4. *Wang Yang-ming ch'üan-chi*, Ch'uan-hsi lu, 2:60–61; tr. adapted from Chan, *Instructions*, p. 164.

5. See his description of how misunderstood or neglected Confucius was in his time (*Ch'uan-hsi lu* 2:62) and compare to Chu's account of the *tao-t'ung* in the preface to the *Mean*.

6. *Ch'uan-hsi lu*, 2:63.

7. *Ibid.*, 2:63.

8. *Wang Yang-ming ch'üan-shu*; I, Wen-lu, 3:190, Hsiang-shan wen-chi hsü.

9. *Ibid.* For a full translation, but somewhat different rendering of the preface, see Julia Ching, *To Acquire Wisdom*, pp. 206–8.

10. *Ch'üan-shu I*, Wen-lu, 4:214, Chi-shan shu-yüan tsun-ching ko chi. A similar tribute (though, as here, not without some reservations) to Lu as the heir to Mencius is found in a letter of 1521. See *Ch'üan-shu II*, Shu-lu 2:26; Yü Hsi Yüan-shan.

11. *Shu-ching*, Shun-tien; Legge, *Classics*, 3:44.

12. *Ch'üan-shu*, Wen-lu, 4:215–17.

13. *Ch'üan-shu*, Wen-lu, 1:1123, Ta hsüeh wen.

14. Chan, *Instructions*, p. 271.

15. *Ch'üan-shu*, Wen-lu, 1:119.

16. Trans. adapted from Chan, *Instructions*, p. 274.

17. *Ch'üan-shu*, Wen-lu, 1:123; cf. Chan, *Instructions*, p. 280.

18. *Ch'üan-shu, Wen-lu,* 1:123.

19. *Ch'uan-hsi lu* (in *Wang Yang-ming ch'üan-chi,* vol. 1), 2:46, Ch'i wen Tao-t'ung shu.

20. *Ch'uan-hsi lu,* 1:24–25, Te-chang yeh . . . : cf. Chan, *Instructions,* p. 69.

21. *Ch'uan-hsi lu,* 1:125.

22. E.g., *Ch'uan-hsi lu,* 1:2; Chan, *Instructions,* p. 7.

23. *Nien-p'u,* 1:4, Hung-chih 15.

24. *Ch'uan-hsi lu,* 2:118; Chan, *Instructions,* p. 118.

25. *Ch'uan-hsi lu,* 2:118; Chan, *Instructions,* p. 119.

26. *Ch'uan-hsi lu,* 2:118; Chan, *Instructions,* p. 120.

27. Chiao Hung, *T'an-yüan chi,* 12:6a–8a.

28. *Ch'uan-hsi lu,* 2:57 (Ta Ou-yang Ch'ung-i), echoing *Analects,* 14:25.

29. The whole work reflects this spirit, but we might cite in particular the conversations recorded by Ch'en Chiu-ch'uan, Huang I-fang, and Huang Mien-shu in *chüan* 3.

30. *Ch'uan-hsi lu,* 3:71; Chan, *Instructions,* pp. 194–5.

31. Hu Ta-shih, T. Chi-sui, SYHA 71:1a.

32. *MJHA,* v.1, "Fan li," pp. 1–2.

33. *Lu Chiu-yüan chi,* 34:423–4.

34. *Ch'uan-hsi lu,* 3:74; Chan, *Instructions,* pp. 194–195.

35. *Ch'uan-hsi lu,* 2:58–59, Ta Lo Ch'eng-an; Chan, *Instructions,* p. 159.

36. *Ch'uan-hsi lu,* 2:60; Chan, p. 164.

37. Cf. Araki Kengo, "Minmatsu ni okeru ju-butsu chōwa ron no seikaku" (The character of Confucian-Buddhist syncretism in the later Ming period), pp. 219–20. Araki believes that it was the intellectual revolution springing from Wang's identification of mind as principle that overcame the intellectual isolation and defensive attitude of Zen Buddhists at this time, and gave them an opportunity to reengage in the intellectual life of the late Ming.

38. The classic example is the discussion of the Four Dicta at the T'ien-ch'üan bridge (see *Ch'uan-hsi lu,* 3:90; Chan, *Instructions,* pp. 241 ff.), which left things as ambiguous as at the start.

39. Cf. Huang Tsung-hsi's classification of the late Ming schools in the Table of Contents of *Ming-ju hsüeh-an* and especially chuan 10–36. The classification of the T'ai-chou school as "left-wing" in contrast to the "right bank" originates so far as I am aware, with Chi Wen-fu. Cf. de Bary, *Self and Society in Ming Thought,* 223, n. 117. See also Okada, "Existentialism," in ibid., pp. 121 ff.

7. WANG CHI AND THE FREEDOM OF INNATE KNOWING

1. For a brief biography and succinct discussion of Wang Chi's teachings, see Julia Ching's account in Goodrich and Fang, *Dictionary of Ming Biography*, pp. 1351–55; also *Records of Ming Scholars*, pp. 114–117.

2. There is considerable scholarly literature on this celebrated issue, but for those unfamiliar with it a succinct discussion may be found in T'ang Chün-i, "The Concept of Moral Mind from Wang Yang-ming to Wang Chi," pp. 108–116; and in Okada Takehiko, "Wang Chi and the Rise of Existentialism in the Late Ming," pp. 121–144. Of the recent discussions in Chinese and Japanese, one of the more significant is found in Mizoguchi Yūzō, *Chūgoku zenkindai shisō no kussetsu to tenkai*, pp. 126–210.

3. *Wang Lung-hsi ch'üan-chi*, 20 chüan, hereafter cited as *Ch'üan-chi*, 20:11a, Hsing-chuang by Ch'ien Hsü-shan.

4. *Ch'üan-chi*, 1:17b, Yü.

5. *Ch'üan-chi*, 17:8b, San-chiao t'ang chi.

6. *Ch'üan-chi*, 15:8a, "Shu Keng Tzu-chien yu-chi hou yü," and 17:15b, "Pu-erh chai shuo."

7. *Lung-hsi ch'üan-chi*, 7:2ab, Nan-yü hui-chi.

8. *Ch'üan-chi*, 3:15a, Ta Nan-ming Wang tzu wen.

9. *Ch'üan-chi*, 16:33ab, Shu Chien-lo chuan chien tseng ssu mo.

10. *Ch'üan-chi*, 1:19a, *Yü-lu*, and 15:4a.

11. *Chou Tzu ch'üan shu*, 2:23.

12. *Ibid.*, 2:23–5.

13. *Ch'üan-chi*, 17:21–41, *T'ai-chi t'ing chi*.

14. See chapter 4, "Individualism and Holism," p. 93.

15. *Chou Tzu ch'üan-shu* (KHCPTS ed.), 2:23–32.

16. For a detailed analysis of these concepts in Wang Chi, see Ueda Hiroki, "O Ryū-kei ni okeru kyo to mu."

17. *Ch'üan-chi*, 16:30a, Shu hsien shih . . . i-mo.

18. *Ibid.*, 16:11b, Pieh yen-tseng Chou Shun-chih.

19. *Ibid.*, 16:11b, Pieh yen-tseng Mei Ch'un-fu.

20. *Ibid.*, 1:32b, Yü lu.

21. *Ibid.*, 2:16a, Yü lu.

22. *Ibid.*, 1:21b–22a, Yü lu.

23. *Ibid.*, 16:37b–38a, also 3:6b–7a, Shu-hsi Ching-she hui-yü.

24. See Tsunoda, de Bary, and Keene, *Sources of Japanese Tradition*, p. 238, 255.

25. *Ch'üan-chi*, 1:25b, Yü-lu.

26. *Ibid.*, 15:20a, Tzu sung . . . erh pei.

27. See de Bary, *The Unfolding of Neo-Confucianism,* pp. 14–16; de Bary and Bloom, *Principle and Practicality,* pp. 12–14.

28. *Ch'üan-chi,* 4:10b–11a, Tung yu Hui yü.

29. *Ibid.,* 1:26b, Yü-lu.

30. *Ibid.,* 2:23b, Yü lu.

31. *Ibid.,* 1:20b, Yü-lu.

32. *Shih Ching,* Chou Sung, Ch'ing miao.

33. *Ch'üan-chi,* 1:25b, Yü-lu.

34. See Yamashita Ryūji, "Nakae Tōju's Religious Thought and Its Relation to Jitsugaku."

35. See de Bary and Bloom, *Principle and Practicality,* pp. 494–495.

36. Cf. *Chüan-chi,* 17:5a, Hsiao yu t'ang chi; and 8:1a, Ta-hsüeh shou-chang chieh-i, *Wang lung-hsi yü-lu,* Kuang-wen ed., 8:1a. The same in Chūbun *Lung-hsi Wang hsien-sheng ch'üan chi,* Chūbun shuppansha.

37. See, for example, the discussion in his Recorded Conversations, *Ch'üan-chi,* 2:28b–31b, 4:6a, and 16:28ab.

8. WANG KEN AND HIS SCHOOL: THE COMMON MAN AS SAGE

1. The discussion of Wang Ken and Ho Hsin-yin here is based on my earlier article in *Self and Society in Ming Thought,* with some additions and revisions. Readers already familiar with the latter may wish to pass on to p. 169.

For this brief account of Wang Ken's life and ideas I have consulted the following sources and selected secondary studies:

Wang Ken [Ming-ju] *Wang Hsin-chai hsien-sheng i-chi,* Peking(?): 1911 (hereafter abbr. *I-Chi*); *Hsin-chai yüeh-yen,* in Tsao Jung, comp., *Hsüeh-hai lei pien:* MJHA, 32 (Wan-yu wen-k'u ed.), 32:62–75.

Hsin-chai Wang hsien-sheng ch'üan-chi; abbr. *Hsin-chai ch'üan-chi.*

Wang Hsin-chai hsien-sheng wen-chi.

Wang Yüan-ting, *Wang Hsin-chai nien-p'u,* in *I-chi,* 3. Biog. in *Ming shih* 283.

Chao Chen-chi, *T'ai-chou Wang Hsin-chai Ken mu-chih-ming,* in Chiao Hung, *Kuo-ch'ao hsien-cheng lu,* 114, pp. 5032–33; abbr. *Mu-chih-ming.*

Hsü Yüeh, *Wang Hsin-chai pieh-chuan,* in *I-chi,* 4:6b–8a; abbr. *Pieh-chuan.*

Keng Ting-hsiang, *Wang Hsin-chai chuan,* in *I-chi,* 4:12a–14a.

Hsu Yü-lüan, *Wang Ken chuan* from *Yang-chou fu-chih,* reprinted in *I-chi,* 4:16a–17b.

Li Chih, *Hsu Ts'ang-shu* (Wan-li ed. of Wang Wei-yen, Nanking), 22:14a; also Chung-hua shu-chü ed., pp. 432–435. Peking, 1959,

Chou Ju-teng, *Sheng-hsüeh tsung-ch'uan*, 34, 16:1a.

DMB, p. 1382, biography by Julia Ching.

Chi Wen-fu, *Tso-p'ai Wang-hsüeh*, ch. 2.

Hou Wai-lu, *T'ung shih*, 4B:958–1002.

Jung Chao-tsu, *Ming-tai ssu-hsiang-shih*, pp. 150–59.

Wu K'ang, *Sung-Ming li-hsüeh*, pp. 324–28.

T'ai-chou hsüeh-pai hsüeh-shu t'ao-lun hui, Chi nien pien-wen chi.

Shimada Kenji, *Zasetsu*, pp. 94–112.

Kusumoto Masatsugu, *Sō-Min jidai jugaku shisō no kenkyū*, pp. 489–94.

Ono Kazuko, "Jukyō no itansha tachi," pp. 25–45.

Forke, Alfred, *Geschichte der neueren Chinesische Philosophie*, pp. 400–402.

Carson Chang, *Development of Neo-Confucian Thought*, 2:25–27, 113–118. Chang's book is the only extended account of the thought of this period, but the limitations of his approach to Wang Ken's thought are clearly indicated by his introductory remark: "I must restrict myself to dealing with it only insofar as it is a mark of the deterioration of the school of Wang Shou-jen. With this end in view, let me point out a few of the peculiarities of the philosopher from Taichou's teaching."

2. Chou Ju-teng, *Sheng-hsüeh tsung-ch'uan*, 16:3a; Shimada, *Zasetsu*, p. 98. *Ken* is hexagram 52 in the *Book of Changes*, where it stands for upright and firm adherence to principle. (See Legge, *I-Ching*, pp. 175–177). The commentary on the hexagram, as well as Wang's courtesy name, Ju-chih, and his honorofic Hsin-chai (taken from Chuang Tzu's "fast of the mind"), all suggest an undistracted and imperturbable state of self-containment.

3. Keng, *Wang Hsin-chai chuan*, 2:12ab.

4. Chao, *Mu-chih ming*, 14:5032a; Hsü Yüeh, *Pieh-chuan*, 4:7b; Keng, *Wang Hsin-chai chuan*, 4:12b; MJHA, 32:68; Hou, *T'ung shih*, 4:261.

5. Chao, *Mu-chih-ming*, 14:5032a; Keng, *Wang Hsin-chai chuan*, 4:12b; Hou, *T'ung-shih*, 4:261.

6. *MJHA*, 32:68, Wang Ken chuan; cf. also Hsü, *Pieh-chuan*, 4:7b.

7. Hsü, *Pieh-chuan*, 4:7b; *Nien-p'u*, 3:2b–3a, 37 *sui*; Hou, *T'ung-shih* 4B:962.

8. *Wang Yang-ming ch'üan-chi*, *Ch'uan-hsi lu*, 2:62, Ta Nieh Wen-wei; tr. adapted from Chan, *Instructions*, pp. 168–169.

9. *Ch'uan-hsi lu*, 2:63.

10. Chao, *Mu-chih-ming*, 5032b; MJHA, 32:68, Wang Ken chuan.

11. Carson Chang's translation of this passage is: "If there is a similarity, then Wang Shou-jen will be a dominating personality for many generations to come. If there is no similarity, then I should follow Wang Shou-jen" (*Development of Neo-Confucianism*, 2:115). Dr. Chang assumes the worshipful tone which would be normal in such a situation, but Chao's epitaph for Wang Ken (see n. 10 above) makes it clear that this was taken as an expression of Ken's amazing self-confidence, and the following encounter with Wang Yang-ming bears out that Ken felt he had as much to give as to get from such a meeting.

12. *MJHA*, 32:69, Wang Ken chuan.

13. *Ibid.*

14. Keng, *Wang Hsin-chai chuan*, 4:12b.

15. *Ibid.;* Chou, *Wang Ken chuan,* 16:4b; Huang, *MJHA*, 32:69; Hou, *T'ung-shih*, 4B:967–968.

16. Hou, pp. 968–969.

17. *MJHA*, 37:71 Yü-lu; Kusumoto, *Sō-Min jugaku*, p. 491.

18. Hsi-tzu B 47; cf. Legge, *I-ching*, p. 392.

19. *MJHA*, 32:69, Wang Ken chuan. This is Huang Tsung-hsi's paraphrase or summary of Wang Ken's position.

20. *MJHA*, 32:69–70, Wang Ken chuan. Again, Huang's paraphrase.

21. *Ibid.*, 32:70, Yü-lu.

22. Cf. *ibid.*, 32:71–75, Yü-lu, and *I-chi*, 1:12b–13a.

23. The expression *Ming-che pao-shen* is drawn from the *Book of Odes*, no. 260, where it is said of a minister that "he is enlightened and wise and so he protects his person," Karlgren, *Book of Odes*, p. 229.

24. *Mencius*, 7A, 15.

25. *I-chi*, 1:12b–13a, Ming-che pao-shen lun.

26. The *Chuang Tzu* refers to a loyal minister cutting off his flesh to feed his sovereign. In the *Hsin T'ang shu* and *Sung shih* there are examples of filial sons slicing flesh from their thighs to make medicine for their parents. See Chan, *Instructions*, p. 107, n. 44. A typical example of this sort of thinking in Ming times was the famous paragon of filial piety, Madam Wang, who, in order to have meat for her parents-in-law, was said to have cut the flesh off her own thighs, cooked it, and served it to them. She was a common figure in moralistic literature and official Confucian indoctrination, and was also represented in painting for moral inspiration down to the nineteenth century. She is included in a set of "Four Illustrations of Filiality" by the Ch'ing painter Ting Kuan-p'eng, modeled after those of an anonymous Yüan artist, at the National Palace Museum, Taipei.

27. Chao, *Mu-chih-ming*, 114:5032a; MJHA, 32:68, Wang Ken chuan.

28. Cf. *I-chi*, 2:9ab, Hsiao chen.

29. For a fuller discussion of this problem in relation to Wang Yang-ming, Wang Chi, and Wang Ken, see Shimada, "Subjective Idealism in Sung and Post-Sung China," pp. 1–9, 40–46.

30. Huang, *MJHA*, 32:70, Yü-lu.

31. Wang Ken, *Hsin-chai yüeh-yen*, 1b–2b, 4b–5b; Kusumoto, *Sō-Min jugaku*, p. 489.

32. *MJHA*, 32:74, Yü-lu.

33. Cf. Kusumoto, *Sō-Min jugaku*, p. 491.

34. *MJHA*, 32:70, Yü-lu. The way of the concubine *(ch'ieh-fu chih tao)* is referred to in Mencius, 3B:2, as characterized by dutiful compliance.

35. *MJHA*, 32:74, Yü-lu.

36. *I-chi*, 1:7ab.

37. *MJHA*, 32:70, 72, 74, Yü-lu.

38. *I-chi*, 2:9b–10; *MJHA*, 32:75, Lo Hsüeh ko.

39. The common reference in Neo-Confucian discourse is to the disciple Yen Yüan who "loved to learn" (*Analects* 7:2).

40. Wang Ken, *Hsin-chai yüeh-yen*, 1a.

41. The original expression *pai-hsing jih-yung* is from the *I-ching*, Hsi-tzu A, p. 40. Hou, *T'ung-shih*, 4B, gives considerable biographical evidence on this point.

42. The term derives from *The Mean*, XII.

43. *MJHA*, 32:72, 73, Yü-lu, *Yüeh-yen*, 3–4.

44. "*Chih-chin erh shen.*" Nien-p'u, 46 *sui*. *I-chi*, 3:4b.

45. Hou, *T'ung-shih*, IVB, pp. 974–95; Jung Chao-tsu, in his *Ming-tai ssu-hsiang-shih*, pp. 150–59, emphasizes practical action, but not a social program to the same extent.

46. This is conceded by Hou, p. 983, and by Ono Kazuko, "Itansha," p. 17.

47. Hou, *T'ung-shih*, 4B:983.

48. *Chuang Tzu*, T'ien-hsia p'ien, Harvard-Yenching Index Series, *A Concordance to Chuang Tzu*, p. 91; tr. in de Bary et al., *Sources of Chinese Tradition*, pp. 82–83.

49. *Ch'iu-shan fu*. I cannot vouch for the ichthyological accuracy of the terms *loach* and *eel*.

50. *I-chi*, 2:10ab, Ch'iu-shan fu.

51. *Mencius*, 3B:2; tr. adapted from Legge and from Chan, *Source Book*, p. 72.

52. *Ch'uan-hsi lu*, 2:44, Ta Ku Tung-ch'iao; tr. adapted from Chan, *Instructions*, p. 124.

53. See Okada, "Wang Chi and the Rise of Existentialism," p. 129.

54. The term *ta-chang-fu* also means "great soul" *(mahāpurusha)* in Buddhism, and Wang Ken's use of it has the double significance of the Confucian and Buddhist ideals of unselfish service to mankind.

55. Shimada, *Zasetsu*, p. 104. Shimada's discussion of this aspect of Wang Ken shows the depth and skill that make this a classic among studies of modern Chinese intellectual history.

56. *Hsin-chai Wang hsien-sheng ch'üan chi*, ch. 6 and ch. 2, hereafter abbr. as *Hsin-chai ch'üan-chi*, 4:25b, Ta ch'eng hsüeh ko.

57. *Hsin-chai ch'üan-chi*, 5:3a, 8a, Huang kung chih tien-wen.

58. *Hsin-chai ch'üan-chi*, 6:5a, Ling kung . . . tzu-t'ang chi. See also Wang Ken's own reference to it in 4:9b, Ta T'ai-shou Jen Kung.

59. *Hsin-chai ch'üan-chi*, 5:1a–2a, Chu Shuang ch'iao . . . tien-wen. A similar account is found in 6:38b, Liu kung tien-wen, and in Chou Ju-teng's preface for the reprinting of the *Complete Works* written in 1604 (see reprint of 1615 in the Naikaku bunko, ts'e 1), though Chou stresses the unmediated "transmission" from mind-to-mind, as if by some mental telepathy.

60. *Hsin-chai ch'üan-chi*, 6:20a, Keng kung . . . chuan-wen.

61. Shimada Kenji, *Chūgoku kindai shii no zasetsu*, p. 87.

62. *Hsin-chai ch'üan-chi*, 6: Ling kung tzu-t'ang chi, and 5:16b, mu ming of Chao Chen-chi.

63. *I-chi*, 4:6b–8a, Pieh-chuan; and in *Hsin-chai ch'üan-chi*, 5: 27a–33a.

64. *I-chi*, 4:14a, Chüan wen; *I-chi*, 3:6a, Nien-p'u for 55 sui.

65. *Hsin-chai ch'üan-chi*, 2:4b, Nien p'u for 36 sui.

66. *Hsin-chai ch'üan-chi*, 3:7a, Yü-lu.

67. *I-chi*, 4:13a, Keng kung . . . chuan-wen.

68. *I-chi*, 3:2b–3a, Nien-p'u 38 sui. *Hsin-chi ch'üan-chi*, 6:11a, Li kung . . . tien-wen.

69. *Hsin-chai ch'üan-chi*, 6:4a, Li kung . . . tz'u chi.

70. *I-chi*, 4:12b, Keng kung . . . chuan-wen.

71. *Mencius*, 4B:29, trans. Legge.

72. *Hsin-chai ch'üan-chi*, 1:1a–2b, "Ch'uan-chi hsü" of Ch'en Li-hsiang.

73. *I-chi*, 4:6b, "Hsü yüeh pieh chuan."

74. *I-chi*, 2:6a, Nien p'u 55 sui; 4:13b–14a, "Keng kung chuan-wen."

75. *Hsin-chai ch'üan-chi*, 4:23b, letter to Hsü Tzu-chih.

76. *Hsin-chai ch'üan-chi*, 3:34b, "Mien jen fang."

77. Kasuga Senan in *Wang Hsin-chai hsien-sheng wen-chi*, Kyoto, 1847 (Koka 4), 4:1a, commentary on Hsiao Chen.

78. *Hsin-chai ch'üan-chi*, 4:2ab, "Ta Hsü Tzu-chih."

79. *I-chi*, 4:7b, "Hsü Yüeh . . . chuan-wen."

80. *Hsin-chai ch'üan-chi*, 3:36b, Mien jen fang; cf. also 2:60ab Preface to Nien-p'u.

81. *Hsin-chai ch'üan-chi*, 3:38a, "Tien-li liang-chih shuo."

82. *Ibid.*, 3:37a–38b.

83. *Hsin-chai ch'üan-chi*, 4:1b, "Yü yü ch'un-fu; cf. also *Hsin-chai ch'üan-chi*, 2:23ab, Nien-p'u, 46 sui.

84. *Ch'üan-chi*, 4:9a–10b, "Ta T'ai-shou Jen kung"; and 2:24b–25a, "Nien-p'u," 47 sui.

85. Chou Tun-i, *T'ung shu*, 7; Chan, *Sourcebook in Chinese Philosophy*, pp. 468–469; *Hsin-chai ch'üan-chi*, 4:10a; 2:24b–25a, "Nien-p'u," 47 sui.

86. *Hsin-chai ch'üan-chi*, 3:30b–31a, "An-ting shu-yüan chiang-hsüeh pieh yen"; 2:19a, "Nien-p'u," 44 sui.

87. *Ch'üan-chi*, 4:38ab; "Yu Liu Tzu-jen."

88. *Ibid.*, 4:38b.

89. As quoted in *Hsin-chai ch'üan-chi*, Preface of Hsiung Shan-wen to 1615 ed., 2b.

90. *Ch'üan chi*, 4:34b. "Shu Ho Hsüan-chüan."

91. Kasuga Senan notes this point in his marginal comments on Wang's letter to Yü Ch'uan fu in his edition of *Wang Hsin-chai hsien-sheng ch'üan chi*, 5:3a.

92. *Hsin-chai ch'üan-chi*, 3:35b–36a, Mien-jen fang.

93. Shimada, *Zasetsu*, p. 113; Hou, *T'ung-shih*, 4B:996–998; Okada Takehiko, "Ō-mon genjōha no keitō (The filiation of the existentialist branch of the Wang Yang-ming school)," p. 36; Carson Chang, *Development*, pp. 26–27.

94. Ping-ti Ho, *The Ladder of Success in Imperial China: Aspects of Social Mobility, 1368–1911*, p. 199 (hereafter abbr. as *Ladder*).

95. See Miyazaki Ichisada, *Ajia shi kenkyū*, 4:306ff., 722ff.

96. See Saeki Tomi, *Sō no shin bunka*, pp. 381ff.

97. See Yoshikawa Kojirō, *Gen Min shi gaisetsu*, pp. 220–222; Saeki, *Sō no shin bunka*, p. 387.

98. See André Levy, *Vogue et Declin d'un Genre Narratif Chinois— Le Conte en Langue Vulgaire du XIIe Siècle*, pp. 231–255. Includes an extensive discussion of the cultural background of the rise of the popular tale in the sixteenth and seventeenth centuries.

99. See Ping-ti Ho, "The Salt-Merchants of Yang-chou, a Study of Commercial Capitalism in Eighteenth Century China."

100. J. L. Gallagher, *China in the Sixteenth Century: The Journal of Matthew Ricci 1583–1610*, pp. 268–269.

101. Miyazaki, *Ajia shi kenkyū*, 4:322. Professor Ho, in a personal

communication, states that the prefectural population was already well over two million by the late fourteenth century and by the late sixteenth century must have been far larger, since by 1776–1850 the population was well over five million.

102. Gallagher, *China in the Sixteenth Century*, p. 317; F. W. Mote, *The Poet Kao Ch'i*, pp. 18, 42–47.

103. Ho, *Ladder*, p. 73.

104. According to Levy, *Vogue et Declin.*

105. These are, with the corresponding reference in the *Ming-ju hsüeh-an* for each case: Hsü Yüeh (32:80); Lin Ch'un (32:95); Chao Ch'en-chi (33:99); Lo Ju-fang (43:1); Yang Ch'i-yüan (34:30); Keng Ting-hsiang (35:35); Chiao Hung (35:45); P'an Shih-tsao (35:50); Chu Shih-li (35:61); Chou Ju-teng (36:64); and T'ao Wang-lin (36:74).

106. Yen Chün, Ho Hsin-yin, and Li Chih were particular beneficiaries of such influence in high places, as will be seen below.

107. Ho, *Ladder*, p. 73; citing *Chen-ch'uan hsien-sheng chi*, 13:ab.

108. Saeki, *Sō no shin bunka*, pp. 388–92.

109. *MJHA*, 32:62.

110. *I-chi*, 1: Fu p'u lun chih t'u, 2b.

111. *MJHA*, 32:77.

112. Hou, *T'ung-shih*, 4B:1000–1002.

113. *I-chi*, 3:4b.

114. *MJHA*, 32:69.

115. Yüan Huang, 1533–1606, *DMB*, pp. 1632–1635, biog. by Tu Lien-che. Sakai Tadao, *Chūgoku zensho no kenkyū*, p. 329.

116. Sakai Tadao, pp. 373–94.

117. *Ibid.*, pp. 330–331; citing the testimony of Wang Chi, Chou Ju-teng, and Li Chih.

118. *Ibid.*, p. 375; see also Sakai, "Confucianism and Popular Educational Works."

119. Takao Giken, *Chūgoku Bukkyō shiron*, pp. 264ff; *DMB*, pp. 322–324, biog. by Chün-fang Yü; and Chün-fang Yü, *The Renewal of Buddhism in China.*

120. Takao, *Bukkyō shiron*, pp. 235–45; Sakai, *Zensho*, p. 377.

121. Sakai, *Zensho*, pp. 377–78.

122. Ch'en, *Buddhism in China*, p. 439, describes it as "a good example of Buddhist-Taoist mixture." I would suggest, however, that it is more than just another case of popular "syncretism." The real impetus here comes not from within Buddhism and Taoism or from a vague eclectic tendency, but from the dynamic humanist spirit of which the

Wang Yang-ming school was the chief expression in the sixteenth century.

123. The range and variety of thought in this school are well represented in Okada Takehiko, *Minmatsu jukyō no dōkō*, and his "Ō-mon genjōha no keitō."

124. See Araki Kengo, "Minmatsu ni okeru jubutsu chōwa-ron no seikaku," pp. 221–223.

125. Shimada's discussion of "The Frustration of Modern Chinese Thought," in his *Zasetsu* (1948), centers on the T'ai-chou school as a means of evaluating the potential for modernization in Ming and Ch'ing China. Hou Wai-lou's more recent work ("Shih-liu shih-chi Chung-kuo ti chin-pu ti che-hsueh ssu-ch'ao kai-hsū," in *Li-shih yen-chiu* [1959, No. 10] and in *T'ung-shih*, 4B) give much attention to the T'ai-chou school as the vanguard of "progressive" thought in the sixteenth century. Earlier, Chi Wen-fu in *Tso-p'ai Wang-hsüeh* and Jung Chao-tsu with his studies of Ho Hsin-yin (*Fu-jen hsüeh-chih*, vol. 6, nos. 1, 2) and *Ming-tai ssu-hsiang shih* (History of Ming thought, 1941) had made some of the more unorthodox thinkers better known. Some of this had stimulated Shimada's own thinking on the subject, but he put the problem in a much broader historical and sociological perspective. For a contrasting view among Japanese scholars, see Yamashita Ryūji, "Minmatsu ni okeru han jukyō shisō no genryū," and Shimada's response in "Ōgaku saharon hihan no hihan." Most recently Ono Kazuko has seen the T'ai-chou school as the first stage in the "quickening of Asia." See Matsumoto Sannosuke, ed., *Taidō suru Ajia*, pp. 1–45.

126. T. Shan-nung, from Chi-an, Kiangsi Province. Dates unknown. See *DMB*, pp. 514–15.

127. Wang Shih-chen, *Yen-chou shih-liao hou-chi*, 35, Chia-lung chiang-hu ta hsia (reprinted in *Ho Hsin-yin chi*, p. 143). On Wang, see *DMB*, pp. 1399–1405, biog. by B. Yoshida-Krafft, and Richard Lynn, "Wang Shih-chen's Theory of Poetry," pp. 217–257.

128. Wang Shih-chen, *Yen-chou shih-liao hou-chi*, p. 35.

129. Original name Liang Ju-yüan, from Yung-feng, Chi-chou, Kiangsi Province. See Huang, *MJHA*, 32:63; *DMB*, pp. 513–515, biog. by Wu Pei-yi and Julia Ch'ing; and Ronald G. Dimberg, *The Sage and Society: The Life and Thought of Ho Hsin-yin*.

130. *MJHA*, 32:62; and in *Ho Hsin-yin chi*, 1:22.

131. T. Tzu-chih, H. Po-shih. *Chin-shih*, 1533. Cf. *MS*, 283:3186; *MJHA*, 32:50.

132. The good deeds of the *yu-hsia* often flouted law or convention or

were undertaken in defiance of the authorities. There is almost as much of the gangster in this conception as of the knight in shining armor. For the tradition of the "knight-errant" in Chinese literature, see James J. Y. Liu, *The Chinese Knight-Errant.*

133. Thinking victory was in his grasp, Hsü allowed himself to be caught off guard by a false surrender trick. See *MJHA,* 32:81, 32:63.

134. Jung Chao-tsu, "Ho Hsin-yin chi ch'i ssu-hsiang" (see n. following) citing *Keng T'ien-t'ai chi* 12.

135. The principal sources for the study of Ho Hsin-yin's thought are contained in the edition of Ho's works edited by Jung Chao-tsu, *Ho Hsin-yin chi.* Prefaced to it is Li Chih's essay on Ho in *Fen-shu* 3 entitled "Ho Hsin-yin lun" (pp. 10–12); an appendix contains several early accounts of Ho's life and thought, of which the following have been most useful here:

Tsou Yüan-piao, Liang Fu-shan chuan in *Ho Hsin-yin chi,* pp. 120–121 (from *Liang Fu-shan i-chi*).

Huang Tsung-hsi, T'ai-chou hsüeh-an hsü, from *MJHA,* 32 (pp. 122–124).

Wang Shih-chen, Chia-lung chiang-hu ta hsia, from *Yen-chou shih-liao hou-chi,* 35 (in *Ho Hsin-yin chi,* pp. 143–44).

The following secondary studies have also been consulted:

Jung Chao-tsu, "Ho Hsin-yin chi ch'i ssu-hsiang," 6(1, 2):129–172.
Hou Wai-lu, *T'ung-shih,* 4B:1003–30.
Shimada Kenji, *Zasetsu,* 134–161.
Okada Takehiko, "Ō-mon genjō-ha no keitō," Part 2, pp. 31–50.

136. Tsou Yüan-piao, *Liang Fu-shan chuan,* in *Ho Hsin-yin chi,* 120; *MJHA,* 32:63 (*Ho Hsin-yin chi,* 123).

137. *Ho Hsin-yin chi,* 68–69, Chü-ho shuai-chiao yü-tsu li-yü; *ibid.,* 70–72, Chü-ho shuai-yang yü-tsu li-yü; Tsou, *Liang Fu-shan chuan,* pp. 120–121; Huang, *MJHA,* 32:63; Jung, "Ho Hsin-yin chi ch'i ssu-hsiang," pp. 130–133.

138. Tsou, *Liang Fu-shan chuan; MJHA,* 32:63; Jung, "Ho Hsin-yin chi ch'i ssu-hsiang," pp. 130–133.

139. *MJHA,* 32:64.

140. *Ibid.,* 32:63.

141. *Ibid.,* 32:64; Tsou, *Liang Fu-shan chuan,* p. 121. The above brief account of Ho's life is offered only as background for the understanding of his type of individualism. More detailed and consecutive accounts are contained in the writings of Jung and Ho cited above.

142. *Ho Hsin-yin chi,* 54, Ta Chan-kuo . . . pu lo i-ch'i.

143. *Ibid.*, 55.

144. *Ibid.*, 40, Kua-yü.

145. *Ibid.*, 42, Pien wu yü; Jung, "Ho Hsin-yin," p. 170.

146. *Ho Hsin-yin chi*, 42, Pien wu-yü.

147. *Ibid.*, 72, Chü-ho lao-lao wen.

148. Thus, the legitimate and irreducible desires were seen as those common to all men. *Ho Hsin-yin chi*, 72, and Jung, "Ho Hsin-yin," p. 170; Ono Kazuko, "Jukyō no itansha tachi," p. 21.

149. *Ho Hsin-yin chi*, 72:3, Hsiu Chü-ho-ssu . . . Ling Hai-lou shu.

150. On these attitudes see de Bary et al. eds., *Sources of Chinese Tradition*, pp. 458–461, 591, 693; and Denis Twitchett, "The Fan Clan's Charitable Estate, 1050–1760."

151. E.g., Hou, *T'ung-shih*, 4B:1018–19; Ono, "Itansha," pp. 20–22.

152. See *Ho Hsin-yin chi*, 2:33–37, Chü, 3:48, Teng Tzu-chai shuo.

153. See Myron L. Cohen, "Variations in Complexity Among Chinese Family Groups: The Impact of Modernization."

154. *Ho Hsin-yin chi*, 28–29, Lun yu, Yü-hui.

155. *Ibid.*, 66, Yü Ai Leng-hsi shu.

156. *Idem.*

157. *Ibid.*, 73–74, Yu shang Hao-lou shu.

158. *Ibid.*, 1–25, Yüan hsüeh, yüan-chiang.

159. *Ibid.*, 11, Ho Hsin-yin lun (from *Li shih fen-shu* 3:87–89).

160. Much of this is summed up in Huang Tsung-hsi's account and evaluation of Ho, *MJHA*, 32:63–64 (Ho *Hsin-yin chi*, 122–24).

161. Cf. Shimada, *Zasetsu*, pp. 133, 142–44; Okada, "Genjōha," pp. 33, 35.

162. *Ho Hsin-yin chi*, 83, Yü Tsou Ho-shan shu.

163. *Ho Hsin-yin chi*, pp. 42, 51–52; Okada, "Genjōha," pp. 32, 34; Ono, *Itansha*, pp. 23–24.

164. *Ho Hsin-yin chi*, 34–35, Chü, 73–74, Yu shang Hai-lou shu; Okada, "Genjōha," pp. 36, 49, no. 5.

9. LI CHIH: ARCH-INDIVIDUALIST

1. Original name Lin Tsai-chih, T. Hung-fu, Ssu-chai, H. Cho-wu, Wen-ling, etc.

Despite the considerable literature on Li Chih, a full-length study of this important figure is still needed. The brief account here is confined to aspects relevant to his individualism, and makes no attempt to settle many of the disputed points concerning his life history. It is based on the following sources and secondary works:

Li Chih, *Cho-wu wen-lü, Fen-shu*, 3:82–87. Brief autobiography.

Yüan Chung-tao, *Li Wen-ling chuan,* from *K'o-hsüeh-chai chin chi:* reprinted in *Fen-shu,* iii–vii. A vivid personal account by a literary friend.

MS, Beijing, Chung-hua ed., 1974, 221:5817. Included in biography of Keng Ting-hsiang; 241:2746, biog. of Chang Wen-ta; Wang Hung-hsü, ed., *Ming shih kao,* 207:6a; P'an Tseng-hung, *Li Wen-ling wai-chi,* 1609 ed. of *Hsü Fen-shu.*

Huang Yün-mei, "Li Cho-wu shih-shih pien-cheng."

Wu I-feng, "Li Cho-wu chi-shu k'ao." A bibliographical study.

Chi Wen-fu, "Li Cho-wu yü tso-p'ai Wang-hsüeh." Li Chih in relation to T'ai-chou school, Wang Chi, etc.

Chi Wen-fu, "Wang Ch'uan-shan yü Li Cho-wu." Wang Fu-chih's criticism of Li Chih.

Jung Chao-tsu, *Li Cho-wu p'ing-chuan,* and *Li Chih nien-p'u.* Major studies by a veteran scholar of Ming thought.

Yeh Kuo-ch'ing, "Li Chih hsien-shih k'ao." On Li's family background, based on a recently discovered family genealogy.

Chu Ch'ien-chih, *Li Chih.* Reviewed by Timoteus Pokora in "A Pioneer of New Trends of Thought in the End of the Ming Period."

Hou Wai-lu, *T'ung-shih,* 4:1031–95. One of the more scholarly and well-documented "Marxist" interpretations, containing much useful information.

Li Hsien-chih, *Li Chih shih-liu shih-chi Chung-kuo fan feng-chien ssu-hsiang te hsien-ch'ü.* Unavailable to me. See R. Crawford's discussion of the relation between Chang Chü-cheng and Li Chih, *Self and Society in Ming Thought,* pp. 401–403.

Ch'iu Han-sheng, "T'ai-chou hsüeh-p'ai ti chieh-chü ssu-hsiang-chia Li Chih, pp. 115–132.

Fung Yu-lan, "Ts'ung Li Chih shuo-ch'i." Li Chih as an example of Mao Tse-tung's thought on contradictions.

Suzuki Torao, "Ritakugo nempu." A pioneering scholarly work done before the reprinting of some of Li's scarcer works.

Hirose Yutaka, *Yoshida Shōin no kenkyū,* pp. 60–149, 182–185. Of interest here mainly for its painstaking research on Li Chih's works preserved or printed in Japan.

Shimada Kenji, *Zasetsu,* pp. 179–251. Li Chih as the central figure in the gestation and abortion of "early modern" thought in China.

Shimada Kenji, "Jukyō no hangyakusha, Ri Shi (Ri Takugo)." A brief report on Shimada's more recent thinking on Li Chih since the publication of his *Zasetsu* in 1949.

Yagisawa Hajime, "Ri Shi." A brief, general account by a specialist in Ming literature.

Okada Takehiko, "Ō-mon genjōha no keitō," Pt. 2. Li Chih in relation to existentialist thought in the Wang Yang-ming school, with special attention to philosophical questions.

Ono Kazuko, "Jukyō no itansha tachi." A semipopular presentation by a specialist in late Ming thought emphasizing Li's practical and social thought.

Mizoguchi Yūzō, *Chūgoku zen kindai shisō no kussetsu to tenkai*. A major portion of this study is devoted to Li Chih as a key figure in the late-Ming/early Ch'ing transition from a "medieval," "idealistic" view of principle *(li)*, denying human desires, to a modern realistic view of it as inclusive of physical desires and the needs of the common man.

O. Franke, "Li Tschi: Ein Beitrage zur Geschichte der Chinesischen Geisteskampfe im 16. Jahrundert," and "Li Tschi und Matteo Ricci." The former is a general introduction to Li's life, works, and thought; the latter a discussion of the brief, cordial, but unproductive contacts between Li and Ricci.

Hok-lam Chan, *Li Chih (1527–1602) in Contemporary Chinese Historiography: New Light on His Life and Works.*

K. C. Hsiao, "Li Chih: An Iconoclast of the Sixteenth Century," and biography of Li in *DMB*, pp. 807–817. The former is a generally sympathetic portrait of Li Chih as seen amidst the intellectual ferment of the '30s in China; the latter reflects the more mature scholarship of the author, an authority on Chinese political thought.

R. Irwin, *The Evolution of a Chinese Novel: Shui-hu-chuan*, pp. 75–86. Li Chih in relation to *Shui-hu chuan* and vernacular literature.

In addition to the bibliographies specifically noted above, the *Nien-p'u* by Jung Chao-tsu has a substantial appendix including a critical bibliography of Li's works (pp. 113–126), as does Hou Wai-lu, *T'ung-shih*, 4:1048–51. A more succinct bibliography is presented by Hsiao in the draft biography listed above. The reader is referred to them for further information of this type.

Following are works of Li drawn upon for this study:

Fen-shu; Hsü Fen-shu, ed. of Chung-hua shu-chü; *Ts'ang shu; Ch'u-t'an chi; Li Cho-wu hsien-sheng i-shu; Li-shih shuo-shu; Li-Wen-ling chi; San I-jen wen-chi*, and [Ming-teng] *Tao ku lu*. The authenticity of the last, earlier questioned by some scholars, is now generally accepted. See Hok-lam Chan, *Li Chih*, pp. 170–171.

2. See Yeh Kuo-ch'ing, "Hsien-shih k'ao," p. 80.

3. *Ibid.*, pp. 81–84; Hou, *T'ung-shih*, 4:1031.

4. Hou, *ibid.*; Ono, "Itansha," pp. 25–27.

5. Hou believes that Li's last testament and burial instructions suggest some connection with Islam, but he does not press the point. See Hou, *T'ung-shih*, Shimada, *Hangyakusha*, 4; Ono, "Itansha," pp. 26–27.

6. See Yeh, "Hsien-shih k'ao," pp. 81–83; Shimada, *Hangyakusha*, 4a–12b (No. 9).

7. Ono Kazuko, "Itansha," pp. 26–27, acknowledging the decline of foreign trade in Ch'üan-chou, nevertheless emphasizes the venturesome, risk-running life of the smuggler as contributing to the "free" spirit of the city, which Li reflected and which she associates with a rising capitalist spirit in sixteenth-century China. Li indeed demonstrated a strong defiance of authority, but the covert defiance of Ch'üan-chou smugglers is certainly a far cry from the open independence of European traders and merchant princes in sixteenth-century Europe.

8. *Fen-shu*, 3:83, Cho-wu lun-lüeh.

9. *Idem*, Jung, *Nien-p'u*, 20. Carson Chang's assertion that Li achieved the *chin-shih* degree at this time is incorrect. (See Chang, *Development of Neo-Confucian Thought*, 2:126.) His relatively low rank certainly has a bearing on what follows, though one must allow that Li's behavior even as a *chin-shih* might have been the same.

10. Shimada discusses this as a problem inherent within the Neo-Confucian revival of the early Ming (*Zasetsu*, pp. 285–289). It is a familiar type to readers of Chinese fiction, especially in *The Scholars (Ju-lin wai-shih)* and *Dream of the Red Chamber (Hung-lou meng)*.

11. *Fen-shu*, 3:83, Cho-wu lun-lüeh; Shimada, *Zasetsu*, p. 181.

12. *Fen-shu*, 3:85.

13. Jung, *Nien-p'u*, 26, citing *Wang Yang-ming hsien-sheng nien-p'u hoy-yü*.

14. H. Lu-yüan, 1528–1611; *MJHA*, 14:36; *DMB*, p. 582.

15. H. Ta-chou, 1508–1576; *MS*, 193:2256; *MJHA*, 33:99; *DMB*, p. 120.

16. *MJHA*, 14:36, Hsü Yung-chien chuan.

17. H. T'ien-t'ai, 1524–1596. *MS*, 221:5815; *MJHA*, 35:35; *DMB*, p. 718.

18. H. Ch'u-k'ung. *MS*, 221:2553b; *MJHA*, 35:43; *DMB*, p. 718.

19. H. T'an-yüan, 1541–1620. *MS*, 288:3237b; *MJHA*, 35:45; *MJCCTLSY*, p. 677; Edward Ch'ien, *Chiao Hung and the Restructuring of Neo-Confucianism in the Late Ming*.

20. In Yunnan he did, it is true, have some intellectual associations with Buddhist monks, but these were not of a kind likely to sustain his

official vocation during a period of great trial. See Jung, *Nien-p'u*, pp. 42–44.

21. *Ibid.*, pp. 45–46.

22. Yüan, *Li Wen-ling chuan*, iii; Jung, *Nien-p'u*, pp. 50–55; Hou, *T'ung-shih*, 4:1036.

23. See *Fen-shu*, 2:42–43, 3:84. In his biography of Li for the *Dictionary of Ming Biography*, pp. 808–809, Hsiao Kung-ch'uan shows that, though Li admired his long-suffering wife, he was not much attached to her and forsook her "to seek the Buddha." Jung's evidence to the contrary (*Nien-p'u*, 65) is less persuasive. To imply deliberate neglect on Li's part would be going too far, but it is clear that the sacrifices necessary for him to follow his chosen course fell more heavily on his family than on him. He seems not to have suffered comparable deprivations.

24. These are discussed by Shimada in *Zasetsu*, p. 184. See also *Hsü Fen-shu*, 1:51, Yü Tseng Chi-ch'üan shu; Yüan, *Li Wen-ling chuan*, iv; Jung, *Nien-p'u*, pp. 64–65.

25. See *Fen-shu*, 4:184, Yü-yüeh, tsao-wan shou t'a. Extracts from this work, emphasizing the same general point, are also given in Lin Yutang, *The Importance of Understanding*, pp. 416–417.

26. Yüan, *Li Wen-ling chuan*, ii–iv, viii.

27. Yüan, *Li Wen-ling chuan*, vi; Shimada, *Zasetsu*, p. 184.

28. The title echoes Ssu-ma Ch'ien's statement that he was storing a copy of his *Shih-chi* in a safe place away from the capital in order to preserve it for posterity. See Pokora, "Pioneers," p. 474, n. 18; Watson, *Ssu-ma Ch'ien, Grand Historian of China*, pp. 57, 214, n. 93.

29. *Fen-shu*, 3:130, Tzu tsan.

30. *Ibid.*, 2:78, Wei Huang-an . . . san shou; 3:87, Ho Hsin-yin lun.

31. Hou (*T'ung-shih*, 4:1051–53) strains greatly to disassociate his hero Li Chih (a "materialist") from the "idealistic" Wang Yang-ming school. He cites the fact that Huang Tsung-hsi classified the T'ai-chou school separately in *MJHA*. But Huang, though he was eager for reasons quite different from Hou to distinguish the T'ai-chou school from the more orthodox Wang Yang-ming school, nevertheless clearly identifies it as a deviant outgrowth of the latter and so far as Li Chih is concerned the evidence is overwhelming that he thinks of himself as carrying on in the spirit of Wang's teaching. Hou's basic position is questioned by Shimada, in *Tōhōgaku hō*, 28, pp. 5–8, 37–41, 46–52. See also Ono, "Itansha," p. 44.

32. *Fen-shu*, 1:1, Ta Chou Hsi-yen.

33. Cf. Hsiao, "Li chih," p. 331; and Hou, *T'ung-shih*, 4:1062.

34. Hou, *T'ung-shih*, 4B:1062.

35. *Hsü Fen-shu*, 1:3–4, Yü Ma Li-shan.

36. *Fen-shu*, 4:137, Nien-fo ta-wen.

37. *Ibid.*

38. *Fen-shu*, 3:97–98, T'ung-hsin lun.

39. *Ibid.*, 3:98.

40. *Ibid.*

41. See Irwin, *Shui-hu-chuan*, pp. 81–86; Pokora, "Pioneer," p. 473.

42. See *Fen-shu*, 3:109, Chung-i Shui-hu chuan hsü; Irwin, *Shui-hu-chuan*, p. 86.

43. *Fen-shu*, 3:109.

44. See *Fen-shu*, 5:205, Ch'in fu; 5:215, I-shao ching-chi; 5:217, Pan-min pei hou; 5:218, Shih hua; also Okada, "Ō-mon genjōha," p. 47.

45. *Fen-shu*, 3:101, Ssu-wu shuo.

46. This appears as the general introduction to the Ming edition of the *Ch'u t'an chi*, but has also been included by Li in the *Fen-shu*, 3:89–90, Fu-fu lun.

47. *Fen-shu*, 2:56–57, Ta i nü-jen hsueh-tao wei chien-tuan shu.

48. *Fen-shu*, 3:90, Fu-fu lun.

49. *Hsu-Fen-shu*, 1:17, Yü Wu Te-ch'ang; 2:78–79, Lun chiao-nan.

50. *Fen-shu*, 1:17, Ta Keng Chung-ch'eng.

51. *Fen-shu*, 1:17, Ta Keng Chung-ch'eng.

52. *Ibid.*, 17, 18, Yu ta Keng Chung-ch'eng.

53. Cf. *Mencius*, 2:8, and *Shu-ching*, 2:3.

54. *Fen-shu*, 1:40, Ch'i ta Keng Ta-chung-ch'eng.

55. *Wu-hsin*. See de Bary et al., *Sources of Chinese Tradition*, p. 561; or Wing-tsit Chan, *A Source Book in Chinese Philosophy*, p. 525.

56. *Ts'ang-shu*, 32:544, Te-yeh ju-chen hou-lun.

57. *Ibid.*

58. *Fen-shu*, 1:36, Ta Teng Ming-fu.

59. *Fen-shu*, 1:4, Ta Teng Shih-yang.

60. *Fen-shu*, 1:37, Ta Keng Chung-ch'eng.

61. *Ts'ang-shu*, viii, Tsung-mu ch'ien-lun.

62. *Ibid.*, 1:2, Shih-chi ts'ung-lun.

63. *Hsü-Fen-shu*, 1:46, Yü Keng Tzu-chien.

64. *Ts'ang-shu*, xx–xxi, Tsung-mu hou-lun; 32:544, Te-yeh ju-chen hou lun.

65. See Carson Chang, *Development*, 2:126.

66. *Hsü Fen-shu*, 1:16, Yü Chiao Jo-hou t'ai-shih.

67. *Ibid.*

68. *Fen-shu*, 3:94–96, Ping shih lun.

69. *Fen-shu,* 3:124–125, Lo Chin-hsi hsien-sheng kao wen.

70. *Ibid.,* 3:88–89, Ho Hsin-yin lun.

71. *Hsu Fen-shu,* 3:94, K'ung Jung yu tzu-jan chih hsing.

72. *Fen-shu,* 4:159, Yin chi wang shih.

73. *Fen-shu,* 2:61, Yü Chiao Jo-hou.

74. *Fen-shu,* 2:46, Yu Yü Chiao Jo-hou.

75. *Ibid.*

76. *Hsü Fen-shu,* 2:78–79, Lun chiao-nan.

77. Hou, *T'ung-shih,* 4:1054; Ono, "Itansha," pp. 41–42, 44–45.

78. *Fen-shu,* 2:47, Yu Yü Chiao Jo-hou.

79. Hou, who cites the foregoing passage *(ibid.),* fails to give the continuation, which puts a very different face on the matter.

80. *Fen-shu,* 2:47.

81. Shimada, *Zasetsu,* p. 90; cf. Max Weber, *Gesammelte Aufsatze zur Religionssociologie,* 1:181; 2:360.

82. *Fen-shu,* 2:78–79, Lun chiao-nan; *Tao-ku lu,* A:14a.

83. *Fen-shu,* 3:102, Hsü-shih shuo.

84. *Fen-shu,* 3:100, *Hsin-ching t'i-kang.*

85. *Hsü Fen-shu,* 1:17, Yu Chiao Jo-hou t'ai-shih.

86. *Fen-shu,* 4:191–92, Han-teng yeh-hua 2; Hsiao, "Li Chih," pp. 336–338.

87. *Ts'ang shu,* 2, Shih-chi tsung-lun; Hou, *T'ung-shih,* 4:1092.

88. *Fen-shu,* 3:93–96, Ping shih lun.

89. *Fen-shu,* 1:7–8, Ta Chiao I-yüan shu; *Hsü Fen-shu,* 1:46, Yü Keng Tzu-chien.

90. *Hsü Fen-shu,* 2:77–78, San-chiao kuei ju.

91. *Ibid.,* 2:77.

92. *Ibid.,* 2:78.

93. *Ibid.*

94. *Hsü Fen-shu,* 4:102, T'i K'ung tzu hsiang yü Chih-fo yüan.

95. The possibility of some interinfluence is alluded to in Irwin, *Shui-hu-chuan,* p. 106, n. 26, and Pokora, "Pioneer," p. 473. On the importance of the Heart Sūtra in the *Journey to the West* (Hsi-yu chi), see C. T. Hsia, *The Classic Chinese Novel.*

96. E.g., *Li Cho-wu hsien-sheng i-shu,* A:8b, Yü Chou Yu-shan (*Hsü Fen-shu,* 1:14); A:47ab, Ta yu-jen shu (*Hsü Fen-shu,* 1:10).

97. Shimada, *Zasetsu,* pp. 222–24, citing *Hsü tsang-shu,* 5:85–6, Sun-kuo ming ch'en, *Wen-hsüeh po-shih Fang kung;* and 7:133, Yü-shih Ch'eng-kung, Li T'u weng yüeh.

98. *Fen-shu,* 4:164, Wu ssu; discussed by Hsiao in his *DMB,* pp. 808–809.

99. *Ibid.*, 3:108, *Chung-i Shui-hu chuan* hsü.

100. *Hsü fen-shu*, 1:20, Yü Keng K'o-nien shu.

101. See de Bary, *The Liberal Tradition*, p. 97.

102. *Hsü Ts'ang-shu*, 21:416. On the authorship and authenticity of the *Hsü Ts'ang-shu*, see Satō Rentarō, "Ri Shi *Zoku/Zōsho* ni tsuite."

103. *Ts'ang-shu*, 32:531–532, 537; 35:604; 41:708; 43:735; 45:770; *Hsü Ts'ang-shu*, 10:186; 21:416; 23:471.

104. *Ts'ang shu*, 32; *Hsü Ts'ang-shu*, 21, 22, 23.

105. See de Bary, *Neo-Confucian Orthodoxy*, pp. 11–12.

106. *Ts'ang-shu*, 32:531–532.

107. *Ts'ang-shu*, 32:517.

108. *Ibid.*

109. *Fen-shu*, 1:3–4, Yu Chiao Jo-hou.

110. *Fen-shu*, 1:3–4, Yu Chiao Jo-hou.

111. Chu Hsi, *Wen-chi*, SPPY, 84:18b; cited by Richard Lynn, "Chu Hsi as Literary Theorist and Critic," pp. 344, 348–49.

112. *Fen-shu*, 1:16, Ta Keng Chung-ch'eng.

113. *Fen-shu*, 1:16, Ta Keng Kung-ch'eng.

114. *Tao ku lu*, A:20b.

115. *Ibid.*, 19b, 21.

116. *Ibid.*, 21a.

117. *Tao-ku lu*, B;19b, 20a.

118. *Chung-yung*, 14.

119. *Tao-ku lu*, B:18b–19a, 20a.

120. *Shuo-shu*, Chung-yung, 2:43b–44a. Portions of this work are of dubious authorship, and may be interpretations of the compiler Lin Chao-en. The ideas expressed here, however, fit with what Li has said elsewhere in works unquestionably his, so there is no reason to suspect another author's hand is at work here. The edition cited here is that of Professor Kusumoto Masatsugu preserved in the Chinese collection of Kyūshu University. On problems of authorship and authenticity, see Okada Takehiko, "Ō-mon genjōha no keitō," p. 37.

121. *Fen-shu*, 1:4, letter to Teng Shih-yang.

122. *Ta-hsüeh chang-chu*, 67a.

123. *Tao ku lu*, B:21a.

124. *Ibid.*, B:21a–b.

125. *Ibid.*, A:8b–9a; B:22a–b.

126. *Ibid.*, B:22a–23b.

127. *Fen-shu*, 1:2a, Ta Chou Jo-chuang.

128. *Ibid.*, 1:2.

129. *Ibid.*, 1:3.

130. Here, and throughout the discussion of Li Chih, my rendering of *jen* shifts from "man" to "human" because Li is explicit in equating men and women as human. For consistency's sake, however, I keep to "noble man" for *chün-tzu* as a concept coming down from Confucius and Mencius.

131. Chu Hsi, *Ta-hsüeh huo-wen*, 4b–5a, 29b–30a; *Chung-yung chang-chü*, 17a. [Wang Ken too had expressed himself in these terms. See chapter 8.]

132. *Chung-yung*, 13, trans. adapted from Legge.

133. *Chung-yung chang-chü*, 2:43b.

134. *Tao-ku lu*, A:22b–23a.

135. *Tao-ku lu*, B:7a–8b.

136. *Ibid.*, A:35a; see also A:32ab.

137. *Fen-shu*, 3:86–88, Lun cheng pien.

138. *Ibid.*

139. *Fen-shu*, 3:101, Ssu-wu shuo.

140. *Tao-ku lu*, B:7b–8b.

141. *Ibid.*, A:12b–13a.

142. *Ibid.*, B:9a.

143. *Ibid.*, B:10a.

144. Chu Hsi, *Chung-yung chang-chü*, 31b.

145. *Tao-ku lu*, B:10ab.

146. *Chung-yung*, 26.

147. Refer to *Shang shu*, Pan keng, A; Legge, *Shoo King*, pp. 226–267.

148. Ref. to *Shih ching*, Ta-ya, Kung liu; Legge, *She King*, p. 483.

149. *Tsang-shu*, 32:544, "Te-yeh ju-ch'en hou-lun."

150. *Tsang-shu*, 32:544–5, Hou lun; *Hsü Fen-shu*, 1:38, Yü yu-jen.

151. See ch. 8, pp. 191–197, and my discussion of this in *The Unfolding of Neo-Confucianism*, pp. 194–204.

152. Ray Huang, *1587, A Year of No Significance*, pp. 215–16.

153. Chu, *Wen-chi*, 76:33b, "Ch'u tzu chi-chu hsü"; cited and translated in part by Richard J. Lynn in "Chu Hsi as Literary Theorist and Critic," p. 346. See also Tai Hsien, *Chu Tzu shih-chi*, 4:20a, p. 197.

154. [Ming-teng] *Tao-ku lu 1*, A:14a–19b; *Fen-shu*, 3:86–87, Lun cheng p'ien; *ibid.*, 3:93–95, Ping shih lun; Hou, *T'ung-shih*, 4:1075; Ono, "Jukyō no itansha tachi," 40–42.

155. Carson Chang, *The Development of Neo-Confucian Thought*, 2:127. Chang does not put all the blame on society, but see also p. 142.

156. *Li Cho-wu hsien-sheng i-shu*, A:150ab, Yüan Chung-tao pa *Li shih i-shu*.

157. See Franke's article, "Li Tschi," which gives considerable information on this point. See also Busch, "The Tunglin Academy," p. 82; Shimada, *Zasetsu*, p. 192. Both Li's admirers and his critics testify to this popularity. Ku Yen-wu's note on Li Chih in *Jih chih lu*, 18, 6:121–22, stresses the point; and the editors of the *Ssu-k'u ch'üan-shu tsung-mu t'i-yao* allude to it in condemning his influence, 50:1111; 178:3401; 179:3950.

158. See Hirose, *Yoshida Shōin*, pp. 60 ff.; Shimada, *Zasetsu*, pp. 192, 240; Irwin, *Shui-hu chuan*, pp. 79–80.

159. Some elements in this situation parallel earlier crises leading to the collapse of great dynasties. At the end of the Han in the second century A.D. there is an intellectual atmosphere characterized by "cynical authoritarianism, Taoist poetry, and revolt against traditions." See Balazs, *Chinese Civilization and Bureaucracy*, p. 225. Thus there appear to be recurring patterns of intellectual frustration and alienation accompanying dynastic decline, which are intermixed in the present case with new trends and more complex social and cultural forces.

160. Shimada, *Zasetsu*, p. 193.

161. The absence of any treatment of Li Chih in the *Ming-ju hsüeh-an* cannot in itself, of course, be considered conclusive evidence on this point. The possibility of censorship cannot be excluded. Huang was unhappy over the deletions in the first edition of *MJHA*, and he expresses satisfaction over Cheng Hsing's more complete edition, which is the one generally in use today. But the chapters dealing with Wang Chi and Chao Chen-chi, with both of whom Li was associated, are remarkably short and deletions may have occurred. The effectiveness of the Ch'ing proscription in suppressing even criticism of Li Chih is indicated by the omission of Ku Yen-wu's condemnation of Li from the Kang-hsi 34 edition of the *Jih-chih lu*. On the other hand, it was restored in subsequent editions, and there are brief accounts of Li in both the *Ming shih* and *Ming-shih kao*. The point requires further investigation, but in any case there can be no doubt of Huang's attitude toward Li and the whole "Wild Ch'an" movement. One of his main reasons for writing the *Ming-ju hsüeh-an* was to rescue Ming thought from Ch'an influence and to counteract Chou Ju-teng's *Sheng-hsüeh tsung-ch'uan*, which gave a strong Ch'anist interpretation to Confucian thought. Cf. Hummel, ed., *Eminent Chinese of the Ch'ing Period* (abbrev. *ECCP*), p. 353; Chang, *Development*, 2:180.

162. Ku Yen-wu, *Jih-chih lu*, 18, Li Chih, 6:122.

163. See Chi Wen-fu, "Wang Ch'uan-shan yü Li Cho-wu," pp. 86–89.

164. The views of both Huang and Ku were widely respected among scholars in and out of office. Both declined honors from the state. Shimada

describes Ku's opinion of Li as the "definitive judgment" in the Ch'ing. See *Zasetsu,* p. 253.

165. See Hummel, ed., *ECCP,* p. 818.

166. Chi Wen-fu, "Wang Ch'uan-shan," pp. 86–87.

167. See Busch, "Tunglin Academy," pp. 47–48.

168. Huang Tsun-su (1584–1626), H. Pai-an. *MJHA,* 61:17; Hummel, ed., *ECCP,* p. 351.

169. *MJHA,* 60:5–6, Shih Yü-ch'ih lun-hsüeh; trans. adapted from Busch, "Tunglin Academy," pp. 87, 89–90.

170. Tsou Shan, H. Ying-ch'üan, *Chin-shih* of 1557. See *MJHA,* 16:55.

171. *MJHA,* 16:64, Ying-chüan hsien-sheng.

172. Jung, *Nien-p'u,* 110–11, citing *Ming Shen-tsung wan-li shih-lu,* 369:14; see also Ku Ken-wu, *Jih-chih lu,* 18, Li Chih.

173. Jung, *Nien-p'u,* 111; Hsiao, *DMB,* p. 814.

174. *Fen-shu,* vi, Li Wen-ling chuan.

175. In Li's case the word "sensual" would certainly be misleading if it did not take into account his primary dedication to the "Way" and his scholarship. On the other hand, he believed in the free and uninhibited expression of emotion and gratification of the appetites as Kenkō, being of a more aristocratic and aesthetic type, did not.

176. *Fen-shu,* 3:99–100, *Hsin-ching t'i-kang.*

177. *Taishō daizōkyō,* 25:1509c, Ta-chih-t'u lun.

178. See Mochizuki Shinkō, *Bukkyō daijiten,* 5:4704b.

179. See Araki Kengo, "Confucianism and Buddhism in the Late Ming," pp. 39–62.

180. Chu-hung, *Chu-ch'uang san-pi,* 21a, Li Cho-wu 1.

181. *Ibid.,* 21b.

182. *Ibid.,* 22a, Li Cho-wu 2.

183. Araki Kengo, "Chōwa ron," p. 220b, citing *Chiai-shu fa-yin,* pp. 342, 358.

184. *Ibid.,* 220b, citing *Ch'an-yü wai-chi* 1, T'i Cho-wu Fen-shu hou.

185. See W. T. deBary, "Buddhism and the Chinese Tradition."

186. See Araki Kengo, *Bukkyō to Jukyō,* pp. 440–48. This reaction is also quite apparent even within the T'ai-chou school itself. Several of its leaders, and even some who were themselves deeply involved with Ch'an, strongly criticized Li. See Araki, "Chōwa ron," pp. 216–217.

187. See *Fen-shu,* 1:23, Ta Liu Hsien-chang; Suzuki, *Nempu,* B, pp. 27–28; Shimada, *Zasetsu,* p. 206.

188. Chang, *Development of Neo-Confucian Thought,* 2:127.

189. See *Hsü Fen-shu,* 2:75–76, Chin-kang-ching shuo. The Great Perfect Wisdom, Li says, objectively and impartially reflects all things,

showing no preferences. Presumably had such rights existed it would have respected them, as Li says it respects the Confucian relations but its function is not to *assert* them. See also Nakamura Hajime, "A Brief Survey of Japanese Studies on the Philosophical Schools of the Mahayana," p. 66, for his discussion of the Madhyamīka in this respect.

190. See de Bary et al., *Sources of Chinese Tradition,* pp. 320–326, where it is translated by Leon Hurvitz.

191. Araki, "Chōwa ron," p. 221, and "Kan Tō-mei" *[Kuan Tung-ming].*

192. Araki, "Kan Tō-mei," pp. 101–102.

193. Huang Tsung-hsi, *Ming-i tai-fang lu,* Yüan-fa, Hsüeh-hsiao; de Bary et al., *Sources of Chinese Tradition,* pp. 585–586, 590.

194. The main purpose, of course, was to entrench Manchu rule, but one important aspect of this was the re-establishment of Chu Hsi orthodoxy. See my *Message of the Mind,* ch. 5.

195. Herbert Butterfield, "Reflections on Religion and Modern Individualism," p. 39.

196. *Ibid.*, p. 35.

10. LÜ LIU-LIANG'S RADICAL ORTHODOXY

1. A standard account of Lü's life may be found in Hummel, *Eminent Chinese of the Ch'ing Dynasty,* pp. 551–552. Pioneering studies of Lü's life and thought are Jung Chao-tsu's *Lü Liu-liang chi ch'i ssu-hsiang* (hereafter cited as Jung, *Lü Liu-liang*); and Ch'ien Mu, in vol. 1, ch. 2, of his *Chin san-pai nien hsüeh-shu shih* (hereafter cited as Ch'ien Mu, *Hsüeh-shu shih*). By far the most exhaustive study of Lü's life and "after-life" is Tom Fisher's "Lü Liu-liang (1629–83) and the Tseng Ching Case (1728–33)," which is recommended for further information on the extensive bibliography of Lü.

2. Jung, "Lü Liu-liang," p. 33; Okada Takehiko, "Ryo Banson no Shushigaku," pp. 51–52.

3. A rare specimen of this type of collection, including sample essay selections and parallel interlinear comments and criticism, organized according to the sequence of passages in the *Analects, Great Learning, Mean,* and *Mencius* is found in the Rare Book Collection of the Starr Library at Columbia University: *T'ien-kai lou ou-p'ing* (Parallel Criticisms from the House of Heaven's Canopy), in six *ts'e,* original ed. of 1675.

4. See Hummel, *Eminent Chinese,* pp. 551–552, 747–749, biography by L. C. Goodrich; Tom Fisher, "Accommodation and Loyalism: The Life of Lü Liu-liang," and "Loyalist Alternatives in the Early Ch'ing."

5. See L. Carrington Goodrich, *The Literary Inquisition of Ch'ien-lung*, pp. 22–23.

6. Ch'en Ts'ung in Lü Liu-liang, *Ssu-shu chiang-i*, Mu-lu 7ab. (Hereinafter abbr. *SSCI*.)

7. Jung, "Lü Liu-liang," pp. 75, 78, quoting Lu Lung-chi, *San-yü t'ang wen-chi*, 12, "Chi Lu Wan-tsun hsien-sheng wen." See also Fisher, "The Life of Lü Liu-liang (1629–1683)," Part 3, 18:3, and Wing-tsit Chan, "The *Hsing-li ching-i* and the Ch'eng-Chu School of the Seventeenth Century," p. 551.

8. Lu Lung-chi *San-yü t'ang wen-chi*, 8:11b. Preface to *Wang-hsüeh chih-i*. The seventeen characters quoted here have been deleted in the *Lu Tzu ch'üan-shu* ed., but are supplied by Jung Chao-tzu in *Lü Liu-liang*, p. 78. A 1701 ed. of the original, in the Library of Peking University contains handwritten reinsertions of the extensive expurgations made during this "purge." According to a note by the copyist, the missing material was supplied from an amended copy in the collection of Professor Ku Chieh-kang.

9. Ch'ien Chen-huang, preface to Lü Liu-liang, *Lü Wan-ts'un hsien sheng wen-chi*, p. 1b. (Hereafter cited as *Wan-ts'un wen-chi*.)

10. *Ibid.*, 2a.

11. *Wan-ts'un wen-chi*, 1:9a, letter to Kao Hui-ch'i.

12. *Ibid.*, 1:9a, letter to Kao Hui-ch'i.

13. *Wan-ts'un wen-chi*, 5:41a, "Ch'eng mo kuan-lüeh lun-wen."

14. *Wan-ts'un wen-chi*, Fu-lu, hsing-lüeh, 8a; also 1:9b–10a, "Fu Kao Hui-ch'i shu."

15. *Hsing-lüeh* and *Yü-lu*, 1:1b.

16. See de Bary, *Self and Society in Ming Thought*, pp. 203–213.

17. *SSCI*, 38:9a, comment on *Mencius*, Wan-chang, Jen yu yen chih yu yü. . . . Quoted by Ch'ien Mu, *Hsüeh-shu shih*, p. 86. See also *SSCI*, 42:10b; 43:7b.

18. *SSCI*, 38:8ab, comment on *Mencius*, Wan chang. Jen yu yen chih yu yü.

19. *Wan-ts'un wen-chi*, Fu lu, Hsing-lüeh, p. 9ab.

20. See my *Liberal Tradition in China*, pp. 40–42.

21. *SSCI*, 1:1b, Ching-i chang; 21:5b–6b. Comment on *Lun-yü*, Tzu-han, Wu yu chih; 43:2b, comment on *Mencius*, "Chin hsin shu"; Jung, *Lü Liu-liang*, p. 19; Okada, "Ryo Banson," p. 56.

22. *Wan-ts'un wen-chi*, Fu-lu, Hsing-lüeh, p. 9a; *SSCI*, 24:4b.

23. *SSCI*, 24:11a, commentary on chapter 1 of the *Mean*.

24. *Wan-ts'un wen-chi*, 5:3a–4b.

25. In a letter to Lo Ch'in-shun included in Wang's *Ch'uan-hsi lu*. See

Wang Yang-ming ch'üan-shu, Ch'uan-hsi lu, 2:63–4; Chan, *Instructions,* p. 163. Wang's criticism of Chu Hsi is less direct and pointed than Lü would have it, but the latter is not unwarranted in seeing this implication in the passage.

26. *Wan-ts'un wen-chi,* 1:15ab; letter to Shih Yu-shan.

27. Lü's is a selective explanation of passages in the Four Books that seem significant to him or that occasion the most discussion. It is not a systematic line-by-line, phrase-by-phrase or word-by-word commentary of the kind given in Chu Hsi's *Sentences and Phrases (chang-chü).*

28. The edition of the *Recorded Conversations* is the *T'ien-kai lou ssu-shu yü-lu,* by Chou Tsai-yen. I have most often given references to both the *SSCI* and *Yü-lu* on the same passage for purposes of ready comparison. Occasionally the treatment in one is a little fuller than the other. The *Yü-lu* often has more comments, but also frequently omits the questions being responded to. In the opinion of Ch'ien Mu there is little, if any, substantive difference between the two, but he most often cites the *SSCI.* Jung Chao-tsu, in his early work, made much use of the later *Lü Tzu p'ing-yü,* which is rare because of its limited circulation before the proscription of Lü's works. A special feature of the *P'ing-yü* is its inclusion of Lü's comments on other recent commentator's observations, only some of which are found in the *SSCI.* Professor Jung confirmed in personal conversation on May 14, 1985, that in his estimation the more selective *SSCI* is probably the single most reliable source. Since it was also the most widely circulated and best known of Lü's works, it may also be taken as most representative of his views as they reached the large audience of examination candidates. See Ch'ien Mu, *Hsüeh-shu shih,* pp. 78–79, Jung, *Lü Liu-liang,* pp. 23–36.

The edition of the *Critical Comments* consulted for this study was the *Wan-ts'un Lu Tzu p'ing yu, cheng-pien,* in the Rare Book Collection of the Beijing Library. Because of limited access to this work I have not been able to provide page references parallel to those of the *SSCI* and *Yü-lu,* but have indicated instead the passages in the Four Books under whose headings the corresponding commentary may be found.

29. *SSCI,* 1:1a, General Introduction.

30. *Ibid.,* 1:1b.

31. *Ibid.,* 1:1b–2a. Comment on Ta-hsüeh chih tao; *Yü-lu,* 1:2a.

32. Sun Ch'i-feng, for instance. See de Bary *The Message of the Mind,* pp. 126–130.

33. *SSCI,* 1:5b, comment on Tung ching an lu *Yü-lu,* 1:7b–8a.

34. See my *Neo-Confucian Orthodoxy,* Part 2.

35. *SSCI,* 5:6b, comment on Lun-yü, 2:4; *Yü-lu,* 14:8a.

36. *Ibid.*, 5:6b; *Yü-lu*, 14:8ab.

37. *Ibid.*, 4:2ab, comment on *Lun-yü*, 1; *Yü-lu*, 13:2a.

38. *I-ching*, Harvard-Yenching Index text, 40 Hsi tzu A, 4.

39. *SSCI*, 24:1a, comment on the *Mean* 1; *Yü-lu*, 5:1a. See also Tom Fisher, "Commentary and Counter-Commentary," p. 5.

40. *SSCI*, 24:1b; *Yü-lu*, 5:2a.

41. *I-ching*, HY Index ed. text, 20:38b.

42. *SSCI*, 24:1b–2a; *Yü-lu*, 5:1b–2a.

43. *Ibid.*, 24:2a; *Yü-lu*, 5:3a.

44. *Ibid.*, 24:2b; *Yü-lu*, 5:5a.

45. *Ibid.*, 24:3a.

46. Chu, *Ta-hsüeh chang-chü*, ch. 1, p. 1.

47. *SSCI*, 42:2a, comment on *Meng-tzu*, 7A:1, Chin ch'i hsin.

48. *Ibid.*, 42:1b.

49. *Ibid.*, 42:2a.

50. *Ibid.*, 43:8a, comment on *Meng-tzu*, 7B:25, Hao sheng pu hai . . . , 43:11a on *Meng-tzu*, 7B:35, Yang-hsin mo shan.

51. *SSCI*, 3:12b–13a, comment on *Ta-hsüeh*, 19, Chih-kuo p'ing t'ienhsia; *Yü-lu*, 4:8b. See also *SSCI*, 42:17b–18a.

52. *Ibid.*, 1:2a, comment on Ming ming-te.

53. *Mean*, 25; *Yü-lu*, 8:2b.

54. *Yü-lu*, 16:7a; *P'ing-yü*, 17; *Lun-yü*, 14, Ku che hsüeh-che.

55. *Yü-lu*, 26:16b; *P'ing-yü*, 17: ibid.

56. *SSCI*, 43:7a; comment on *Meng-tzu*, Hsien-che i ch'i chao chao.

57. An expression found in the *Sung History*'s account of the Ryukyuans, who were regarded as naked savages—a description which, apart from its view of "savages," could hardly be less appropriate for the beautiful dress of the Okinawans.

58. Chu Hsi, *Chung-yung huo-wen*, 45b–47a (pp. 90–93), comment on Chung yung, 25; *SSCI*, 25:10b; *P'ing-yü*, 39 on *Chung-yung*, 14.

59. *Yü-lu*, 7:7a.

60. *SSCI*, 25:10a; *P'ing-yü*, 39, comment on *Chung-yung*, 14, Tzu te.

61. This particular comment, which follows the passage cited in note 60, is found in the *P'ing yü* but not in the *SSCI*.

62. *Yü-lu*, 7:7a–8a.

63. *Ibid.*, 40:6b–7a.

64. *Ibid.*, 40:7a.

65. *Ibid.*, 40:7ab.

66. *SSCI*, 37:5a; *Yü-lu*, 40:7a.

67. *Ssu-shu chi-chu*, *Lun-yü chang chü*, shang lun, 1:9.

68. Chu Hsi, *Chu Tzu yü-lei*, 24:8b–9a.

69. *SSCI*, 5:11b, comment on *Lun yü*, 2:11; *Yü-lu*, 14:14ab.

70. Yüan Huang, T. K'un-i, H. Hsüeh-hai, *DMB*, p. 1632, and de Bary, *Self and Society in Ming Thought*, pp. 175–176, 319–330, 335–336.

71. *SSCI*, 5:11b–12b; *Yü-lu*, 14:14ab.

72. *SSCI*, 5:12b; *Yü-lu*, 14:15a.

73. *Ibid.*, 37:5b; *Yü-lu*, 40:7b.

74. *Ibid.*, 37:5b.

75. *SSCI*, 7:14ab; *Yü-lu*, 16:16ab.

76. Not all critics of Wang Yang-ming linked him to Ch'en Hsien-chang. Earlier T'ang Po-yüan, who opposed Wang's enshrinement in the Confucian temple, defended Ch'en, a follow Kuangtung man, from the charge of heterodoxy. See T'ang Po-yüan, *T'ang Chu-t'ai hsien-sheng chi*, in *Kuang li-hsüeh pei-k'ao, Wu-ching*, t'ang ed., 1:14a, *Yü-lu*; *MJHA*, 42:76.

77. See the discussion of Ch'en Chien and the *Hsüeh-pu t'ung-pien*, in de Bary, *The Message of the Mind*, pp. 95–103.

78. Ch'ien Mu, *Hsüeh-shu shih*, p. 87.

79. See de Bary, *The Unfolding of Neo-Confucianism*, pp. 17–19, 23–38, 170–175; and de Bary and Bloom, *Principle and Practicality*, pp. 12–13, 21–27, 41–42, 129, 132, 139; Rodney Taylor, *The Cultivation of Sagehood as a Religious Goal in Neo-Confucianism: A Study of Selected Writings of Kao P'an-lung, 1562–1626*, esp. pp. 77–88.

80. See de Bary and Bloom, *Principle and Practicality*, pp. 21, 251–252, 419.

81. See my *Neo-Confucian Orthodoxy*, pp. 128–131.

82. *SSCI*, 24:5b, on *Chung-yung*, Shen tu.

83. Wang Yang-ming's view of quiet-sitting was somewhat ambivalent since his later teaching greatly qualified his early endorsement of the practice. However, in his preface to the *Collected Writings of Lu Hsiang-shan (Hsiang-shan wen-chi hsü)*, Wang speaks of Lu as carrying on the teachings of Chou Tun-i and the Ch'eng brothers, who had emphasized the practice of quiescence, as did both Wang Chi (see chapter 7) and the quietist wing of the Wang Yang-ming school later. See *Wang Yang-ming ch'üan-shu*, Wen-lu, 3:190. See also Rodney Taylor, "Subitist and Gradualist: A Simile for Neo-Confucian Learning," for the Conference on Sudden and Gradual Enlightenment (pp. 16–17, 26–27).

84. *SSCI*, 2:12–13, *Ta-hsüeh*; Ch'eng-i; *Yü-lu*, 5:7a–11a, *Chung-yung*,1, Shen-tu; Okada, "Ryo Banson," p. 66.

85. *Chin-ssu lu*, 46a; Chan, *Things at Hand*, p. 151.

86. *SSCI*, 24:7b, on *Chung-yung*, 1, Shen-tu; *Yü-lu*, 5:9b.

87. *SSCI*, 24:8a, comment on *Chung-yung*, 1; *Yü-lu*, 5:9b–11a.

88. *Yü-lu*, 5:10b.

89. *SSCI*, 24:8b, on *Ta-hsüeh*, 1.

90. *SSCI*, 24:8b, comment on *Chung-yung*, 1, Shen tu.

91. *SSCI*, 1:13b, comment on *Ta-hsüeh*, 1; *Yü-lu*, 1:12b.

92. Ch'ien Mu, *Hsin hsüeh-an*, I, 132:3, 138.

93. E. O. Reischauer and J. K. Fairbank, *East Asia, The Great Tradition*, p. 240.

94. Wang Yang-ming was given the honorary title of Earl of Hsinch'ien in 1521. His enemies at court had it stripped from him six years later, but it was posthumously restored in 1567.

95. These criticisms are found particularly in Wang's "Preface to the Old Text of the Great Learning" (*Ku-Wen Ta-hsüeh hsü*) and "Questions on the *Great Learning*" (*Ta-hsüeh wen*). See *Wang Yang-ming ch'üan-shu*, Wen-lu, 1:119, 3:191. Chang Huang's *Tu-shu pien*, contains a collection of Wang Yang-ming's comments on this question (64:60a–77a).

96. This may well refer to Li Yung (Erh-ch'ü) who lectured at the Tunglin Academy and elsewhere in Kiangsu during the early 1670s. Li's interpretations of these same passages fit Lü's characterization exactly. See Li's *Ssu-shu fan-shen lu* in *Li Erh-ch'ü hsien-sheng ch'üan-chi*, 1:4ab, 2:2b–3b.

97. *Lun-yü*, 7:28.

98. *SSCI*, 2:10ab.

99. *Yü-lu*, 6:6b, comment on *Chung-yung*, Tsun ch'i ta chih.

100. *SSCI*, 24:5b, comment on *Chung yung*, 1.

101. On Li Yung, see Hummel, *Eminent Chinese*, pp. 498–499, biography by Dean Wickes.

102. These lectures were later published in Li Yung's *Ssu-shu fan-shen lu* and much later in his *Complete Works*.

103. *SSCI*, 40:12, on *Meng tzu*, 7A, Jen jen hsin; *Yü-lu*, 43:14b–15a.

104. *SSCI*, 40–12a; *Yü-lu*, 43:15ab.

105. *Yü-lu*, 43:15a–16a.

106. *SSCI*, 18:1b, on *Lun-yü*, 15:2, To-hsüeh erh shih chih.

107. *SSCI*, 18:1b.

108. *Ibid.*, 18:1b.

109. *SSCI*, 7:14a, on *Lun-yü*, 41, I i kuan chih; *Yü-lu*, 16:16b.

110. *SSCI*, 18:1b–2a.

111. *Ibid.*, 7:14a.

112. *Yü-lu*, 16:16a. The analogy of a small stream deriving from the main source (corresponding to a branch emerging from the stem or trunk) is one more apt for people in a hydraulic civilization, which thinks in terms

of water being drawn off some main source and being dissipated through use, than it is for those who think of small streams as tributary to larger rivers.

113. *SSCI*, 7:14ab; *Yü-lu*, 16:17a.

114. *SSCI*, 7:11b; on *Lun-yü*, 4, Chün-tzu chih yü t'ien hsia.

115. *SSCI*, 7:14a; *Yü-lu*, 16:16ab, on *Lun yü*, 4, I i kuan chih.

116. *Yü-lu*, 16:17a.

117. *SSCI*, 5:8ab; on *Lun-yü*, 2 Shih yu wu; *Yü-lu*, 14:9a.

118. Ch'ien Mu, *Hsüeh-shu-shih*, pp. 28–29. On this point my own judgment may be open to some question. Coming from one whose work in this field already owes so much to both Huang and Ch'ien Mu, it can perhaps be discounted.

119. *Wan-ts'un wen-chi*, 3:18a. Reply to Ch'en Shou-ch'eng cited with emphasis by Jung, p. 26.

120. *SSCI*, 1:7b–8a, on ch. 1 of *Ta-hsüeh*; *Yü-lu*, 1:9ab.

121. *Wan-ts'un wen-chi*, 4:24b, letter to Wu Yü-chang.

122. *Wan-ts'un wen-chi*, as cited above, gives *hsin chih hua* for what I have translated as "brush strokes of the heart"; Ch'ien Mu, citing the same source, gives *hsin chih shu*, "writings of the heart," but gives no clue as to his basis for this.

123. *Ibid.*, 4:24b. The passage is much quoted by those who have studied Lü Liu-liang; by Ch'ien Mu, on p. 77, by Okada, p. 57; and Fisher, p. 13. To the best of my knowledge Jung Chao-tsu does not quote it, perhaps because it does not fit his characterization of Lü as an extreme conservative.

124. On Hu Yüan's dictum see my comment in *East Asian Civilizations*, pp. 47–48.

125. See de Bary, *The Liberal Tradition*, pp. 17–20.

126. See my *Neo-Confucian orthodoxy*, pp. 9–10, 69–70, 99–100.

127. Jung, *Lü Liu-liang*, p. 18, describing the intellectual situation just prior to Lü's appearance on the scene, characterizes the thought of Ch'en Hsien-chang and Wang Yang-ming in terms of "getting it oneself" and giving expression to one's own innate learning.

128. See de Bary, *Self and Society in Ming Thought*, pp. 195–197.

129. *Wan-ts'un wen-chi*, 4:24b, letter to Wu Yü-chang.

130. *Wan-ts'un wen-chi*, 3:25b–26a; *SSCI*, 1:1ab.

131. Ch'ien Mu, *Hsüeh-shu shih*, pp. 77–78.

132. T. S. Fisher, "The Life of Lü Liu-liang," Part 3, "The Later Years," 18:19.

133. *Lü Wan-ts'un tsa-chi*, vol. I, no pagination, "Chia hsün," edition under the general supervision of Wang Yün-wu.

134. Jung, *Lü Liu-liang*, pp. 33–37.

135. Ch'ien Mu, *Hsüeh-shu shih*, pp. 86–87.

136. See my "Some Common Tendencies in Neo-Confucianism," pp. 35–38.

137. *SSCI*, 29:10ab, on *Chung-yung* 32.

138. *Ibid.*, 26:4a, on *Chung-yung* 17.

139. *SSCI*, 11:2ab, on *Lun-yü* 8.

140. *SSCI*, 3:13b, on *Ta-hsüeh*, Chih-kuo, p'ing t'ien-hsia; *Yü-lu*, 45:10a; quoted by Ch'ien Mu, p. 80.

141. *SSCI*, 3:13b.

142. *SSCI*, 3:14a; *Yü-lu*, 4:10b.

143. *SSCI*, 38:8ab, on *Meng-Tzu* 5a:6.

144. *SSCI*, 6:10ab, on *Lun-yü* 3:19; *Yü-lu*, 15:13b–14a.

145. *SSCI*, 17:9a, on *Lun-yü* 14:18; *Yü-lu*, 26:2a. Quoted in part by Ch'ien Mu, p. 83.

146. *SSCI*, 37:1b–2a, on *Meng-tzu* 4B:3; *Yü-lu*, 40:2ab. Quoted by Ch'ien Mu, p. 83.

147. *SSCI*, 6:10ab.

148. *SSCI*, 29:2b, on *Chung-yung* 27; *Yü-lu*, 11:10b.

149. *SSCI*, 29:10ab, on *Chung-yung* 32; *Yü-lu*, 12:6a.

150. *SSCI*, 3:13b–14a, on *Ta-hsüeh* 9, 19; *Yü-lu*, 4:10ab.

151. *SSCI*, 3:13b; *Yü-lu*, 4:10ab.

152. See my discussion of Huang Tsung-hsi in chapter 5, *Liberal Tradition*, p. 84.

153. *SSCI*, 37:2b–3a, on *Meng Tzu* 4B:6; *Yü-lu*, 40:3b–4a.

154. *SSCI*, 29:1b–2b, on *Chung-yung* 27; *Yü-lu*, 11:8ab.

155. See Ch'iu Chün, *Ta-hsüeh yen-i'pu*, 13:5b. See also my "Neo-Confucianism and Human Rites."

156. *SSCI*, 41:1ab, on *Meng-Tzu* 6B:1; *Yü-lu*, 44:1ab.

157. *SSCI*, 3:12a–13b on *Ta-hsüeh* 9; not in *Yü-lu*.

158. See Ch'ien Mu, *Hsin hsüeh-an*, pp. 107–122.

159. See de Bary et al., *Sources of Chinese Tradition*, ch. 22.

160. *SSCI*, 34:7b, on *Meng-tzu* 3A:3; *Yü-lu*, 37:16b–17a.

161. *SSCI*, 39:4b–5a, on *Meng-tzu* 5B:2; quoted in part by Ch'ien Mu, p. 82.

162. See further discussion of this problem in my *The Trouble with Confucianism*, chapters 1, 6.

163. *SSCI*, 24:4a, on *Chung-yung* 1; *Yü-lu*, 5:3b.

164. *SSCI*, 1:19b, on *Ta-hsüeh* 1; *Yü-lu*, 1:25b.

165. *Yü-lu*, 1:25b.

166. *SSCI*, 1:19ab, on *Ta-hsüeh* 1; *Yü-lu*, 1:25a.

167. *SSCI*, 29:12a–14a, on *Chung-yung* 33; *Yü-lu*, 12:8b–11b.

168. *SSCI*, 29:14b–15a; *Yü-lu*, 12:12a–13a.

169. *SSCI*, 29:11b; *Yü-lu*, 12:7b.

170. *SSCI*, 29:11b; *Yü-lu*, 12:7b.

171. See Araki Kengo, *Yomeigaku no kaiten to Bukkyō*, pp. 282–90; Jung, *Lü Liu-liang*, p. 35.

172. *Wan-ts'un wen-chi*, 1:31b, letter in reply to Chang Chu-jen; Ch'ien Mu, *Hsüeh-shu shih*, p. 86.

173. *SSCI*, 29:1a, on *Chung-yung* 27.

174. *SSCI*, 34:10a, on *Meng tzu* 3A:3; Ch'ien Mu, pp. 80–81.

175. *SSCI*, 29:1a.

176. Jung, *Lü Liu-liang*, p. 29.

177. Jung himself acknowledges this, p. 21.

178. See Herbert Fingarette, "Human Community as Holy Rite."

179. See my *Neo-Confucian Orthodoxy and the Learning of the Mind-and-Heart*, pp. 94–95.

180. *Ibid.*, pp. 10–13.

181. *SSCI*, 38:8b, on *Meng-tzu* 5A:7.

182. *Hsing-li ta-ch'üan* 38 (Chūbun shuppansha ed., pp. 617–621).

183. Wing-tsit Chan, "The *Hsing-li ching-i* and the Ch'eng-Chu School of the Seventeenth Century," p. 568.

184. Chan, "*Hsing-li ching-i*," p. 568.

185. Li Kuang-ti, *Jung-ts'un ch'üan-chi*, 10:2b–3a.

186. Chan, "*Hsing-li ching-i*," pp. 554–55.

187. *SSCI*, 29:1a.

188. Tu Wei-ming, "Yen Yüan: From Inner Experience to Lived Concreteness" (hereafter referred to as Tu, "Yen Yüan"), pp. 511–515, includes a brief review of the principal modern literature on Yen Yüan.

189. See Chung-ying Ch'eng, "Practical Learning in Yen Yüan, Chu Hsi, and Wang Yang-ming," p. 40.

190. Tu, "Yen Yüan", pp. 532–535.

191. *Ibid.*, p. 527.

192. See de Bary, *Liberal Tradition*, p. 83; and *Unfolding*, pp. 192–193.

193. *Analects*, 14:18.

194. *SSCI*, 17:9a.

195. Tu, "Yen Yüan," pp. 526, 533.

196. *Ibid.*, p. 532.

197. *Ibid.*, pp. 534–535; see also Chung-ying Ch'eng, "Practical Learning," p. 40.

198. *Yü-lu*, 24:7b.

199. *SSCI*, 15:1b–2a; *Yü-lu*, 24:3ab; *P'ing yü* 15; *Lun yü* 12:1.

200. *SSCI*, 15:5a; *Yü-lu*, 24:10a; *P'ing-yü* 15; *Lun yü* 12:1.

201. See my *Neo-Confucian Orthodoxy and the learning of the Mind-and-Heart*, Part 2.

202. *SSCI*, 5:8b.

203. Chan, "*Hsing-li ching-i*," pp. 543, 559, 564–565.

204. Ch'ien Mu, *Hsüeh-shu shih*, 78; Fisher, "Later Life," pp. 20–21.

205. Lu Lung-chi, *San-yü t'ang wen-chi*, 2:4b.

206. Chan, "*Hsing-li ching-i*," p. 557.

207. See de Bary and Bloom, *Principal and Practicality*, pp. 131, 149.

208. *Po Lü Liu-liang Ssu-shu chiang-i*, compiled by Chu Shih. See also de Bary, *The Message of the Mind*, pp. 195–199.

209. Fisher draws attention to the wide dissemination of Lü's works in several of his articles. See his "Loyalism," pp. 95–96; "Accommodation," pp. 127–129; "Later Years," pp. 2–3; "Loyalist Alternatives," pp. 96, 122. See also Ch'ien Mu, *Hsüeh shu-shih*, p. 79.

210. Tom Fisher, in a preliminary report on research in progress, indicates his intention to make a much fuller study of this matter. See his "Commentary and Counter-Commentary: Private and Imperially-sponsored Exegeses of the Four Books in Qing China," p. 4.

211. See de Bary, *Liberal Tradition*, pp. 88–89; *Unfolding*, pp. 4, 193–194.

212. For some examples see my *Message of the Mind*, pp. 153, 160–61, 171, 175, 179, 186, 231, 235.

213. On this point see the very apt discussion by Tom Fisher in his "Commentary and Counter-Commentary," pp. 2–4; and in "Accommodation and Loyalism," pp. 98–102.

214. These issues are discussed further by Araki Kengo in his *Yōmeigaku no kaiten to Bukkyō*, pp. 275–294.

215. See Matsumoto Sannosuke, "Nakae Chōmin and Confucianism," p. 251; "The Idea of Heaven: A Tokugawa Foundation for Natural Rights Theory," pp. 181–97; and see also Matsumoto, *Kinsei Nihon no shisōzō*, pp. 49–73.

216. See Jung, *Lü Liu-liang*, pp. 25–26.

217. Chan, "*Hsing-li ching-i*," pp. 564–65.

218. See Tu, "Yen Yüan," pp. 511–515.

219. Ch'ien Mu, *Hsüeh-shu shih*, pp. 30–31.

Glossary

An-ting shu-yüan 安定書院
Chan Jo-shui (Kan-ch'uan) 湛若水 (甘泉)
Ch'an 禪
Chang Heng-ch'ü 張橫渠
Chang P'u 張溥
Chang Chü-cheng 張居正
Chang Tsai 張載
Chao Chen-chi 趙貞吉
Chao Ch'i 趙歧
Chao Ju-yü 趙汝愚
chen-k'ung 真空
Chen Te-hsiu 真德秀
Ch'en Ch'i-chih 陳器之
Ch'en Chien (Ch'ing-lan) 陳建 (清瀾)
Ch'en Ch'un 陳淳
Ch'en Hsien-chang 陳獻章
Cheng Ch'iao 鄭樵
cheng-chi erh wu-cheng 正己而物正

Cheng-i t'ang ch'üan-shu 正誼堂全書
ch'eng i-ko jen 成一個人
cheng-hsüeh 正學
ch'eng 誠
Ch'eng-Chu 程朱
Ch'eng Hao 程顥
Ch'eng I 程頤
chi (self) 己
chi (end, pole) 極
chi (trace) 跡
Chi tzu 箕子
chi-wen chih hsüeh 記問之學
chia 家
chiang-hsüeh 講學
Chiao Hung 焦竑
chien-i 簡易
chieh-shen 戒慎
Ch'ien Mu 錢穆
ch'ien sheng chih chüeh-hsüeh 千聖之絕學
Ch'ien Te-hung 錢德洪
chih (reach, arrive) 至
Chih-fo yüan 芝佛院
chih-chih 致知
chih-li 支離
chih pen-mo 知本末
chih-shan 至善
chih-shih 知識
ch'ih ching 持敬
Chin-chiang 晉江
Chin Lü-hsiang 金履祥
Chin-hsi (Lu Hsiang-shan) 金溪
chin-shih 進士
Chin-ssu lu 近思錄
ching (reverent seriousness) 敬
ching (quiescence) 靜
Ching-chai (Hu Chü-jen) 敬齋
ching-shen 敬身
ching-tso 靜坐
ching-tso tu-shu 靜坐讀書
ch'iu 求
Chou 周

Chou Tun-i 周敦頤
Chu Ch'en-hao 朱宸濠
chu ching 主靜
Chu Hsi 朱熹
Chu-hung 袾宏
Chu Tzu chia-li 朱子家禮
Chu Tzu yü-lei 朱子語類
Chu Yün-ming 祝允明
ch'u hsiung-chung so tzu-te chih 出胸中所自得之
Ch'u-t'an chi 初潭集
Ch'u tz'u 楚辭
Ch'uan-hsi lu 傳習錄
Chuang Tzu 莊子
Chung-yung huo wen 中庸或問
chu tsai 主宰
chü-ching 居敬
chü-ching ch'iung-li 居敬窮理
Chü-ho t'ang 聚和堂
Ch'ü-fu 曲阜
Ch'üan-chou 泉州
chüeh-hsüeh 絕學
chüeh-wu 覺悟
chün-tzu 君子
chung 忠
chung-chieh ming-ch'en 忠節名臣
fa-ming 發明
Fan Chung-yen 范仲淹
fan-nao chi p'u-t'i 煩惱即菩提
Fan Tsu-yü 范祖禹
Fang Hsiao-ju 方孝孺
fei-i chih i 非義之義
fei-li chih li 非禮之禮
fen 分
Fen-shu 焚書
feng-shui 風水
fu-jen 輔仁
Fu Kuang 輔廣
Fu-she 復社
Fung Yu-lan 馮友蘭
Hai Jui 海瑞
Han Chen 韓貞

hao-chieh 豪傑

hao-chieh chih shih 豪傑之士

Ho Chi 何基

Ho Hsin-yin 何心隱

hsi-ching 習靜

hsien li yü ch'i ta 先立於其大

Hsi-ming 西銘

hsi-ning 熙寧

Hsi-yang-li chih hsü 西洋歷志序

hsiao-jen 小人

Hsieh 契

hsien t'ien chih hsin-fa 先天之心法

hsin 心

hsin-fa 心法

hsin-hsüeh 心學

hsing 性

Hsing-li ching-i 性理精義

Hsing-li ta-ch'üan 性理大全

hsing-lüeh 行略

hsiu-chi chih-jen 修己治人

hsiu-tsai 秀才

hsü 虛

Hsü Heng 許衡 (Chung-p'ing 仲平)

Hsü Ts'ang-shu 續藏書

Hsü Yüeh 徐樾

Hsü Yung-chien 徐用檢

hsüan 玄

hsüeh 學

Hsüeh Hsüan 薛瑄

Hsüeh-pu t'ung-pien 學部通辨

Hsün Tzu 荀子

Hu Chi-sui 胡季隨

Hu-kuang 湖廣

Hu Yüan 胡瑗

Hua yen 華嚴

Huai-nan Tzu 淮南子

Huai-nan ko-wu 淮南格物

Huang-an 黃安

Huang Kan 黃幹

Huang T'ing-chien 黃庭堅

Huang Tsung-hsi 黃宗羲

Hui-yüan 慧遠
hun-jan yu wu t'ung-ti 渾然與物同體
huo-jan kuan-t'ung 豁然貫通
Huo-wen 或問
i-ch'i 意氣
I-ch'uan 伊川
i-jen chih jen 以人治人
i-kuan 一貫
I-li 儀禮
iro bōshi 色坊子
i-tao tzu-jen 以道自任
i t'ien-hsia wei chi-jen 以天下為己任
I-t'ung shu 易通書
jen 仁
jen-che 仁者
jen-hsin 人心
Jen-shuo 仁說
jen-yü 人欲
Jih chih lu 日知錄
ju 儒
Jung Chao-tsu 容肇祖
K'ang-chai 康齋
K'ang-hsi 康熙
Kao P'an-lung 高攀龍
Kao Tzu 告子
Kasuga Senan 春日潛菴
ken 艮
Kenkō 兼好
Keng Ting-hsiang 耿定向
ko-jen chu-i (Japanese:kojin shugi) 個人主義
ko-wu chih-chih 格物致知
ko-wu chih pen 格物知本
ko-wu ch'iung-li 格物窮理
k'o-chi fu-li 克己復禮
Ku Hsien-ch'eng 顧憲成
Kuan Chung 管仲
kuan-t'ung 貫通
kung 公
kung-fu 工夫
Kuei Yu-kuang 歸有光
kung-kuo ko 功過格

k'ung 空
li (rites) 禮
Li Ao 李翱
Li Chih 李贄 (Cho-wu 卓吾)
li-hsüeh 理學
li-hsüeh ming-ch'en 理學名臣
li-i fen shu 理一分殊
Li Kuang-ti 李光地
li-shen 立身
Li T'ung 李侗
Li Yung 李顒
liang-chih 良知
Liu Tsung-chou 劉宗周
Liu Yin 劉因
Lo 洛
Lo Ch'in-shun 羅欽順 (Cheng-an 整菴)
Lo Hung-hsien 羅洪先
Lo Ju-fang 羅汝芳
Lou Liang 婁諒
Lu Hsiang-shan 陸象山
Lü Lung-chi 陸隴其
Lü Liu-liang 呂留良 (Wan-ts'un 晚村)
Lü-shih hsiang-yüeh 呂氏鄉約
Lü Tsu-ch'ien 呂祖謙
Lun-yü ching-i 論語精義
Lung-hsi 龍溪
Ma Tuan-lin 馬端臨
Meng Tzu huo-wen 孟子或問
miao-yung 妙用
mien-jen 勉仁
min (people) 民
Min (Fukien) 閩
Ming 明
ming-che pao-shen lun 明哲保身論
ming ch'i tzu-jan chih ku 明其自然之故
Ming-i tai-fang-lu 明夷待訪錄
Ming-ju hsüeh-an 明儒學案
ming ming-te 明明德
Ming-te 明德
mo-tso ch'eng-hsin 默坐澄心
Mo Tzu 墨子

Morohashi Tetsuji 諸橋轍次
Nakae Tōju 中江藤樹
Nan-k'ang 南康
nien-p'u 年譜
Ou-yang Hsiu 歐陽修
Ou-yang Hsüan 歐陽玄
pa t'iao-mu 八條目
pai-hsing jih-yung 百姓日用
pi-jan chih li 必然之理
po-hsüeh 博學
Po Lü Liu-liang Ssu-shu chiang-i 駁呂留良四書講義
pu-i 不已
pu-li wen-tzu 不立文字
Ren Jiyu 任繼愈
sa-lo 洒落
San i-jen chi 三異人集
san kang-ling 三綱領
shan-jen 山人
shan-shu 善書
Shan-yin 山陰
Shao Yung 邵雍
shen 身
shen-tu 慎獨
sheng-chih 生知
sheng-li 生理
sheng-sheng 生生
shen-tsao erh tzu-te chih 深造而自得之
shen-tsao ssu-tao 深造斯道
sheng-yüan 生員
shih 士
shih-hsüeh 實學
Shih-ku shu-yüan 石鼓書院
shih-shih 實事
shih-ta-fu 士大夫
Shimada Kenji 島田虔次
shu 恕
Shui-hu chuan 水滸傳
shun (follow, accord with) 順
Shun 舜
so-i-jan chih ku 所以然之故
so-tang-jan chih tse 所當然之則

so yu chih tzu 所有之自
ssu 私
ssu-chi 私己
Ssu-ma Kuang 司馬光
Ssu-shu chang-chü 四書章句
Ssu-shu chiang-i 四書講義
Ssu-shu yü-lu 四書語錄
ssu-wen 斯文
ssu-yü 私欲
su 素
su-hsüeh 俗學
Su Shih 蘇軾
sui-ch'u t'i-jen t'ien-li 隨處體認天理
Sung 宋
ta-chang-fu 大丈夫
Ta-ch'eng hsüeh-ko 大成學歌
Ta chih tu lun 大智度論
Ta-hsüeh chang-chü 大學章句
Ta-hsüeh huo-wen 大學或問
Ta-hsüeh wen 大學問
Ta-hsüeh yen-i 大學衍義
ta-jen 大人
Ta-kuan 達觀
ta-t'ung 大同
Ta-Yü mo 大禹謨
ta-yüan ching-chih 大圓鏡智
t'ai-chi 太極
T'ai-chi t'u-chieh 太極圖解
T'ai-chou 泰州
tao-hsin 道心
tao-hsüeh 道學
tao-i yu shih-yu yu chih 道義有師友有之
Tao-ku lu 道古錄
tao-t'i 道體
tao-t'ung 道統
te chih yü chi 得之於己
te-i 得義
t'i 体(體)
ti-hsüeh 帝學
t'i-jen tzu-te 體認自得
t'ien-fu 天賦

t'ien hsia wan wu shih chieh yu i-ting chih fa 天下萬物事皆有一定之法
t'ien-hsing 天性
t'ien-li 天理
t'ien-ming 天命
t'ien-ti wan-wu i-t'i chih jen 天地萬物一體之仁
t'ien-wei 天位
Ts'ang-shu 藏書
tsao 造
tsao-i 造詣
Tseng Ching 曾靜
Tseng Tzu 曾子
tso-chan 坐禪
tu-kung 篤恭
tu-shu jen 讀書人
tsun te-hsing tao wen-hsüeh 尊德性道問學
Tsure-zure gusa 從然草
T'ung-an 同安
T'ung chih 通志
t'ung-hsin 童心
T'ung-shu 通書
tzu 自
tzu-cheng 自正
tzu-ch'eng (self-fulfillment) 自成
tzu-ch'eng (sincerity, genuineness) 自誠
tzu-chi i-p'ien 自己一片
tzu-ch'i 自欺
tzu-chia 自家
tzu-ch'ieh 自慊
tzu-ch'ien 自謙
tzu chih (self-knowledge) 自知
tzu-chih (self-governance) 自治
Tzu-chih t'ung-chien 資治通鑑
tzu ch'iu te-chih 自求得之
tzu-hsing 自省
tzu-hua 自化
tzu-jan 自然
tzu jan chih ming-chüeh 自然之明覺
tzu-jan ti tao-li 自然的道理
tzu-jen 自任
Tzu-lu 子路
tzu-shih 自失

Tzu Ssu 子思

tzu-sung 自訟

tzu-te 自得

tzu-te ch'i pen-hsin 自得其本心

tzu-te chih hsüeh 自得之學

tzu te t'ing 自得亭

tzu-tsai 自在

tzu-tsun 自尊

tzu-yu 自由

tzu-yu chu-i (Japanese: jiyu shugi) 自由主義

tz'u 慈

Wan-ts'un Lü Tzu p'ing-yü, cheng-pien 晚村呂子評語, 正編

Wang An-shih 王安石

Wang Chi 王畿

Wang Fu-chih 王夫之

Wang Ken 王艮

Wang Po 王柏

Wang Shih-chen 王世貞

Wang Tao-k'un 汪道昆

Wang Yang-ming 王陽明 (m. Shou-jen 守仁)

wei 偽

wei-chi 為己

wei-chi chih hsüeh 為己之學

Wei Liao-weng 魏了翁

wei wei 惟危

wen 文

Wen-hsien t'ung-k'ao 文獻通考

wen-ku chih-hsin 溫故知新

wo 我

wu (nothingness) 無

Wu 武

Wu Ch'eng 吳澄 (Yu-ch'ing 幼清)

wu-chi (no-self) 無己

wu-chi (non-finite) 無極

wu-chi erh t'ai-chi 無極而太極

wu chiang-hsüeh chih kung 無講學之功

wu chih 無知

wu-hsin 無心

wu hsing 悟性

wu ssu 無思

wu t'i 無體

wu-wang wu-chu 勿忘勿助

wu-wei 無為

wu-wei erh ch'eng 無為而成

wu-yü 無欲

Wu Yü-pi 吳與弼

Yamashita Ryūji 山下龍二

Yamazaki Ansai 山崎闇齋

Yang 陽

Yang Chi 楊楫

Yao 堯

Yen Chün 顏鈞

Yen Hui 顏回

Yen-p'ing ta-wen 延平答問

Yen Tzu 顏子

Yen Yüan 顏淵

Yen Yüan 顏元

Yi T'oegye 李退溪

yin (shade) 陰

yin (silver) 銀

yin-yü chi shih tao 淫欲即是道

ying-hsiung chih shih 英雄之士

yu-hsia 游俠

yu so tzu-te 有所自得

yu wei 有為

Yü Chi 虞集

Yü 禹

yü-chung ti-i shih 宇中第一事

yü-fu yü-fu 愚夫愚婦

yü-lei 語類

yü-lu 語錄

Yü-shan chiang-i 玉山講義

Yüan Chung-tao 袁中道

Yüan Hsien 元賢

Yüan Huang 袁黃

Yün-ku 雲谷

Yüeh-ch'uan 月川 (Tsao Tuan 曹端)

yung 用

Yung-cheng 雍正

Yung-lo 永樂

CHINESE, JAPANESE, AND KOREAN SOURCES

Abe Takeo 安部健夫. *Gendai no kenkyū* 元代の研究. Tokyo: Sōbunsha, 1972.

Araki Kengo 荒木見悟. *Bukkyō to Jukyō* 仏教と儒教. Kyoto: 1963.

—— "Kan Tō-mei" [Kuan Tung-ming] 管東溟. *Nippon chūgoku gakkai hō*, 12:101–102.

—— "Minmatsu ni okeru jubutsu chowa-ron no seikaku" 明末における儒仏調和論の性格. In *Nihon Chūgoku gakkai hō*, no. 18, pp. 210–223.

—— *Yōmeigaku no kaiten to Bukkyō* 陽明学の開展と仏教. Tokyo: Kembun shuppan, 1984.

Chan Jo-shui 湛若水. *Kan-ch'uan wen-chi* 甘泉文集. 1580 ed., and in Shiga Ichirō: *Tan Kansen* 湛甘泉.

Chang Huang 章潢. *T'u-shu pien* 圖書編. 127 *chüan* ed. of Wan-li, 41 (1613).

Chang Sankyon 張三植. *Tae han han chachŏn* 大漢韓辭典. Seoul: Song-munsa 省文社, 1968.

Chang Tsai 張載. *Chang Tzu ch'üan-shu* 張子全書. KSKSSK ed.

Ch'en Ch'ang-fang 陳長方. *Wei-shih chi* 唯室集. Ssu-k'u ch'üan-shu chen-pen ed. Shanghai: Commercial Press, 1935.

Ch'en Hsien-chang 陳獻章. *Pai-sha Tzu ch'üan-chi* 白沙子全集. Hong Kong: Ch'en Pai-sha Cultural and Educational Foundation, 1967; repr. of 1710 ed.

Ch'eng Hao 程顥, *I-shu*, 遺書. In *Erh Ch'eng ch'üan-shu*, 二程全書. SPPY ed.

—— *Ming-tao wen-chi* 明道文集. In *Erh Ch'eng ch'üan-shu*, SPPY ed.

Ch'eng I 程頤. *I-ch'uan wen-chi* 伊川文集. In *Erh Ch'eng Ch'üan-shu*, SPPY ed.

Ch'eng shih chia-shu tu-shu fen-nien jih-ch'eng 程氏家塾讀書分年日程. In Ts'ung-shu chi-ch'eng ed.

Chi Wen-fu 嵇文甫. "Wang Ch'uan-shan yü Li Cho-wu" 王船山與李卓吾. *Li-shih yen-chiu*, pp. 86–89. 1961–1966.

——. "Li Cho-wu yü tso-p'ai Wang-hsüeh" 李卓吾與左派王學. *Honan ta-hsüeh hsüeh-pao*, I–II, June 1934.

——. *Tso-p'ai Wang-hsüeh* 左派王學. Shanghai, 1934.

Chiang Fu-tsung 蔣復璁, gen. ed. *Ming-jen chuan-chi tzu-liao so-yin* 明人傳記資料索引 (abbr. MJCCTLSY). Taipei: National Central Library, 1965.

Chiao Hung 焦竑. *Kuo-ch'ao hsien-cheng lu* 國朝獻徵錄. In *Chung-kuo shih-hsüeh tsung-shu* 中國史學叢書 (photographic reprint). Taiwan: 1965.

—— *T'an-yüan chi* 澹園集. Chin-ling tsung-shu ed.

Ch'ien Mu 錢穆. *Ts'ung Chung-kuo li-shih lai k'an Chung-kuo min-tsu hsing chi Chung-kuo wen hua* 從中國歷史來看中國民族性及中國文化. Taipei: 1979.

—— *Chung-kuo chin san-pai nien hsüeh-shu shih*, 中国近三百年學術史. 2 vols. Taipei: Commercial Press, 1937; 8th reprint 1983.

—— *Chung-kuo hsüeh-shu ssu-hsiang shih lun-ts'ung* 中國學術思想史論叢. Tung-ta t'u-shu kung-ssu. Taipei: 1978.

—— *Chu Tzu hsin hsüeh-an* III 朱子新學案. Taipei: San min shu-chü, 1971.

Ch'iu Chün 邱濬. *Ta-hsüeh yen-i pu* 大學衍義補. 160 *chüan* edition of Chia Ching 38 (1559). Reprint of Hung chih (1488) ed. preserved in the National Central Library, Taipei.

Ch'iu Han-sheng 丘漢生. "T'ai-chou hsüeh-p'ai ti chieh-ch'u ssu-hsiang-chia Li Chih" 泰州學派的傑出思想家李贊, pp. 115–132. *Li-shih yen-chiu*, 1964.

Chou Ju-teng 周汝登. *Sheng-hsüeh ts'ung-ch'uan* 聖學宗傳. Wan-li ed.

Chou Tsai-yen 周在延 ed. *T'ien-kai lou ssu-shu yü-lu* 天蓋樓四書語錄. 46 *chüan* ed. of 1684.

Chou Tun-i 周敦頤. *Chou Tzu ch'üan shu* 周子全書. KHCPTS ed.; also in KSKSSK ed., *Chou-Chang ch'üan-shu* 周張全書.

—— *T'ung-shu* 通書. Taipei: Commercial Press, 1978.

Chu Ch'ien-chih 朱謙之. *Li Chih* 李贊. Wuhan: 1957.

Chu Hsi 朱熹. *Meng Tzu huo-wen* 孟子或問. Chu-tzu i-shu ed. 朱子遺書.

—— *Wen chi* 文集. See *Hui-an hsien-sheng Chu Wen-kung wen-chi*.

—— *Chu Tzu ta-ch'üan* 朱子大全. SPPY ed. Taipei: Chung-hua shu-chü, 1970.

—— *Chu Tzu yü-lei* 朱子語類. Taipei: Cheng-chung shu-chü, 1970, and Kyoto, Chūbun shuppansha, 1979; also Beijing, *Chung-hua shu-chü*, 1986.

—— *Chung-yung huo-wen* 中庸或問. Chūbun KSKSSK ed.

—— *Hui-an hsien-sheng Chu wen-kung wen-chi* 晦庵先生朱文公集, SPTK and Chūbun shuppansha ed., 1977.

——. *Ta-hsüeh huo-wen* 大學或問. In KSKSSK ed., *Shisō sampen*.

—— *T'ai-chi-t'u chieh* 太極圖解. In *Chou-Chang ch'üan-shu* 周張全書, KSKSSK ed., Shisōhen, vol. 1. Kyoto: Chūbun shuppansha, 1972.

—— *Chung-yung chang-chü* 中庸章句 (Commentary on the Mean). In *Ssu-shu chi-chu*. Taipei: CKTHMCCC ed., 1978.

—— *Ssu-shu chi-chu*, 四書集註. Taipei: CKTHMCCC ed., 1978.

—— *Yen-p'ing ta-wen* 延平答問. KSKSSK ed., Shisōhen no. 8. Kyoto: Chūbun shuppansha.

———. *Yen-p'ing ta-wen fu pu-lu* 延平答問附補錄. KSKSSK ed., Shisōhen no. 8.

—— *Chu Tzu ch'üan-shu* 朱子全書. 1713 ed.

Chu-hung 袾宏. *Chu-ch'uang san-pi* 竹窗三筆. 1615 ed.

Chu Shih 朱軾, comp. *Po Lü Liu-liang Ssu-shu chiang-i* 駁呂留良四書講義. Preface dated 1731.

A Concordance to Chuang-tzu 莊子. Harvard-Yenching Index Series, Supplement No. 20.

Erh Ch'eng ch'üan-shu 二程全書. SPPY ed.

Erh Ch'eng i-shu 二程遺書, in *Erh Ch'eng ch'uan-shu*, SPPY ed. and KSKSSK ed.; also in *Erh Ch'eng chi* 二程集, Chung-hua shu-chü ed. Beijing: 1981.

Erh Ch'eng wai-shu 二程外書. In SPPY and KSKSSK *Erh-Ch'eng ch'üan-shu* and in *Erh Ch'eng chi*, Chung-hua shu-chü ed.

Fan Hao-ting 范鄗鼎. *Kuang li-hsüeh pei-k'ao* 廣理學備考. Wu-ching t'ang ed. 五經堂.

Fan Tsu-yü 范祖禹. *Ti hsüeh* 帝學. CKTHMCCC ed.

Fung Yu-lan 馮友蘭. "Ts'ung Li Chih shuo-ch'i" 從李贄說起. *Chung-kuo che-hsüeh-shih lun-wen erh chi* 中國哲學史論文二集. Shanghai: 1962.

———. "Lüeh-lun tao-hsüeh ti t'e-tien, ming-ch'eng ho hsing-chih" 略論道學的特點,名稱和性質. *She-hui k'o-hsüeh chan-hsien* (1982), 3:35–43.

Hirose Yutaka 廣瀬豐. *Yoshida Shōin no kenkyū* 吉田松院の研究. Tokyo: Musashino shoin, 1943.

Hou Wai-lu 侯外廬. *Chung-kuo ssu-hsiang t'ung-shih* 中國思想通史. Beijing: Jen-min ch'u-pan she, 1960, vol. 4B.

Hsi-shan wen-chi 西山文集. KHCPTS 2 vol. ed. Taipei: Commercial Press, 1968.

Hsü Heng 許衡. *Lu-chai ch'üan-shu* 魯齋全書. Kinsei kanseki sōkan, 2d. series ed. Kyoto: Chūbun shuppansha, 1975.

—— *Hsü Wen-cheng kung i-shu*, 許文正公遺書. T'ang shih ching kuan ts'ung-shu ed.

A Concordance to Hsün Tzu 荀子. Harvard Yenching Sinological Index Series, Supplement 22.

Hu Kuang 胡廣. *Hsing-li ta-ch'üan* 性理大全. Ssu-k'u chen-pen ed., 5th series. Taipei: Commercial Press, 1974; also in Chūbun shuppansha ed., Kyoto, 1981.

Huai-nan Tzu 淮南子. Ssu-pu ts'ung-k'an ed.

Huang T'ing-chien 黃庭堅. *Yü-chang Huang hsien-sheng wen-chi* 豫章黃先生文集. SPTK ed.

Huang Tsung-hsi 黃宗羲. *Ming-i tai-fang lu* 明夷待訪錄. Erh lao ko ed. 二老閣.

―――― *Ming-ju hsüeh-an* 明儒學案. Commercial Press, Wan-yu wen-k'u ed.

Huang Tsung-hsi 黃宗羲 and Ch'üan Tsu-wang 全祖望. *Sung Yüan hsüeh-an* 宗元學案. Taipei: Ho-lo t'u-shu ch'u-pan-she, 1975.

Huang Yün-mei 黃雲眉. "Li Cho-wu shih-shih pien cheng" 李卓吾事實辨正. *Chin-ling hsüeh-pao* (May 1932), vol. 2.

A Concordance to I-ching 易經. Harvard Yenching Sinological Index Series, Supplement No. 10.

I-ch'uan wen-chi Supplement 伊川文集. In KSKSSK ed. of *Erh Ch'eng ch'üan shu*, vol. 1, and *Erh Ch'eng chi*, Chung-hua ed., vol. 1.

Iki, Hiroyuki. "Empei tōmon wo yomu." (On reading *Responses of Yen-p'ing*). In Okada Takehiko, ed., *Tōyō no risō to eichi* (The Ideals and Wisdom of the East). Fukuoka: Tōyō Shisō Kenkyūkai, 1963.

Juan Yüan 阮元, gen. ed., *Shih san ching chu-su* 十三経注疏, Taipei, I-wen yin-shu kuan, reprint, 1955.

Jung Chao-tsu 容肇祖 ed., *Ho Hsin-yin chi* 何心隱集. Beijing: Chung-hua, 1960.

―――― "Ho Hsin-yin chi ch'i ssu-hsiang" 何心隱及其思想. *Fu-jen hsüeh-chih* (1937), 6(1-2):129-172.

―――― *Li Chih nien-p'u* 李贄年譜. Peking: 1957.

―――― . *Li Cho-wu p'ing-chuan* 李卓吾評伝. Shanghai: Commercial Press, 1937.

―――― "Lü Liu-liang chi ch'i ssu-hsiang" 呂留良及其思想. *Fu-jen hsüeh chih* 輔仁學志 (December 1926), 5(1-2):1-86. Reprinted. Hong Kong: Ch'ung-wen shu-tien, 1974.

―――― *Ming-tai ssu-hsiang-shih* 明代思想史. Reprint. Taipei: 1966.

Kuei Yu-kuang 歸有光. *Chen-ch'uan hsien-sheng chi* 震川先生集.

Ku Yen-wu 顧炎武. *Jih chih lu* 日知錄. Commercial Press, 1934.

Kusumoto Masatsugu 楠本正繼. *Sō-Min jidai jugaku shisō no kenkyū* 宋明時代儒学思想の研究. Chiba ken, Kashiwa-shi, 1962.

Li Chih, 李贄. *Ch'u-t'an chi* 初潭集. 30 *chüan*. Undated Ming edition, National Central Library, Taipei.

―――― *Cho-wu wen-lü* 卓吾文錄. *Fen shu* 焚書. Beijing: 1961.

―――― *Fen-shu* 焚書. Ed. of Chung-hua shu-chü. Beijing: 1961.

―――― *Hsü Fen-shu* 續焚書. 1609 ed.; also ed. of Chung-hua shu-chü, Beijing: 1959.

―――― *Hsü Ts'ang-shu* 續藏書. Wan-li ed. of Wang Wei-yen, Nanking. Also Chung-hua shu-chü ed. Beijing: 1959.

—— *Li Cho-wu hsien-sheng i-shu* 李卓吾先生遺書. 3 chüan ed. of Wan-li 40 (1613). National Central Library, Taipei.

—— *Li-shih shuo-shu* 李氏説書. 9th undated Ming ed. In Chinese collection of Kyūshu University, Fukuoka, Japan.

—— *Li-wen-ling chi* 李溫陵集. 20 *chüan*. Ming ed. National Central Library, Taipei.

—— *San I-jen wen-chi* 三異人文集. 18 *chüan*. Ming ed. National Central Library, Taipei.

—— *Ts'ang shu* 藏書. Ed. of Chung-hua shu-chü. Beijing: 1959.

—— [Ming-teng] *Tao-ku lu* 明燈道古錄. 2 *chüan*. Ming ed. Collection of Yoshikawa Kojirō. Preface dated c. 1599.

Li Hsien-chih 李謙之. *Li Chih shih-liu shih-chi Chung-kuo fan feng-chien ssu-hsiang ti hsien-ch'ü* 李贄十六世紀中國反封建思想的先驅. Wuhan: 1957.

Li Kuang-ti 李光地. *Jung-ts'un ch'üan-chi* 榕村全集. Preface dated 1829.

—— *Ssu-shu chieh-i* 四書解義. 1825 ed.

Lin-ch'uan Wu Wen-cheng kung chi 臨川吳文正公集. Wan-li 40 (1612), ed., in National Central Library, Taipei.

Li Yung 李顒 (Erh-ch'ü) 二曲. *Li Erh-ch'ü hsien-sheng ch'üan-chi* 李二曲先生全集. Shanghai: Sao-yeh shan fang ed. 掃葉山房, 1925.

Liu Yin 劉因. *Ching-hsiu wen-chi* 靜修文集. Chifu ts'ung-shu ed. 畿輔叢書.

Lou Liang 婁諒. "K'ang-chai hsien-sheng hsing-chuang" 康齋先生行狀. In *Ming ming-ch'en wan-yen lu* 明名臣琬琰錄, Ssu-k'u chen-pen ed., 6th Series. Taipei: Commercial Press, 1976.

Lu Chiu-yüan chi 陸九淵集. Beijing: Chung-hua shu-chü, 1980; also Taiwan: Commercial Press edition.

Lu Lung-chi 陸隴其. *San-yü t'ang wen-chi* 三魚堂文集. Lu Tzu ch'üan-shu ed.

Lü Liu-liang 呂留良. *Lü Wan-ts'un hsien-sheng wen-chi*, 呂晚村先生文集. Dated 1929 (1869?).

—— *Lü Wan-ts'un tsa-chi* 呂晚村雜集. Taipei: Taiwan Commercial Press, 1973.

—— *Ssu-shu chiang-i* 四書講義. 43 *chüan*. Ed. of 1686.

—— *Ssu-shu yü-lü* 四書語錄. In T'ien-kai lou 天蓋樓. 26 chüan ed. of 1684.

—— *T'ien-kai lou ou-p'ing* 天蓋樓偶評. In six *ts'e*, original edition of 1675.

—— *Wan-ts'un Lu Tzu p'ing yu, cheng pien*, 晚村呂子評語, 正編. 42 *chüan* ed. of K'ang Hsi 55 (1716) in the rare book collection of the Beijing Library.

Lun-yü chi-chu, 論語集註. *Ssu-shu chi-chu* 四書集註. CKTHMCCC ed.

Lun-yü ching-i 論語精義. Chu Tzu i-shu ed.

Makino Shūji 牧野修二. "Gendai no jugaku kyōiku" 元代の儒学教育. *Tōyōshi kenkyū* (March 1979), 37(4): 71–74.

Mao Hsing-lai 茅星來. *Chin-ssu-lu chi-chu* 近思錄集註. Ssu-k'u shan-pen ts'ung-shu 四庫善本叢書. Taipei: I-wen shu-chü, n.d.

Matsumoto Sannosuke 松本三之助. *Kinsei Nihon no shisōzō* 近世日本の思想像. Tokyo: Kembun shuppan 研文出版, 1984.

Matsumoto Sannosuke, ed. *Taidō suru Ajia* 胎動するアジア. Tokyo: 1966.

Meng Tzu 孟子. In *Shih-san ching chu-shu* 十三經註疏. Taipei: I-wen yin-shu-kuan reprint of Chia-ching 20 ed. Nanching: 1915, vol. 14.

Ming shih 明史 (MS). Beijing: Chung-hua ed., 1974.

Miyazaki Ichisada 宮崎一定. *Ajia shi kenkyū*, IV アジア史研究. Kyoto: Dōbōsha, 1964.

Mizoguchi Yūzō 溝口雄三. *Chūgoku zenkindai shisō no kussetsu to tenkai*, 中国前近代思想の屈折と展開. Tokyo: Tokyo University Press, 1985.

Mochizuki Shinkō 望月信亨. *Bukkyō daijiten* 仏教大字典. Tokyo: Bukkyō daijiten hakkōsho, 1931–36.

Morohashi Tetsuji 諸橋轍次. *Dai kanwa jiten* 大漢和辞典. Tokyo: Taishūkan 大修館, 1960.

—— *Jukyō no mokuteki to Sōju no katsudo* 儒教の目的と宋儒の活動. Tokyo: Taishūkan 大修館, 1926.

Mou Tsung-san 牟宗三. *Hsin-t'i yü hsing-t'i* 心體與性體. 3 vols. Taipei: Cheng-chung Book Co. 正中書局, 1969.

Nihon kokugo daijiten 日本国語大辞典. Tokyo: Shogakkan, 1976.

Okada Takehiko 岡田武彦. *Minmatsu jukyō no dōkō* 明末儒教の動向. Kyūshu daigaku bunkakubu, Sōmin shisō kenkyūshitsu, 1960.

—— "O-mon genjōha no keitō" 王門現成派の系統 (The Filiation of the Existentialist Branch of the Wang Yang-ming School). *Teoria* (December 1961), 5, pt. 1, pp. 59–86; and no. 6, pt. 2, pp. 31–50.

—— "Ryo Banson no Shushigaku" 呂晩村の朱子学. *Teoria*, March 1968, no. 11.

—— "Shushi no chichi to shi" 朱子の父と師. *Seinan gakuin daigaku bunri ronshū* (March 1974), 14(2): 70.

Okada Takehiko, ed. *Ōyōmei zenshū* 王陽明全集. Tokyo: Meitoku, 1983.

Ono Kazuko 小野和子. "Jukyō no itansha tachi" 儒教の異端者達. In Matsumoto Sannosuke, ed., *Taidō suru Ajia* 胎動するアジア, pp. 25–45. Tokyo, 1966.

Ōta Tatsuo 太田辰夫. *Chūgoku rekidai kogobun* 中国歴代口語文. Tokyo: 1947; reprint Kyoto: Hoyū shōten 朋友書店 1982.

Ou-yang Hsüan 歐陽玄. *Kuei-chai wen-chi* 圭齋文集. SPTK ed.

Pan Ku 班固. *Han shu* 漢書. SPTK Po-na ed.

Ren Jiyu 任繼愈. "Ju-chia yü ju-chiao" 儒家與儒教. *Chung-kuo che-hsüeh*, No. 3.

Sakai Tadao 酒井忠夫. *Chūgoku zensho no kenkyū* 中国善書の研究. Tokyo: 1960.

Saeki Tomi 佐伯富. *Sō no shin bunka* 宋の新文化. Tokyo: Jimbutsu ōraisha 人物往來社, 1967.

Satō Rentarō 佐藤錬太郎. "Ri Shi *Zoku zōsho* ni tsuite" 李贄續藏書について. In *Tōhōgaku* (January 1984), 67:76–90.

Shiga Ichirō 志賀一郎. *Tan Kansen no kenkyū* 湛甘泉の研究. Tokyo: Fuma shobō, 1980.

Shih Ching 詩經. In *Shih san ching chu-su* 十三經註疏. Vol. 4.

Shih san ching chu-su, *see* Juan Yüan.

Shimada Kenji 島田虔次. *Chūgoku ni okeru kindai shii no zazetsu* 中国に方ける近代思惟の挫折. Tokyo: 1949; revised ed. 1970.

—— "Jukyō no hangyakusha, Ri Shi (Ri Takugo)" 儒教の叛逆者李贄. In *Shisō* (1962) no. 462 (1597–1609), nos. 1–13.

—— "Ōgaku saharon hihan no hihan" 王学佐派論批判の批判. In *Shigaku zasshi* (1952), vol. 61, no. 9.

—— *Shushigaku to Yōmeigaku* 朱子学と陽明学. Tokyo: Iwanami, 1967.

—— "Subjective Idealism in Sung and Post-Sung China: The All Things Are One Theory of *Jen*." *Tōhōgaku-hō* (March 1958), No. 28.

Shu-ching 書經. In *Shih san ching chu-su* 十三經注疏.

Ssu-k'u ch'üan-shu tsung-mu t'i-yao 四庫全書總目提要. Commercial Press, 1922 ed.

Sung shih 宋史. Beijing: Chung-hua shu-chü, 1977.

Suzuki Torao 鈴木虎雄. "Ritakugo nempu," 李卓吾年譜. In *Shinagaku* (February 1934), 7(2):139–197; (July 1934), 7(3):299–347.

Ta-hsüeh chang-chü 大學章句. In *Ssu-shu chi-chu* (CKTHMCCC ed.).

T'ai-chou hsüeh-p'ai hsüeh-shu t'ao-lun hui, Chi-nien pien-wen chi, 泰州學派學術討論會. T'ai-chou (Kiangsu): T'ai-chou hsüeh-p'ai chi-nien kuan, 泰州學派紀念館, 1987.

Tai Hsien 戴銑. *Chu Tzu shih-chi* 朱子實紀. In *Kinsei kanseki sōkan*, Shisōhen no. 22. Kyoto: Chūbun shuppansha; Taipei: Kuang-wen Publishing, 1972.

Taishō shinshū daizōkyō 大正新修大藏經. Tokyo, 1914–22.

Takao Giken 高雄義堅. *Chūgoku Bukkyō shiron* 中国仏教史論. Kyoto: Heirakuji, 1952.

T'ang Chün-i 唐君毅. *Chung-kuo che-hsüeh yüan-lun, Yüan chiao p'ien* 中國哲學原論,原教篇. Hong Kong: Hsien-ya yen-chiu-so, 1975.

Tomoeda Ryūtarō 友枝龍太郎. Introduction to *Yen-p'ing ta-wen* 延平答問. KSKSSK, Shisōhen ed.

—— *Shushi no shisō keisei* 朱子の思想形成. Rev. ed. Tokyo: Shunju-sha, 1979.

Ts'ao Jung, comp. 曹溶. *Hsüeh-hai lei-pien* 學海類編. Wan-yu wen-k'u ed.

Tzu-hai 辭海. Shanghai: Chung-hua shu-chü, 1937; revised ed., Hong Kong: 1979–84.

Tzu-yüan 辭源. Shanghai: Commercial Press, 1926.

Ueda Hiroki 上田弘毅. ''O Ryū-kei ni okeru kyo to mu'' 王龍溪に於ける虚・無. In [*Shūkan*] *Tōyōgaku* (October 1981), no. 46.

Uno Seiichi 宇野精一. *Shōgaku* 小学. Tokyo: Meiji hoin, 1965.

Wang Chi 王畿. *Wang lung-hsi ch'üan chi*, Tao-kuang 2 (1822) ed., also in *Lung-hsi Wang hsien-sheng ch'üan-chi* 龍溪王先生全集. KSKSSK, Shisōzokuhen, Chūbun shuppansha ed.

Wang Lung-hsi yü-lu 王龍溪語錄. Taipei: Kuang-wen ed., n.d.

Wang Ken 王艮. *Wang Hsin-chai hsien-sheng wen-chi* 王心齋先生文集. Ed. of Kasuga Senan 春日潜菴. Kyoto: 1847. Preserved in Kyoto University Jimbun kagaku kenkyūjō.

—— *Hsin-chai Wang hsien-sheng ch'üan-chi* 心齋王先生全集. 1615 ed. of Wang Yüan-ting. Preserved in the collection of the Naikaku bunko.

—— *Ming-ju Wang Hsin-chai hsien-sheng i-chi* 明儒王心齋先生遺集. Beijing: 1911.

Wang Yang-ming 王陽明. *Wang Yang-ming ch'üan-chi* 王陽明全集. Shanghai: Ta-tung 大東 shu-chü, 1935.

—— *Wang Yang-ming ch'üan-shu* 王陽明全書. Taipei: Cheng-chung shu-chü ed. 1953.

Wei Liao-weng 魏了翁. *Ho-shan hsien-sheng ta-ch'üan chi* 鶴山先生全集. SPTK ed.

Wu Ch'eng 吳澄. *Ts'ao-lu Wu Wen-cheng kung ch'üan-chi* 草廬吳文正公全集. Ch'ung-jen Wan Huang chiao-k'an 崇仁萬潢校刊本 ed. of Ch'ienlung 21, 1756.

Wu I-feng 烏以鋒. ''Li Cho-wu chu-shu k'ao'' 李卓吾著述考. *Wen-shih yen chiu-so chi-k'an* (June 1932), vol. 1.

Wu K'ang 吳康. *Sung-Ming li-hsüeh* 宋明理學. Rev. ed. Taipei: 1962.

Wu Yü-pi 吳與弼. *Jihlu* 日錄 in *K'ang-chai chi* 康齋集. Ssu-k'u chen-pen ed., 4th series. Taipei: Commerical Press, 1973.

Xiandai hanyu cidian 現代漢語辭典. Hong Kong: Commercial Press, 1977.

Yagisawa Hajime 八木澤元. ''Ri Shi'' 李贄. In *Chūgoku no shisōka*, 中国の思想家. Compiled by Tōkyō daigaku chūgoku tetsugaku, kenkyūshitsu. Tokyo: 1963.

Yamashita Ryūji 山下龍二. "Minmatsu ni okeru han jukyō shisō no genryū" 明末における反儒教思想の源流. *Tetsugaku zasshi*, June 1951.

Yamazaki Michio 山崎道夫, ed. *Chin-ssu lu* 近思錄 (selections). *SSGTK*, vol. 9.

Yeh Kuo-ch'ing 葉國慶. "Li Chih hsien-shih k'ao" 李贄先世考. *Li-shih yen-chiu* (1958), vol. 2.

Yeh Ts'ai 葉采. *Chin-ssu-lu chi-chieh* 近思錄集解. Kinsei kanseki sōkan, 3d series. Kyoto: Chūbun shuppansha, 1979.

Yoshikawa Kōjirō 吉川孝次郎. *Gen Min shi gaisetsu* 元明詩概説. Tokyo: Iwanami, 1963.

Yü Chi 虞集. *Tao-yuan hsüeh-ku lu* 道元學古錄. Ch'ien-lung 41 (1775) ed., of Ch'ung-jen Ch'en Chao-li.

Yüan Chung-tao 袁中道. "Pa Li shih i-shu" 跋李氏遺書. In *Li Cho-wu hsien-sheng i-shu* 李卓吾先生遺書. 3 chuan ed. of Wan-li 40. National Central Library, Taipei.

Bibliography

Ames, Roger T. "Chinese Conceptions of the Body." *International Philosophical Quarterly* (March 1984), 24(1):39–54.

Ames, Roger T. "Co-extending Arising, *Te*." *Journal of Chinese Philosophy* (1984), 2:121.

Analects. In James Legge, tr., *The Chinese Classics*. 2d ed. rev., vol. 1. Oxford: Clarendon Press, 1892; Taipei reprint, 1966.

Araki, Kengo. "Confucianism and Buddhism in the Late Ming." In W. T. de Bary, ed., *The Unfolding of Neo-Confucianism*. New York: Columbia University Press, 1975.

Balazs, Etienne. "Nihilistic Revolt or Mystical Escapism." In Arthur Wright, ed., *Chinese Civilization and Bureaucracy*, pp. 226–254. New Haven: Yale University Press, 1964.

Busch, Heinrich. "The Tunglin Academy." *Monumenta Serica*, 14:1–163.

Butterfield, Herbert. "Reflections on Religion and Modern Individualism." *Journal of the History of Ideas* (January–March 1961), 22(1):33–46.

Chaffee, John W. *The Thorny Gates of Learning in Sung China*. Cambridge: Cambridge University Press, 1985.

Chan, Hok-lam. " 'Comprehensiveness' and 'Change' in Ma Tuan-lin's Historical Thought." In Hok-lam Chan and W. T. de Bary, eds., *Yüan Thought*. New York: Columbia University Press, 1982.

Chan, Hok-lam. *Li Chih (1527–1602) in Contemporary Chinese Historiography: New Light on His Life and Works*. White Plains, N.Y.: M. E. Sharpe, 1980.

Chan, Wing-tsit. "Chinese Theory and Practice." In Charles Moore, ed., *Philosophy and Culture, East and West*. Honolulu: University of Hawaii Press, 1962.

Chan, Wing-tsit. "Chu Hsi's Completion of Neo-Confucianism." In Françoise Aubin, ed., *Sung Studies in Memoriam Etienne Balazs*, Series 2, No. 1. Paris and the Hague: Mouton, 1973.

Chan, Wing-tsit. "The *Hsing-li ching-i* and the Ch'eng-Chu School of the Seventeenth Century." In W. T. de Bary, ed., *The Unfolding of Neo-Confucianism*, pp. 543–572. New York: Columbia University Press, 1975.

Chan, Wing-tsit. "Neo-Confucian Philosophical Poems." *Renditions* (Spring 1975), no. 4, pp. 5–21.

Chan, Wing-tsit. "Patterns for Neo-Confucianism: Why Chu Hsi differed from Ch'eng I." *Journal of Chinese Philosophy* (June 1978), 5(2): 101–126.

Chan, Wing-tsit. *Source Book in Chinese Philosophy*. Princeton: Princeton University Press, 1966.

Chan, Wing-tsit, tr. *Instructions for Practical Living*. New York: Columbia University Press, 1963.

Chan, Wing-tsit, tr. *Reflections on Things at Hand*. New York: Columbia University Press, 1967.

Chang, Carson. *The Development of Neo-Confucian Thought*. Vol. 2. New York: Bookman Associates, 1962.

Ch'en, Kenneth. *Buddhism in China*. Princeton: Princeton University Press, 1964.

Ch'eng, Chung-ying. "Practical Learning in Yen Yüan, Chu Hsi, and Wang Yang-ming." In W. T. de Bary and Irene Bloom, eds., *Principle and Practicality*, pp. 37–68. New York: Columbia University Press, 1979.

Ch'ien, Edward. *Chiao Hung and the Restructuring of Neo-Confucianism in the Late Ming*. New York: Columbia University Press, 1986.

Ching, Julia. *To Acquire Wisdom*. New York: Columbia University Press, 1976.

Ching, Julia. "The Goose Lake Monastery Debate." *Journal of Chinese Philosophy* (1974), vol. 1, no. 2.

Cohen, Myron L. "Variations in Complexity Among Chinese Family Groups:

The Impact of Modernization." *Transactions of the New York Academy of Sciences* (March 1967). Series 2, 34(5):638–644.

Dardess, John. "Confucianism, Local Reform and Centralization in Late Yüan Chekiang, 1342–1359." In H. L. Chan and W. T. de Bary, eds., *Yüan Thought*, pp. 327–374. New York: Columbia University Press, 1982.

de Bary, W. T. "Buddhism and the Chinese Tradition." *Diogenes*, no. 47, pp. 102–124.

de Bary, W. T. "Chu Hsi's Aims as an Educator." In W. T. de Bary and J. Chaffee, eds., *Neo-Confucian Education, the Formative Stage*. Berkeley: University of California Press, 1989.

de Bary, W. T. *East Asian Civilizations: A Dialogue in Five Stages*. Cambridge: Harvard University Press, 1987.

de Bary, W. T. and Hok-lam Ch'an. *Yüan Thought: Chinese Thought and Religion under the Mongols*. New York: Columbia University Press, 1983.

de Bary, W. T. "Individualism and Humanitarianism in Late Ming Thought." In *Self and Society in Ming Thought*, pp. 145–248. New York: Columbia University Press, 1970.

de Bary, W. T. *The Liberal Tradition in China*. Hong Kong: Chinese University Press; New York: Columbia University Press, 1983.

de Bary, W. T. *The Message of the Mind in Neo-Confucianism*. New York: Columbia University Press, 1989.

de Bary, W. T. *Neo-Confucian Orthodoxy and the Learning of the Mind-and-Heart*. New York: Columbia University Press, 1981.

de Bary, W. T. "Neo-Confucianism and Human Rites." In Irene Eber, ed., *Confucianism, the Dynamics of a Tradition*, pp. 109–132. New York: MacMillan, 1986.

de Bary, W. T., ed. *Self and Society in Ming Thought*. New York: Columbia University Press, 1960.

de Bary, W. T. "Some Common Tendencies in Neo-Confucianism." In D. Nivison and A. Wright, eds., *Confucianism in Action*, pp. 24–49. Stanford: Stanford University Press, 1959.

de Bary, W. T. "The Trouble With Confucianism." *Tanner Lectures 1988*. University of Utah Press, 1989.

de Bary, W. T., ed. *The Unfolding of Neo-Confucianism*. New York: Columbia University Press, 1975.

de Bary, W. T. and I. Bloom, eds. *Principle and Practicality*. New York: Columbia University Press, 1979.

de Bary, W. T. and J. Chaffee, eds. *Neo-Confucian Education: The Formative Years*. Berkeley: University of California Press, 1989.

de Bary, W. T., W. T. Chan, and B. Watson. *Sources of Chinese Tradition.* New York: Columbia University Press, 1960.

Deuchler, Martina. "Self-Cultivation for the Governance of Men." *Asiatische Studien* (1980), 34(2):9–39.

Dimberg, Ronald G. *The Sage and Society: The Life and Thought of Ho Hsin-yin.* Honolulu: University of Hawaii Press, 1974.

Fingarette, Herbert. "Human Community as Holy Rite." *Harvard Theological Review,* January 1966.

Fisher, Tom. "Accommodation and Loyalism: The Life of Lü Liu-liang," *Papers on Far Eastern History.* Canberra: Australian National University (March 1977), 15:97–104; September 1977, 16:107–145; September 1978, 18:1–42.

Fisher, Tom. "Commentary and Counter-Commentary: Private and Imperially-Sponsored Exegeses of the Four Books in Qing China." Paper presented to the Columbia University Regional Seminar on Neo-Confucianism, February 1, 1985.

Fisher, Tom. "Loyalist Alternatives in the Early Ch'ing." *HJAS* (June 1984), 44:88–123.

Fisher, Tom. "Lü Liu-liang (1629–83) and the Tseng Ching Case (1728–33)." PhD. dissertation, Princeton, 1974.

Forke, Alfred. *Geschichte der Neueren Chinesische Philosophie,* Hamburg: 1938.

Franke, O. "Li Tschi: Ein Beitrage zur Geschichte der Chinesischen Geisteskampfe im 16. Jahrhundert." *Abhandlungen der Prussichen Akademie der Wissenschaften* (1937), no. 10.

Franke, O. "Li Tschi und Matteo Ricci." *Abhandlungen der Prussischen Akademie der Wissenschaften* (1937), no. 5.

Gallagher, J. L. *China in the Sixteenth Century: The Journal of Matthew Ricci 1583–1610.* New York: Random House, 1953.

Goodrich, L. Carrington. *The Literary Inquisition of Ch'ien-lung.* Baltimore: Waverly Press, 1935.

Goodrich, L. C. and C. Y. Fang, eds. *Dictionary of Ming Biography.* New York: Columbia University Press, 1976.

Hall, David and Roger Ames. "Getting It Right: On Saving Confucius from the Confucians." *PEW* (January 1984), 34(1):3–24.

Hartwell, Robert. "Patterns of Settlement, the Structure of Government, and the Social Transformation of the Chinese Political Elite, ca. 750–1550." Paper presented to the Columbia University Seminar on Traditional China, September 9, 1980.

Hightower, J. R. "Individualism in Chinese Literature." *Journal of the History of Ideas* (April–June 1961), 22(2):147–168.

Ho, Ping-ti. *The Ladder of Success in Imperial China: Aspects of Social Mobility, 1368–1911*. New York: Columbia University Press, 1962.

Ho, Ping-ti. "The Salt Merchants of Yang-chou, A Study of Commercial Capitalism in Eighteenth Century China." *HJAS* (June 1954), 17(1–2):130–168.

Houn, Franklin. "Rejection of Blind Obedience as a Confucian and Maoist Concept." *Asian Thought and Society*, vol. 7, no. 21. White Plains: M. E. Sharpe, 1982.

Hsia, C. T. *The Classic Chinese Novel*. New York: Columbia University Press, 1968.

Hsiao, K. C. "Li Chih: An Iconoclast of the Sixteenth Century." *T'ien Hsia Monthly* (April 1938), 1(4):317–341.

Huang, Ray. *1587, A Year of No Significance*. New Haven: Yale University Press, 1981.

Hummel, Arthur. *Eminent Chinese of the Ch'ing Period*. Washington, D. C.: Library of Congress, 1943.

Irwin, R. *The Evolution of a Chinese Novel: Shui-hu-chuan*. Cambridge: Harvard University Press, 1953.

Ishida Ichirō. "Tokugawa hōken shakai to Shushigakuha no shisō" (Tokugawa feudal society). Partial English translation in *Philosophical Studies in Japan* (1964), 5:17–24.

Jen Yu-wen. "Ch'en Hsien-chang's Philosophy of the Natural." In W. T. de Bary, ed., *Self and Society in Ming Thought*. New York: Columbia University Press, 1970.

Jiang, Paul. *The Search for Mind: Ch'en Pai-sha, Philosopher-Poet*. Singapore: Singapore University Press, 1980.

Karlgren, B., tr. *The Book of Odes*. Stockholm: Museum of Far Eastern Antiquities, 1950.

Kelleher, Theresa. "Personal Reflections on the Pursuit of Sagehood: The Life and Journal of Wu Yü-pi (1392–1469)." Ph.D. Dissertation, Columbia University; Ann Arbor: University Microfilms, 1982.

Lau, D. C., tr. *Mencius*. London: Penguin, 1960.

Lee, Thomas H. C. "Life in the Schools of Sung China." *Journal of Asian Studies* (November 1977), 37(1):58–59.

Legge, James, tr. *Doctrine of the Mean (Chung-yung)*. In *The Chinese Classics*. 2d. ed., rev. Oxford: Clarendon Press, 1892; reprint, Taipei: 1966.

Legge, James, tr. *I-Ching*. New York: University Books, 1964.

Legge, James, tr. *Mencius*. In *The Chinese Classics*, vol. 2, 2d. ed., rev. Oxford: Clarendon Press, 1892.

Legge, James, tr. *She King.* In *The Chinese Classics,* vol. 4, 2d ed., rev. Oxford: Clarendon Press, 1892.

Legge, James. *The Shoo King.* In *The Chinese Classics,* vol. 3, 2d ed., rev. Oxford: Clarendon Press, 1892.

Levy, André. *Vogue et Declin d'un Genre Narratif Chinois—Le Conte en Langue Vulgaire de XVIe Siècle.* Paris: Collège de France, 1981.

Lin, Yutang. *The Importance of Understanding.* Cleveland: World, 1960.

Liu, James J. Y. *The Chinese Knight-Errant.* Chicago: University of Chicago Press, 1967.

Liu, James T. C. *Ou-yang Hsiu.* Stanford: Stanford University Press, 1967.

Liu Shu-hsien. "The Functions of Mind in Chu Hsi's Philosophy." *Journal of Chinese Philosophy* (June 1978), 5(2):195–208.

Loehr, Max. "Individualism in Chinese Art." *Journal of the History of Ideas* (April–June 1961), 22(2):147–168.

Lynn, Richard. "Chu Hsi as a Literary Theorist and Critic." In Wing-tsit Chan, ed., *Chu Hsi and Neo-Confucianism,* pp. 337–354. Honolulu: University of Hawaii Press, 1986.

Lynn, Richard. "Wang Shih-chen's Theory of Poetry." In W. T. de Bary, ed., *The Unfolding of Neo-Confucianism,* pp. 217–270. New York: Columbia University Press, 1975.

Maruyama, Masao. *Studies in the Intellectual History of Modern Japan.* Princeton: Princeton University Press, 1975.

Matsumoto, Sannosuke. "The Idea of Heaven: A Tokugawa Foundation for Natural Rights Theory." In T. Najita and I. Scheiner, eds., *Japanese Thought in the Tokugawa Period,* pp. 181–197. Chicago: University of Chicago Press, 1978.

Matsumoto, Sannosuke. "Nakae Chōmin and Confucianism." In Peter Nosco, ed., *Confucianism and Tokugawa Culture,* pp. 251–266. Princeton: Princeton University Press, 1984.

Metzger, Thomas. *Escape from Predicament.* New York: Columbia University Press, 1977.

Mote, F. W. *The Poet Kao Ch'i.* Princeton: Princeton University Press, 1962.

Murck, Christian. "Chu Yün-ming (1461–1527) and Cultural Commitment in Suchou." Ann Arbor: University Microfilms International, 1979.

Nakamura Hajime. "A Brief Survey of Japanese Studies on the Philosophical Schools of the Mahayana." *Acta Asiatica,* 1:56–88. Tokyo: 1960.

Okada Takehiko. "Wang Chi and the Rise of Existentialism in the Late

Ming." In W. T. de Bary, ed., *Self and Society in Ming Thought*, pp. 121–144. New York: Columbia University Press, 1970.

Pokora, Timoteus. "A Pioneer of New Trends of Thought in the End of the Ming Period." *Archiv Orientalni* (1961), 29:469–475.

Reischauer, E. O. and J. K. Fairbank. *East Asia, the Great Tradition*. Boston: Houghton Mifflin, 1958.

Ren, Jiyu. "Confucianism as a Religion." *Social Sciences in China* (1980), 2:128–152.

Sakai, Tadao. "Confucianism and Popular Educational Works." In W. T. de Bary, ed., *Self and Society in Ming Thought*, pp. 331–362. New York: Columbia University Press, 1970.

Schirokauer, C. "Chu Hsi's Political Career: A Study in Ambivalence." In Arthur Wright, ed., *Confucian Personalities*, pp. 162–188. Stanford: Stanford University Press, 1962.

Sellman, James D. "Three Models of Self-Integration in Early China." *PEW* (October 1987), 37(4):372–390.

Shiba, Yoshinobu. *Commerce and Society in Sung China*. Mark Elvin, ed. Michigan Abstracts of Chinese and Japanese Works on Chinese History, No. 2. Ann Arbor: Center for Chinese Studies, 1970.

T'ang Chün-i. "The Concept of Moral Mind from Wang Yang-ming to Wang Chi." In W. T. de Bary, ed., *Self and Society in Ming Thought*, pp. 93–119. New York: Columbia University Press, 1970.

Taylor, Rodney. *The Cultivation of Sagehood as a Religious Goal in Neo-Confucianism, A Study of Selected Writings of Kao P'an-lung, 1562–1626*. Missoula, Mont.: Scholar's Press, 1979.

Taylor, Rodney. "Subitist and Gradualist: A Simile for Neo-Confucian Learning." *Monumenta Serica* (1984–86), 36:1–31.

Thompson, Kirill O. "A Comparative Study of Chu Hsi's and Kant's Ethical Theories." Paper presented for the International Conference for Asian and Comparative Philosophy, Honolulu, August, 1984.

Thompson, Kirill O. "The Maturation of Chu Hsi's Mind and Moral Self-Cultivation." Unpublished MS., 1985.

Tsunoda, R., W. T. de Bary, and D. Keene, eds. *Sources of Japanese Tradition*. New York: Columbia University Press, 1958.

Tu, Wei-ming. "Toward an Understanding of Liu Yin's Confucian Eremitism." In Chan and de Bary, eds., *Yüan Thought*, pp. 511–542. New York: Columbia University Press, 1982.

Tu, Wei-ming. "Yen Yüan: From Inner Experience to Lived Concreteness." In W. T. de Bary, ed., *The Unfolding of Neo-Confucianism*, pp. 511–542. New York: Columbia University Press, 1975.

Twitchett, Denis. "The Fan Clan's Charitable Estate, 1050–1760." In Arthur Wright, ed., *Confucianism in Action*, pp. 97–133. Stanford: Stanford University Press, 1959.

Watson, Burton, tr. *Complete Works of Chuang Tzu.* New York: Columbia University Press, 1968.

Watson, Burton. *Ssu-ma Ch'ien, Grand Historian of China.* New York: Columbia University Press, 1958.

Weber, Max. *Gesammelte Aufsatze zur Religionssociologie.* Tübingen: 1922–33.

Yamashita Ryūji. "Nakae Tōju's Religious Thought and Its Relation to Jitsugaku." In W. T. de Bary and I. Bloom, eds. *Principle and Practicality*, pp. 307–336. New York: Columbia University Press, 1979.

Yü, Chün-fang. *The Renewal of Buddhism in China: Chu-hung and the Late Ming Synthesis.* New York: Columbia University Press, 1981.

Index

Abiding in reverence *(chü-ching)*, 83

Abiding in reverence and fathoming principle, 74

Academies, 139, 269, 321

Academy of the White Deer Grotto, 15, 56

Actuality, 147

Advance unceasingly, 45

"Advancing in learning," 46

Affections, 58, 65

All things forming one body, 168, 211, 223

Ames, Roger, 21

Analects, 53, 58, 60, 101, 156, 195

Anarchism, 228

Anti-intellectualism, 301

Archaism, 359

Arriving at principle, 117, 118

Articles of the Academy of the White Deer Grotto, 56, 116, 317

Authenticity, 256

Autonomy, 291

Beyond good and evil, 153, 256

Bodhisattva, 108, 152, 227, 232

Book learning *(tu-shu)*, 10, 54, 59, 85, 116, 150, 212, 213, 220, 314, 348

Book of Changes *(I-Ching)*, 67, 73, 145, 300

A Book to Be Hidden Away *(Ts'ang-shu)*, 208, 218, 219, 229, 233, 234, 260

A Book to Burn *(Fen-shu)*, 208, 209

Bourgeois, 204

Breakthrough to integral comprehension *(huo-jan kuan-t'ung)*, 81, 83, 92, 104, 127, 309, 342

Broad learning, thorough inquiry, careful reflection, clear discrimination and conscientious action, 62, 94, 102, 114, 316, 317, 318

Buddha, 231, 240

Buddhahood, 262, 263

Buddhism, 142, 143, 150, 264, 263, 280, 318

Buddhist compassion *(tz'u)*, 81

Carson Chang, 266

Case Studies of Ming Confucians (Ming-ju hsüeh-an), 135

Centrality, 308, 311

Ceremonial Rites *(I-li)*, 332

Chan, Wing-tsit, 18, 50, 345

Chan Jo-shui (Kan-ch'uan, 1466–1560), 113, 141

Ch'an (Zen) Buddhism, 5, 8, 84, 85, 123, 137, 138, 188, 189, 190, 212, 220, 252, 282, 308, 310, 313, 319, 322, 336, 358

Ch'an meditation, 220

Chang Chü-cheng (1525–1582), 194

Chang Po-hsing (1652–1723), 303, 355

Chang Pu (1602–1641), 323

Chang Tsai (1027–1077), 66, 81, 86, 88, 89, 105, 111, 178, 246, 290, 304

Changes, see Book of Changes (I-ching)

Chao Chen-chi (1508–1576), 192, 205, 209

Chao Ch'i (d. 201), 46

Chao Ju-yü (1140–1196), 257

Chen Te-hsiu (1178–1235), 20, 67, 99, 320, 327, 331, 332, 353, 360

Ch'en Ch'ang-fang (1108–1148), 50

Ch'en Chien (1497–1567), 303

Ch'en Ch'un (1159–1223), 320

Ch'en Hsien-chang (1428–1500), 107, 110, 117, 136, 156, 165, 167, 168, 175, 278, 303, 313, 320

Cheng Ch'iao (1104–1162), 94

Cheng-i t'ang ch'üan-shu, 303

Ch'eng brothers, 56, 99, 105, 111, 121, 175, 234, 290, 327, 345

Ch'eng Hao (1032–1085), 31, 51, 67, 108, 174

Ch'eng I (1033–1107), 13, 14, 15, 20, 23, 32, 35, 36, 38, 48, 50, 56, 57, 58, 64, 66, 67, 73, 75, 76, 281, 307, 351

Ch'eng-Chu orthodoxy, 343, 346

Ch'eng-Chu school, 8, 31, 66-68, 74, 76, 233, 250, 255, 286-87, 290, 299, 306, 332, 346

Cherish the old while learning the new, 59, 299, 301

Chiang-hsüeh, *see* Discussion of learning

Chiao Hung (1541–1620), 134, 206

Ch'ien Mu, 312, 319, 361

Ch'ien Te-hung (1497–1574), 127, 129

Childlike mind *(t'ung-hsin)*, 211, 212, 213

Chin Lü-hsiang (1232–1303), 277

Chin-ssu-lu, see Reflections on Things at Hand

Ching-shen, see Reverencing the self

Ching-tso, tu-shu, see "Quiet sitting and book learning"

Ch'iu Chün (1420–1495), 332, 334

Chou Tun-i (1017–1073), 20, 37, 74, 82, 92, 94, 105, 111, 143-45, 172, 174, 180, 195, 234, 307

Chu Hsi (1130–1200), 7, 12, 14, 16-18, 20, 23, 28, 29, 33-35, 56, 64, 66, 67, 72, 80, 86, 88, 92, 94, 96, 99-101, 108, 111, 121, 126, 133-35, 145, 149, 150, 171, 176, 196, 201, 237, 238, 242, 246, 256, 257, 275, 277, 279-81, 290, 292, 301, 303, 309, 310, 313, 318, 320, 322, 326, 327, 332, 340, 344, 345, 349, 352, 357, 361

Chu Yüan-chang (1328–1398), 183

Ch'u Yüan, 257

Ch'üan-chou, 204

Chuang Tzu, 44, 148, 167

Chu-hung (1533–1615), 189, 263

Chü-ching ch'iung-li, see Dwelling in reverence and fathoming principle

Chüeh-hsüeh, 143

Chüng-yung, see Mean

Ch'u-t'an chi, 214

Civil service examinations, 103, 331

Clan community, 198

Clarifying of moral nature, 61

Clarifying of lucent virtue, *see* Manifesting lucent virtue

Classic of Filial Piety, 156

Classics, 43, 56, 57, 59, 61, 63, 64, 66, 67, 212

Classified Conversations (Yü-lei), 28, 55, 112

Clear wisdom and self-preservation, 163, 164, 165, 223

Cognitive learning, 91, 122, 314, 316, 317, 351, 353, 355

Collegiality, 69

Common good, 16, 249

Commoner, 159, 185, 186

Common man *(min)*, 162, 173, 227, 231, 250, 341, 342, 363

Common man as sage, 155, 169, 245

Compendium on Human Nature and Principle (Hsing-li ta-chüan), 86

Comprehending the Changes (T'ung-shu), 20, 37, 40, 92, 94

Comprehensive Inquiry into Literary Remains (Wen-hsien t'ung-k'ao), 94

Comprehensive Mirror for Aid in Government (Tzu-chih t'ung-chien), 94

Comprehensive Treatises (T'ung-chih), 94

Comprehensiveness *(t'ung)*, 94

Concrete affairs of daily life *(shih-shih)*, 350

Confucian Classics, 212

Confucius, x, xi, 68, 122, 133, 143, 145, 167, 171, 174, 176, 195, 215, 218, 230, 237, 242, 287, 290, 316, 351

Conquer self and restore riteness *(k'o-chi fu-li)*, 16, 17, 18, 90, 249, 255, 350-52

Consciousness, 209, 210

Conservatism, 325, 359

Contemplative practice, 355

Correct learning *(cheng-hsüeh)*, 15

Critical Comments of Master Lü (Lü Wan-ts'un Lü Tzu p'ing-yü cheng pien), 284

Cultivating the person, 115

Culture *(wen)*, 53

Curriculum, 272

Desirelessness (wu-yü), 146, 148, 195, 307

Diagram of the Supreme Ultimate Explained (T'ai-chi-t'u chieh), 73

Diamond Sutra, 210

Dignity of the individual, 96

Directly pointing to the mind, 287

Discourses on the Four Books (Ssu-shu chiang-i), 275, 282, 284

Discriminating and singleminded, 125

Discussion of learning (discursive learning, *chiang-hsüeh*), 117, 118, 153, 261, 278, 282

Dispositions of the Sages and Worthies, 82

Diversity of particularizations, *see* Unity of principle

Doing nothing *(wu wei)*, 148, 251, 252, 254, 267, 297

Dwelling in reverence and fathoming principle *(chü-ching ch'iung-li)*, 10

Dynastic rule, 328, 331, 333, 336, 337

Educated class, 260, 352, 357

Education, 202, 221

Egalitarianism, 152, 155, 210, 220

Eight Items or Specifications *(pa tiao-mu)*, 284

Eight-legged essay, 273, 274, 322

Elegies of Ch'u (Ch'u tz'u), 257

Elementary Learning (Hsiao-hsüeh), 39, 55, 332

Elitism, 153

Emotions, 212, 292, 293, 304, 321, 335

Empathetic response, 143

Emperor Wu of Han (r. 140–87 B.C.), 251

Empirical learning, 358

Emptiness *(hsü)*, 63, 85, 142, 144, 145, 147, 148, 256, 293, 304

Empty spirituality, 292

Empty learning (of Buddhism), 82

Emulating sages and worthies, 110, 339

Enfeoffment system, 326, 329, 338

Enlightenment *(chüeh-wu)*, 85, 156, 308, 310

Equilibrium (centrality), 313

Equilibrium and correctness, 145, 146, 147

Equilibrium of the unmanifest (a priori) state, 116

Essential Ideas Concerning Human Nature and Principle *(Hsing-li ching-i)*, 86, 345, 346, 354

Essential Meaning of the Analects (Lun-yü ching-i), 14

Establishing the self *(li-shen)*, 174

Everyday needs of the people *(pai-hsing jih-yung)*, 167, 188

Everyman, 129

Examination essays, 273, 322, 343

Examination system, 348

Exercising the mind, 77

Expediency and utilitarianism, 337

Expedient adaptability, 336

Extended Meaning of the Great Learning (Ta-hsüeh yen-i), 331

Extending innate knowledge *(chih liang-chih)*, 114, 129, 283

Extension of knowledge *(chih chih)*, 114, 118, 249, 310, 311

Extension of learning, 342

Extinction, 143, 144

Family (or household) *(chia)*, 163, 199

Family Instructions, 324, 345

Family Ritual of Master Chu (Chu Tzu chia-li or Wen-kung chia-li), 250, 332

Fan Chung-yen (989–1052), 360, 361

Fan Tsu-yü (1041–1098), 33, 345

Fang Hsiao-ju (1357–1402), 37, 232, 233, 360

Father and son, 214, 328, 329

Fathoming of principle *(ko-wu ch'iung-li)*, 77, 83, 288, 314

Feed the starving tiger, 90

Fen-shu, see A Book to Burn

Filial piety, 164, 174

Finding the Way in oneself (through personal experience) *(t'i-jen tzu-te)*, 39, 85, 92, 122, 149, 240, 359

First emperor of the Ch'in, 251

First set up the greater part [of one's nature] *(hsien li yü ch'i ta)*, 58, 148

Fisher, Tom, 322

Five Classics, 102, 257

Five human relations, 213

Fixed principle, 308

Following one's heart's desire without transgressing the norm, 287

Forgetting (the moral nature), 28, 148

Forming one body with Heaven, Earth and the myriad things, 113, 120, 126, 153

Four Beginnings, 130

Four Books, 66, 80, 101-3, 109, 111, 173-76, 245, 257, 274, 281-84, 301, 310, 318, 322, 332, 343, 351

Free discussion, 201

Free, pure, and unobstructed, 83

Friend-friend relationship, 199, 200, 213, 215, 329

Friendship, 199, 329

Fu Kuang (fl. c. 1210), 277

Full employment of the mind *(chin hsin)*, 285, 293

Function(ing), 85, 90-92, 95, 146

Fundamental human rights, 266

Fundamentalism, 271, 281, 284, 285, 320, 324, 332, 343

Fung Yu-lan, 22

General Critique of Obscurations to Learning *(Hsüeh-pu t'ung-pien)*, 278

Getting it [the Way] oneself *(tzu-te)*, 8, 13, 31, 32, 43, 47-52, 56, 57, 59, 60, 65, 92, 100-4, 107, 109-11, 113, 114, 116, 118, 133-35, 141, 148, 172-75, 177, 238, 239, 241, 279, 291, 296-300, 302, 316, 343, 355, 359

Giving primacy to quiescence *(chu-ching)*, 307, 311

Goodness of human nature, 67, 264, 290

Governance of men through self-cultivation *(hsiu-chi chih jen)*, 244, 245

Govern men through men (or according to the human being) *(i-jen chih jen)*, 182, 244, 245, 247, 248, 255

Grain, 40

Grand Unity, 122, 168

Great Compendium on Human Nature and Principle (Hsing-li ta-ch'üan), 47, 281, 301

Great Learning, 15, 18, 27, 64, 65, 80, 96, 108, 112, 119, 126-29, 143, 156, 176, 181, 193, 194, 199, 238, 242, 243, 283-86; *see also* Inquiry into the Great Learning

Great Man *(ta-chang-fu or ta jen)*, 52, 108, 112, 140, 169, 170, 177, 178, 180, 182, 202, 222, 226, 231

Growing grain, 40

Hai Jui (1513–1587), 37

Han and T'ang scholarship, 67

Han Chen (n.d.), 187

Han Kao-tsu (r. 202–195 B.C.), 327

Having no mind [of one's own] *(wu-hsin)*, 27, 252

Heart Classic, 20

Hear the Way in the morning, 36, 52, 72, 115, 181, 205, 230, 363

Heart Sutra, 263

Heaven's endowment *(t'ien-fu/tempu)*, 289, 358

Heaven's imperative *(t'ien-ming/ten-mei)*, 174, 289, 291, 292, 325, 326, 340, 341, 358

Heaven's position *(t'ien-wei)*, 328, 330

Heaven's principle *(t'ien-li/tenri)*, 18, 19, 84, 113, 114, 116, 117, 138, 141, 287, 334, 355, 358

Heavenly nature or moral nature *(t'ien-hsing)*, 79, 238, 289, 290, 294, 304, 349, 358

Hero *(hao-chieh chih shih)*, 29, 51, 52, 105, 106, 109, 143, 144, 169, 177, 178, 193, 202, 227, 229, 232, 236, 237, 275, 279, 361; heroic scholars *(ying-hsiung chih shih)*, 107; heroic leaders *(hao-chieh chih shih)*, 170; heroism, 107, 169, 191, 197

Heterodoxy, 201, 231, 335

Highest good, 75, 91, 96, 165, 244

Ho Chi (1188–1268), 135, 277

Ho Hsin-yin (1517–1579), 191, 192, 193, 195, 205, 207, 213, 215, 222, 269

Hold fast the Mean, 125, 171, 308

Holding to reverence *(chih-ching)*, 83, 85

Holism, 80, 86, 88, 93, 95, 113, 182

Honoring the moral nature (virtuous nature, *tsun te-hsing)*, 238, 246, 286, 314

Hou Wai-lu, 187

Hsiang-shan, *see* Lu Hsiang-shan

Hsin-fa, see Method of the Mind

Hsing-li ching-i, see Essential Ideas of Human Nature and Principle

Hsiu-chi chih-jen, see Human governance

Hsü Heng (1209–1281), 100, 101, 108, 112, 183, 277, 303, 320, 346, 354, 360

Hsü Yüeh (c.s. 1532), 173, 192, 193, 209

Hsüeh Hsüan (1389–1464), 346

Hsüeh-pu t'ung-pien, see General Critique of Obscurations to Learning

Hsün Tzu, 12, 44, 250

Hu Chü-jen (1434–84), 278, 279
Hu Yüan (993–1059), 180, 321
Huai-nan [method of] investigation of things, 162, 176
Huai-nan tzu, 44
Huang Kan (1152–1221), 277
Huang, Ray, 256
Huang T'ing chien (1045–1105), 82
Huang Tsung-hsi (1610–1695), 135, 136, 162, 186, 187, 261, 268, 272, 317, 337, 348
Hui-yüan (333–416), 9, 267
Human desires *(jen yü)*, 131, 197, 294, 296, 335-37, 349, 357
Humaneness *(jen)*, 17, 19, 76, 81, 169, 175, 179, 216, 243, 312, 350
Humaneness and rightness, 146, 197, 312
Humaneness forming one body with heaven, earth, and all things, 81, 86, 130, 146, 178, 180
Human governance through self-cultivation *(hsiu-chi chih-jen)*, 357
Humanitarianism, 218, 220, 221, 226, 244, 264
Humanity as the principle (substance) of love, 89, 163, 197, 221
Human mind, 19, 93, 125, 127, 286, 306, 308; human mind is precarious, 122
Human nature *(hsing)*, 75, 165, 215
Human relation(ships), 213, 215, 217, 218
Human rights, 267
Husband-wife relationship, 131, 214
Hypocrites, 223

I-ching, see Book of Changes
Individual, 162, 168, 170, 171, 188, 190, 201, 207, 215, 216, 218, 219, 255; individual freedom, 265; individual lot *(fen)*, 82; individual moral responsibility *(tzu-jen)*, 109

Individualism, xii, 1, 2, 4-6, 8, 23, 25, 26, 69, 94-97, 106, 107, 130, 133, 182, 183, 190, 202, 228, 244, 246, 264, 265, 269, 270, 333, 361; individualism of disassociation, 269
Individuality, 4, 79, 82, 209; individuality and collegiality, 69
Individual rights, 153
Infinite nothingness, 147
Innate knowledge or knowing *(liang-chih)*, 101, 127-29, 133, 136, 140-43, 146, 148-52, 159, 161, 163, 165-67, 172, 176, 177, 180, 195, 210, 222-24, 310, 311, 330, 334, 342, 361
Innate moral imperative, 291
Inner and outer [principles], 62, 309
Inquiry into the Great Learning (Ta-hsüeh wen), 15, 18, 27, 64, 65, 80, 96, 108, 112, 119, 126-29, 143, 156, 176, 181, 193, 194, 199, 238, 242, 283-85
Instructions for Practical Living (Ch'uan-hsi lu), 134
Integral comprehension *(kuan-t'ung)*, 64, 65, 78, 93, 361
Intellectual freedom, 258
Investigation of things *(ko-wu)*, 113, 114, 117, 126, 159, 161, 310, 311
Investigation of things and extension of knowledge *(ko-wu chih-chih)*, 65, 76, 288, 309
Investigation of things and the fathoming of principle *(ko-wu ch'iung-li)*, 83, 275
Investigation or rectification of things, 283
Islam, 203
I-tao tzu-jen, see Take up the Way as one's own responsibility

Jen, see Humaneness
Jih-chih lu, 261
Joy in learning, 166

Ju, 54
Jung Chao-tsu, 325

K'ang-hsi Emperor (r. 1662–1722), 357
K'o-chi fu-li, 19, 21
Kao P'an-lung (1562–1626), 306
Kasuga Senan (1811–1878), 175
Keng Ting-hsiang (1524–1596), 172, 174, 175, 177, 193, 207, 222, 237, 266
Knight-errant *(hsia)*, 192, 193, 279
Knowing nothing *(wu-chih)*, 148
Ko-wu, *see* Investigation of things
Ku Hsien-ch'eng (1550–1612), 303
Ku Yen-wu (1613–1682), 260, 337, 349
Kuan Chung (d. 645 B.C.), 351
Kuan-t'ung, see Integral comprehension
Kuei Yu-kuang (1507–1571), 186
Kung, see Public good

Lao Tzu, 228, 231
Learning by discussion *(chiang-hsüeh)*, 118, 181, 221, 280
Learning for one's self *(wei-chi chih hsüeh)*, x, 7, 10-16, 18, 30, 31, 39, 43, 49, 52, 54, 80, 92, 94, 103, 111, 118, 124, 134, 141, 149, 177, 178, 216, 237, 273, 295, 342, 343, 355, 360
Learning of the Emperors *(ti-hsüeh)*, 200
Learning of the Great Man, 285
The Learning of Great Realization *(Ta-ch'eng hsüeh-ko)*, 170
Learning of the Mind-and-Heart *(hsin-hsüeh)*, 122, 124, 125, 144, 171, 173, 262, 285-287, 292, 306, 313, 320, 333, 335
Learning of the sage(hood), 144, 146, 234, 252, 254, 278, 287; learning to be a sage, 129, 289
Learning of the Way *(tao-hsüeh)*, 54, 99, 103, 236, 276

Learning that is fragmented *(chih-li)*, 241
Learning that is plain and simple (Chien-i), 241
Learning that has been cut off *(chüeh-hsüeh)*, 143, 171
Learning to get it oneself *(tzu-te chih hsüeh)*, 110, 173
Lecturer from the classics mat, 31
Lecturers *(chiang-hsüeh che)*, 222, 223
Lecturing, 191
Lecturing and discussion, 200, 321
Ledgers of merit and demerit *(kung-kuo ko)*, 189
Legal institutions, 61
Legalism, 228; legalist "law," 268; legalist methods, 266; legalist philosophy, 255
Legge, James, 46
Li Ao (774–836?), 20
Li Chih (1527–1602), 183, 203, 204, 206, 207, 215, 233, 234, 238, 241, 243, 256, 258, 259, 260, 262-64, 266-69, 279, 321, 324, 332, 342, 361, 362
Li Kuang-ti (1642–1718), 346, 354
Li T'ung (1093–1163), 12, 80, 82, 84, 86, 88, 100, 104, 111, 175
Liberalism, xii, 25, 27
Libertarianism, 245
Liberty, 8
Licentiates, 332
Li-i fen shu, see Unity of principle and diversity of its particularizations
Limitless *(wu-chi)*, 93
Lin-chi, 313
Literate discourse, 321
Liu Tsung-chou (1578–1645), 165, 261
Liu Yin (1249–93), 100-102, 260
Lo Ch'in-shun (Ch'eng-an) (1465–1547), 293, 303
Lo Hung-hsien (1504–1564), 170
Lo Ju-fang (1515–1588), 209
Lord-on-high, 151

Lot or share in life *(fen)*, 76, 96
Lotus Sutra, 108, 149
Lou Liang (1422–1491), 109
Love of goods and sex, 335
Loving the people, 115, 120, 243, 244
Loyalism, 272, 325, 348
Loyalty, 233, 314, 315
Lu Hsiang-shan (1139–1193), 8, 58, 74, 103, 123, 133, 148, 150, 238, 241, 275, 277, 278, 280, 285, 313
Lu Lung-chi (1630–1693), 276, 346, 354
Lü Family Community Compact (Lu-shih hsiang-yüeh), 332
Lü Liu-liang (1629–1683), 320, 346, 348, 354-56, 358, 362
Lü Tsu-ch'ien (1137–1181), 13
Lucent virtue, *see* Manifesting lucent virtue
Lun-yü ching-i, see Essential Meaning of the Analects
Lustful desires are identical with the Way *(yin-yü chi-shih tao)*, 263

Ma Tuan-lin (1254–1325), 66
Mahayana Buddhism, 210
Making one's intention sincere, 115, 248, 249, 327
Male-female relationship, 214
Mandate, 341
Manifesting (or clarifying) lucent virtue *(ming-ming te)*, 108, 120, 127, 143, 242-44, 255, 285, 292, 295
Manifesting the moral nature, 78, 115, 181
Martyrdom, 232, 258, 258, 268
Material desires, 165, 195
Mean (Chung-yung), 49, 60, 64, 96, 122, 127, 137, 163, 173, 181, 238, 242, 245, 246, 252, 291, 295, 296, 313, 320, 326, 344-42
Mean and correctness, 38, 181
Mencius, 12, 28, 35, 44, 46, 50, 58, 60, 68, 83, 89, 101, 105, 111, 114, 122,

123, 129-31, 143, 157, 169, 171, 176, 255, 283, 284, 290, 312, 339, 345
Meng-tzu huo-wen, see Questions on the Mencius
Merchants, 185, 204
Methodical effort *(kung-fu)*, 352
Method of advancing in the Way, 298
Method of moral practice, 298
Method of the mind-and-heart *(hsin-fa)*, 122, 128, 143, 171, 306, 311-13, 319
Middle-class, 34, 185, 269
Military and penal affairs, 61
Mind, 30, 67, 77, 305
Mind-and-heart, 18, 62, 64, 65, 74, 83, 84, 107, 108, 112, 114, 119, 146, 149, 174, 217, 246, 319
Mind coordinating the nature and the emotions, 294, 304, 312
Mind-in-itself, 305, 356
Mind of the Way, 19, 93, 122, 124, 125, 126, 127, 287, 306, 310
Ming-i tai-fang lu, 269
Ming-ju hsüeh-an, 191
Ming-te, moral nature, 120
Ministership, 31, 233, 236, 328, 330
Moon and its reflection, 40
Moral imperative, 289, 290, 300
Moral nature *(ming-te)*, 40, 120, 289, 325, 339, 340
Moral practice, 319
Moral principles, 211, 296
Morality books *(shan-shu)*, 189
Mo Tzu, 105, 169, 283, 284
Mountain-men (shan-jen), 224
Mysterious being *(miao-yu)*, 85

Nakae Chōmin (1847–1901), 358
Nakae Tōju (1608–1648), 152
Nanking, 184, 206
Nationalism, 325
Natural awakening *(tzu-jan chih ming-chüeh)*, 141
Natural goodness of man, 227

Naturalness *(tzu-jan)*, 28, 30, 50, 115, 140, 240, 251, 252, 254, 267, 290, 291, 336
Natural spontaneity *(tzu-jan)*, 113, 165
Necessary principles *(pi-jan chih li)*, 342
Neither forget *(wu-wang)* nor abet *(wu-chu)*, 28, 113
Neo-Confucian discourse, 55
Neo-Confucianism, 20, 152
Neo-Confucian orthodoxy, 274
Neo-Taoists, 28, 252
Nobility of Heaven, 12, 37, 339
Noble man *(chün-tzu)*, x, 49, 104, 146, 162, 182, 226, 227, 231, 237-41, 245, 247, 250, 296-99, 312, 316, 331, 339, 359, 360
Non-dependence on words, 319
Nondiscrimination, 318
Non-finite *(wu-t'i* or *wu-chi)*, 144, 145, 148, 308
Non-finite and yet the Supreme Ultimate *(wu-chi erh t'ai-chi)*, 73, 123, 144, 145, 147, 234
Nothing, nothingness *(wu)*, 142, 144, 147, 148, 215

Official recruitment, 322, 352
Older and younger brother, 329
One moon with many reflections, 314
Oneness with Heaven and earth and all things, 127
One Thread Running Through It All *(i-kuan)*, 4, 94, 313, 315, 316, 318
Orthodox tradition, 171, 235, 236, 280, 346
Orthodoxy, 93, 201, 271, 280, 303, 318, 323, 355
Outward Confucianism/covert Buddhism, 275, 283, 285, 289, 292, 318, 350
Ou-yang Hsiu (1007–1072), 66

Parent-child relationship, 131, 214, 328
Pariah capitalism, 225

Passions are enlightenment *(fan-nao chi p'u-t'i)*, 263
Path of inquiry and learning, 314
People's daily needs, 217
Personal experience, 116, 117
Personalism, 4, 8, 23, 94, 95, 182
Personal realization of Heaven's principle, 114, 115
Personhood, 16, 22, 95
Philosophical discussion, *see* Discussion of learning
Physical nature, 79
Plan for the Prince (Ming-i tai-fang lu), 333
Platform Sutra, 173
Popular education, 112
Practice *(kung-fu)*, 282, 353, 355
Prajnaparamita philosophy, 206
Preface to the *Great Learning*, 41
Preface to the *Treatise on the Western Calendar (Hsi-yang-li chih hsü)*, 283
Preserving one's moral nature and pursuing scholarly inquiry *(tsun te-hsing, tao wen-hsüeh)*, 10
Principle, 63, 67, 73, 75, 77, 85, 91, 100, 123, 214, 215, 243, 286, 288-90, 293, 302-4, 307, 309, 312, 314, 315, 318, 321, 330, 336, 337, 339-41, 343, 344, 353
Principle is one, its particularizations diverse *(li-i fen-shu)*, 40, 341; *see also* Unity of principle
Principle of Heaven (nature, *t'ien-li)*, 48, 90, 130
Promised land, 359
Prophetic role, 359
Psycho-physical consciousness *(hsin)*, 304, 305, 307, 309, 312
Psycho-physical nature, 349
Public discourse (discussion), 137, 153, 258, 321
Public education, 193
Public good, common good *(kung)*, 16
Public lecturing, 194
Public morality, 192, 261

Public philosophy, 182, 357
Puritanism, 169
Pursuing the path of scholarly inquiry, 238

Questions on the Great Learning (Ta hsüeh huo-wen), 75, 80, 84, 309
Questions on the Mean (Chung-yung huo-wen), 56, 296
Questions on the Mencius (Meng tzu huo-wen), 45
Quiescence (ching), 144, 145, 146, 147, 157, 178, 252, 307
Quietism, 178, 201
Quiet-sitting, 10, 57, 84, 85, 111, 113, 150, 156, 223, 306, 308, 311, 349, 350, 354
Quiet-sitting and book learning (ching-tso, tu-shu), 10, 85

Radical individualism, 152
Radicalism, 95, 271, 324, 332, 333, 343
Reach deeply within and get the Way for himself (shen-tsao erh tzu-te chih), 115, 174
Reach or arrive (tsao-i) at the principle in things and affairs, 114
Reading method, 62, 64, 300
Real or practical learning, 82
Reciprocity (shu), 162, 245, 246, 314, 315
Recorded Conversations on the Four Books (Ssu-shu yü-lu), 284
Record of Rites, 67
Rectification of affairs, 161
Rectifying one's intentions, 118
Rectifying the mind, 115
Rectify oneself and others will become rectified (cheng chi erh wu cheng), 177
Reducing one's desires, 146, 196
Refined and coarse [natures], 62
Refinement, 146, 308, 318
Refinement and singleness (oneness), 122, 123, 126, 128, 171, 308, 312

Reflections on Things at Hand (Chin-ssu-lu), 13, 17, 18, 23, 37, 41, 55, 66, 72, 82, 83, 86
Relationship of friend and friend, 199, 200, 213, 215, 329
Relationship of husband and wife, 131, 214
Relationship of male and female, 214
Relationship of older and younger brother, 329
Relationship of parent and child, 131, 200, 214, 330, 331
Relationship of ruler and minister (subject), 36, 131, 199, 200, 214, 236, 328, 329, 330
Religiosity, 19
Renewing the people, 61, 78, 108, 133, 181, 256, 285, 295, 338, 340
Ren Jiyu, 22
Repossession of the Way (tao-t'ung), 99, 100, 102, 105, 109, 119, 121, 122
Respect for the moral nature (tsun te-hsing), 58
Respect the self, 165
Responses of Yen-p'ing (Yen-p'ing ta-wen), 80, 82, 100, 111
Responsibility for the Way, 109
Resting in the highest good, 61, 104, 115, 287
Restoration, 325, 359, 360
Restoration Society (Fu she), 323
Restoring riteness, 250
Reverencing the self (ching-shen), 39
Reverent seriousness (ching), 30, 57, 252, 288, 307, 342
Revisionist critique, 343
Ricci, Matteo, 184, 185
Rightness, 76, 197, 312, 329, 330, 333, 334
Rights or entitlements for the individual, 256
Rigorism, 361
Rising bourgeoisie, 225

Rites or riteness *(li)*, 3, 16, 17, 18, 21, 76, 213, 250, 251, 327, 331-36, 341-43, 345

Rote learning *(chi-wen chih hsüeh)*, 300

Rulership, 330

Ruling elite, 229, 250

Sage, 30, 39, 163, 166, 168, 227, 229, 232, 237, 248, 262, 360

Sagehood, 38, 39, 40, 71, 140, 157, 231, 234, 237, 242, 244, 279, 357, 359, 362

Sage-king, 200, 331

Sage Learning, 285, 308

Sages and worthies, 238, 240

San i-jen chi (Works of Three Nonconformists), 232

Scholar-officials, 11, 33, 152, 155, 158, 224, 269, 323

Scholarly associations, 200

Scholarship, 54, 220

School of the Mind *(hsin-hsüeh)*, 220

School of the Way *(tao-hsüeh)*, 171, 234

Schools, 198, 200, 269, 346

School system, 337, 341

Seed of grain, 79

Self *(chi)*, 20, 21, 27, 29, 199, 201, 250, 342

Self-accusation *(tzu-sung)*, 103

Self-authentication *(tzu-ch'eng)*, 103

Self-control *(tzu-chih)*, 18

Self-correction [as a basis] for others' correcting of themselves *(cheng-chi erh wu cheng)*, 173

Self-cultivation *(hsiu-chi chih jen)* as the key to good government, 243, 254

Self-deception *(tzu-ch'i)*, 27, 241, 248

Self-enjoyment *(tzu ch'ieh)*, 57

Self-enlightenment *(tzu-ming)*, 103

Self-examination *(tzu-hsing)*, 103

Self-fulfillment *(tzu-ch'eng)*, 221

Self-governing, 247

Self-interest *(ssu)*, 215, 217, 225, 231, 249, 251, 252, 254, 294

Selfish desires *(ssu-yü)*, 16, 19, 84, 166, 332, 350

Selfishness, 195, 327, 330, 331, 338, 353, 357

Self-knowledge, 177

Self-negation *(tzu-shih)*, 44

Self or person *(shen)*, 164, 168, 172, 199

Self-reformation *(tzu-cheng)*, 103

Self-respect *(tzu-tsun)*, 174

Self-satisfaction *(tzu-ch'ien)*, 28

Self-transformation *(tzu-hua)*, 103

Self-watchfulness *(shen-tu)*, 241, 306, 308, 342

Sentences and Phrases of the Great Learning (Ta-hsüeh chang-chü), 76, 80, 281

Setting up a model for oneself, 110

Shan jen, *see* Mountain Men

Shao Yung (1011–1077), 105

Shen, see Self or person

Sheng-yüan, see Stipendiary or licentiate

Shih-ta-fu, 250

Shinto devotionalism, 152

Sincerity or Integrity *(ch'eng)*, 75, 256, 297

Singleness of mind, 146, 310, 313

Sitting in meditation *(tso-ch'an)*, 84

Sitting in silence and clearing the mind *(mo-tso ch'eng-hsin)*, 84

Six Classics, 56, 101, 149, 150, 174, 175

Sixth Patriarch of Ch'an Buddhism, 173

Skeptical attitude, 66

Small man, 146

Social or economic program, 168

So-i-jan chih ku, 79

Solitariness *(tu)*, 307

Son of Heaven, 340-43

Soochow, 184, 185

So-tang-jan chih tse, 79
Sovereign Ultimate, 145
Special transmission outside the scriptures, 314
Spontaneity, 308
Sprouts of capitalism, 34
Ssu-wen, see This culture, 9
Ssu-yü, see Selfish desires
Steep oneself in the Way *(shen ts'ao i tao),* 297, 298
Stipendiary or licentiate, 273
Studying, inquiring, thinking, sifting, and practicing, 56
Substance, 85, 146
Substance, function and literary expression, 319
Substance of the mind *(pen-t'i or jen),* 90, 92, 147, 282, 288, 305, 308, 309, 313, 317, 318
Substance of the Way, 217
Substance and function, 89, 95, 178, 352
Succession to the mind of the sages, 129
Succession to the Way *(Tao-t'ung),* 99, 319, 345, 354; *see also* Repossession of the Way
Sudden enlightenment, 84, 308
Sung, 94
Sung autocracy, 33
Sung learning, 343, 354
Supplement to the "Extended Meaning of the Great Learning," 334
Supreme Ultimate or Supreme Norm *(t'ai-chi),* 73–76, 79, 91, 92, 96, 144, 145, 147, 214, 301, 308, 309, 341, 342
Su Tung-p'o (1036–1101), 8, 34

Ta-chang-fu, see Great man
Ta-chih-t'u lun, see Treatise on the Great Perfection of Wisdom
Ta-hui (1089–1163), 278
Ta-jen, see Great Man
Ta-kuan, 268

Take the whole world as one's own responsibility *(i t'ien-hsia wei chi-jen),* 351
Take up the Way as one's own responsibility *(i-tao tzu-jen),* 32, 121, 172, 277
Taking responsibility [for the Way] oneself *(tzu-jen or chi-jen),* 29, 31, 32, 99, 106, 122, 171, 172, 270, 275, 277, 297, 355, 356, 359, 360
T'ai-chou, 156, 184, 191, 212
T'ai-chou School, 112, 183, 186, 187, 189, 190, 197, 205, 212, 222, 264, 279, 361
T'ang T'ai-tsung (r. 626–649), 327
Tao-hsin, see Mind of the Way
Tao-hsüeh (Learning or School of the Way), 250
Taoism, 5, 142, 150, 231, 252, 336
Tao-t'ung, see Tradition of the Way; Succession to the Way
Things-and-affairs, 312
Things at Hand, see Reflections on Things at Hand
Things brought to light *(fa-ming),* 68
Thinking nothing *(wu-ssu),* 148
This culture *(ssu-wen),* 9, 10, 52
Three Dynasties, 327, 330, 343, 344
Three Guiding Principles or Mainstays (san kang-ling), 96, 243, 244, 284, 285, 295
Three Teachings, 142, 206, 208, 229, 230, 263, 264, 266
Tien-li, see Principle of nature
To be an individual *(ch'eng i-ko-jen),* 207
To love fish and love bear-paws, 196
Totally forming the same body [substance] with things *(hun-jan yü wu t'ung-t'i),* 81
Tradition of the Way *(tao-t'ung),* 50, 127, 129, 171, 235, 280, 345, 346, 354
Traditionalism, 259
Transcendence of the world, 240

Trans-moral enlightenment, 244
Treatise on the Great Perfection of Wisdom *(ta-chih-t'u lun)*, 263
Treatise on the Western Calendar *(Hsi-yang-li chih hsü)*, 285
True emptiness *(chen-k'ung)*, 241
Ts'ang-shu (A book to be hidden away), 208, 218, 219
Tsao Tuan (1376–1434), 229, 233, 234, 260, 279, 363, 346
Ts'ao-tung school, 313
Tsao-i, reach, attain, fathom, 114
Tseng Ching (1679–1736), 274, 357
Tsou Shan (c.s. 1556), 262
Tsun te-hsing, see Respect the moral nature
Tu-shu jen, 353
T'ung, see Comprehensiveness
Tung Chung-shu (179?–104? B.C.), 44
Tung-lin Academy, 261
T'ung-shu, see Comprehending the Changes
Tzu-ch'eng, see Self-fulfillment
Tzu-ch'i, see Self-deception
Tzu-ch'ieh, see Self-satisfaction
Tzu-chia (oneself), 28, 29
Tzu-chih, see Self-control, 18
Tzu-jan, see Naturalness
Tzu-jen, see Taking responsibility oneself
Tzu-jen yü tao, see Taking responsibility for the Way
Tzu-ssu, 50, 111, 290
Tzu-te, see Getting the Way oneself
Tzu-tsun (self-respect), 174

Ultimate directional norm, 296
Unceasing advancement, 298
Unceasingness, unceasingly (pu-i), 290–92, 300
Undifferentiated compassion, 352
Undifferentiated unity, 314
Uneducated persons *(yü-fu, yü-fu)*, 167, 182
Uniqueness of the individual, 130, 215

Unity and diversity, 92, 302
Unity of mind and principle in innate knowing, 126, 134
Unity of principle and diversity of its particularizations *(li-i fen-shu)*, 22, 81, 82, 85, 86, 89, 91, 130, 294, 296, 315, 356
Unity of the Three Teachings, 230, 263
Universality of the Buddha-nature, 108
Universal love, 88
Universal schooling, 112, 339, 352
Utilitarianism, 178, 337

Vimalakīrti, 170
Virtuous nature or moral nature *(te-hsing)*, 242, 246

Wang An-shih (1021–1086), 34
Wang Chi (1498–1583), 139, 143, 147-9, 152, 153, 187, 189, 205, 209, 221, 222, 244, 251, 256, 307, 308
Wang Fu-chih (1619–1692), 261, 337
Wang Ken (1483?–1540), 152, 155-61, 164, 165, 168, 170-73, 176, 178, 179, 181-83, 187, 188, 190-92, 193, 197, 205, 206, 209, 223, 242, 251
Wang Po (1197–1274), 277
Wang Shih-chen (1526–90), 191, 192
Wang Yang-ming, xii, 93, 112-14, 117, 119, 134, 136, 144, 149, 150, 152, 156-61, 167, 168, 170, 172, 176, 190, 191, 196, 197, 205, 206, 209, 220, 223, 242, 276, 277, 280, 282, 285, 301, 303, 310, 313, 320, 337, 361
Wang Yang-ming school, 190, 202, 221, 222, 260, 262, 269
The Water Margin (Shu-hu-chuan), 212
Way (The), 237, 246, 248, 254, 258, 291
Way of humankind, 235
Way of parent and child, 200
Way of ruler and minister, 200
Way of Sagehood, 234, 235

Way of self-respect, 192
Way of the concubine, 166
Way of the Sage Kings, 360
Way of the Sage(s), 71, 102, 151, 344
Way of the Measuring Square, 336
Way of the teacher, 180
Wei Liao-weng (1178–1237), 99
Wei-chi chih hsüeh, see Learning for one's self
Well-field system, 337, 338, 344
Wen, 9, 52, 53
Western individualism, 269
Western Inscription *(Hsi-ming)*, 66, 81, 86, 89, 178
What Yen Tzu loved to learn, 37
Whole substance and great functioning (of the mind-and-heart), 65, 77, 79, 85, 86, 91, 92, 297
Wild Ch'an, 190, 212
Winning the hearts and minds of the people, 55
Wiping out old ideas, 68
Wisdom, 76
Without desires *(wu-yü)*, 20
Wondrous functioning *(miao-yung)*, 85
Works of Three Non-conformists *(San i-jen chi)*, 232
Written words the brushstrokes of the heart, 319
Wu Ch'eng (1249–1333), 28, 102, 107, 112, 277, 279, 320
Wu-chi (Non-finite), 74, 75, 91
Wu-yü, see Without desires

Wu Yü-pi (1392–1469), 107, 109, 175, 233, 278, 346, 360

Yamashita Ryūji, 151
Yamazaki Ansai (1618–1682), 306
Yang Chi (1142–1213), 257
Yang Chu, 105, 283, 284
Yang-chou, 184
Yen Chün (n.d.), 191, 192, 193, 194, 209
Yen Hui (disciple of Confucius), 148, 175, 215, 360
Yen Sung (1480–1565), 194
Yen Tzu (*see also* Yen Hui), 38, 111, 176
Yen Yüan (1635–1704), 21, 281, 353, 356
Yi T'oegye (1501–1570), 306
Yung-cheng Emperor (r. 1723–1735), 276
Yu Chi (1272–1348), 102, 106, 107
Yüan Chung-tao (1570–1624), 207, 258
Yüan Huang (1533–1606), 188, 189, 301
Yüan-hsien (Yung-chüeh Yüan-hsien, 1578–1657), 264, 267
Yu-hsia, 192
Yü-fu yü-fu, see Uneducated persons, 167, 182

Zen, *see* Ch'an Buddhism

Other Works in the Columbia Asian Studies Series

NEO-CONFUCIAN STUDIES

Instructions for Practical Living and Other Neo-Confucian Writings by Wang Yang-ming, tr. Wing-tsit Chan   1963

Reflections on Things at Hand: The Neo-Confucian Anthology, comp. Chu Hsi and Lü Tsu-ch'ien, tr. Wing-tsit Chan   1967

Self and Society in Ming Thought, by Wm. Theodore de Bary and the Conference on Ming Thought. Also in paperback ed.   1970

The Unfolding of Neo-Confucianism, by Wm. Theodore de Bary and the Conference on Seventeenth-Century Chinese Thought. Also in paperback ed.   1975

Principle and Practicality: Essays in Neo-Confucianism and Practical Learning, ed. Wm. Theodore de Bary and Irene Bloom. Also in paperback ed.   1979

The Syncretic Religion of Lin Chao-en, by Judith A. Berling   1980

The Renewal of Buddhism in China: Chu-hung and the Late Ming Synthesis, by Chün-fang Yü   1981

Neo-Confucian Orthodoxy and the Learning of the Mind-and-Heart, by Wm. Theodore de Bary 1981

Yüan Thought: Chinese Thought and Religion Under the Mongols, ed. Hok-lam Chan and Wm. Theodore de Bary 1982

The Liberal Tradition in China, by Wm. Theodore de Bary 1983

The Development and Decline of Chinese Cosmology, by John B. Henderson 1984

The Rise of Neo-Confucianism in Korea, by Wm. Theodore de Bary and JaHyun Kim Haboush 1985

Chiao hung and the Restructuring of Neo-Confucianism in the Late Ming, by Edward T. Ch'ien 1985

Neo-Confucian Terms Explained: The Pei-hsi tzu-i by Ch'en Ch'un, ed. and trans. Wing-tsit Chan 1986

Knowledge Painfully Acquired: The K'un-chih chi, by Lo Ch'in-shun, ed. and trans. Irene Bloom 1987

To Become a Sage: The Ten Diagrams on Sage Learning, by Yi T'oegye, ed. and trans. Michael C. Kalton 1988

The Message of the Mind in Neo-Confucianism, by Wm. Theodore de Bary 1989

COMPANIONS TO ASIAN STUDIES

Approaches to the Oriental Classics, ed. Wm. Theodore de Bary 1959

Early Chinese Literature, by Burton Watson. Also in paperback ed. 1962

Approaches to Asian Civilizations, ed. Wm. Theodore de Bary and Ainslie T. Embree 1964

The Classic Chinese Novel: A Critical Introduction, by C. T. Hsia. Also in paperback ed. 1968

Chinese Lyricism: Shih Poetry from the Second to the Twelfth Century, tr. Burton Watson. Also in paperback ed. 1971

A Syllabus of Indian Civilization, by Leonard A. Gordon and Barbara Stoler Miller 1971

Twentieth-Century Chinese Stories, ed. C. T. Hsia and Joseph S. M. Lau. Also in paperback ed. 1971

A Syllabus of Chinese Civilization, by J. Mason Gentzler, 2d ed. 1972

A Syllabus of Japanese Civilization, by H. Paul Varley, 2d ed. 1972

An Introduction to Chinese Civilization, ed. John Meskill, with the assistance of J. Mason Gentzler 1973

An Introduction to Japanese Civilization, ed. Arthur E. Tiedemann 1974

Ukifune: Love in the Tale of Genji, ed. Andrew Pekarik 1982

The Pleasures of Japanese Literature, by Donald Keene   1988
A Guide to Oriental Classics, ed. Wm. Theodore de Bary and
    Ainslie T. Embree; third edition ed. Amy Vladeck Heinrich   1989

TRANSLATIONS FROM THE ORIENTAL CLASSICS

Major Plays of Chikamatsu, tr. Donald Keene. Also in paperback
    ed.   1961
Four Major Plays of Chikamatsu, tr. Donald Keene. Paperback text
    edition   1961
*Records of the Grand Historian of China, translated from the Shih
    chi of Ssu-ma Ch'ien,* tr. Burton Watson, 2 vols.   1961
*Instructions for Practical Living and Other Neo-Confucian Writ-
    ings by Wang Yang-ming,* tr. Wing-tsit Chan   1963
Chuang Tzu: Basic Writings, tr. Burton Watson, paperback ed.
    only   1964
The Mahābhārata, tr. Chakravarthi V. Narasimhan. Also in paper-
    back ed.   1965
The Manyōshū, Nippon Gakujutsu Shinkōkai edition   1965
Su Tung-p'o: Selections from a Sung Dynasty Poet, tr. Burton
    Watson. Also in paperback ed.   1965
Bhartrihari: Poems, tr. Barbara Stoler Miller. Also in paperback ed.   1967
Basic Writings of Mo Tzu, Hsün Tzu, and Han Fei Tzu, tr. Burton
    Watson. Also in separate paperback eds.   1967
The Awakening of Faith, Attributed to Aśvaghosha, tr. Yoshito S.
    Hakeda. Also in paperback ed.   1967
Reflections on Things at Hand: The Neo-Confucian Anthology,
    comp. Chu Hsi and Lü Tsu-ch'ien, tr. Wing-tsit Chan   1967
The Platform Sutra of the Sixth Patriarch, tr. Philip B. Yampolsky.
    Also in paperback ed.   1967
Essays in Idleness: The Tsurezuregusa of Kenkō, tr. Donald Keene.
    Also in paperback ed.   1967
The Pillow Book of Sei Shōnagon, tr. Ivan Morris, 2 vols.   1967
*Two Plays of Ancient India: The Little Clay Cart and the Minister's
    Seal,* tr. J. A. B. van Buitenen   1968
The Complete Works of Chuang Tzu, tr. Burton Watson   1968
The Romance of the Western Chamber (Hsi Hsiang chi), tr. S. I.
    Hsiung. Also in paperback ed.   1968
The Manyōshū, Nippon Gakujutsu Shinkōkai edition. Paperback
    text edition   1969

Records of the Historian: Chapters from the Shih chi of Ssu-ma Ch'ien. Paperback text edition, tr. Burton Watson — 1969

Cold Mountain: 100 Poems by the T'ang Poet Han Shan, tr. Burton Watson. Also in paperback ed. — 1970

Twenty Plays of the Nō Theatre, ed. Donald Keene. Also in paperback ed. — 1970

Chūshingura: The Treasury of Loyal Retainers, tr. Donald Keene. Also in paperback ed. — 1971

The Zen Master Hakuin: Selected Writings, tr. Philip B. Yampolsky — 1971

Chinese Rhyme-Prose: Poems in the Fu Form from the Han and Six Dynasties Periods, tr. Burton Watson. Also in paperback ed. — 1971

Kūkai: Major Works, tr. Yoshito S. Hakeda. Also in paperback ed. — 1972

The Old Man Who Does as He Pleases: Selections from the Poetry and Prose of Lu Yu, tr. Burton Watson — 1973

The Lion's Roar of Queen Śrīmālā, tr. Alex and Hideko Wayman — 1974

Courtier and Commoner in Ancient China: Selections from the History of the Former Han by Pan Ku, tr. Burton Watson. Also in paperback ed. — 1974

Japanese Literature in Chinese, vol. 1: *Poetry and Prose in Chinese by Japanese Writers of the Early Period,* tr. Burton Watson — 1975

Japanese Literature in Chinese, vol. 2: *Poetry and Prose in Chinese by Japanese Writers of the Later Period,* tr. Burton Watson — 1976

Scripture of the Lotus Blossom of the Fine Dharma, tr. Leon Hurvitz. Also in paperback ed. — 1976

Love Song of the Dark Lord: Jayaveda's Gītagovinda, tr. Barbara Stoler Miller. Also in paperback ed. Cloth ed. includes critical text of the Sanskrit. — 1977

Ryōkan: Zen Monk-Poet of Japan, tr. Burton Watson — 1977

Calming the Mind and Discerning the Real: From the Lam rim chan mo of Tsoṅ-kha-pa, tr. Alex Wayman — 1978

The Hermit and the Love-Thief: Sanskrit Poems of Bhartrihari and Bilhana, tr. Barbara Stoler Miller — 1978

The Lute: Kao Ming's P'i-p'a chi, tr. Jean Mulligan. Also in paperback ed. — 1980

A Chronicle of Gods and Sovereigns: Jinnō Shōtōki of Kitabatake Chikafusa, tr. H. Paul Varley — 1980

Among the Flowers: The Hua-chien chi, tr. Lois Fusek — 1982

Grass Hill: Poems and Prose by the Japanese Monk Gensei, tr. Burton Watson — 1983

*Doctors, Diviners, and Magicians of Ancient China: Biographies of
Fang-shih,* tr. Kenneth J. DeWoskin. Also in paperback ed.   1983
Theater of Memory: The Plays of Kālidāsa, ed. Barbara Stoler
Miller. Also in paperback ed.   1984
*The Columbia Book of Chinese Poetry: From Early Times to the
Thirteenth Century,* ed. and tr. Burton Watson. Also in paper-
back ed.   1985
*Poems of Love and War: From the Eight Anthologies and the Ten
Songs of Classical Tamil,* tr. A. K. Ramanujan. Also in paper-
back ed.   1985
The Columbia Book of Later Chinese Poetry, ed. and tr. Jonathan
Chaves. Also in paperback ed.   1986
The Tso Chuan: Selections From China's Oldest Narrative History,
tr. Burton Watson.   1989

MODERN ASIAN LITERATURE SERIES

Modern Japanese Drama: An Anthology, ed. and tr. Ted Takaya.
Also in paperback ed.   1979
*Mask and Sword: Two Plays for the Contemporary Japanese The-
ater,* by Yamazaki Masakazu, tr. J. Thomas Rimer   1980
Yokomitsu Riichi, Modernist, by Dennis Keene   1980
*Nepali Visions, Nepali Dreams: The Poetry of Laxmiprasad Dev-
kota,* tr. David Rubin   1980
Literature of the Hundred Flowers, vol. 1: *Criticism and Polemics,*
ed. Hualing Nieh   1981
Literature of the Hundred Flowers, vol. 2: *Poetry and Fiction,* ed.
Hualing Nieh   1981
Modern Chinese Stories and Novellas, 1919–1949, ed. Joseph S.
M. Lau, C. T. Hsia, and Leo Ou-fan Lee. Also in paperback ed.   1984
A View of the Sea, By Yasuoka Shōtarō, tr. Kären Wigen Lewis   1984
*Other Worlds: Arishima Takeo and the Bounds of Modern Japanese
Fiction,* by Paul Anderer   1984
Selected Poems of Sŏ Chŏngju, tr. with intro. by David R. McCann 1989

STUDIES IN ORIENTAL CULTURE

1. *The Ōnin War: History of Its Origins and Background, with a
   Selective Translation of the Chronicle of Ōnin,* by H. Paul
   Varley   1967
2. *Chinese Government in Ming Times: Seven Studies,* ed. Charles
   O. Hucker   1969

3. *The Actors' Analects (Yakusha Rongo)*, ed. and tr. by Charles J. Dunn and Bungō Torigoe 1969
4. *Self and Society in Ming Thought*, by Wm. Theodore de Bary and the Conference on Ming Thought. Also in paperback ed. 1970
5. *A History of Islamic Philosophy*, by Majid Fakhry, 2d ed. 1983
6. *Phantasies of a Love Thief: The Caurapañcāśikā Attributed to Bilhana*, by Barbara Stoler Miller 1971
7. *Iqbal: Poet-Philosopher of Pakistan*, ed. Hafeez Malik 1971
8. *The Golden Tradition: An Anthology of Urdu Poetry*, by Ahmed Ali. Also in paperback ed. 1973
9. *Conquerors and Confucians: Aspects of Political Change in Late Yüan China*, by John W. Dardess 1973
10. *The Unfolding of Neo-Confucianism*, by Wm. Theodore de Bary and the Conference on Seventeenth-Century Chinese Thought. Also in paperback ed. 1975
11. *To Acquire Wisdom: The Way of Wang Yang-ming*, by Julia Ching 1976
12. *Gods, Priests, and Warriors: The Bhrgus of the Mahābhārata*, by Robert P. Goldman 1977
13. *Mei Yao-ch'en and the Development of Early Sung Poetry*, by Jonathan Chaves 1976
14. *The Legend of Semimaru, Blind Musician of Japan*, by Susan Matisoff 1977
15. *Sir Sayyid Ahmad Khan and Muslim Modernization in India and Pakistan*, by Hafeez Malik 1980
16. *The Khilafat Movement: Religious Symbolism and Political Mobilization in India*, by Gail Minault 1980
17. *The World of K'ung Shang-jen: A Man of Letters in Early Ch'ing China*, by Richard Strassberg 1983
18. *The Lotus Boat: The Origins of Chinese Tz'u Poetry in T'ang Popular Culture*, by Marsha L. Wagner 1984
19. *Expressions of Self in Chinese Culture*, ed. Robert E. Hegel and Richard C. Hessney 1985
20. *Songs for the Bride: Women's Voices and Wedding Rites of Rural India*, by W. G. Archer, ed. Barbara Stoler Miller and Mildred Archer 1986
21. *A Heritage of Kings: One Man's Monarchy in the Confucian World*, by JaHyun Kim Haboush 1988

INTRODUCTION TO ORIENTAL CIVILIZATIONS
Wm. Theodore de Bary, Editor

Sources of Japanese Tradition 1958; paperback ed., 2 vols., 1964
Sources of Indian Tradition 1958; paperback ed., 2 vols., 1964; second
    edition, 1988
Sources of Chinese Tradition 1960; paperback ed., 2 vols., 1964